A
DARK
AND
BLOODY
GROUND

BOOKS BY DARCY O'BRIEN

A Dark and Bloody Ground (1993)

Margaret in Hollywood (1991)

Murder in Little Egypt (1989)

Two of a Kind, the Hillside Stranglers (1985)

The Silver Spooner (1981)

A Way of Life, Like Any Other (1978)

Patrick Kavanagh (1975)

W. R. Rodgers (1970)

The Conscience of James Joyce (1968)

A DARK AND BLOODY GROUND

DARCY O'BRIEN

HarperCollins*Publishers*

Photographs follow page 152.

HarperCollins books may be purchased for educational, business, or sales promotional use. For information, please write: Special Markets Department, HarperCollins Publishers, Inc., 10 East 53rd Street, New York, NY 10022.

FIRST EDITION

Designed by George J. McKeon

Library of Congress Cataloging-in-Publication Data
O'Brien, Darcy.
   A dark and bloody ground: outlaw love, a miser's hoard: lust, greed, and killing from the beaches of Florida to the mountains of Kentucky / by Darcy O'Brien.—1st ed.
     p. cm.
ISBN 0-06-017958-9 (cloth)
   1. Hodge, Benny. 2. Criminals—Southern States—Biography. 3. Murderers—Southern States—Biography. I. Title.
HV6248.H463027 1992

364.1′523′09769163—dc20   92-54451

93 94 95 96 97 ❖/HC 10 9 8 7 6 5 4 3 2 1

To Thomas Flanagan

"I was born on Bullskin Creek, and I have told many a tale, but never under oath."

—LESTER H. BURNS, JR.

1

So RICH WAS THE SOIL, so plentiful were the fish and game and various the beauties of Kentucky, that its original inhabitants, including Shawnee and Cherokee, fought continuously over tribal boundaries and called it "the dark and bloody ground." The phrase, from which the name Kentucky derives, gained currency during the period of white settlement, when Daniel Boone and others wrote of the new land as a Garden of Eden well worth bloodshed. Over the past two hundred years, however, Kentucky has become known and celebrated for so many things—bourbon, moonshine, tobacco, railroading, coal mining, country and bluegrass music, thoroughbreds, not to mention Colonel Sanders's fried chicken—that the old epithet no longer seems fair.

The state ranks second to Wyoming in coal production; the Humana hospital chain, with its headquarters in Louisville, has become an equally conspicuous enterprise, economically and politically powerful. To travel through Kentucky today is to be confronted by change—new industries, new architecture, the urban intensities of getting and spending—and by the lack of it. If Louisville feels up to date, Lexington, in the heart of the Bluegrass country, a limestone plateau that nourishes horses' bones, does not. With its elegant old neighborhoods, set in a countryside that resembles a manicured park, Lexington clings to an earlier era. It has been the breeding center of American thoroughbred racing since at least 1875, when the Lexington-bred Aristides won the first Kentucky Derby. Recently it was the site of the U.S. Open Polo Championships, an event harmonious with the city's atmosphere of monied Southern languor, epitomized by mint juleps, horse farms that are fiefdoms, the Idle Hour country club, and Keeneland, one of the three most beautiful racetracks in the nation, where love of tradition forbids even a public address system and where the annual yearling sales attract sheiks and other bankrolled gamblers smitten by long-legged possibilities. Urban sprawl and the presence of a Toyota plant only fifteen miles to the north may portend change, but for now the local ambience values aesthetics over utility. The Lexington airport offers floral displays and art exhibitions; at a downtown restaurant with a French name, you will find snails broiled in goat cheese, and no grits.

Down in one corner of the Commonwealth, where the border skirts West Virginia, Virginia, and Tennessee, still another culture prevails. Here are the rugged hills and mountains where, sixty and seventy years ago, folklorists convened, excited that the people seemed so odd that they must be throwbacks to Elizabethan times, on the evidence of quaint turns of phrase and the survival of several ballads. That the natives might be backward was thought to be important. Their Anglo-Saxon stock was celebrated; that about a third of the native surnames were Celtic was played down. In romantic zeal the folklore and folk song industries sought to persuade these Appalachian mountaineers to cast off their mail-order banjos in favor of dulcimers and to forsake drinking and roaring for morris dancing. It seems not to have occurred to these interventionists that they were altering forever what they praised as pure and that in music as in language, it is the poor and the isolated who preserve the old, unaffected as they are by the fashionable and phony.

Idealists from the Bluegrass and from as far away as the Seven Sisters colleges of the Northeast, most of them women of means drawn toward social work when many other professions remained closed to them, adopted Eastern Kentucky as a focus of cultural and religious missionary activity. They established settlement schools modeled after Hull House. Motivated by a well-meaning condescension and offended by raw music and moonshine, they taught coal miners' children the niceties of a genteel Christmas, encouraged local crafts such as carving, quilting, and weaving, and organized folk festivals. Some of the locals learned to sing the way the antiquarians wanted them to; others, clinging to their natural styles, caught the attention of commercial recording companies and achieved national popularity after 1924, when the first "hillbilly" record was cut.

Here in the thirties, Bill Monroe invented what he called blue-grass music: it has no connection whatever to the actual Bluegrass region, but the name is free from the taint of ignorance that dogs hill-billy. Here lies Butcher Hollow, birthplace of those coal miner's daughters Loretta Lynn and Crystal Gayle. The antiquarians were correct in this, that Eastern Kentucky has a distinctive voice, one that does derive from Britain and Ireland but whose genius was too hardy to be tamed and has flowered at the Grand Ole Opry.

This is a stretch of Appalachia as mountainous and shadowy as the Bluegrass is broad and as poor as the horse country is rich. And here the old Indian epithet is still apt, because the murder rate in most counties of Eastern Kentucky yearly exceeds that of New York, Chicago, or Los Angeles, and has done so as long as statistics have been kept. Only Washington, D.C., three hundred miles away, and a portion of Illinois called Little Egypt rival Eastern Kentucky in per capita homicides.

History, poverty, and tradition—this last including what is often referred to as "the mountain philosophy," a very loose definition of the permissible boundaries of self-defense—combine to encourage and perpetuate crime and violence. The first white settlers, freed after seven-year terms as indentured servants in Virginia and the Caroli-nas, drifted into these mountains a generation or two before Daniel Boone, learned from the Cherokee the technique of the log cabin, and gained a deserved reputation for rude and hostile behavior, shooting first or pulling up stakes whenever someone moved within five miles of them. They did not establish towns, preferring the isolation of cab-ins hidden in hollows, living off the land. In 1775 Boone entered the territory through the Cumberland Gap on his way to a leveler land-scape—disdaining a coonskin cap, current scholarship compels us to accept, but, surely, using what came to be called a long Kentucky rifle. Boone, a sociable man, headed north; other whites turned south to settle the Cumberland Plateau, into what became Tennessee, what the Indians had known as the richest of hunting grounds.

After the Civil War, during which Kentuckians, like East Ten-nesseans, divided on the issues of slavery and states' rights, the Hat-fields and McCoys and other clans feuded Eastern Kentucky into new, bloody legends. Later, moonshiners blasted "revenuers," as the liquor-tax collectors and agents were called, with homemade shrapnel fashioned from nailheads. The coming of the railroad and the coal industry changed much about the region, but not its inclination to violence. "They used to say Kentucky was Eden," a grandfather wrote to his progeny in 1869. "If it was, the snakes took it."

And it grew worse. Railroad and coal barons sent in their agents to buy up timber and mineral rights at fractions of their worth, as little as a dollar an acre, hoodwinking locals and strong-arming the courts to invalidate long-held titles or discover that titles were up for grabs. Coal wars raged, union against management, union men against scabs; one county became known as Bloody Harlan; sixty years later, Leslie (twenty-eight homicides annually per hundred thousand inhabitants), Breathitt, and Harlan counties alternate as rural murder capitals of the U.S. The coal fields have known sporadic prosperity, but the blessings have been mixed, creating wild economic swings and doing violence to the earth. While private companies have done their share of damage, the chief environmental villain has been the Tennessee Valley Authority, which introduced, financed, and promoted strip mining in Eastern Kentucky to feed its generators to the south with cheap coal, destroying the watershed and making floods annual disasters. It is hardly surprising that mountain people continue to view outsiders with suspicion.

Today second-growth timber covers many of the scars left by stripping, stricter regulations have modified the floods, and the impressions a traveler receives of mountain life are confusing. Luxury automobiles and jalopies on the roads and parked in driveways; expensive-looking houses with trimmed lawns and shrubs next to rusting-out mobile homes where chickens range freely amid litter; dreary villages and isolated hovels along the highway to tidy, bustling towns—the area seems a patchwork of contrasts.

In 1991 at the Holiday Inn in Hazard, in Perry County, there were always a few Mercedeses and BMWs with local license tags in the parking lot. The inn itself was bankrupt: it had been built atop a filled-in strip mine; half the rooms had cracked and sunk. But the cars were not for sale. One seventy-thousand-dollar Mercedes belonged to the motel's owner, another to the manager, a third to the young woman behind the reception desk, who provided this information cheerfully, as if anyone ought to be able to afford decent transportation. Over at Whitesburg, in Letcher County, the Commonwealth's Attorney had recently traded his Jaguar plus twenty-five thousand dollars for a Rolls-Royce, a transaction widely discussed and recorded in court documents related to a sensational murder trial; yet a few miles away at Fleming-Neon, people stared idly from the porches of miners' shacks built seventy years ago. In a grocery store at Jenkins, one shopper paid with food stamps, another flashed a fat wad of bills. (The actual percentage of people receiving food stamps in Eastern Kentucky is about one in three, or three times the national average; welfare dependency spanning generations is widespread and is unrelated to race, the number of blacks being minuscule and in decline, down to only one hundred and ninety in Letcher County according to 1990 census data; the family names of the original settlers continue to appear on most headstones, reflecting a continuity that is nearly unknown elsewhere in America.)

For a partial explanation of these disparities in wealth, one can look back to the mid-seventies, when the world oil shortage sent coal prices soaring, and Eastern Kentucky's mines briefly boomed again. A fellow could load up his truck for forty dollars a ton and sell the coal for a hundred. Some people made fortunes in illegal, wildcat mining, untaxed and unencumbered by expensive permits and environmental restrictions. Locals recall that at that time even the high school parking lots filled up with expensive cars. Today, however, the price of coal has dropped again; as through the eighties, unemployment ranges in most counties from fifteen to twenty percent, officially, and is in reality higher than that. Even if one assumes that small businessmen and local officials managed to come by their sleek machines without ever deviating from the straight and narrow, something peculiar has to be going on here to explain the anomalous prosperity.

The answer lies in a thriving illegitimate economy. As the mines close, unions weaken or collapse, and more miners lose their jobs, many see a choice only between welfare and crime, and some choose both. The richest fields have as high a concentration of low-sulphur, high-b.t.u. coal as any in the world, lying just beneath the surface. Even at depressed prices, handsome profits can be made from wildcatting. And with good reason, many Eastern Kentuckians believe that they were cheated out of their mineral rights generations ago anyway, so why not claim what's rightfully theirs?

There are other, still riskier ways to make more than a few bucks. Marijuana, as in several other states, has become Kentucky's largest cash crop. Representatives of national crime syndicates come in yearly to make deals for the harvest; cultivation flourishes especially in Leslie County, where the Daniel Boone National Forest offers a solution to the problem of having your land seized if the authorities spot your crop. Over a hundred thousand plants, worth from a thousand to twenty-five hundred dollars apiece, were confiscated and burned in Leslie County during the first eight months of 1991. Untaxed, the profits enrich a few and do nothing for the many.

Along with what is referred to locally as the pot industry, narcotics dealing, intricate theft rings, and bootlegging have replaced moonshining as the principal highly private enterprises. Bourbon and white lightning aside, Kentucky was the birthplace of Carry Nation, and the majority of its counties have always been dry; others are "moist," permitting liquor sales only in incorporated areas that vote wet. As in the days of Prohibition, and as with narcotics, this situation invites entrepreneurship. Today a bootlegger can make ten dollars a case on liquor and up to forty on beer. Up-to-date, high-tone *booticians* offer delivery to your doorstep and operate out of mobile homes with drive-up windows, selling *piña coladas* topped with decorative umbrellas and other exotica as well as basic hootch.

The informing, double-crossing, and enforcing attendant on all these activities, in which county sheriffs often play the pivotal conspiratorial role, make the territory a place where being deaf and dumb has much to recommend it and where, as the saying goes, if they don't like the way your hair is parted, they'll part it for you. A stranger can expect friendly greetings in towns, but he had better not venture up into the hollows unarmed, if at all.

While both the FBI and the Kentucky State Police maintain vigorous presences—in one week alone in 1991, the sheriffs of Lee, Wolfe, and Owsley counties were convicted in drug and extortion cases— they confront a rich and romantic outlaw tradition in the region, where the belief is widespread that no one ever made a pile of money without being at least a little crooked. Scant shame or disgrace attaches to singing those lonesome jailhouse blues: if you haven't done some time yourself, your uncle or your cousin probably has. Being clever enough to get away with something is as likely to inspire an admiring wink as disdain; in this, as in other traits, Eastern Kentuckians resemble the Irish from whom so many of them are descended.

As for violence, mountaineers, or highlanders as they often call themselves with a bow toward Scottish roots, make a distinction between killing and murder. Killing is what you may have to do to defend your property or honor. Murder implies something vicious, gratuitously brutal; killing occurs spontaneously, as between husbands and wives, wives and husbands. And, in an oft-heard phrase, "Some people just needs killing." It is the mountain philosophy.

In 1980 a mountain jury hung nine to three for acquittal of a preacher who had gunned down a fellow preacher and distant cousin in a dispute over a driveway. When the retrial was moved out of the mountains to Lexington, in Fayette County, the killer received ten years. "My feeling is that in Fayette County they don't believe in self-defense as we do in Eastern Kentucky," the defendant's lawyer said. "They don't understand the mountain philosophy."

Lester H. Burns understands the mountain philosophy and everything else about his native grounds. Until 1987, when he was sentenced to eight years in the federal penitentiary, Lester Burns was the most famous, probably the most prosperous, and certainly the most colorful lawyer in the Commonwealth. Like the economy, his income fluctuated, but it was rarely much under a million dollars a year. If his client had money, Lester's fees were enormous, the highest in Kentucky, he liked to boast. Occasionally he took a case for a dollar "to help the needy—and for the publicity," he openly admitted. He owned property in several counties, along with cattle, interests in coal mines and shopping centers, and various glamorous and antique automobiles. He sometimes wore diamond rings on eight fingers, two or three rings on one, and toured the back roads in a two-hundred-and-fifty-thousand-dollar customized Blue Bird motor home—or bus, as he preferred to call it, beaming with false modesty—with "Lester H. Burns, Jr." emblazoned across the front in golden script. He was a member of the bars of and practiced in seven states. When Lester pulled into some county seat to defend a killer or to argue a civil action, he always drew a crowd. Sometimes he contrived to arrive a day or two early, just to stir things up. Spectators filled the courtroom to hear him ring the rafters with rhetoric and watch him fall to his knees and weep before the jury. Only prosecutors were glad when he left town.

But on May 14, 1987, Lester's world collapsed. He had already resigned his license to practice law. Gone were the diamonds and fancy suits. One newspaper compared him to a dethroned heavyweight. He was fifty-five.

Stooped and abject, he stood before a federal judge, having waived his right to a trial, and wept not for a client, but for himself. His family and friends, admirers and hangers-on averted their eyes as he clasped hands and pleaded guilty and said:

"Your Honor, I am begging for mercy. I did what I am accused of. I have a good past record. I could wear out a miner's kneepads until the day of my death and I couldn't apologize enough to make me feel like a human being. I am humiliated. As long as I live, I'll apologize to my family and my friends and the whole world."

The two counts to which he had pleaded guilty carried a maximum penalty of five years each. When Judge Eugene E. Siler, Jr. sentenced him to four years on each count, with the terms to run consecutively, Lester Burns looked as if he had been stabbed in the back. His life was destroyed, everyone said. A legend was finished.

How had it happened? How could Lester Burns have gone, as his own lawyer described it, from the pinnacle of his profession to total degradation? It had happened in scarcely more than a year. How could a man so intelligent, so clever, so experienced, and so rich have behaved, as Lester himself phrased it, like a nitwit?

He had made several crucial mistakes. One of them had been not hanging up when a call reached his unlisted number on the evening of August 15, 1985. The caller, a former client, asked Lester if he had heard about the robbery and attempted murder of Dr. Roscoe Acker and the murder of Dr. Acker's daughter in Letcher County a week before. Of course he had heard about it, Lester said. It was all over the papers and on television. A terrible thing. How much money had been taken? Four hundred thousand in cash, wasn't it? That was an awful lot of money for anyone to be keeping around the house. That poor old man. That poor girl.

It might have been more money than that, the caller said, a lot more. Three men had been arrested down in Florida. One of them was Roger Epperson, who wanted Lester Burns for his lawyer.

Lester thought for a minute. He knew the Eppersons. They were from around Hazard. Roger had always been a strange young man, in and out of trouble. What was particularly odd about Roger, especially given this phone call, was that from about the age of fourteen or fifteen, he had been a fan of Lester's. That had been ten, twenty years ago. Roger would follow Lester around like a groupie, showing up at all the big-time murder trials, rushing to congratulate him if he won and asking to buy him a sandwich or a cup of coffee. In another boy such an interest might have signalled an aspiring lawyer. As a young man Lester himself had studied and become enthralled by the courtroom performances of great attorneys. Roger Epperson's fascination appeared to have sprung from different motives.

The idea settled quickly like a cloud on Lester's mind that the three men who had been arrested were guilty. He knew they were, that was all there was to it. And he had another flash of insight. In following him around all those years ago, observing how he was able to instill doubts in a jury's mind and win technical points from a judge and drive a prosecutor to distraction, Roger Epperson had come to the conclusion that if you had Lester Burns as your lawyer, you could get away with just about anything. Now Roger had done something horrendous and, the second he was arrested, was trying to contact the great Lester Burns.

It was unnerving. An old man robbed, brutalized, his daughter murdered—Lester felt like an accomplice. He could feel Epperson's eyes on him. Epperson had stalked him; now he beckoned. Lester was already so rich that he had begun to cut down on his practice. There would be other cases. His instincts told him to pass this one up.

Yet four hundred thousand dollars, maybe more than that ... Lester ruminated. He was a man who rarely saw things in black and white, nor in gray, either, but most often in all the colors of the rainbow. Whoever did the killing would face the death penalty; they all might. And Roger's family had money, too, although how much of it they would be willing to part with to defend a scumbag like Roger was another matter.

Every man, even the lowest wretch on earth, even the rottenest son of a bitch who ever drew breath, deserves a fair trial, Lester reminded himself, and, as he always added, deserves to *believe* that he has had a fair trial and the best legal counsel that money can buy.

"Well, what do you say, Lester?" the caller asked. "Can I give Roger your number?"

"I will consider the matter," Lester said. "Yes, give him my number."

Years later, trying to account for the errors that had caused his fall, Lester recalled that moment, that fateful instant of acquiescence, and said, "I felt the darkness closing in."

2

Down in the basement den of Lester Burns's house, a long room panelled with weathered wood from barns, lies a violin case. It rests in a corner next to the Xerox machine, Lester's name spelled out on one side in pasted-on silver block letters.

"An old man gave that to me," Lester says. "He was the best fiddle maker in the mountains. I did some legal work for him, helped him with his Social Security. He could never pay me, so he gave me this fiddle."

Lester opens the case to reveal an unfinished instrument, a violin still in-the-white, as musicians say, the strings in place and waiting for a bow but the wood unvarnished.

"He gave it to me for Christmas. He wanted me to have it on the day, even though he had more work to do on it. I was supposed to give it back so he could put the varnish on. But by New Year's Eve, he was dead."

Lester conjures up the image of an old man dead in his cabin among the violins, bloodsoaked shavings on the floor, the smells of varnish and glue and gunpowder.

"His son killed him. The little son of a bitch. I prosecuted the bastard, nailed him for ten years. Maybe he should've got the chair. I believe in the death penalty, as deterrent and as retribution.

"Sometimes when I'm feeling low I take out that fiddle and pluck on those strings and think about that old man."

The story of the unfinished violin illuminates Lester Burns from several angles. Whenever Christmas came and Lester sat down at the head of the table with his family, he silently asked a special blessing for the holiday season because family quarrels would soon be erupting all over Eastern Kentucky, somebody would kill somebody, and Daddy would have new clients. The story of the violin also illustrates why Lester sometimes worked for free: "The fellow you help today for nothing may become a killer or a victim tomorrow, and that family will call you." Someone would come up with the money, or a farm. Under a Kentucky law since repealed, Lester for many years was employed by the families of victims to assist the Commonwealth's Attorney in prosecuting. The legislature repealed the law, it is Lester's opinion, because he annoyed the state's lawyers by outshining them and taking over the case. Defending a client, he would go to almost any length, but as a prosecutor he was hard-nosed. His unsentimental, law-and-order, conservative attitudes and politics were those of a self-made man who had fought himself out of a hole in the ground to become as dramatic as Tom Mix and as solvent as the Toyota Motor Company.

Born on Bullskin Creek on October 7, 1931, Lester H. Burns, Jr., was the first baby in Clay County delivered by the Mary C. Breckinridge Frontier Nursing Service, one of several mountain projects established by women of the prominent Breckinridge family of the Bluegrass. The "H" in the name had been added by Lester Sr., to make life easier for the postman, and stood for nothing. The nurse arrived on horseback to bring Lester into a world of mule-drawn ploughs, oil lamps, and dawn-to-dusk physical labor, of anvils and haystacks, of steam locomotives and gob piles.

Never destitute, Lester's family did struggle like everyone else during the Depression, without going on relief or taking WPA jobs, an independence that shaped Lester's character. His father farmed and, after the repeal of Prohibition, operated a small mill that manufactured white-oak staves for whiskey barrels. There was always enough to eat. After moving the family briefly to Ohio, his father managed to expand the Clay County farm and to acquire minor interests in coal mines here and there. Like all the other boys he knew, Lester by the age of twelve was laboring in the underground mines after school, on Saturdays, and throughout the summers. He soon concluded that this was not the life for him.

Whenever he had the chance, he hung around the courthouse, entranced by the dramatic spectacles enacted by country lawyers and by the excitement of the entire scene, which he enjoyed as much as his other youthful passion, Western movies. In the fifth grade, when his brother, James, was in the sixth, both boys wrote essays proclaiming that one day they would become soldiers, policemen, and lawyers. They both became all three.

Up Bullskin Creek Lester discovered a hollow with a natural echo. There he climbed atop a pine stump and delivered orations to the mountains, flailing the air, mesmerized by reverberations of himself, training his voice to scale peaks and plummet into valleys in a style derived in equal parts from the courtroom, the political rally, and the evangelist's tent. The subject was always some wretched innocent who had only Lester Burns standing between himself and the rope.

"The copperheads crawled out to listen," he says. "The birds stopped singing when I spoke."

He attended high school at the Oneida Baptist Institute, which had been founded by a cousin, and graduated at fifteen as valedictorian of his class. To escape the mines and to save money for college, he drove a Pepsi-Cola truck, learning the twists of mountain roads through twelve counties, stopping to chat with each delivery. Folks hung around to visit with him, this emissary from the wider world. He gathered stories from miners, farmers, shopkeepers, gas station attendants, and moonshiners, storing up intimacies of the highlanders' ways and figuring that one day when he was successful, maybe as a lawyer come back to defend them, they would remember him as the boy who drove the Pepsi truck.

After two years at Eastern Kentucky State College, in Richmond, Lester grew bored with his studies and joined the Air Force in search of adventure. He found plenty of it flying combat missions in Korea. The war over, he returned to finish college with the intention of going on to law school. By the time he graduated, however, he was married; his wife, Asonia, was soon pregnant with their first child. Lester became a state trooper, at a salary of two hundred and fifty dollars a month.

One of his fellow troopers, later the Lexington police chief, remembers him as "a character, that's the best way I can describe him. Very ambitious. And he was a hard-nosed officer, a hustler. He'd lock you up or give you a ticket in a minute." There was no question that Lester would rise rapidly in the police bureaucracy, but that was not what he wanted. He took advantage of the considerable amount of time a trooper has to spend testifying in court to absorb the law and to study lawyers. His favorite, who became something of a mentor to him, was the celebrated John Y. Brown, Sr., whose son, John Y. Jr., would later buy up Kentucky Fried Chicken, become governor, and marry Miss America. From the start, Lester had a knack for making the right contacts.

The most important of these was the governor at that time, A. B. "Happy" Chandler, the most popular figure in modern Kentucky history. First elected in 1935, Happy Chandler was appointed commissioner of baseball after World War II and by 1956 was into his second term as governor. In that year Lester managed to land frequent assignments as the official chauffeur of the governor and Mrs. Chandler.

As commissioner, Chandler left mixed impressions. He helped to integrate the sport by assisting Branch Rickey in bringing Jackie Robinson up to the Brooklyn Dodgers; but in the eighties Chandler compromised that distinction by uttering the word "nigger" at a meeting of the University of Kentucky Board of Regents, a slip that prompted demands for his resignation from the board. In 1947 he suspended Leo Durocher for the season for allegedly having consorted with gamblers; but many people, including Leo the Lip, believed that Durocher's crucial mistake was in complaining to reporters about the commissioner's hypocrisy in not suspending a Yankee owner for entertaining the same gamblers, Memphis Engleberg and Connie Immerman, in a private box at a ball game in Havana. "Baseball typifies the great American dream," Chandler wrote in his preface to the *Encyclopedia of Baseball* (1949), "where a boy may rise from direct poverty to become a national hero. No pull—no inside track is necessary. The only requirements are the development of a skill and the willingness to work hard in the development of that skill." In anointing Lester Burns as a protégé, however, Chandler must have believed that some pull and the inside track would do the boy no harm. In Lester, Governor Chandler spotted a fellow with political instincts, down-home charm, and shrewdness not unlike his own. The two developed a father-and-son closeness.

Lester was by then a handsome stripling, as he might have

phrased it, just under six feet tall, his physique toughened by work in the mines and lifting those Pepsi crates. High cheekbones, a tanned, coppery complexion, and a regal carriage exuding confidence suggested a Shawnee chief, maybe Tecumseh himself somewhere in the background ennobling the tough Scottish strains. His hair was sandy; his eyes gleamed turquoise.

"Momma and I just about raised him," Governor Chandler recalled twenty-five years later in speaking to a reporter who was preparing a front-page feature story on Lester. "He just had that Clay County determination about him. Under other circumstances, he might have had an average life. But he had that spark."

One October afternoon Lester drove Mrs. Chandler to the Keeneland races, a journey of more than an hour, plenty of time for him to spin a few mountain yarns. He also gave her a tip on the big race.

"Lester, honey," Momma said on the return trip, "do you want to be a trooper all your life?"

"No, Momma," Lester said, "I have always dreamed of becoming a lawyer."

"Then why don't you do it?"

"I can't afford it. I've got a wife and a baby daughter, and besides, I can't choose my hours. They don't have classes at night, and half the time I'm working days."

"Lester, honey, didn't you finish first in your class at the Police Academy?"

"Yes, ma'am, I did."

"Well, Lester, I want you to call your supervisor first thing Monday morning, you hear? You tell him the governor told you to call. From now on, you're working nights, and you can attend law school during the day."

"I don't think the supervisor will agree to that," Lester said. "Everybody has to work different shifts."

"Honey, the head of the State Police works for my husband. If he doesn't like it, Happy will fire him."

Lester enrolled at the University of Kentucky School of Law that week, his books and tuition taken care of by a special scholarship granted by the governor's office. He gave out very few tickets during the next few years. Usually he parked his cruiser on some lonely road to study. Another trooper gave him a book rack with a light attached that hooked onto the steering wheel. When he received his degree, other graduates urged him to sign up for special courses to cram for the bar examination.

"Why would I need to do that?" Lester asked. "I've been going without sleep for three years. If I don't know the law by now, I must be some kind of an idiot."

Lester passed the bar on his first try in September 1959, argued his first case the same day, and won. He borrowed five hundred dollars to move his family—Asonia had given birth to a second daughter by then—back to Manchester, the Clay County seat, where he knew he had enough contacts and understood the people well enough to give himself a running start. He opened a twenty-dollar-a-month office and began immediately to establish the theatrical style that would mark his career.

The nearest Cadillac dealer was over in Corbin. Lester walked into the showroom wearing a new suit he had just purchased on credit, pointed to a white 1959 Coupe de Ville, and announced that he did not have a dime to his name but was the best lawyer in Kentucky and would never miss a payment. When the salesman laughed at him, Lester demanded to see the owner and drove off in the Cadillac with no money down. In his first four months of practice, he made twenty-five thousand dollars and paid off the car.

Lester knew he had brains and was willing to work harder than anyone else; he also knew that that was not enough. To be the kind of success he was determined to be, he knew he had to appear it and act it, and he understood which symbols meant success to mountain folk. There was the Cadillac, that was a prerequisite, and there had to be clothes to match and the panache to wear them as if he belonged in them—the mountain boy who had made it and with whom everyone could identify, or nearly everyone. Lester was so meticulous and imaginative about his clothes that if he had been born a Parisian, he might have outstyled Christian Dior. He often wore a touch of bright blue, in a tie or a silk handkerchief billowing from his breast pocket, to call attention to his eyes. To complement the white Caddy with its red leather upholstery he chose several pastel suits, added diamond rings, and made sure his shoes never showed a speck of dust. When he descended on a dingy mining town he looked as if he had flown in from a holiday in Florida or maybe Las Vegas, tan, sparkling, rich, exuding bravado.

"I can't understand these small-town lawyers with their Sears Roebuck suits and *shop rags* for ties," Lester said. "You know what a *shop rag* is? That's what a grease monkey uses to change your oil. All those lawyers wear them. No wonder they're broke."

When Lester began handing out business cards with his name engraved in gold on a black background, the state bar association came after him. Lawyers in those days were forbidden to advertise. He was not advertising, Lester insisted. His only advertisement was himself. The cards displayed only his name, not a word about his being an attorney-at-law. Surely the Constitution protected the right of every American citizen to print his name on a little-bitty card! The association backed off.

In court, Lester adjusted his wardrobe to fit the circumstances, gearing sartorial selections to appeal to the jury. He often visited a territory two or three days beforehand incognito, wearing bib overalls if necessary to mingle for coffee or a few beers with the locals, to gauge the temper of a place. He found out what color suit the prosecutor was wearing on any given day and, dressing in his motor home, chose something that contrasted with his adversary. When jurors began showing up wearing Lester's colors, he knew he had the case won. Nosing around before one trial in 1983, he learned that the whole town had gone mad for a certain brand of imported Taiwanese clothing that a local merchant had on sale under the Frenchified label "Etienne Augère." He bought two suits and a leather jacket and began carrying a briefcase bearing that label, which he left open for the jury to see.

"I Augered 'em to death," Lester crowed, pronouncing the name as if it were something used to bore holes. It took the jury twenty minutes to reach a verdict of acquittal.

The premise of his courtroom tactics was that anyone who believed that twelve randomly selected human beings were capable of reaching a unanimous decision on the basis of a cool disinterested weighing of the evidence was an idiot. You had to play psychological games, you had to distract and entertain a jury to persuade them and make them grateful to you for giving them something better than anything on TV. And you had to be able to anticipate their gut reactions. Supposing, for instance, that one of your key defense witnesses had something ghastly in his background that, if unskillfully elicited, would undermine his credibility. The key was to bring that skeleton out of the closet right off the bat, so that by the time the jury was ready to deliberate, they had forgotten about it or at least had relegated it to the backs of their minds. Thus he might begin examining a witness by saying, "Mr. Smith, it's true that several years ago you had the misfortune of getting into an argument with your cousin and shooting him, isn't it? And you were convicted of manslaughter and spent time in prison satisfying your debt to society, isn't that also true?" That out of the way, Lester could get down to business. If he left damaging information to be brought out by the prosecutor, a mere distraction could turn into a bombshell.

Everyone conceded Lester's cleverness, even brilliance; no one doubted his knowledge of the law or the thoroughness with which he usually prepared a case. It was his theatrics that offended other members of the bar and some judges. There were those who called him a buffoon. John Y. Brown, Sr., once advised a certain client to plead guilty and accept a sentence of ten years in prison. The client consulted Lester, who asked how much John Y. was charging him. The man said fifteen hundred dollars, and Lester said that that was about fourteen-ninety-nine too much. What did he need a lawyer for? He could go to prison on his own. The man went back to John Y. Brown and fired him, saying he was hiring Lester Burns.

"But—Lester Burns has no *finesse!*" John Y. protested.

"You tell John Y.," Lester retorted when he heard this, "that Lester Burns has finessed everything he ever started."

When Lester purchased the first of his twenty-foot-long motor homes displaying his name across the front and sides, the bar association again took exception. Lester told them that if they didn't care for this one, he had another bus that lit up in neon with the slogan, "If You Cough, Call Us!" The facetious reference was to his advocacy of black lung disease cases on behalf of miners. He would roll into the coalfields with an entourage of assistants and gofers—some of them former clients paying off debts to him by working for nothing—and open up for business on the spot, doing minor legal work for free and taking black lung cases on a contingency basis. He was a pioneer in this litigation, which did more than anything else to build his reputation and income.

When the government tightened the rules on black lung suits, making it difficult for Lester to turn a wheeze into money, "I could feel the darkness closing in," he remembers in one of his favorite asides. Quick to adjust, he began to specialize in criminal defense, which occupied about seventy-five percent of his practice, with personal injury and medical malpractice taking up most of the rest. By one means or another, he continued to enhance his reputation as the champion of the little man—or woman. First it had been the injured miner against the corporation; now it was the accused against an oppressive system of justice and a vindictive prosecutor, or, if Lester was himself prosecuting, the victim's family crying out for retribution. Lester was careful, whatever the economic temptations, never to represent the obviously rich and powerful unless he could somehow cast them in the role of the oppressed. And he continued to do some work for free or for next to nothing. He took on for one dollar, for instance, any case in which a state trooper was charged with any sort of crime—out of warm memories of his days on the force, he said, and because troopers were shamefully underpaid public servants who daily risked their lives for the common good. Whatever his motives, this public-spirited generosity did no harm in terms of publicity and may even, some cynics claimed, possibly have caused troopers called to testify in criminal cases to modify, to soften, perhaps to shape their testimony in Lester's behalf without, of course, ever stepping over the perilous line of perjury.

As Lester became more and more identified with criminal cases, his flamboyance—the word reporters associated with him more than any other—increased, his sense of drama growing bolder. He had the instincts of a P. T. Barnum or a Mike Todd, that if the public likes what you are giving them, give them more of it.

ATTORNEY LESTER BURNS TURNS THE COURTROOM INTO A STAGE read a front-page headline in the *Lexington Herald-Leader,* under a three-column photograph of Lester standing grinning beside his bus, dressed in a Western-cut suit, rings flashing, an enormous gold-on-silver belt buckle gleaming. He had discovered that, although Kentucky was hardly the Wild West, Western clothing, including handmade ostrich-, snake-, and turtleskin boots, always played well.

"I would have no quarrel with the word flamboyant," he said. "I've been known to get down on the floor and I've been known to wrap myself in the American flag." He meant all of this literally.

"But if working to the fullest extent of my abilities for my clients, if wearing expensive clothes and expensive diamonds and giving myself fully to every case I take is being flamboyant, then I plead guilty to being flamboyant."

His theatrics included high-powered firearms. Explaining his need for bodyguards, automatic rifles, pistols, and shotguns, Lester claimed that "the cases I have are not ones that enhance popularity," a judgment with which most Eastern Kentuckians would have disagreed. "It's sad, but I have to go heavily armed. When the crooks and killers of this country know you're packing a gun they won't be so quick to go out there and shoot people down in the streets." Here he walked a tightrope, because he was defending crooks and killers at the same time that he presented himself as their enemy. The people saw no contradiction: it was a variation on the mountain philosophy.

To Lester the principle was simple and obvious, that ordinary people, the common people if you like, will always admire and covet what they cannot have and will continue to admire the person having it, as long as he never forgets where he came from and never loses the common touch. He was the millionaire who was still the country boy. He was a Will Rogers figure, tweaking the establishment and, it was true, scorned by it even as he bought up tracts of land and collected rent in six counties. He was a law-and-order man even as the assumption grew, and he began to worry about it, that anyone Lester Burns defended must be guilty, whatever the verdict.

When he tried a murder case at Greenup on the Ohio River, he leased a sternwheel riverboat for himself and his entourage. After all, he said, there were so few motel rooms. Lester Burns deserved adequate accommodations just the same as any rock or country music star; the public expected it. When he drove into a mountain town in his Rolls-Royce, he sat down on the courthouse steps to chat with the folks and a crowd gathered. The sheriff asked if Lester would allow him to open the doors and rope off the car so everyone could examine it without damaging it. "Sure," Lester said, "but doesn't anyone want to take a spin?" Several hands went up. Lester tossed the keys to the crowd, and people drove that Rolls around as carefully as if it had been their own.

One old man, however, came up and told Lester that he was worried about him:

"Lester, are you in trouble? Have you lost all your money?"

"What do you mean?" Lester asked.

"That car."

"Why, that's a Rolls-Royce. That's the most expensive car in the world."

"I don't care what you're telling me," the old man said. "What's happened to your Cadillac?"

Although he continued to concentrate on the mountains, Lester's fame brought him cases all over the Commonwealth and into neighboring states. His country-boy tricks played well in all rural areas. On a foray into Ohio, he arranged to be followed by a pickup truck loaded with Kentucky country hams, and he began handing them out as soon as he arrived at the courthouse. When he went to see his client, the jailer, giving Lester a hostile, contemptuous stare, told him that visiting hours were over. He would have to come back tomorrow, like everyone else.

"This is a legal matter," Lester said. "I am the gentleman's attorney."

"I don't care who you are," the jailer said.

Lester summoned a gofer and offered the jailer a ham.

"Your wife will love it," Lester said. "You've never tasted anything like it, and there's enough here for the whole family. They say that a man alone with a Kentucky ham is a definition of eternity."

The jailer took it but suggested that it might be a good idea to give the sheriff one, too, and a couple of the deputies might like one. Lester obliged and was able to see his client day or night after that. When someone suggested that this was bribery, Lester replied, "When the time comes in America that our great system of justice can be perverted by a country ham, we might as well give in to the Russians."

It was inevitable that Lester Burns would take a fling at politics. In the mid-sixties he was elected Commonwealth's Attorney for Clay, Leslie, and Jackson counties, a part-time post that he won in a walk and that permitted him to carry on his private practice while reinforcing his law-and-order image. In 1967 he ran for Attorney General as a Republican populist, attacking "those ruthless, cutthroat, moneystealing politicians in Frankfort," calling Democratic gubernatorial candidate Henry Ward "a liar, a thief, a rat, and a little weasel," ex-Governor Bert Combs "Dirty Bert the Little Squirt," President Johnson "Lightbulb Lyndon," and Vice President Humphrey "Hubert Heartbeat." He lost, narrowly, to Democrat John Breckinridge. In a try for the governorship, he enlivened a commercial television spot by grabbing the Stars and Stripes and using it as a shawl, but he failed to gain the Republican nomination.

Lester was too outrageous for statewide office. His popularity in his native and other rural areas was solid; but many educated urban and suburban voters could not take him seriously, and some called him a clown, an embarrassment to Kentucky's attempts to shake its backwoods reputation. As a Republican who appealed to the working class and sensed that working people resented welfare, high taxation, and the politics of promises and preferred to identify with material success rather than with the poor, Lester was ahead of his time, anticipating the national Republican strategy of the eighties. But as a man who gloried in his hillbilly roots, he seemed an anachronism. And he had stepped on too many establishment toes over the years. He went back to being "the people's lawyer," as he had always called himself.

He also left the mountains, although his criminal practice continued to be centered there, where most of the crime was. In 1972 he and his family moved fifty miles west to Somerset, on Lake Cumberland, a gentler landscape and perhaps the most picturesque in Kentucky, soon to become a prospering tourist mecca, much to the enhancement of Lester's investments in land. There he built a large office with a balcony cantilevered over the lake. He also bought the building next door, leasing it to a psychic, astrologer, and palm reader who was always on time with the rent.

Somerset, the home grounds of the patrician Republican U.S. Senator John Sherman Cooper, was named for the Duke of Somerset and had about it a certain leisureliness and even elegance. Lester built a handsome, four-bedroom house beside the fairways of the Eagle's Nest Country Club and a stone farmhouse overlooking the lake, where on lush acres he raised Black Angus cattle, fished, shot the breeze and drank a little with his buddies, and drove heavy equipment to let off steam. For his widowed mother, Ruby, he purchased a condominium and dropped by to share with her the latest results from the Kentucky and other state lotteries.

At the Eagle's Nest house, decorated by Asonia, who had conservative taste and was as shy as he was bold, Lester played the soft-spoken country gentleman in blue blazer, designer jeans, and cordovan loafers. In his garage he tinkered with classic automobiles—"I love knocking them down and putting them back together again screw by screw"—including the first air-conditioned American car, a 1938 Packard that eventually brought nearly two hundred thousand dollars at auction in New York. Not to disappoint his mountain faithful, he had customized to his specifications a "Saturn-bronze" Cadillac Fleetwood 75 limousine with crushed-velvet bronze upholstery and curtains, a bar, refrigerator, television set, and a rear window in the shape of the ace of spades.

"I am going day and night" was his byword. In 1982 he was back in politics as Commonwealth's Attorney for Pulaski and Rockcastle counties, winning ninety-three percent of the vote in one and eighty-six percent in the other; but even his loyalists thought he took his knack for publicity a bit far when he had himself photographed arresting drunk drivers at gunpoint.

In 1983 he outfitted a new motor home with a satellite dish, burglar-alarm system, charcoal grill, gun racks, sleeping accommodations for five, three computers, a basic law library, and a horn that played Willie Nelson's "On the Road Again."

"I'm always raring to go," he exulted. "Just put me in that starting gate! You have to love life and love humanity, isn't it the truth? Otherwise, what's the point? I'm still the boy from Bullskin Creek. What I need is to find more folks in trouble who're rich enough to pay my fee!"

3

THE MAN TELEPHONING Lester Burns that August evening in 1985 with the news that Roger Epperson needed a lawyer was Hurley "Sonny" Spencer, who lived in the mountains of Perry County in a village called Viper. The Kentucky State Police knew Spencer as an associate of the late Muggs Cummins, a local drug czar whose body had been discovered one day on the side of a hill, the skull bashed in with a two-by-four. The last time Lester had counseled him, Sonny Spencer had been residing in the Clark County jail; he was now out on parole.

Within a few minutes of Spencer's call, a woman was on the line from Florida. Sounding agitated, she identified herself as Carol Epperson, Roger's wife. Roger had been arrested that afternoon and was locked up in the Orange County jail. He wanted no one but Lester Burns for his lawyer. She rattled on nonstop, saying that she would be able to pay Lester's standard fee in a murder case, which Roger had informed her was one hundred thousand dollars.

He did not have a standard fee, Lester advised. He did not believe in them. His fee depended on a number of variables. Knowing nothing about the case and what would be required of him, he could hardly be asked to estimate as yet what he would have to charge. He was not an auto mechanic or a plumber. Murder was a serious matter. He would come down to Orlando tomorrow to see what he could do.

On Friday, August 16, Lester flew out of Lexington, taking with

him Ralph Gibson, a recent law school graduate who was working in
Lester's office that summer. The morning papers told of the arrests of
Roger Dale Epperson, Benny Lee Hodge, and Donald Terry Bartley,
who had apparently been cornered by the FBI on the previous day
and taken to the Orange County jail, where they were booked on
charges of first-degree burglary, first-degree robbery, attempted murder, and capital murder. They were suspects in the robbery and
attempted murder of Dr. Roscoe J. Acker and the murder of his
daughter Tammy, a University of Kentucky student, at the doctor's
residence in Fleming-Neon, Letcher County, Kentucky, on August 8.
Approximately five hundred thousand dollars in cash and five thousand dollars in jewelry and other valuables had reportedly been taken
from the house.

Lester noted that the amount of money supposedly taken had
risen by a hundred thousand since the first reports and that most of it
was said to be still missing. The papers did not indicate what had led
the police to identify these three men as suspects, nor how the FBI
had been able to find them down in Florida within a week of the
crimes.

At the Orlando airport Lester rented a car and drove downtown
to the Best Western Catalina Inn, on 33rd Street near the county jail.
He telephoned Carol Epperson, who was also staying at the motel.
She said that she would be right over to Lester's room. She was
bringing along a friend of hers, who she said was Benny Hodge's girlfriend.

Lester took an instant dislike to Carol Epperson. It was obvious
to him that she was on drugs—"a full-blown dopehead" was the way
he characterized her—as he had already deduced from her mile-a-
minute babbling on the phone. This would make negotiating with her
and keeping her under control a big headache. She was also untidy,
Lester thought—cleanliness was important to him in judging anyone's character; he noticed what looked like ketchup on her blouse
and spots on her tight pants. Another count against her, from his
point of view, was that she looked Japanese. "I can never forget or
forgive Pearl Harbor," Lester liked to say, although he had been ten
years old at the time of the attack.

Carol introduced her companion as Sherry Wong, which seemed
peculiar, as the woman did not appear to be Chinese or Asian in any
respect. She was an inch or two taller than Carol, about five-three or
-four, and a few years older, maybe in her mid-thirties. Her hazel eyes,

magnified behind clear-rimmed glasses, had deep circles underneath. Dressed in pressed jeans and a T-shirt, she seemed as tidy as Carol was unkempt, as steady and cool as Carol was fidgety. When Sherry spoke, the accent was pure hillbilly.

"How do I know you're who you say you are?" she asked. "How do I know you're a lawyer? You could be FBI. Let's see some I.D."

Lester showed her his business card. When that didn't satisfy her, he emptied the contents of his wallet—credit cards, driver's license, the works. He said that he admired her caution. She was correct, the FBI must be crawling all over the place. After all, some of the money was missing, wasn't it? Neither woman indicated yes or no.

"This is Ralph Gibson," Lester said, "a dandy young lawyer who's here to assist me."

Carol took this as an invitation to start talking again. She was impossible to follow. Lester thought he heard something about going to college and Patty Hearst.

"Turn off that mouth, Chop," Sherry Wong said.

"Why don't you ladies have a seat?" Lester said. "You all must be worn out. It's a terrible strain, having loved ones locked up. How about a soda or something?"

It was a standard motel room. Carol and Sherry took the chairs. Gibson and Lester perched on the beds.

Sherry wanted to know what they were supposed to do next. She asked about Lester's fee.

"I understand that I've been asked to represent Roger Epperson," Lester said. "I've known Roger for a long time, and his mother and daddy. They must be suffering, with their boy in the clutches of the law and all. Are they coming to town?"

"What is this going to cost?" Sherry said.

"My fee will be a confidential matter between me and my client. I can tell you this much, I'll require a retainer up front, so I can give Roger all the attention he deserves, right out of the chute. I would say that he is in a mighty precarious position. One wrong move—"

"How much is your retainer?" Sherry demanded.

"Twenty-five thousand."

Sherry and Carol agreed that he could have that by sometime tomorrow. Lester said that would be satisfactory. In the meanwhile, to show good faith and because there was no time to lose, he would head right over to the jail to see Roger.

When the women left, Lester could hear them arguing outside.

Their voices rose above the air conditioner, which was going full blast. He peeked through the window and saw Sherry poking an index finger at Carol's shoulder.

"Feuding and fussing," Lester said. "Isn't it sad, what money will make people do. Dear oh dear, I do believe those two are going to kill each other."

As Lester feared, Roger Epperson acted as if he had little to worry about. He seemed to regard his attorney as someone who must already have figured out how to set him free. The other two suspects, whom Lester glimpsed in their cells, did not radiate this optimism. Bartley looked like a caged rodent; Hodge, burly and sullen, stared from behind the bars with eyes that said nothing.

Lester consulted with Epperson in a room at the jail set aside for that purpose. Roger had put on weight in the years since Lester had last seen him and had lost some hair. He was thirty-five, six-foot-one, two hundred and twenty pounds, according to the booking sheet. He was pale, flabby, puffed like a pastry. He looked as if he had been on dope; it would have been an interest he and Carol had in common.

He told Lester that there was only one man he wanted to defend him, and that was Lester Burns. He asked Lester if he remembered how he used to watch him in court. Lester acknowledged that he did. Roger cited a couple of murder cases that had ended in acquittals.

"Have you ever been in serious trouble before?" Lester asked.

Roger said not much. A few minor scrapes. And he wasn't worried about this time, either, not with Lester on his side.

"You've been charged with murder," Lester said, "and attempted murder. The robbery's one thing, but that girl was twenty-three years old. I understand that she was stabbed to death. With a butcher knife."

Roger said he knew nothing about that. He had not been present. If somebody had stabbed the girl, it had been someone else, not that he knew or was saying who. He was not worried. They had nothing on him.

What about the robbery? Lester wanted to know. According to the newspapers and what the cops were saying, a good deal of money had been found in the condominium Roger had been sharing with Hodge and Bartley, and Hodge had had money on him. What about the briefcase found in Roger's car? Hadn't that had about sixty thousand in it? Was this money from the Acker robbery, or did Roger have another explanation for it? Roger hesitated.

Lester said that it was in Roger's best interest to tell his lawyer the truth. He did not care whether Roger was guilty; if he was, it was his lawyer's duty to keep the truth from coming out, and to see to it that he had a fair trial. If Lester didn't know what had happened, he could not be expected to fashion an effective defense. He couldn't be put in a position where the authorities knew more than he did. That was suicide. Had Roger participated in the Acker robbery? How much money was involved?

"More than a million," Roger said, grinning.

"You got more than a million from that old man? From his house? Cash money?"

"Make it a million-two," Roger said. "We never finished counting."

"You mean a million two hundred thousand? You don't mean two million, do you?"

"Could be," Roger said, acting coy. "You never know. There's piles of it. Some of it's so old, it stinks."

Where was the money? Lester asked as casually as he could. Sherry had it stashed somewhere, Roger said, he didn't know where. She might have buried it. Carol was angry about that, so was Donnie Bartley, but Roger wasn't worried. Sherry wasn't about to run off, she was too stuck on Benny Hodge. She had the best head for figures, Carol was too strung out, so Sherry was the banker. They had agreed to divide everything three ways. The women had been down in Miami, getting passports and seeing about a boat, when the boys had been arrested. It was shitty timing. They had planned to leave the country. They probably still would, when they got out.

"So most of the money is still out there?" Lester asked, making it sound like a matter of mere idle curiosity. "Over a million, you say?"

"That's right."

"My fee will be four hundred thousand," Lester said. "That's over and above the retainer."

Roger exploded. Lester must be kidding. This was robbery!

Lester suggested that Roger go back to his cell to think things over. The sooner he came to a decision, the better, because if he was not going to hire Lester Burns, he had better get someone else, quick. There would be an extradition order coming down from Kentucky.

There wasn't any time to waste at all, but Roger could sleep on it, if he wished.

"You don't hire the best for peanuts," Lester told him.

As he headed for his car, Lester ran into Carol and Sherry, who were with two other women Carol introduced as Louise Farley and Sharon Wilson, Donnie Bartley's mother and sister.

"You are not Lester Burns," Louise Farley said. "I have seen Lester Burns, and you're not him. Lester Burns wears cowboy boots."

The next morning Lester waited for Carol in the motel coffee shop. He was feeling a bit jittery. What with thinking about all those piles of money lying around somewhere, just waiting to be put to some good use or to be found by the FBI, and what with the pain he had been feeling in his arthritic left hip, Lester, alone in his room the previous night, had made too deep an impression on the whiskey bottle. The hip needed an operation, but he had been putting that off. He had a prescription for Percodan, but he was afraid of getting hooked; the aspirin and the whiskey did help the pain, and his ideas grew wild. What if this gang really had made off with more money than anyone, including the FBI, suspected? What if Dr. Acker had been reluctant to admit how much money he had been hoarding, or what if he didn't even know how much? Lester had already learned that Roger had been arrested earlier that summer for a robbery in Rome, Georgia; he had been out on bond for that at the time of this new arrest. How many other robberies had there been and how much was the total take? The suspects weren't ratting on each other, not yet anyway. They might have been together long enough to have done many jobs and to have developed loyalties based on who knew how many secrets.

As Lester excited himself with visions of heaps of cash, he became anxious. It would not be easy to show that he had no idea where his fee was coming from. Every criminal lawyer faced this difficulty, but here it was acute. This crew was unlikely to have legitimate assets. The prudent course would be to pack up and go home.

Still, if no one knew how much cash there was, who was to know how or how much Lester was being paid? And Roger's family had money of their own. Obviously they were not rushing to their son's aid, they were nowhere within sight; but they might prove helpful one way or another once they realized that Roger might be facing the electric chair. If Roger could get money to them, and they could pay Lester …

The thing to do, Lester more or less decided in his reverie, was to wait to receive the retainer and go from there. He had gone this far. He had already devoted time and money to this case. He deserved something. Was it his responsibility to know where every penny of his fee was coming from? If it were, what criminal would ever be able to hire a lawyer? This had become a hotly debated aspect of the law, especially because of the enormous cash resources of drug dealers and organized crime figures. A lawyer who knowingly accepted stolen goods could be prosecuted, but to what lengths a lawyer ought to go to ascertain the origin of a fee was not clearly defined. The key to avoiding prosecution and conviction was to be able to show that you had good reason to believe that your client had legitimate assets from which the fee could conceivably be paid.

When Carol appeared at the coffee shop she was antsy as usual and, this time, irate. There was no way, she said, that Roger would agree to such an outrageous fee. Roger was insisting that she should not pay Lester a cent over a hundred thousand.

"The money won't do him much good after he fries," Lester said. His spiel unreeled automatically; he had been giving versions of it for twenty-five years. "You may not even find another lawyer who'll take this money. I notice the other two boys don't have one. What kind of a wife wouldn't do more for her husband than hire some no-good two-bit shyster who doesn't know his ass from his elbow about Kentucky and how we do things there? Don't you love your husband?"

Of course she loved him, Carol said. Technically, they were not man and wife. Her real name was Ellis. Actually it was Keeney. They had planned to get married. Then this had happened.

Lester leaned toward her across the table, his face assuming furrows of worry and concern. He was not one to question other people's domestic arrangements, he said. He and his wife had celebrated their thirty-second wedding anniversary, but not everyone could be so fortunate in these troubled times. Unfortunately, he told her almost in a whisper, not everyone was so broad-minded. The law was a cruel, impartial thing. The law made an important distinction between people who were actually married and those who were not. If she was not in fact Roger's lawful wedded wife, she would more than likely be called to testify. She could be charged with criminal facilitation, at the very least. Hadn't she been making plans to leave the country? If the FBI found out about that, and they were very likely to find out, she could be looking at years behind bars. And there was a more serious likelihood. She could become her loved one's executioner.

"You may end up being the instrument that sends Roger to the chair. I have seen it happen. If you're not his wife, they will compel you to testify against him. I have seen lives wrecked. Even if they let you off, you won't have much to spend your money on, except flowers for his grave. What a pitiful story! I am telling you this for your own good. People do not understand how vulnerable and helpless they are. The law can grind you to bits."

He said that he felt so sorry for her that he would be willing to represent her, too, at no charge. His fee for her would be a dollar—assuming that Roger wised up and came to an agreement. Roger's situation was dire. The authorities had already turned up evidence that Lester was not yet at liberty to disclose. This case would require every ounce of his experience and ingenuity. What price could you place on a human life?

4

THAT EVENING CAROL SUMMONED LESTER to her room at the motel. He took Ralph Gibson with him and found Carol waiting with Sherry, Louise Farley, and Sharon Wilson. The women did not appear glad to see him. His attempt at pleasantries fell flat.

Carol handed Lester a brown paper bag. Hefting it, he took it into the bathroom and closed the door. The counter beside the sink was wet and strewn with toiletries, so he emptied the bag out onto the floor. There were five bundles of bills, each secured at both ends with rubber bands. It was all in hundreds, five bundles of five thousand dollars each. It occurred to him that carrying that amount around in a paper bag probably was not such a good idea, so he tucked the bundles under his shirt in the small of his back. Through the door he could hear the women.

When he came out, Sherry was saying that nobody called her a bitch and a thief and got away with it. If it weren't for her, they wouldn't have any money to pay a lawyer. Carol would have lost it or spent it on coke. Ralph Gibson stood in a corner, looking alarmed. Lester stepped between Sherry and Carol and told everyone to calm down and listen to him. They should put everything in his hands, it was the best thing they could do.

"Roger wants me to have his share," Carol shouted.

"I'll have to hear that from Roger himself," Sherry said.

"Ladies! Please!" Lester begged them. "Keep it down!"

Lester went to the window, leaned against the air conditioner and pushed the curtains apart an inch. The money bulged under the back of his shirt.

"The FBI are everywhere," he said. "I'll bet they have a hundred agents on this thing. They're scouring the state for that money. I wouldn't go out with any money on you, if I were you. I wouldn't keep any in the room, either." He turned to face the women. "What about the attorneys for Benny and Donnie? Of course, you could try to get the court to appoint some nobody to defend them, if you think you can prove they're broke. It's too bad I'm not in a position to help, the way things are at the moment. I can only do so much. I could do a lot for all of you. I know how you must be suffering," he said to Louise Farley, "as a mother." He reached out and put his arms around her. "These are trying times. You're a fine-looking woman and I know you love your son. Don't cry." She wasn't.

Back in his room, Lester told Ralph Gibson that he ought to fly back to Kentucky the next day. Things at the office would be piling up. Lester pulled out his shirt and tossed the money onto the bed, bundle by bundle.

"There's twenty-five grand there. You can take it with you and keep it for me till I get back."

Gibson stared at the money silently. Then he said that he did not think he wanted to do that. It was one thing to receive this money. It was another to transport it across state lines. The law against doing that with stolen money was clear.

"How do you know it's stolen?" Lester asked. "You know more than I do. How do we know this is Acker money? For all I know, one of the girls inherited it from her grandmother. Maybe Epperson's parents are paying my expenses."

Gibson looked Lester in the eye.

"All right," Lester said. "I understand. You're young. I wouldn't dream of asking you to do something you don't want to do. You go home, and I'll take care of this end of things."

In the morning Lester stuffed the money into the sack his whiskey had come in and hid it under the spare tire in the trunk of his car. He realized that he was now beyond a certain threshold.

He decided to take a Sunday drive over to Ormond Beach, fifty miles northeast, where the automobiles Epperson and the others had been driving were impounded and where Lester thought he might pick up some information. He was nervous about the money in the trunk. Because of its heavy drug traffic, Florida was the worst place in the country to be caught with loose cash you couldn't explain, and besides, he didn't trust the people he was dealing with. They might decide to fire him and take the money back, and they might find his existence an inconvenience, given what he already knew. If and when he received more, he would have to get hold of a gun to protect himself.

At the Ormond Beach police compound, Lester turned on the charm and learned that Letcher County Assistant Commonwealth's Attorney Mike Caudill, two Kentucky state troopers, and a couple of FBI agents had already been there with warrants to search the three cars, a Dodge conversion van, a Datsun 300ZX sports car, and a flaming red Corvette, all brand new, all purchased during the week after the Acker robbery, although registered in names other than those of the suspects. He heard again about the briefcase stuffed with money that had been found in Roger's car, the Corvette. Guns had been discovered in Hodge's van; marijuana, cocaine, a boot knife, and a portable two-way radio had turned up in Bartley's Datsun. Lester would have learned all this officially soon enough, but he could use it now.

Back at the county jail in Orlando, Lester confronted Epperson with the evidence and suggested that buying all those cars immediately following the robbery had not been the brightest idea. There were other cars, too, Roger admitted, six in all. The Toyota MR2 that Carol was driving was one of them.

Yet Roger remained adamant against paying Lester the four hundred thousand. Lester dropped it to three. Roger went up to a hundred and twenty-five thousand and said he would throw in a Corvette, not the 1985 one that was impounded, but a 1963 classic that was not part of the Acker spoils. In a sense, you could call it a legitimate car. He had paid eleven thousand down for it and still owed about six; Lester could pay it off and it was his. Lester accepted, but they remained far apart overall.

Leaving the jail again that afternoon, Lester encountered a pair of Kentucky state troopers who were down gathering evidence. Lester knew them both and struck up a friendly chat. He told them that he was representing Epperson but that there were questions about his fee. He would probably end up with nothing but automobiles and jewelry, and he had no use for either.

One of the troopers, Detective Lon Maggard, said that he had been one of the first people to arrive at the Acker house on the night of the robbery and murder. The scene was horrendous. The house had been ransacked, and Maggard said he had never seen so much blood. Tammy Acker had been stabbed eleven times. The photographs were enough to make you throw up.

"I'll be interested to see them," Lester said. He would take a look at them soon and would probably run into the troopers later in the week.

"We'll be taking those boys back to Kentucky," Maggard said.

"Maybe so, maybe not," Lester said.

But Lester knew that all three of the suspects would be going back to Kentucky to stand trial. It was not only a question of the evidence found in the cars and at the Ormond Beach condominium where they had been staying with Sherry, Carol, and apparently a third woman or girl. According to the *Orlando Sentinel* and what Lester had heard was being reported in papers at home and broadcast over the news, the boys were in deeper water than they had thought. In addition to the Acker case and the Georgia robbery, they were also suspects in another Letcher County robbery, in the murders of an elderly couple up in Jackson County, and in the murder of someone described only as "a prominent Florida businessman." Roger denied a connection to any of these other crimes. It was just a typical case of the police and the FBI putting out a lot of bullshit to try people in the press and to clean up a bunch of crimes they couldn't solve. The next thing you knew, he'd be charged with robbing Fort Knox and killing his grandmother. Once they had you locked up, they'd stop at nothing to keep you there. Cops were nothing but crooks and liars.

"That's why you need a good lawyer," Lester reminded him.

By Tuesday, August 20, Lester had reached an agreement with Roger. Lester accepted one hundred and seventy-five thousand dollars, inclusive of the retainer, plus the 1963 Corvette, as his fee. He had guessed all along that negotiations would end up at around that figure; by holding out as long as he had, he made himself look generous and made Roger and Carol believe that they were getting the great Lester Burns at bargain-basement prices. He also had already formulated in his mind a plan for getting his hands on more of the money—but that would take some time, maybe a couple of weeks. Then, he was willing to bet, more cash would fall into his lap like apples off the tree.

Carol said that she would get the remaining one hundred and fifty of his fee to him as soon as Sherry produced it. Roger had told Sherry in no uncertain terms to turn over his full share to Carol.

On Tuesday, over at the jail, Lester ran into Detective Maggard again, who this time was in the company of Detective Frank Fleming, whom Lester knew well from the Hazard KSP post. The troopers had obtained court orders for the impoundment of two more cars traced to Epperson, another Dodge van and some kind of English sports car; that brought the number of vehicles in evidence up to five. Lester told the detectives that he had decided to waive extradition on Epperson, which meant that they could take at least one prisoner back to Kentucky by the end of the week.

Where were the troopers staying? Lester asked. Were they going to catch some sunshine while they were down in Florida? They weren't going to waste the whole trip working, he hoped. Fighting crime all day long could get kind of depressing, didn't they agree? Maybe they'd even have time for a cocktail or two.

Fleming, a square-jawed, humorous fellow who Lester knew was not one to pass up a chance to party, admitted somewhat sheepishly that he wasn't about to go home without trying out the beach in front of their hotel. They were staying at the Inn on the Beach at Daytona, just a few miles down the road from Ormond Beach, where they'd been doing most of their snooping around. It was a beautiful spot, and the girls were enough to lead a grown man into temptation.

"Tell you what," Lester said. "I could use some company. What do you say we have dinner Thursday night at your place?"

Having built a bridge to the troopers, Lester got another idea, with future questions about his fee in mind. From Carol's room at the Catalina Inn, he telephoned Lieutenant Danny Webb at the KSP post in Hazard. He had just run into a pair of Webb's crack detectives, Lester told the lieutenant. He wanted Webb to know that his men were working their butts off.

And, by the way, in the next couple of days he would be bringing a large cash fee back with him to Somerset. He wanted Webb to know that, just in case some trooper stopped him and accused him of robbing a bank. Webb thanked Lester for the information.

Why would I be telling the police about the money, Lester calculated, if I thought it was stolen?

5

LESTER WAS NO STRANGER TO FLORIDA. He owned considerable property there, residential and commercial, including a vacation house at Okeechobee, on the shore of the lake. About a hundred and seventy-five miles south of Orlando, Lake Okeechobee (which means "plenty big water" in the Seminole language) is the largest lake in the South. Its southern end marks the upper limits of the Everglades; at its northern tip the town of Okeechobee (pop. 4,225) sits in a marshy area of tall sawgrass and cypress swamps. Just as the Gold Coast—from Miami north roughly to Delray Beach—attracts visitors and retirees from New York and New Jersey, Okeechobee is the favored spot of those Eastern Kentuckians who can afford a second house or a condo—far enough away and different, tropical, but not too far, and full of homefolks. On either side of Lester's street of ranch-style houses, most of the neighbors were people he knew from Kentucky. A number of them were former or present clients.

Normally Lester confined his Okeechobee visits to the winter months, but he decided to make the three-hour drive through the soggy heat in order to deposit at least some of the money he was already carrying around. He put eight thousand dollars into his account at an Okeechobee bank. He planned to draw on that for the six thousand still owed on the 1963 Corvette. He needed to keep the total of any single deposit well under ten thousand, because federal law requires banks to report all transactions and to record the serial numbers of all cash at or above that amount. In Florida, moreover, because of the drug traffic and the active enforcement of drug laws, anyone depositing a large amount of cash could expect to be interviewed about it immediately by the Drug Enforcement Agency or the FBI.

As for the seventeen thousand remaining from his retainer, Lester went to his house as unobtrusively as he could and hid it in the garage. He also retrieved from his house a .41 caliber Magnum pistol, an Uzi machine gun, and plenty of ammunition, for protection after he received the rest of his money. The more he thought about actually receiving such a large amount of cash, of such dubious origin, the more frightened he became. Not that he seriously considered backing out. By then he may as well have been dreaming, unable to conceive of controlling a scenario written by some unseen hand. Before leaving his house that evening, he fixed himself a couple of stiff whiskies and popped a few aspirin. His hip hurt. He had not been sleeping much that week.

Carol continued to fail to come up with Lester's money. Sherry had supposedly gone for it and hadn't returned. The next morning, Lester delivered an ultimatum. He told Carol that he was moving over to Daytona, where the Kentucky police were staying; he gave her that number and one in Okeechobee where he said he could be reached on Saturday, if it came to that. He would give them through the weekend. After that, if they had still not produced his money, they could forget the whole business. He was beginning to wonder whether they really had as much cash as Roger had claimed.

Lester phoned a friend in Okeechobee, saying he was down in Florida to receive a fee and would visit with her over the weekend. Would it be possible for her to drive him back to Kentucky? For certain reasons, he didn't want to fly. Lillian Davis said that she would be glad to help out. She needed to drive back to Kentucky anyway.

By the time Lester sat down to dinner that evening with the detectives, after an hour or so at the bar, everyone was on very friendly terms. Lester had them falling out of their chairs with laughter at his stories about Happy Chandler and giving out speeding tickets before the days of radar and the mountain judge who used to fine himself for being drunk on the bench. He made sure that glasses stayed full and everyone ordered plenty of food and the waitress knew that these were the finest law enforcement officers in the

United States. Lester himself ate prodigiously, as always; he was worried about his weight but expressed disappointment that there wasn't a buffet, so he could sample something of everything. When he started talking about the Acker case, it was as if he and the police were on the same side, colleagues in a world that criminals had made. He wondered aloud how much money had actually been taken from the Acker house.

As far as they knew, the detectives said, it was half a million, just as had been reported in the press. That was what Dr. Acker had estimated. They also recalled some firearms and pieces of jewelry, including a lady's Rolex watch.

Saying nothing about it, Lester thought he remembered that Sharon Wilson, Donnie Bartley's sister, had been wearing a gold and stainless-steel Rolex; but he could not be sure, and besides, it needn't have been stolen and it might have been a fake.

They had gotten a big break only that afternoon, one of the detectives volunteered. The FBI had found a 1978 Oldsmobile sedan that had been sitting for days in a motel parking lot in Fort Lauderdale. The Olds matched the description of the car several witnesses claimed to have seen Epperson, Hodge, and Bartley driving in Kentucky just before the Acker murder. It had Kentucky plates and was registered to Carol Malone, which was an alias of Epperson's girlfriend, Carol Ellis. They were going to issue a warrant for her arrest.

Lester changed the subject to give himself time to think. It certainly would make things difficult if Carol were taken into custody before she was able to give Lester his money. He had to think of some way of gaining time.

He told them that he was also representing Carol Epperson or whatever her name was. They would be taking Roger Epperson up to Kentucky tomorrow. It would be a great help to Lester if Roger could be housed in the Pulaski County jail, in Somerset, so that Lester could have easy access to him rather than having to drive all the way over to Letcher County to see his client. If the KSP could fix that up, Lester would promise to have Carol there within a matter of days to make a statement. He would personally guarantee her appearance.

They did not have the authority, the detectives said, as Lester knew, but they would see what they could do about his requests. It would make life easier for them, too, if Lester could get Carol to appear in Kentucky voluntarily.

When Fleming and Maggard reached for their wallets, the waitress told them that Mr. Burns had already picked up the check.

On Saturday morning Frank Fleming watched from a balcony as Lester was getting into his car. Fleming shouted a farewell; Lester waved to him with a paper sack he was carrying. Fleming assumed the sack contained a bottle.

Lester took possession of the 1963 red-and-cream Corvette that morning at a Daytona garage, paid a mechanic to return his rental car, and took off for Okeechobee, managing to hit a hundred and fifteen on the Florida Turnpike with the radio blasting Conway Twitty and the Statler Brothers. At his house he re-hid what was left of his retainer in the trunk of the Corvette and locked the car away in his garage. Then he walked over to Lillian Davis's duplex, just behind the Treasure Island Motel.

Lester had once owned the Treasure Island. But in 1982 he sold the motel for three hundred and fifty thousand dollars to Dr. Billy Davis, Lillian's husband, a Somerset physician. Dr. Davis had hired Lester, whom he had read about in the newspaper, to defend him on a charge of involuntary homicide. Because he could not afford Lester's fee, Dr. Davis paid twenty-two thousand down for the motel and also gave Lester a 1982 Corvette, a motorcycle, a bass boat, furniture out of a condominium, and ten thousand in cash to defend him.

The case went before a jury in Elliott County, Lester gave a memorable performance, and the judge directed a verdict of acquittal. Lester then set Dr. Davis up in medical practice in Somerset, financing the opening of a clinic and becoming the doctor's landlord. Dr. Davis owed his freedom to Lester—and so much else that Lester had had little doubt when he had asked Mrs. Davis to drive him to Kentucky that she would not hesitate to do him the favor. She was down in Okeechobee that week to see about putting a new roof on the motel, which was in need of several repairs.

As it turned out, Lillian Davis was required to do more for Lester than drive him home. He arrived at her door dripping with sweat. Breathing hard, he locked the door behind him and announced that he was being watched. He showed her the pistol he was carrying in a paper sack and the Uzi in a shopping bag. He needed a drink.

Within minutes a woman was on the phone asking for Lester Burns.

"You better have it this time!" Lester shouted into the phone. "I am not driving all the way back there unless I'm getting my money, you hear? All right. This is absolutely your last chance. Where are you?"

When he hung up, Lester asked Lillian to drive him to Orlando the next day. He did not want to go alone; he might need both hands free in case trouble started. These were not nice people he was dealing with. He told her who they were and that he needed help to collect part of his fee tomorrow.

It was not how Lillian Davis had planned to spend her Sunday, but she agreed. They were on the road to Orlando by noon, Lillian behind the wheel of her black Bronco, Lester beside her with the Uzi at his feet and the .41 Magnum shoved into the side pocket of the door. From time to time Lester sipped from a bottle and chewed aspirins.

Carol and the others had switched motels. Lester directed Lillian to the Days Inn and told her to circle the parking lot twice, as he tried to spot FBI agents. Then he told her to park as close as she could to 121, a ground-floor room.

Lillian stayed in the car as Lester knocked on the door of the room and went inside. When he returned and climbed back into the car, he told her to wait. Carol Epperson was coming out with his money. Lester inspected the pistol and made sure that it was loaded. Lillian pointed out a rather short middle-aged woman standing a few doors down with a younger dark-haired woman; they appeared to be watching. Lester said that they were Donald Bartley's mother and sister.

Carol came out of her room carrying something wrapped in white motel towels. She climbed past Lester into the back seat, and he closed the door and locked it. Carol unwound the towels and let Lester peek into a paper sack that was filled with stacks of bills secured with rubber bands.

"I understand that this is my fee, ninety thousand dollars," Lester said, lying to conceal the actual amount from Lillian.

"No," Carol said. "There's more than that. It's all there." She spoke rapidly, complaining about two men who were out by the motel pool watching her.

Lester told Carol to get out of the car. He would see her in Somerset in a few days, he said. In the meantime, she should stay out of sight and off the highway and be careful. He would be in touch with her.

Lillian threw the Bronco into reverse and screeched the tires. Lester told her for God's sake to cool it and act perfectly normal. He wrapped the sack back up in the towels, put it under his feet next to the machine gun, and instructed Lillian not to exceed the speed limit on the way to Okeechobee.

Lillian dropped Lester off at his house. Alone in his garage, he counted the money. There were thirty bundles of five thousand dollars each. He counted out ninety-two thousand and replaced that in the sack, wrapping it again in the towels. Then he hid the remaining fifty-eight thousand along with the other money in the trunk of the Corvette.

Back at Lillian's duplex, Lester unwound the towels again and emptied the sack onto the floor and began counting the money, riffling through the stacks and dropping them as if he did not like touching them. Once or twice he went to the window and looked into the street. Lillian watched him count. He was acting paranoid, she said. She brought him a drink.

"Ninety-two thousand," Lester finally announced. "She was right, there's a little more than I thought. Actually they're paying four hundred twenty-five thousand, can you believe it? Plus automobiles."

Lester said that he was worried about fingerprints on the money. Some of it was old, 1970s series, and mildewed. He didn't know that this was Acker money, of course, there was no way he could know that, but it would be better not to take chances. He would have to wash it.

"You mean launder it?" Lillian asked.

"No, for now, what I need to do is wash it."

He took the money into the bathroom and began wiping it, bill by bill, with a facecloth wrung out with soap and warm water. It was mostly in hundreds, but there were fifties, too, and a scattering of twenties. With a glass of whiskey beside him, he worked at his washing steadily for hours, calling for fresh facecloths, meticulously wiping both sides of each bill. Around midnight he was done. He scrubbed his hands with surgical thoroughness, as if to rid himself of some contaminant.

He wondered at himself. What was he getting himself into? But it seemed impossible to stop now. What was he going to do, return the money, saying sorry, I've changed my mind? It would be dangerous on the road tomorrow. These people would stop at nothing. The way they fought among themselves, some of them might come after him. There might be others out there who had not been caught. Who knew how many murders they had already committed? He decided he needed a bodyguard.

The sack of money clutched in his hand, limping from the pain in his hip, Lester lurched into the street. He made his way to the house next door to his own and banged on the door. A light came on. Someone asked who it was at that hour. Lester called out his name. A man peered through a window and opened up.

"Griff, I've got a problem."

"Lester. Christ, have a drink."

Somewhere in his early sixties, Houston J. Griffin was a big old boy the size of a linebacker. Divorced and retired, he was originally from Eastern Kentucky; he now lived in Georgia and came down to Okeechobee for the fishing. Lester pushed past him and dumped the money out onto the middle of the living room floor. He told Griffin that this was only part of a fee he had collected. His client was charged with murder. Lester was afraid that some of the cohorts were trying to take the money back. He needed help in bringing it to Kentucky. He would pay Griffin whatever he demanded to make the trip.

Griffin said he would do it for expenses plus one of Lester's Black Angus bulls.

They did not get an early start. In the morning, Lester strolled around the neighborhood flashing wads of bills, boasting that he had just landed one of the biggest cases of his life. A stranger might have thought him deranged, the way he pranced and poured talk of riches into every ear; those who knew him understood it as typical Lester Burns behavior, if somewhat more grandiose than usual. Around Lester, you always felt within reach of a fortune. You wanted to touch him, hoping his magic was catching.

They set off in tandem, Lester riding with Lillian, Griffin following in his white LTD with the money stashed in the trunk in a blue plaid gym bag. Keeping to the speed limit, they figured it might take twenty hours or more up the length of Florida, through Georgia and Tennessee to the shores of Lake Cumberland.

Lester held the Uzi in his lap and checked out every car that passed. His thoughts were of this gang of thieves. Epperson seemed to be their leader. Lester had not had much contact with the others, but he had the impression that Hodge was the most dangerous, Bartley a wimp who yet might be capable of anything if cornered. Together they were an arrogant bunch who brought to mind the James boys or the Dalton gang, tearing around the country. They had been on quite a spree, there was no doubt of that.

As for the women, Bartley's girlfriend was staying out of sight somewhere in the Tennessee hills, apparently. Carol was a mess, yapping and intolerable. Early in the day, clean and with black hair shining, she did present allurements—sinuous, exotic as opium, she was plausible as an attraction in some joss house, an amber-skinned geisha mindlessly open to possibilities. Nor, in a sense, was she ignorant, her druggie but grammatical prattle sprinkled with references to oddball books, pop psychology. Lester classed her as a fading flower child turned crook.

Among them, men and women, only Sherry might be an actual human being. Her eyes showed weariness and worry. She seemed the most intelligent. She was kind of a loner.

6

S HE WAS BORN SHERRY LORAINE SHEETS on January 15, 1951, in Rockwood, Roane County, East Tennessee, a region similar historically, culturally, and geographically to Eastern Kentucky, which lies immediately to the north. The accents are alike. When hill people from either place say, "The far truck blowed a tar afore Ah pulled mah paints awn and Ah shouldah took thet kaemper of urine," they mean, "The fire truck blew a tire before I pulled my pants on and I should have taken that camper of yours." The economy of East Tennessee is more diversified and healthier, but it is also a high-crime area, most of it drug-related; and as in Eastern Kentucky the linchpin in the drug trade is often the county sheriff.

Roane County, where Sherry Sheets was still living when she met Benny Hodge, was known among local criminals as Little Chicago, and not because of the wind or stockyards or even a city. It happens to be a convenient tankful of gas from Central America, and on a given night you might spot a plane loaded with cocaine touching its pontoons down on one of several wide rivers and lakes created by the TVA. Interstates 40 and 75 provide links west to Nashville, east to Knoxville, and north through Kentucky to Cincinnati and other midwestern markets. It is pretty country, romantic when the black CSX trains come barreling out of the mountains and rumble over bridges that cross the Clinch River and the Tennessee; but the drugs are everywhere.

Sherry did not take drugs, or hardly ever. Although she had done a little selling here and there, and one or two other things that could have landed her in jail or, at least, lost her a job, she had managed to stay out of trouble through her twenty-nine years. "I put forth my best effort, whether it's legal or illegal," she liked to say, "and ain't nothing's illegal till you're caught." For Sherry, however, nothing was ever the same after the day she first laid eyes on Benny Hodge, September 3, 1980. Her daughter, Sherri Renee, happened to be celebrating her fifth birthday on that date; but a child was one thing, Benny Hodge another.

On that Wednesday, Sherry drove up to Brushy Mountain State Prison, in Morgan County, to apply for a job as a guard. The pay was good—eight hundred and forty-seven a month take-home, plus full benefits—and Sherry thought it sounded like a better way to earn a living. Where else could you get paid, as she expressed it, to sit on your butt all day watching men? It beat being a cashier or a beautician, jobs she had held since her 1972 marriage to Billy Pelfrey, a welder at one of the big government plants in Oak Ridge. Billy's sister, Charlene, had told her about the opening at Brushy. Charlene was already a guard there and described it as a piece of cake—a little scary sometimes, but what was wrong with excitement? Sherry had an itch. She was as bored with her marriage as with her work.

Years ago Brushy Mountain had been notorious for its harsh treatment of prisoners. You could still see the corner of the exercise yard where men were hung up by their thumbs and whipped. It remained one of the few prisons in the country from which no one had ever escaped, owing mainly to the physical situation of this castellated fortress, surrounded on three sides by sheer rock cliffs and rugged hills thickly forested and infested with snakes. James Earl Ray, who for a few months was Benny Hodge's cellmate at Brushy, made an escape attempt in 1977. Along with several other inmates, Ray staged a fight during a baseball game and scrambled over the rear wall while the guards were distracted. One prisoner who bolted spontaneously without his shoes fell and was quickly captured. Ray and others scattered up into the mountains.

Warden Herman Davis directed his men to forget about the other escapees until Martin Luther King's assassin was run to ground. Fifty-five hours later, a mile or so into the forest, they heard twigs snapping, and the bloodhounds found Ray in a hole, trying to cover himself with leaves, dehydrated and exhausted. At Brushy a man may make it over the wall, but he soon discovers that he has nowhere to run. This absence of hope could partially explain why there were seven murders at Brushy between 1976 and 1980.

When Sherry filled out her application, she already knew from her sister-in-law something about how it was on the inside; and Sherry had been selling marijuana and Quaaludes (downers) to two other guards, a fellow she knew from high school and his buddy. (She was able to buy the pot from friends at a hundred and eighty dollars per quarter pound and sell it to the guards for six to eight hundred dollars; the pills she bought for two dollars and fifty cents each and sold for twenty dollars apiece.) She understood how the prison's microeconomy ran on drugs at wildly inflated prices. Still, she had much to learn.

When she passed her interview, Warden Davis told her she could start work in two weeks. She and Charlene were walking through the front gate, heading for the parking lot, when a state car pulled up. In the back seat, staring straight ahead, was the best-looking man she had ever seen. The sight of him made her gut flip.

"Who's the hunk?" she asked Charlene.

"That's Benny Hodge." Charlene explained that Hodge had been let out for the day to go see his new baby at the hospital in Knoxville.

"He was messing with some girl," Sherry asked, "while he was locked up in here?"

"He sure did. He married her, too. That's Benny."

"Lord have mercy."

For the next two weeks Sherry thought about Benny Hodge. She tried to imagine how he had managed to knock a girl up while he was behind bars. There were no conjugal visits allowed at Brushy and besides, they hadn't even been married when she became pregnant. Had he sneaked her into his cell? Had Benny been able to slip it to her in the visiting room under the eyes of the guards? It must have been some quickie, that was for sure, and Benny must be hung like a bull. Sherry dreamed about him day and night.

She spotted him again on the job at Brushy. She was in Shack Number One, a wooden structure directly in front of the main prison building, with a clear view of an alleyway to the left. Through a window she watched Benny Hodge unloading big cases of canned produce from a truck and carrying them down the steps to the basement storeroom. The other prisoners working with him staggered under a single case. Hodge was lifting three and four cases at a time and carrying them effortlessly. He barked at the other men, directing them like a foreman.

If Sherry had not known Hodge for a prisoner, she would have thought he ran the place. She watched him bending and lifting, never breaking a sweat. When he turned toward the stairs with his load, he was only fifteen or twenty feet from her window. She admired his forearms and saw the muscles in his back working under his denim shirt. The bright early-fall light made his hair shine brownish-blondish and look so soft when it fell forward that she wanted to feel it on her face and smell it.

He was different from the other prisoners. Except when he shouted orders, he spoke to no one, and no one to him. Sherry had not been close enough to him to look into his eyes, but she saw that they were a pale blue, baby blue she guessed, and she thought that she detected in them a pent-up anger that she understood. He had a soft-looking Fu Manchu mustache that she liked. His only flaw that she could see was that his chin was maybe a little weak and gave him a baby face—not that she minded; it made him seem sweet. But she thought he might look even better and stronger with a beard. Sherry was crazy about beards.

Sometimes his eyes looked sad, then they would go cold. She bet that he could be ruthless when somebody crossed him, yet he looked as if he needed love and could accept tenderness, the poor guy, who must have known precious little love in his sad life.

She learned that Hodge had been at Brushy for five years and was serving the ninth of a twenty-year sentence for armed robbery. Nine years! He was only twenty-nine, seven months younger than herself; they had been born in the same year. He had had no life to speak of. If there was something in him that made him mean sometimes—there must have been, or he would not have received such a stiff sentence—it wasn't God-given. He must have been hurt. She could sense his goodness and bet that she could bring it out if she got the chance.

The authorities helped to set Hodge apart, permitting him greater freedom than most of the other prisoners. He slept in what was called the White Building, at the front of the prison complex with only a wire fence between it and the road, set up like a dormitory with beds in rows and no barred cells. He had discovered a talent for cooking while in jail and lately had been appointed chief cook for the staff's commissary. Sherry found herself going back for seconds of his chili and cornbread.

None of the other prisoners bothered Hodge or challenged his status. Everyone said that he was strong enough to snap a neck with one hand. He had built himself up and kept in shape by lifting weights.

The social strata at Brushy were clearly defined. Authorities and prisoners alike made a distinction between two kinds of prisoners: convicts and just plain inmates. An inmate was someone who was merely doing time and had neither allegiance to nor power over his fellow prisoners; nor was he trusted by them. Convicts, by contrast, were tightly knit, organized within their own society and its hierarchies, arranged informally but like the military into ranks. The more physical strength, aggressiveness, and cunning you had, and the more cigarettes, marijuana, and other dope you controlled, the higher up you were in the convict pecking order. Those at the highest level even had "green money" (actual currency) hidden in one place or another. Once you understood it, Sherry decided, the organization of life within the prison was a mirror of life on the outside, minus hypocrisy.

The convict-inmate split did not cut across racial lines. At Brushy the ratio of whites to blacks was a fairly steady sixty-forty. Both groups divided into convict-inmate segments; blacks and whites, as on college and university campuses, mixed hardly at all, eating and socializing separately, but on the basis of spontaneous mutual aversion, rather than distinct and formal gangs. (Tennessee prison populations, to this day, have never organized themselves into the gangs— Aryan Brotherhood, Mexican Mafia, Black Guerillas—that dominate West and, to a lesser extent, East Coast prison life. Random drug testing and the segregation of violent and sexually aggressive prisoners have, since the mid-eighties, altered prison hierarchies somewhat. Prison officials continue to observe the convict-inmate division, but it is less of a factor than before. As in the outside world, loyalties have come to count for less than individual interests. Violence toward certain kinds of offenders, particularly "baby rapers" or child molesters, continues, but with far less frequency. The prevailing prison ethos is a fashionable moral relativism.) The threat of racial conflict was constant. A few months before Sherry began working there, three white prisoners smuggled a gun inside, climbed up an air shaft, and shot two blacks dead in their cell. From what authorities could determine, the motive was purely racial.

Sherry preferred the convicts to the inmates or the male guards. The guards resented her because she was a woman and were constantly hitting on her and making ugly remarks. The convicts were con artists, so they were polite, and she enjoyed the way they bullshitted her with rapid-fire chat and had her thinking that she was the grandest thing that ever put on shoes, with their "Yes, ma'ams" and

"Thank you, ma'ams" and cornball endearments—"A gal like you could cause the world a heartache." She could see how they studied her, that was what they did best, reading people; they were so street smart they could fool you upside down six ways a minute with sweet talk and flattery, and they were always manic-high on something. The next thing you knew, one of them had sliced somebody open with a homemade knife or split somebody's skull with a meat cleaver. They were liars, first and foremost; all criminals were, that was the point and purpose of their existence; but once you were onto their game, and they knew it, they could be fun.

"I'm gonna marry you when I get out," one called Lefty would say. "We'll head for California and you'll be in the movies."

"You know why there are no left-handed people in the insane asylum?" Sherry would shoot back. "Because they drive everybody else crazy."

The ordinary inmates, Sherry thought, were nothing but slime and as boring as nine-to-five types anywhere, putting in time and always ready to snitch. The convicts were her allies in a system that ran on lies and accomodations, threats and power. She knew enough, for instance, to turn a blind eye to the wall-to-wall homosexuality, as to the drugs. What else was a locked-up man supposed to do? Like most people, most of them were sheep and went along with the sex because it was the accepted thing. A handful were brutally gay, punishing the sexual slaves they called punks; some took on girlish-looking boys as punks and pretended they were women. Others merely did what they could to fill the isolated hours with the human warmth available, which happened to be male. It was no different from becoming a cannibal if you were starving to death; it didn't mean you would pass up ham and eggs if they were offered. A man who wasn't a natural fruiter, Sherry was told and believed, would go back to women once he was free. She thought that people in prison understood human nature better than hypocrites on the outside. At Brushy you had to face reality. There was nothing else.

It was the same with the dope: she ignored it unless it was blatant, and even then, she'd tell a guy to get smart rather than bust him. She had stopped selling to the guards once she became one; she did not trust her male fellow workers not to snitch on her just to get rid of a woman. They had other sources, and the wives and girlfriends of the prisoners smuggled in plenty of dope, usually inside a condom or a balloon hidden in pants or vaginas. The men swallowed it or inserted it into their rectums, in case they were cavity-searched. (Visitors were never cavity-searched unless strongly suspected.) It was a game that was more or less ignored. Marijuana or downers, after all, kept the men calm. They could get away with smoking pot in their cells in any number of ways, combining it with apple-scented pipe tobacco, smoking it with the water running in the basin so the fumes went down the drain, perfuming the air with spray deodorant or baby powder.

Sherry's growing infatuation with Benny Hodge helped her catch on fast. He was obviously a convict, a general who took orders from no one. She gathered that he controlled a lot of dope but was himself clean, being so health-conscious. Nor did he resort to men for sex. Apart from visitors—the story was that Hodge had made his new wife pregnant when she sat on his lap at the prison picnic grounds— he was also involved with another woman who worked at the prison with a face like a bad stretch of road but a great figure.

This woman was always disappearing with Hodge. A prisoner was supposed to be accompanied by a prison employee whenever he left the cellblock, so Hot Pants, that was what Sherry called her, was always saying, "I'm taking Hodge down to bring this here stuff up," and down they went together into the storeroom. She would come up looking mighty smug. What did she think people thought they had been doing, taking inventory?

Sherry was jealous. It didn't seem right that a man like Hodge was doing the Texas two-step with a pruneface.

The exercise yard was at the rear of the main building. Beyond the yard lay the ball field, the wall, and the mountains. Sherry discovered that she could stand on the third floor at the end of a row of cells and look down into the yard to see Hodge lifting weights. He was there every afternoon, stripped to the waist, lifting.

Sherry wondered about the wisdom of leaving those weights where anyone could pick them up. A couple of years before, one prisoner had been heaving a barbell over his head when another ran up and smashed down on his face with a hundred-pound weight. The victim had required extensive plastic surgery. But no one came within thirty feet of Hodge when he exercised. If someone dared, Sherry imagined, they could feed the guy to the dogs, for all that would be left of him.

As often as she could, Sherry stole time to watch from her perch as Hodge lifted. She guessed that he must be pressing four hundred pounds. It was the most gorgeous body she had ever seen, perfectly proportioned, with more muscles than you would have guessed from the way he looked with his shirt on; but his was an athlete's body, not a muscle freak's. She heard his grunts echoing off the concrete and dug her nails into her palms.

He lifted standing first, straining, grimacing, triumphant. Then he lay on his back on the bench with his crotch toward her, legs bent, sweat streaming. He was not too hairy, just some on his chest.

All around her there were men, five hundred of them, men in their cells jerking off and touching each other, men swabbing floors, men in the kitchen working and in the dining room eating in shifts, always eating, men watching from the towers. And in the center was Benny Hodge.

It wasn't easy at home at night in the marriage bed, thinking about Hodge in the yard or Hodge in the basement with that horny old bitch.

Sherry had been a tomboy. She had never thought of herself as pretty; an older sister was the beautiful one. But Sherry didn't think she had to be a prom queen to be attractive to men. She wore no makeup; it was her way of saying take me as I am or leave me the hell alone. She believed that she had certain qualities, including more determination than the next ten women combined, that compensated for whatever knockout looks God had neglected to provide her. Another thing she knew about herself was that when someone told her that she could not have something, she found a way to get it. She had been that way as far back as she could remember, like a running back who found a way around when he couldn't go straight through. And when someone had something else she wanted, especially when that something was a man, then watch out.

Not that she was always preying on other women's men. She had had only two affairs since her marriage, both of them as a way of getting back when she believed her husband had been cheating on her. Both affairs had been with married men, but in her view this had been merely a practical choice. You had better not mess with a single man, because he might want you permanently and cause a big fuss and endanger your marriage. Sherry could have told Dear Abby a thing or two.

She held off until it was already a week into October. She had been watching Benny Hodge for more than three weeks; she could not resist the excitement any longer. She did not care what happened, she had to get with him. They had locked eyes a few times. They still had not spoken to one another, but she was certain that he knew who she was and that he felt something, too—or was she imagining this? She had to find out. Sherry's way of dealing with temptation was to try to keep calm, devise a plan, see how things played out, and deal with the consequences later. "You can't change life," was the way she put it, "but you can learn to live with it."

By ten in the morning, Sherry knew from studying Hodge's routine, he would be starting to prepare lunch in the staff kitchen. There was a phone nearby which Hodge had the privilege of using and answering. Just after ten on a Tuesday, she rang that phone from another out of sight near the warden's office.

"Hodge here," he answered.

"This is Sherry Sheets. You know me?"

"Yeah, I know you."

"Well, I think you're pretty cute."

"Is that right."

"I do. I been watching you. I have went to a lot of trouble to watch you, and I'm going to miss you so much, it hurts."

"What, you quitting? They fire you?"

She felt her knees shake, hearing his voice and knowing she could get caught.

"No," she said, "I ain't quitting and I ain't fired and I ain't no quitter, neither. I've got Wednesdays and Thursdays off and what that means is, I won't be able to see you for two whole days. I don't know if I can stand it. I mean, all I've got between then and now is my husband, and I don't think he'll do, know what I mean?"

"You a married woman? You shouldn't be talking like that."

"Well, you ain't nobody to talk, Benny Hodge, Lord knows. You are married, too, and I know what you've been up to. You're as bad as they come. You still haven't told me what I'm supposed to do. What do you want me to do, Hodge? Aren't you going to tell me? What's a girl supposed to do with herself?"

"You know where the men's bathroom is near the kitchen?"

"Yes."

"I'll be there. And don't pay no attention to the guy standing outside the door. Just come on in. I'll give you five minutes to get there."

The way he said it, Sherry didn't think Hodge believed that she would dare. He didn't know her. Nobody ever accused Sherry Sheets of being chicken.

She covered by reporting to the operations desk that she was going to the commissary and popped into the dining room to make sure that she was seen. Then she shot down a flight of stairs. As Hodge had said, another prisoner was standing by the door to the men's room. He motioned her inside with his thumb. Sherry understood that he was the pinner, the guy who would keep his eyes pinned so he could warn them if anyone was coming in.

Inside there was space for a urinal and a washbasin, and there was a stall, where Hodge stood waiting.

They started kissing, not saying a word. Sherry was scared and excited. His mustache was as soft as it had looked, and she loved how soft the skin on his cheeks was against hers. He sat down on the toilet, and she crawled onto his lap and propped her feet against the wall so if anyone came in they would see only a man's pair of shoes on the floor.

"Benny," she said, enjoying hearing his name in her voice. "Benny." She felt his big hard arms.

He was just getting into her shirt when the pinner came in and whispered "Hodge! Hodge, they're looking for her!"

Sherry jumped up and tidied herself and hurried out when the pinner said the coast was clear. She headed straight for the operations desk.

"What do you all want with me?" Sherry asked, acting annoyed.

"Where have you been?"

"What do you mean, where have I been? I been in the dining room."

"No you didn't. We went there looking for you."

"They was complaining about that men's room. I made sure it got cleaned up."

They managed to meet a couple of times more during the next few weeks in the storeroom, where they kissed in the dark and got to know each other against flour sacks. Necking was what it was, Sherry said to herself, high school making out and heavy petting where you might get caught and you enjoyed it more because you were "getting over on somebody." They did not graduate beyond that stage until, on Halloween, Benny left Brushy.

7

I F A PRISONER WAS WITHIN TWO YEARS of becoming eligible for
parole and had a record of good behavior, Brushy Mountain Prison
sometimes loaned him out as contract labor to local sheriffs, who
could use him for anything from washing dishes to polishing patrol
cars and sometimes for less wholesome duties. Reformers occasionally denounced these arrangements as a form of indentured servitude,
but they kept county taxes down, and prisoners competed for them
the way professors do for paid sabbatical leaves. Compared to the
claustrophobic regimen of a place like Brushy, half a lungful of fresh
air was something to covet.

In the fall of 1980, Anderson County Sheriff Dennis O. Trotter
needed someone at the county jail in Clinton to help out with the
cooking. The regular cook for the past eighteen years, Minnie Webster,
whom everyone called Maw, was eighty-four years old. She wasn't
ready to retire, but she was not as agile with the spatula as she had
been. Because he would be eligible for parole in January 1982 and had
stayed out of trouble and not tried to escape since being moved to
Brushy from Nashville in 1975, Benny Hodge was the obvious candidate to become Maw Webster's sous-chef. Administrators and staff at
Brushy, from the warden on down, were so impressed with Hodge's
work ethic and culinary skills that they hated to see him go and said
that they would welcome him back anytime, should circumstances
compel his return. He would not have landed his new post, however,

had his admirer Hot Pants not demonstrated an understanding of political science by slipping Sheriff Trotter some cash.

Or that was what Sherry believed, because Benny told her so. Sherry kept quiet; she had the same motivation as Hot Pants in wishing Hodge moved toward freedom. But once the transfer was completed, Sherry confronted her rival and warned her to keep her mitts off Hodge from now on or find herself accused of bribing a public official. Sherry was not about to continue sharing Benny with anybody.

She could hardly believe the luck. Clinton was only twenty miles east of Brushy and thirty miles northeast of Harriman, where Sherry lived with her husband and daughter, surrounded by a host of relatives and in-laws. Benny was not quite in the free world, but he was halfway there; he had to live at the jail, but one of his duties was to do the grocery shopping. All he had to do was to sign out, indicating where he was going and when he would be back, and sign in on return.

The first time she visited him at the jail, Benny introduced her to Maw Webster, who treated him like a favorite grandson. Maw said that Benny was nearly as good a cook as she was and had Sherry sample a batch of brownies he had just pulled out of the oven. They were so thick and moist, they melted in her mouth. The rich chocolate smell mingling with pork loin and potatoes roasting and applesauce bubbling on the stove made Sherry say that if she were ever sent to jail, she hoped it would be in Anderson County. She was especially appreciative because she did not cook herself, ever; it was one thing she was adamant about. Another was not eating beans.

Maw said that she had to keep an eye peeled or the deputies would steal Benny's creations, especially his biscuits, and the poor prisoners would have nothing to eat. In fact Maw's eyesight was failing, and she was hard of hearing. Under the pretence of conducting a tour, Benny led Sherry into the pantry and shut the door. They were locked in, he whispered, but he knew how to unlock the door from the inside. Other prisoners had showed him; they were always bringing girlfriends in there. He switched off the light. They embraced and started yanking down each other's jeans.

They made love for the first time there on that pantry floor. At the height of it, Sherry screamed so that Benny had to clamp his big hand over her mouth.

The next time, they used the ladies' bathroom.

* * *

When Brushy sent Sherry to Nashville for a two-week training course, she missed Benny so much that she telephoned him two or three times a day and rushed home to visit him on the weekend. As a wife and mother, she knew that there would be hell to pay if she were caught. No one would understand what she saw in a convict. But Sherry's regard for the opinions of others had rarely governed her conduct, and when it had, she believed, she had always ended up unhappy. She had married her husband to please her relations, who liked the idea of an ex-Marine and ex-football player with a steady job.

She ought to have cashed in her chips on her wedding night, she believed, when she had accused him of being sauced and had thrown her ring at him and gone to bed without touching him. On his part, Billy told her she was a fanatic on the subject because her father had been an alcoholic and she didn't drink herself. He denied being anything more than a fellow who liked to party, and what was wrong with that? Sherry did not question that Billy was a good provider and a good father, and she admitted that it was probably not easy for a man to live with such an independent-minded woman, who took no guff and refused to cook. But did he have to turn their house into a saloon every weekend? He was never abusive, that was true, and his lapses from fidelity had been brief, especially when she paid him back in kind. But he was the type who had to have his buddies over starting Friday night and into Sunday, going through a gallon of whiskey and God knew how many cases of beer while she shut herself up in the bedroom watching television. The minute she heard those balls begin to click on his nine-foot Brunswick pool table and the ice clinking and smelled the first joint, she knew that she might as well subside into a coma. It was not that anyone misbehaved, usually. One afternoon she had caught a kid in the kitchen tying a rubber tourniquet around his arm, preparing to shoot up, but she had kicked him out pronto. It was just so boring, with nearly everyone drunk or stoned. Billy himself never became obnoxious—it was just that he was more involved in playing host than husband. Football season was the worst. About the only way she was able to make herself noticed was to enrage the guests by rooting for Alabama against Tennessee, irritating everybody by insisting that Bear Bryant was more of a man than anyone in the room. Their house was so well known as a playground that the prison guards came to her to buy pot because they knew she knew the dealers. At least she made some spending money from that behind Billy's back.

Before Brushy and Benny, the principal excitement in any week had come at her job at Kroger's supermarket, where she fiddled the cash register. Sherry was so quick with figures and her fingers flew so fast that no one could catch her or even suspected her. She cheated less for money than for kicks. Let others drink or smoke or pop pills, she got her thrills through private enterprise. She had numerous accounting tricks. The simplest was to have a girlfriend buy groceries for the both of them. Sherry would ring up half the total and split the difference with her friend, helping her out, saving money herself, and sharing a few laughs in the bargain.

But there was nowhere for Sherry to go at Kroger's. The woman who held the head cashier's job was not about to move over; even the assistant manager's job would always go to a man. She held a certificate from beautician's school and was skilled at styling hair, but that was tiring work at low pay with zero opportunities to steal, and you had to put up with so many bitches. The other jobs for women in the region were mostly in textile and clothing factories, again with low pay and no chance to help yourself. Her first job out of high school had been at Roane Hosiery, where she worked as a crotch-slitter in a pantyhose factory. The pantyhose came off the line in one piece, crotchless, so you had to make a slit with a razor-sharp knife where the extra piece of material would go between the legs. She was not about to go back to that; the work numbed the brain.

Sherry had been hoping that sooner or later her husband would grow up and pay more attention to her. They never did anything together except take care of little Sherri Renee, to whom Sherry admitted her husband was more attentive than most fathers. He had even changed diapers and prepared the formula; now he enjoyed watching television with her, taking her to McDonald's and the county fair. Probably he would have enjoyed having more children, especially a son, but Sherry had witnessed too many women in her family worn down by over-breeding. Her mother, who had had hair as luxuriant and long as Crystal Gayle's, had died three months after giving birth to Sherry, the last of eight children, five of whom had survived infancy. After Renee, Sherry had chosen to undergo a tubal ligation.

Not long before taking the job at Brushy, Sherry had made a last attempt to put some zest into her marriage. Instead of partying away another weekend, she asked, why couldn't they do something alone for a change?

"Gee, Peaches," Billy said, "I can't think of anything, can you?"

When she came up with the idea, he agreed to take her off-roading in the mountains. They would pack a lunch, Billy could take a six-pack if he liked, and make a day of it, tearing through the hills in a cloud of dust.

Sherry borrowed her brother's four-wheel-drive truck. They weren't a mile from the house when Billy spotted a friend, a black guy called Wild Man, standing on a corner drinking beer out of a can in a sack. He looked as if he didn't know what to do, with the usual Pelfrey party cancelled. Billy pulled up. Oh, no, Sherry thought.

"Hey, Wild Man!" Billy called. "Whatcha doing? Wanta go four-wheeling?"

Wild Man jumped into the truck and that was that. Sherry tried to enjoy herself, but by the time the men were into their third six-pack she was angry and depressed, and she ended up being the one to drive home. It was as if Billy was afraid to be alone with her. Did he need protection, for Christ's sake? Did he think she was going to bite his balls off? He knew how pissed she was when she didn't speak to him all day Sunday after church.

On Monday when she got home from work he greeted her with a microwave oven with a ribbon tied around it. He must have thought that this would appease her and maybe even inspire her to nuke a frozen dinner from time to time.

Sherry was not mollified. On previous occasions, he had demonstrated contrition by buying her a new TV, a Mr. Coffee, a dishwasher, an electric can opener, ultimately a trash compactor. She had everything to make the little woman happy. What a dope.

One Saturday afternoon in mid-December, Sherry shouted through the smoky din that she was going Christmas shopping, leaving Billy and the boys and the scattering of zonked bimbos in charge of Renee. As she drove off she noticed the cars lined up halfway around the block. It looked like honky-tonk Saturday night, and I ain't nobody's honky-tonk angel, she muttered, scanning the radio dial and settling happily on Willie Nelson's "Stardust" to put her in the right mellow mood. She had not slept a wink last night, but she was alert and did not even mind that the rain was turning to sleet. Because in my heart the sun is shining, she thought, was that from a song? Thinking of what the next day promised was what had kept her awake all night, not the partying. Around four, with Billy snoring in the bed, she had gotten up and gone outside in the cold to feel the mist rolling down off the mountains and listen for a train. She had checked on Renee and given her a kiss, silently wishing her health and happiness and love, most of all love.

At a stoplight in Oliver Springs she fumbled in her purse for her perfume and dabbed some behind her ears. She reminded herself to put some in the crooks of her arms and behind her knees and elsewhere when she could get out of her jacket and jeans.

At Clinton she passed the jail and headed straight for the motel next to the McDonald's. It was called the Family Inn. She registered as Loraine Sheets. In the room she telephoned Benny to tell him the room number and to hurry. Then she took off everything except her bra and panties, put on what she decided was too much perfume and tried to wash some off, and got into bed to wait. She had asked for a king-size. It was going to be their first time off the floor.

Standing in the doorway, dripping from the rain, Benny took her breath away. He looked so fantastic in the beard he was growing just for her and that she had promised to keep trimmed for him, she wanted to throw herself on the carpet and die down at his feet. He tore off his windbreaker and sneakers and climbed into bed with his clothes on to let her undress him.

When he took her, something gave way, a check, a barrier that had always been there before with everyone else, a burst dam that could no longer hold back the flood. She made so much noise that Benny kidded her and said that she'd better calm down or someone would call the police; and when he rolled over she saw that she had made four long scratches down his back with her nails. She told him that it was the first time for her, like that; with him it was as if everything were for the first time. This was the first day of the rest of her life. She knew she wasn't that pretty, she said, but did she make him happy? He said she was beautiful. She had a body that was perfect for—it. If she walked into a room naked, every man would jump on her. She said that was such a nice thing to say.

"Oh, Benny, what're we going to do?"

"I'm getting out," he said, "and I ain't never going back to jail no more. You got to help me."

She held him and stroked his hair and rubbed herself against his beard. He needed her. Her husband didn't need her, he lived in his own world and might as well be married to an inflatable woman. Somehow she would help Benny get his fresh start. Everything would be new. It would be like rescuing and reviving someone who had been given up for dead.

"Hodge-Podge," she called him, hugging him. "Now you've found me, everything's going to be all right."

They were in each other's arms when the pounding started on the door. Someone was trying to bust in! Benny leapt out of bed, fists clenched.

"Open up, Hodge! We know you're in there, you son of a bitch!"

Sherry glanced at her watch. Nearly five! Benny had written in the jailhouse log that he would be back from doing the grocery shopping by four.

"Open up! Or we'll knock this fucking door in!"

The next day two of Sheriff Trotter's deputies, the same pair, as it happened, who had accompanied the sheriff to find Benny Hodge, transported a prisoner from Clinton for delivery to Brushy Mountain. Filling out papers in Warden Davis's office, they talked about how funny it had been catching Hodge buck naked in a motel room with a woman. It hadn't taken ten minutes to locate him. He was supposed to have been buying groceries at French's market. Right down the street, they spotted his county car outside the motel room door.

"He must've been thinking with his pecker," a deputy said. "Son of a bitch must be some pussyhound. Old Trotter about busted a gut laughing. Hodge ain't been with us six weeks and he's already got hisself some poontang." The sheriff had scared Hodge by threatening to send him back to Brushy, but Trotter would not do that. You had to kind of admire the boy's determination, and besides, he was a hell of a cook. "We figure Hodge'll be real cooperative from here on out. I figure we can tie a string around his dick."

"Put a bell on it," the other deputy suggested.

Warden Davis was intrigued. Hodge had had quite a reputation around Brushy, too, though he had never given any trouble. Had they happened to get a look at the girl? Did they know her?

They did not know her but described her as frizzy-haired. She had put on a pair of glasses when Hodge let them in.

"She had the sheet pulled up to her chin. Must be a real fine lady, har de har-har."

"Maybe this will help," the warden said. He opened a file and took out some photographs of women and spread them across his desk. The deputies immediately pointed to one.

Warden Davis asked his secretary to get him Sherry Sheets's home number.

"I hate spoiling her Sunday," the warden said.

8

SHERRY POSTPONED TELLING HER HUSBAND that she had been fired from Brushy. It was not necessary for him to know yet, and it was Sherry's way to react to necessity rather than to force matters prematurely. She had always taken this circumspect, deliberative approach to life. During her senior year in high school, for instance, when her grades began to fall, she waited until she received her midterm report card and changed the F's and D's to B's with the stroke of a pen. By the end of the next quarter she had discovered the store in Harriman that sold blank report cards; for six cents she was able to convert herself into an honor student. She knew that eventually the people she called Mom and Dad, who were actually her sister and brother-in-law, would discover the ruse. They would be angry and disappointed, and she would be unable to qualify for entrance to nursing school. But all that could be dealt with in its proper time, and meanwhile, there was the thrill of getting away with something for months on end.

She pretended to leave for work as usual, fabricating an erratic work schedule so she could see Benny when she wished, lolling around the house when Billy was at work and Renee at kindergarten. She relished having more time to devote to Benny, but she was resentful. She did not blame Warden Davis; he had no choice but to fire her, and she knew him as a decent and honest man with concern for the welfare of his prisoners and a belief in the possibility of rehabilitation for some of them. But she thirsted for vengeance against Hot Pants, who must have snitched on her. How else would the warden have suspected her? What also galled her was that Benny the jailbird had scarcely been reprimanded—not that he deserved worse, since his only crime had been in acting like a real man—while she, the supposedly free woman, had lost her job for doing nothing more than loving someone. That was what the world called justice. She was out of a job, while Sheriff Trotter was even talking about giving Benny weekend passes if he behaved himself. The next thing you knew, Benny would have himself deputized.

It was Sherry who handled the family finances—just as she was always the designated driver and the one who went down to bail friends out when they were DUI'd and the one who did the shopping and took Renee to the doctor—and she prided herself on her skills in the field of domestic economy. But with her salary stopped, she quickly ran into a cash-flow problem.

The Pelfreys' house, three bedrooms and a carport, had been willed free and clear to Billy and his two brothers and two sisters by their mother. Sherry and Billy had taken out a mortgage to buy up his relatives' shares. At the end of each month, Sherry went to the bank to make the payment in cash. What with only Billy's salary coming in and buying presents for more than a dozen relations and decorating the house with a tree and lights and stocking up on holiday goodies, Sherry was flat broke by the end of December. She thought of selling or pawning something, but Billy might notice. A scheme to stall for time formed in her fertile mind.

At the loan window to the bank, she asked the teller to check the balance on her mortgage. She said that she and her husband had come into some money and were trying to decide whether to pay down some of their debt or refinance. While the teller was off looking up the figures, Sherry reached through the window and snatched up the stamp used to mark her payment book and slipped it into her purse. The teller returned with the numbers; she thanked him and said that she would discuss the matter with her husband.

At home, she stamped the book "Paid" and filled in the date in a hand copied from previous entries. At the end of January, she stamped the book again.

One day in February, Billy confronted her. What in hell was going on? Mr. Terwilliger had called from the bank today at work. They were two months behind in their mortgage payments. If they didn't pay up, the bank would plant a For Sale sign in their front yard. What had Sherry been doing with the money?

"Terwilliger's a fool," Sherry said. "You can tell him his horse-and-buggy bank's fouled up, and it's no surprise, some of the morons he's got working for him. You wonder how they stay in business." She had been paying up faithfully, as always. To prove it, she showed him the payment book. There was her receipt, in black and white. Nor did she appreciate Billy's making accusations.

Billy was convinced. There was quite a to-do, but the bank gave in and marked their account current. As Sherry had assumed would happen, the teller had never reported the missing stamp, undoubtedly having blamed himself for misplacing it; he would be afraid now to admit his mistake. You could get away with a lot, Sherry took satisfaction in knowing, never underestimating how timid and slow-witted people were.

At the end of the month she was still broke and out of ideas. A notice arrived that the electricity was about to be shut off, then the phone. Circumstances dictated that it was time to tell the truth.

She told her husband everything, or almost. She announced that she was in love with another man and wanted a divorce. She would file herself. And yes, she would ask for custody of Renee.

Billy was more stunned, at first, than angry. Sherry refused to say who the other man was. He was no one Billy knew, she assured him. If he didn't mind, she would stay on in the house until she located a place of her own.

Billy tried to talk her out of her decision, but no, she said she had to do it, she was deeply in love and Billy ought to admit that their marriage had been in trouble for a long time. "You have a drinking problem, and I have a running-around problem," was the way she put it. Her advice to him was to "bow out gracefully." She was asking for very little, only her personal belongings, her car, and her daughter.

When Billy found out who his wife's lover was, he vowed to fight for custody of Renee, and he and Sherry could no longer speak without screaming at each other. She was counting on the courts to recognize the sacred bond between mother and child.

Sherry took a job in Clinton with Protective Apparel, a factory that manufactured bulletproof vests, camouflage jackets, and other paramilitary fashion items. She worked as a cashier in the retail shop. She also moved to Clinton, into one room in the house of a girlfriend whose husband was working in Arkansas. Benny was able to visit her there because Sheriff Trotter, a broad-minded man, had made good on his promise of weekend passes.

Renee remained with her father for the time being, but Sherry took her on outings and began telling her about Benny and preparing her to meet him. The prospect made Sherry anxious. Benny had often said how much he liked children and animals, but you never knew how a man would react to your child, especially when he had his own. Stepchildren caused trouble in every instance she could remember.

One bright blue Saturday in May, Sherry picked up Renee and drove to the Clinton jail, where Benny was waiting for them and climbed into the car. They were all in the front seat. Sherry noticed that when Benny tried to put his arm around Renee, the child flinched and started nattering on about the Flintstones. Benny let her talk. Sherry pulled into the drive-up window at McDonald's and ordered Big Macs, fries, and shakes for everyone to go and headed for a spot she had picked out on the banks of the Clinch River.

There were yellow and blue flowers everywhere in the new grass. A houseboat drifted by on the wide, dark river, a man and a boy taking the sun on the deck. On the opposite bank a man fished from the end of a dock, and upriver you could see two or three big houses that looked as if they had been there forever, with lawns sloping down to the water's edge. Sherry spread out the blanket she had brought and handed out the food. She couldn't think of anything to say.

Then, only a couple of bites into her own, Renee asked for a bite of Benny's hamburger. Sherry was about to tell her not to be so greedy, but before she could get the words out, Benny handed his hamburger to Renee. She took a big bite and offered it back to him.

"You can have it if you want," Benny said. "Does it taste better than yours?" he laughed.

Sherry swallowed the lump in her throat. Billy would never have done that, she thought, he was too selfish. Now she knew that everything was going to be all right.

The only serious complication in this new life, from what Sherry could see, was Benny's wife, Lona Kay, who brought his one-year-old daughter, Krystal Dawn, to visit him at the jail. There had been more than one unpleasant confrontation when the wife had appeared with the baby when Sherry was there or just leaving. No words had been exchanged, but Lona Kay had looked at Sherry with hatred.

Had she been unfair to Hot Pants? Sherry wondered. It could have been Lona Kay who had tipped off Warden Davis. The woman was no stranger to Brushy, after all, having met Benny there when she had been visiting another prisoner. The warden, according to Benny, had been about to remove her from the approved visitors list when Benny had managed to get her pregnant. Once he married her, she was safely back on the list, as a wife was normally not prevented from visiting her husband, the prison's gesture toward family life. Benny had baked the wedding cake, chocolate mint with cherries on top.

Benny also had another daughter, Sharon Annette, by a woman he had married just before he had been sent to Nashville State Prison. Sharon, who was now eleven, lived in Benny's hometown of Morristown, east of Knoxville. She had never seen her father out of prison. She visited him several times a year and wrote to him every week without fail. Sherry had read some of the letters, which had drawings on them of father and child and told him over and over that he was the greatest daddy in the world. Benny cared a lot for little Sharon. Sherry looked forward to meeting her.

He cared for little Dawn, too, and it was clear that he had room in his heart for Renee. It would take time to straighten everything out—to achieve what up-to-date therapists choose to call a "blended family."

Maw Webster fell ill in October and relinquished her post to her apprentice. She vowed gallantly to return, but it looked as if Benny could be the head cook as long as he wanted the job. He was only two months short of eligibility for parole, which would be a cinch. His behavior had been exemplary except for the one incident of unauthorized absence.

On Christmas Eve 1981, the *Clinton Courier-News* carried a front-page story about the new jailhouse cook. A photo showed Benny posed plunging spoons into a bowl of stuffing, wearing a Snoopy sweater Sherry had given him for Christmas. His hair and beard were neatly trimmed. He looked into the camera with sad, suspicious eyes. He was preparing a dinner of roast turkey, baked country ham, green beans, mashed potatoes, giblet gravy, cranberry sauce, hot rolls, and pecan pie for twenty prisoners.

The story referred to Benny's "culinary magic" and suggested that the dinner the prisoners "will sit down to is bound to be as good as many would get if they could be at home for the holidays.

"'My main concern is I want to see prisoners fed right. I didn't get fed right when I was a prisoner,' the quiet-spoken, friendly Hodge said over a cup of coffee in the jail kitchen."

He was planning to open his own restaurant after he received parole but said he would continue working at the jail until Maw Webster returned. "'I'm more interested in getting my own place than anything. I'd like to have it in Anderson County. That's home now. Everybody is friendly around here and I'm just not used to that. ... I'd like to be a chef but it would take some training. I can make it taste good but I can't make it look pretty.'"

Bena Mae Seivers, a secretary at the sheriff's department, disputed Benny's self-deprecations. His meals were not only delicious and nutritious, they were pleasant-looking. "'He doesn't just fix those all-white plates, you know.'"

The prisoners' plight, the story concluded, "may not give them much to be cheerful about but they at least can dig into a holiday spread prepared by a future professional who has personal reasons to see them enjoy it."

A sign posted on the wall outside the entrance to the Anderson County Sheriff's Department read:

> Through These Portals Pass
> The Finest Law Enforcement
> Officers in the World
> Professional Dignity
> PRIDE.

With the possible exception of Maw Webster, a generous soul, no one who worked for Sheriff Dennis O. Trotter or who had been arrested by his deputies could take the sign as anything but a joke.

The sheriff, who was into his second term of office by the time Benny Hodge went to work for him, maintained his perennial popularity with voters by insisting on a liberal policy toward motorists. He instructed deputies to treat county residents who exceeded the speed limits with the utmost courtesy, forgiveness, and understanding. His concept of law enforcement was based on a principle of fairness, that is, that if he did a favor for you, it was only fair that you did him the favor of voting for him. To receive anything more than a warning for speeding in Anderson County, you had to be either an outsider or guilty of some additional offense, such as being imprudent enough to display a bumper sticker supporting one of the sheriff's opponents. Trotter was also popular with drug dealers, fences, moonshiners and bootleggers (Oak Ridge was the county's only wet city), prostitutes, bookies, and operators of poker machines and other illegal forms of gambling, all of whom paid protection to him if they cared to stay in business. Four hundred years ago, when freebooting chieftains along the Scottish border exacted tribute in return for freedom from plunder, the way Sheriff Trotter operated was called blackmail. In the eighties in East Tennessee, they called it politics.

Of the sheriff's several sources of payoffs, drug dealers were by far the most lucrative for him. Aside from its geographical and topographical advantages to the drug trade, the presence of Oak Ridge within its boundaries meant that Anderson had more cash floating around than other counties in the area. Oak Ridge, which used to call itself The Atomic City, is home to the Oak Ridge National Laboratory, Oak Ridge Associated Universities, the American Museum of Atomic Energy, and numerous government plants. It has been the nation's leading center for nuclear research since the forties, when, because of the abundance of water and power nearby, the government created it as part of the effort to make the bomb, displacing more than a thousand local families and bringing in scientists and technicians from around the country. Its population once exceeded fifty thousand, later dwindling to around thirty thousand—a well-paid, highly educated group, distinct from and with more money to spend than most East Tennesseans on everything, including recreational drugs.

Oak Ridge had its own police force, but Sheriff Trotter's jurisdiction included smaller communities and unincorporated areas favored for their obscurity by drug drealers and other crooks, who could slip into the larger city on business or let the traffic come to them. People in the know understood that Sheriff Trotter and his chief deputy controlled Anderson County. And the sheriff's power derived from more than taking bribes. Several of his deputies and plainclothes enforcers spent a good deal of their time making the rounds to collect payoffs, but another key to his success was being able to get the drugs back into circulation once they were seized in a well-orchestrated raid. Recycling, some called it; through it Trotter was able to share in the actual profits from drug sales, horning in on the retail end of the action.

Typically a dealer, or sometimes a lower-level snitch, would tip off the sheriff to where a cache of drugs could be found. The sheriff would stage a raid, making sure reporters knew about it so he could reap publicity. The headline might read DRUGS SEIZED, SUSPECTS FLEE. If anyone was actually arrested, a portion of the drugs would be kept for evidence, the rest returned immediately to the street. Deputies routinely stored evidence in their lockers, from where it had a way of disappearing.

Every few weeks the sheriff made a show of destroying material no longer needed as evidence. He would put a match to heaps of drugs at the county landfill—except that what was burned was bogus, the real stuff being back on the street. He would unseal samples returned from the state toxicological lab, sell the genuine narcotics, and replace them with baking soda, sugar, or over-the-counter pills obtained through burglary and hijacking. If open crime got out of hand and citizens began to squawk, the sheriff's underworld connections enabled him miraculously to solve a few cases and return the stolen goods.

While the structure of Sheriff Trotter's organization was hardly innovative—muckraking journalists uncovered identical practices in America's largest cities nearly a hundred years ago; reforming that sort of corruption was the basis of the Progressive Movement—the violent nature of the narcotics trade made it especially vicious and dangerous. It thrived because by no means all of the deputies were on the take or privy to the sheriff's nefarious activities, although many were aware of them; Trotter, like any successful gangster, understood the importance of confiding in only a few intimates. One key was that each raid, whether legitimate or phony, had to be cleared beforehand with the sheriff or his chief deputy, Tim Schultz, who could decide whether to lay off this or that dealer or gambling joint. At least two deputies quit during 1982 but, valuing their health, reported nothing. One of them was asked to resign by her husband, who feared for her

safety; another enrolled in a creative writing course and began com-
posing tales of police corruption, disguised as fiction.

By January 1982, when he was finally released on parole, Benny
Hodge was familiar with Sheriff Trotter's philosophy of law enforcement. Trotter had not been so understanding about Sherry and free
with weekend passes merely to foster his trusty's love life. Technically
Benny had violated the conditions of his position and had jeopardized
his release date. After the incident at the Family Inn, the sheriff had
an arm on him.

Trotter began using Benny as a bag man, to deliver drugs from
the jail and collect payment for them. Benny was not only physically
right for the job, the sheriff could make use of him without spending
an extra dime. Whether Benny would have been willing to perform
these services of his own free will was beside the point. The alternative for him was back to Brushy.

Once Benny achieved parole, he moved in with Sherry in the
house she was sharing; a week later they rented a trailer together at
the Cedar Grove Mobile Home Park on Laurel Road in Clinton. He
continued on as the jailhouse cook and, occasionally, as the sheriff's
bag man, aware of Trotter's power over him. Sherry urged him to
look for another, full-time job, but Benny hesitated. He was unused to
being free, and finding other work would not be easy for an ex-con.
Cooking was the first legitimate employment he had had since high
school.

One day Sheriff Trotter summoned Benny to his office, which
was decorated with marijuana plants and fruit jars of moonshine—
evidence, of course. The sheriff sipped from a jar and, patting his
beer gut happily, offered some to Benny, who declined, saying he
didn't drink.

"I guess pussy's your vice. Right, Hodge? Biggin, I got plans for
you."

Some people, the sheriff observed, did not understand how
important it was to pay their debts. They had no sense of honor or
responsibility, and sometimes they needed persuading to cough up.

Trotter offered Benny a job as an enforcer. Benny could go on as
cook if he wished; the sheriff would even see to it that he got a raise.
But the real money would be in his new position. He would be guaranteed a percentage of every debt he managed to collect. Whatever
techniques he used would be up to him. Big as Hodge was, the sheriff

did not think that many delinquents would choose to argue with him. He could carry a gun, however, and use it whenever and however necessary. All in the line of duty, no questions asked. Was it a deal?

Benny said that he would talk the matter over with his girlfriend. He was just getting started in his new life. He had children to worry about. He didn't want to mess things up.

"You do that," the sheriff said. "Get you some of that butt and talk it over with her. Tell 'er old Trotter can't think of a better way for a fella on parole to stay out of trouble than helping the sheriff fight crime, hear?"

Sherry was strongly opposed. It wasn't the physical risk; she figured Benny could take care of himself. It was the idea of getting in so deep with Sheriff Trotter, whom only a damn fool would trust and who sooner or later would set Benny up and hang him out to dry. For a few extra bucks, he would be buying himself a one-way ticket back to Brushy.

Benny told Trotter that he appreciated the offer but preferred to stay on strictly as the cook for the time being.

"Sure, I understand," the sheriff said. "Now you can haul ass out of here. You dumb idiot, you're fired!"

9

OTHER THAN THROUGH SHERRY, whose friends and relations were being cool toward her, and through his wife and children, Benny's only contacts in the free world were people from the jail and former convicts, who for better or for worse maintained a certain solidarity. One former Brushy Mountain prisoner who had managed to start a contracting business gave Benny a job painting apartments in Oak Ridge. Most of Benny's fellow workers were also ex-cons; the only way to endure the boredom of house painting is to listen to the radio, get high, talk, or manage a combination of two or three of these; among ex-cons the conversation naturally turned to what else they might be doing for a living and who was into what. Benny was not a talker, but he did plenty of listening; and to supplement his meager wages, as well as to gain the satisfaction of some revenge against Sheriff Trotter, Benny visited the Clinton jail from time to time and helped himself to drugs with the aid of a deputy who remained friendly. Sherry approved of this. The drugs had already been stolen, she reasoned, and would soon be on the street again anyway. Why shouldn't she and Benny sell them, rather than leaving them to fatten Trotter's wallet?

But the sheriff took his own revenge, or so Sherry believed, against Benny because of his defiance. On June 28, 1982, deputies arrested Benny. At the jail, an elderly lady identified him as one of two men who had broken into her house on the night of June 16.

On learning of Benny's arrest, Sherry went immediately to his parole officer to try to stave off trouble. Merely having been arrested and charged with second-degree burglary was enough to have Benny cited with parole violation. Sherry begged for leniency. This was a setup, she pleaded. Benny was trying to go straight, but Sheriff Trotter had framed him out of resentment at him, she thought. Didn't everybody know what kind of a crooked bastard the sheriff was?

The officer reacted sympathetically. For his part, he had more work than he could handle anyway; he agreed not to cite Benny—"I won't violate him," was the way he phrased it—unless an actual conviction came down. Sherry assured him that it would not. Not only was there no evidence, the only witness was an old biddy who couldn't see any better than a common garden mole.

If Sherry did care for her boyfriend as much as she appeared to, the parole officer said, she should try to keep him on the straight and narrow and make sure he sent in the ten dollars every parolee was required to remit each month to pay for the paperwork. If Benny did that and stayed out of trouble, the officer would be just as happy to mark him reported and clean and to forget about him. Sherry gladly forked over two months in advance and told the officer she would keep Benny honest. It was a pleasure to meet an understanding gentleman for a change. She had begun to think that there were none left in the world.

With money saved from drug sales, Sherry managed to make Benny's bond. Whether arresting him had been solely the sheriff's idea, or whether the other suspect, who had been arrested first, had been offered a deal to name Benny was unclear. Benny had been told by deputies that the corruption and misuse of informants was standard practice in this sheriff's office, where criminals were frequently paid, threatened, or induced to incriminate others in order to save their own necks.

Sherry, who was by then working as a cashier at the Bi-Lo market in Oak Ridge, claimed that Benny had been in the store at the time of the incident; another cashier backed her up. The victim, moreover, had been unable to identify Hodge from photographs shown her by deputies prior to his arrest and had described him as smaller than his accomplice, whereas he turned out to be taller and heavier. She had caught a glimpse of him by only the light from a television set. There was no physical evidence because, the woman said, the burglars had fled when they determined that she and her husband were armed.

The judge dismissed the charges for lack of evidence. Sherry and Benny were only slightly relieved. What if, the next time he felt like harassing Benny, Trotter built a better case?

When the deputy who had been giving Benny access to drugs was himself fired, Benny and Sherry, reduced to living on their salaries, fell behind in the rent on their trailer and moved in with a friend, one of the ex-cons Benny had met house painting. The man's apartment was a rathole, so filthy and depressing that Sherry could not bring Renee there to visit. Under the circumstances, and because Billy Pelfrey had refused to pay child support while Sherry was shacked up with an ex-con—a position Sherry considered unfair but one she knew that the court would uphold—she gave up seeking custody of her daughter. If she had been able to accept that this loss of her child would be permanent, she would have been more upset. She believed, however, that she could regain custody after she helped Benny get back on his feet—or onto his feet for the first time in his life. As it was, she began having nightmares in which Renee was snatched from her arms and carried off. She awoke to find Benny beside her and took comfort from him. Somehow she knew, or hoped or tried to believe, they would work things out. His wife was divorcing him. Sherry went down to the court every month to make his support payment, when they had the money.

She also believed that for the time being, not forever but during this trying and tumultuous transitional period, Renee might be better off without her. Benny himself was like a newborn child requiring all of her attention. Not that he wasn't a man. To her he was a man like no other. They made love day and night. She would wait naked in the bed for him to come home from work and crawl in with her. There was nothing she had to do to attract him. It was enough for her to be there. Sometimes she would manage to get through to him on the phone while he was working and she would tell him what she wanted and what she planned to do to him when he got home, and by the time he arrived there was no stopping him. He would get a little rough sometimes, plowing away and yanking her hair and calling out blunt words, but that was fine, it thrilled her, and it made her all the more his, she thought, the one person in the world he could say anything to and do anything with.

When they lay exhausted between bouts, she called him Honey

and Hodge-Podge and Sweetpete. He was especially tender when they were totally fucked out. He called her Booger, as in "You little Booger," his snot-nosed kid, and other endearments she loved hearing. I have lived thirty years on this earth, she thought, and I never knew what it was supposed to be like, and it turns out to be more than I could have imagined. Sometimes her Sweetpete, he was so dear and seemed so lost in the world. He wasn't like her husband, who could never be alone with her; Benny wanted no one else around, just the two of them. At times she felt more like the mother of this homeless boy, the big abandoned baby. She wished she could nurse him.

They were like two kids in a rowboat, she told him, floating down the river of life—but that was funny, because he was such a big strong boy, his arms the size of her thighs. She asked him how and when he had started building himself up. When he stood and posed naked for her, it took her breath away; and she noticed that he was always looking at himself in the mirror. Why not? His pride was in his body. He had worked out daily at the county jail, as before at Brushy; now he was anxious to join a health club as soon as they had the money. He never took a drink and smoked a joint only once or twice a week. He did go through about a pack of Camels a day, and Sherry smoked, too. That's our only vice, she told him, that and each other.

He told her that he had started lifting weights when, at nineteen, he had been convicted on a robbery charge and was sent to prison at Nashville. He had been in the reformatory before, but never prison, and he had not been prepared for it. The first week, three black prisoners had jumped him and tried to rape him. He had managed to fight them off long enough for the guards to come and rescue him, but he knew that this was the way it was going to be if he didn't do something about it. He wasn't strong enough to defend himself.

In desperation he managed to escape but was quickly caught, with extra time tacked onto his sentence. He was facing at least two years before parole. Another prisoner showed him the weights and how to work with them. It had not taken long before nobody dared touch him.

When, a year and a half after his release, he was caught robbing a store with a gun and sentenced to twenty years, he had all the more motivation to keep strong. Of course he had thought about escape, every day, but once he was moved to Brushy Mountain, he knew it was futile. He had seen what had happened to James Earl Ray and others who had tried. There was no way to break out of Brushy.

And then something happened that changed his attitude about doing time.

Throughout his first few years in prison, Benny had thought of little else but escape and had kept to himself, shunning contact with authorities and with fellow prisoners. He was with the convicts, not the inmates, but he was not a leader and had not developed his cooking skills beyond performing routine tasks in the kitchen. Then in 1977, a few weeks after James Earl Ray's escape attempt, Benny's father died, killed in a bar fight. This was not his real father, whose name was Vernon Troubaugh—that was about all Benny knew about him, because he had disappeared so long ago. The man killed in '77 was the third of Benny's seven stepfathers and the one he remembered the best, because his mother had been married to him for six years while Benny was growing up, and he was the most hateful person Benny had ever met, in or out of prison.

His name was Billy Joe Hodge. The first thing Benny hated him for was forcing him to take the name Hodge. Benny hated his mother, too, for allowing this to happen; but there were numerous other reasons to hate her, such as her marrying Billy Joe to begin with. She ought to have had enough sense and enough regard for her children not to have married a man who had made his reputation in Morristown at the age of sixteen when he had slit open his brother's stomach with a knife and watched the entrails spill out onto the sidewalk. Everybody in Morristown knew about that incident.

On the other hand, once she had married him, his mother could never have stood up to Billy Joe, who beat her something awful, in front of the children. She ought never to have left Benny's previous stepfather, Junior Hickey, who was the father of Benny's half-sister, Donna Kay. Sometimes Benny would run and hide at the Hickeys' house when Billy Joe went berserk beating his mother, Eula Kate, and taking whacks at Benny and his two full sisters, Carol Sue and Patricia Ann. Billy Joe was such a jealous man, he hardly ever let Eula Kate out of the house and beat her if she so much as acknowledged her firstborn, Donna Kay Hickey, on the street.

So when Billy Joe marched over to the school and had the records changed so that Benny Lee Troubaugh became Benny Lee Hodge, Eula Kate did not dare object. Billy Joe never actually adopted Benny. The truth was, his name was legally still Troubaugh, but it was too late to change it back now. Every time he heard the name Hodge or signed it, he had to think of that son of a bitch.

Benny told Sherry that he had never talked to anyone else about these things. He tried not to think about them, but they haunted him. Now as they lay in bed, smoking a cigarette or maybe a joint, Sherry urged him to unburden himself. It was a way of getting over something and going on, and she cajoled him by revealing secrets of her life, too. Benny said that in facing up to the past, he was beginning to realize what an effect Billy Joe had had on his life.

Oh, yes, he could thank Billy Joe for introducing him to crime when he was only twelve years old. Billy Joe had written a bad check to a hardware store in Morristown. That night, he took Benny by the hand and dragged him to the store, which was closed at that hour, the street deserted. He handed Benny a brick and told him to heave it through the window. "Go ahead, son, do as I say, or I'll beat the hide off of you." Benny broke the window. He was terrified. Billy Joe lifted him through the window, pushed him in and told him to retrieve the check from the cash register. It was his first crime. Up till then, he had been just another kid, a good boy as far as he could remember. His teachers had liked him and had been kind to him. Neither of his sisters nor his half-sister had ever been in trouble.

By the time he was in high school he was in hot water all the time, fighting and stealing, and he ended up being sent to the state reformatory. Billy Joe, he knew, was happy to have him out of the house and off the grocery list. When, after six months, he was due to be released, his mother failed to sign the required papers saying that he had a home to go to and was wanted there. He could never forgive her for that, because it meant that he had to stay another six months in the reformatory. Billy Joe must have threatened to beat her if she did sign, but still, Benny hated his mother for having done that to him.

Benny's happiest childhood memory was also his saddest, because of Billy Joe. Benny had a dog named Queenie, black and white and mostly St. Bernard, who ate too much, or so Billy Joe complained. Every time Benny petted Queenie and talked to her and let her up on the bed to snuggle, Billy Joe became so jealous that he flew into a fury and called Benny a sissy and an ingrate. He said he hated that dog so much that he was going to kill it.

One day Billy Joe, waving a pistol, chased Benny and Queenie out of the house and into the street and shot the dog dead, right before Benny's eyes. Benny remembered this so vividly, it could have happened yesterday. The first shot hit Queenie in the hind leg. She fell, yelping. Billy Joe walked up, calm as could be, and shot her through the head.

He didn't know why he hadn't fainted right there, Benny said, or why he hadn't run and kept on running. Instead he had rushed inside to his mother, screaming, "Why did he kill my dog? Why did he kill Queenie?" What a mistake that had been! Eula Kate asked him if he wasn't sure that a policeman hadn't done it. A policeman! There weren't any policemen around. "Why would a policeman shoot a dog in front of my young'un?" his mother had wailed. She must have been too terrified of Billy Joe to tell the truth.

So it was that when Warden Davis informed him that his father had died, he had felt more like offering up a prayer of thanks than anything else. Whoever had killed him, Benny wished he could give the guy a medal. When the warden offered to let him go to the funeral, Benny was inclined to say no. But any prisoner will jump for a glimpse of the free world. He had not been on the outside for years. He might get a chance to spit on the coffin. And, you never knew, he might be able to escape.

But the warden attached a condition. He would let Benny go to the funeral in street clothes, and he would even permit the shackles and handcuffs to be removed and would instruct the guards to remain inconspicuous, so as not to embarrass Benny in front of his relatives. In exchange, however, Benny would have to promise not to escape. Warden Davis was giving him this chance to get a breath of fresh air and to prove that he had truly changed, could take responsibility, and was on his way toward rehabilitation. Benny would have to give his word of honor.

He could not possibly do that, Benny told the warden. He knew that Davis was being straight with him and, like a true convict, Benny would do the same. He had to tell the truth, that if he got the chance to run, he could do nothing else.

Back in his cell, Benny gave the warden's offer more thought. He understood it as more than a gift of one day outside. It was a test, and if Benny passed, he sensed he could expect further rewards. What if he did run? They would catch him anyway, sooner or later, and his parole date would be set back. Why not show the warden that he could trust Benny Hodge? It was a game, like the whole system, and the prize for winning was freedom. He gave the warden his word.

At the funeral home, Benny's guards waited outside on the steps during the service. Benny was able to chat with his sisters and cousins. He even kissed his mother on the cheek, which wasn't easy.

A cousin came up to him and whispered in his ear that there was a Camaro parked outside with the keys in the ignition and a full tank of gas and a roll of money in the glove compartment. Benny could slip out the side entrance and get a good start.

Benny said no thanks. He had given his word to the Man, who was trying to help him.

It was after that that Benny worked on his cooking, found he enjoyed it, got appointed cook for the staff commissary, and was permitted to bunk in the White Building. If it hadn't been for Warden Davis's showing faith in him, he would probably still be behind bars.

All this pillow talk, which went on in fits and starts over many weeks, deepened Sherry's attachment to Benny. It gave her a sense of mission about him. He was her man, her lover, but he was still the frightened little boy, needing a chance, hurt into meanness and ripe for healing. It was as the Bible said, be you as little children to enter the kingdom. She determined to devote herself to his healing. One thing she knew she had to do was to try to reconcile Benny, somehow, with his mother and to encourage him to forgive her. There was a saying that you can never trust a man who hates his mother, or a woman who hates her father. Sherry had every reason to believe that the saying was true.

One of the secrets Sherry revealed to Benny—and she had never spoken to anyone about it before—was that she hated her own father. Charles Sheets had never been what you would call much of a provider after he married Samantha Hill and fathered eight children by her in nineteen years. Charles cut timber in East Tennessee most of the year and picked oranges in Florida the rest, so he was often away; and when he was home, he was usually drunk. When her mother died, Sherry's sister Louise, who was then nineteen, and Louise's husband, E. L. Smith, agreed to take in Sherry along with her two surviving brothers, who were three and fifteen. Another older sister, Brenda, then eighteen, was on her own. Although the Smiths soon had three children themselves, E. L. and Louise always treated everyone alike. Sherry called them Mom and Dad and loved them, she said, with all her heart. If it hadn't been for them, she would have ended up in an orphanage.

But Charles Sheets was a hateful man and, unfortunately, never left the picture until he died in 1976. He contributed nothing; the family survived on E. L.'s salary from an Oak Ridge government plant, but Charles would show up every so often and act as if he had rights in the house, drinking and cursing and behaving like such a pest that everyone was always glad to see him leave.

He would get drunk and turn on Sherry, making fun of her hair, which wasn't long and straight and shiny as her mother's had been. He would hold up a photograph of Samantha and taunt Sherry with it, asking her why she couldn't look like that, or like her sister Brenda, who was the beautiful one and the successful one. It wasn't only her father who compared Sherry unfavorably to Brenda; everyone did. It was as if no one expected Sherry to turn out anything but bad. Brenda was admirable, Sherry admitted; she was now the head of security for the entire K-25 plant in Oak Ridge; and she was beautiful, except for her butt, which was flat. If she had a butt, she'd be perfect, and she was still a lot prettier than Sherry, with creamy skin and straight dark hair. Sherry had darker skin. She wasn't so dark that she could be taken for a Negro, but at school she had been called an Indian.

When Sherry's father would get thoroughly drunk, he would blame her for her mother's death. "If it hadn't been for you, you no-good frizzy-headed little bitch, your mother would be alive today. I should've pinched your head off when you was born." He blamed Sherry for Samantha's death at least once every time he'visited. You could count on it.

And he was always complaining about her hair. She remembered her father cursing her unruly hair and spitting in his hands and rubbing the spit all over her head. Her mom and dad had asked him to leave when he did that, but the damage was done. It made her feel filthy and rotten and worthless, and she hated him.

But she truly hated him for something he had done one night when she was eleven years old. Her father had been visiting, misbehaving as usual. He came in one night drunk when everyone else was asleep. There was no bed for him, with five children in the house at that time. Usually he slept on a couch, but that night he stumbled in and crawled into bed with Sherry. She pretended to stay asleep, but he began fondling her, and before she knew it she could feel his hard thing against her back and he was turning her over and crawling on top of her and trying to rape her.

Sherry screamed. Everyone woke up and came running. Her father whispered to her that she had better say she had been dreaming.

"A nightmare!" she managed to choke out. "I been having a nightmare!" So her mom made her some warm milk.

She kept her distance from her father after that. It always irked her when Louise asked why she wasn't nicer to their father, but Sherry never said anything. Maybe someday she would tell them, to let them know how she felt. They ought to have figured it out. It didn't take a brain surgeon to understand what Charles Sheets had been after, drunk in the bed with his own daughter.

That was the way her mom and dad were. E. L. and Louise were Christian people, church every Sunday, always finding the good in folks, leading a life that to Sherry was uptight but that she was sure was how life should be lived, even if she couldn't quite live it without throwing up. They were good to her. They sent her to the eye doctor to get glasses as soon as they figured out she was shortsighted; nor did she mind being a four-eyes, it was what she was, and anyone who made fun of her, she was ready to punch out, so they stayed clear. It was just that her parents didn't understand her. They loved her and raised her as their own, when it would have been so easy for E. L. to turn her out, saying that is not my child, that girl already has a father. It was just that they made her feel like some kind of a prisoner. Not their fault.

E. L.'s idea of a good time was sitting at the family dinner table. When she looked back on it, she loved it; but at the time, she had wanted to roam the woods. Everyone took meals on time, fingernails clean, at the table, period, the end. She remembered this with joy, even though at the time she wanted to be off to meet Tarzan. One of the things that had bothered her about Billy Pelfrey and his family was that they would grab a plate and go their separate ways as if they lived in a zoo and didn't know what a table was for. Monkeys! Maybe when you didn't have a real mom and dad, you didn't take eating at a table for granted. When they got a place of their own, she would insist that they sit down to meals together. It would be an example to the children.

Sherry said that as a child she had never been permitted to leave the yard without permission. That was the way it should be; she wished she still had that yard. When she fought with her brothers, which she had to do to keep from being crushed, she was so rebellious, with such a sassy mouth on her, that no one could keep her down, not even her dad when he whipped her. There was no one who could restrain her, no matter who or what. Nobody messed with her. She might stay in the yard, but she was king of it, or queen.

She remembered the time that she and her brother had fought at the table over a piece of cornbread. It was the last piece. He took it off her plate and she socked him, hard, on the shoulder.

Her dad jumped up and grabbed the two of them and said if they didn't stop fighting, he would whip them both.

"You all going to fight at this table anymore?"

"I will," Sherry said, "if he eats my cornbread."

From then on, every time they sat down, her brothers stole something from her plate, and she bopped them in the nose.

"You don't tell me you ain't going to fight at this table," E. L. said, "I'm going to have to whip you."

"Then whip me for telling a lie," Sherry said.

"Why is that?"

"Because if he keeps stealing, I'm going to keep on fighting."

Spanking and whipping never worked with her. If she thought she was right, you might as well have been talking to the wall as to her; and if you whipped her, she would wait until it stopped hurting and then go on doing whatever it was that she had been punished for.

She didn't know what had made her the way she was, always ready to stand up for herself and fight, and always wary of trusting people. Maybe it was not having a real father and mother; maybe it was what her father had done to her and how little others thought of her; maybe it was just the way people were. She considered herself naturally generous, just like Benny; but at school she had soon noticed that the other children always tried to take advantage of her giving nature, the way her brothers did. If some kid whined that he didn't have milk money, Sherry would give it to him; the next thing she knew, that kid would be demanding milk money from her every day. She'd have to fight to hang onto her own lunch.

Benny agreed with her about people. You could not trust anybody. The only thing that counted was strength.

"And brains," Sherry said. "Don't you never try to fool me, Hodge-Podge, 'cause I'll be three steps ahead of you. I can outsmart anybody, but ain't nobody outsmarts Sherry. With those muscles of yourn and my brains, we'll make a team nobody cain't beat. But don't you never try to cross me."

"Who, me?" Benny said. "I ain't that dumb."

Men were the worst, Sherry said, except for women, who would sooner stab each other in the back than say how do you do. It had taken her some time to figure men out, because she had had so little experience of them, outside of her family, before marriage. E. L. and Louise were so strict, Sherry had had to learn to be a good liar even to get out of the house at all. She remembered one time when E. L. was working the second shift and had forbidden her brother and her to go to a basketball game. They had conned Mom into letting them go, as long as they got back before midnight, when E. L. was due home. Unfortunately, they'd had a car wreck.

The next morning, E. L. asked Sherry what was that cut on her chin. She was prepared.

"I was in the bathroom at school," she said without hesitating, "and the bell rang to go to class and I was getting up to run quick and this girl stabbed me with a pencil."

The lie had worked. The secret to lying was, you had to get it out quick and you had to make it big enough and interesting enough for people to buy it. You had to use a little imagination, so that the person you're fooling gets involved in the story enough, he forgets you might be making it up.

Because E. L. was so strict, Sherry had had only one real date in high school, and that was with a hoodlum she asked to the prom just to upset her parents. She had gone out with the dude to spite them; she had married Billy Pelfrey to please them. That made her a two-time loser, the way she figured it.

It was after she had dated the hood that her grades had begun to fall. She supposed that she had started failing in school in order to bug her mom and dad, too. E. L. had been so keen on her going to nursing school that he had helped her get a summer job at the hospital, something she had enjoyed, even if it paid next to nothing and was mostly emptying bedpans, because helping sick people made her feel good. E. L. had personally selected her high school courses for her, tough ones like chemistry and advanced algebra, which she would need to qualify as an R.N. It was not that she couldn't handle them; she had always found math and science a breeze. She had deliberately chosen to fail. She did not like anyone telling her what to do, and there were other reasons. Why not piss them off?

"I take responsibility for everything I do," Sherry said. "If a man wants me instead of his wife, I don't blame him. I know it's some-thing about me, or maybe I'm coming on to him. It's the way I am. Good or bad, I don't believe in whining and blaming other people for my mistakes. Hell, it ain't wrong till I'm caught anyway, and if I'm caught, it's my fault. I hate a whiner."

Why would she have wanted to spite her parents, Benny won-dered, if they had been so good to her? He wished he'd had parents like that. Hadn't she told him that, give or take a few things, she'd had a happy childhood?

"I'd give up my life for my dad," Sherry said, meaning her brother-in-law, "anytime. As for my mom, I'd have to think twice about it." Sherry often made this statement. She'd pause, let it sink in, let curiosity simmer, then go on, as if it were a rehearsed speech. "She's jealous of me. Always was. Because E. L. loves me so much. My mom thinks he loves me more than he does her. Maybe he does. And I love him. I love to see the way he sits on that porch when the leaves change in the fall, that's the best time, when he's painting pic-tures of trees and animals and birds. He's a real good artist, you know that? He paints on wood and on rocks and saws and everything. Do you know E. L. give me this picture of a eagle he painted on a saw?" She started to cry. A big sob welled up and broke. "It's so pretty. I wish I didn't have to do nothing to hurt him. I wish I hadn't've had to fail my grades. I had to do it. I wish I hadn't've had to do a lot of things and disappoint him and fail him. It's the way I am. I wish I could help him. He's sick. His lungs don't work no more.

"I don't want to hurt him. You do things. Never mind." She was having trouble speaking. "Maybe I'll talk about it some day. Maybe I won't. You better let sleeping dogs ..."

And Benny, being less inquisitive a person than she, asked no more. Sherry reached for him in the bed and told him that she loved him.

"Come here, Outlaw. You *are* my outlaw. Let me do something for you."

"I love you, too, Booger," Benny said. He confided that he had truly loved only one person before in his life. That had been a long time ago. Her name was Sandy. Poor Sandy, she had been messed up in a drug deal and got her throat slit.

10

THE BURDENS OF THEIR PASTS, low horizons, shady companions, Sherry's capacity for rationalization, prejudice against ex-convicts, infantilism, delusions of grandeur, a commitment to progress, dissatisfaction with the minimum wage, the corruptness of public officials, the prevalence of narcotics, the sheriff as role model, the chaos of modern American life, defects of character, weakness of will, the habits of lifetimes, an outlaw tradition, circumstance, biology, fate—numerous factors must have figured into Sherry and Benny's taking up crime as their principal source of income. The immediate reason was that they were short of cash.

As long as they were living in that cramped dump with Benny's friend, who was a slob and proud of it, they were able to make it financially, taking into account the regular payment to the parole officer, money Benny sometimes sent to his wife and ex-wife for his daughters, eating in restaurants because there was no stove in the apartment, and the occasional amusement. But any unexpected expense, as when Sherry's car broke down, was a setback. Luxuries such as presents for each other or family members were out of the question. Worst of all, they had nowhere to bring the kids for a visit.

When they scraped up the money to see the movie *E.T.*, they were so moved by the story of the cuddly alien and his earthling companion, the boy living in a suburban heaven chock-full of toys and friends and relatives, that they wept—or at least Sherry did. Although she saw aspects of herself in the bug-eyed, scaly creature, she identified more with the boy who was so eager to help and protect his strange friend: E.T. was her Biggin. E.T.'s cry of *"Home!"*, his plaintive longing to return to an extraterrestrial hearth, was meant for them, they both felt. It was time to create for themselves the home they had never known, a place of their own they could fill with love and laughter and material goods. The quickest and surest means to this end, they decided, was armed robbery.

To Sherry it was obvious that the reason most criminals got caught was because they were stupider than the police. Yet most cops were stupid, too. If you were smarter than the cops, you could stay ahead of them time after time, as long as you watched your step and never got careless. Cops did not so much solve crimes, Sherry believed, as criminals tripped themselves up one way or another. Leaving clues was obviously one; calling attention to yourself was another, such as by driving a flashy car or wearing clothes you could not possibly have come by legitimately; talking too much was another, and leaving a paper trail still another.

Other than school texts, Sherry had never read a book all the way through. She was an avid student of local newspapers, however, reading at least one every day from front to back. She gave national and international news only cursory attention—in a given year she might not have been able to name the President of the United States, and she could not have found China on a map to save her life—but she knew what was going on in Anderson, Roane, and surrounding counties as well as any local editor did. She pored over feature stories, social notes, and the want ads with a proofreader's eye. Sports mattered little more to her than the stock market. Most avidly of all she followed crime stories, especially accounts of arrests, trials, convictions, or acquittals. Why one criminal got nailed and another went free were questions of insatiable curiosity to her. Ask her about any local case and she could provide means, motive, evidence, alibi, or have read between the lines to catch a whiff of payoff. Her obsession was a source of wonder and irritation to Benny. "Booger," he would say, "why you got your nose in that damn paper again? Ruin your eyes." She also studied people incessantly at work or when she was out and around, priding herself on being able to guess their occupations, whether someone was cheating on a husband or wife, how much this or that item of clothing or jewelry had cost and whether a face showed misery or joy, innocence or guilt. If cops had brains, they would have hired me to go undercover, she often said.

Add to all this what she had learned at Brushy, from Benny, from her own small-time misdemeanors and felonies, and from the numerous scrapes friends and relatives had experienced, and one could count Sherry Sheets as a woman of the world. If her circles did not encompass the rich, she believed that she understood them and that she certainly knew more about them than they did about her. To Sherry, the rich were different from her because they were bigger crooks.

She could not drive through the prosperous neighborhoods of Oak Ridge, with their flowering lawns and shiny, expensive cars in every driveway and two or three TVs and stereos blasting and people sipping drinks in Jacuzzis, without thinking that she deserved all that as much as anyone. In the stores at the Oak Ridge mall she studied the spoiled little girls in pressed designer jeans dealing from decks of Daddy's credit cards and wondered what swindle had gone down, what money passed under the table to float this game? Were there that many nuclear scientists pulling down a bundle? You didn't make that kind of bucks being an egghead. The honest day-to-day laborer didn't stand a chance. She knew what her dad and her ex-husband earned at the plants, good salaries, but peanuts compared to real money. They would die never knowing the good life. You had to have an angle.

Sherry wasn't so much envious as impatient of ignorance and irritated by hypocrisy. The way she saw it, there was a certain amount of wealth in the world. The people who had most of it had figured out when the fix was on. Benny's approach was similar but simpler. To him, if the other dog had the bone and you could sink your teeth into it, it was yours.

In that neck of the woods, Sherry concluded, the angle was drugs. Drugs were the common denominator that linked rich to poor, poor to middle class. Money might be scarce, but drugs were everywhere, and once you had the drugs, money followed.

With their cash crunch acute, it was only logical for Sherry to ask why, if Sheriff Trotter could get away with it, she and Benny also couldn't profit from the same scam, confiscating drugs and selling them. There was one thing about drug dealers, they were not about to blow the whistle. What were they going to do, call the police? Hey, these people got my drugs and my money! I want them caught and prosecuted!

The prospect of robbery with virtual immunity from arrest proved irresistible. This would be no crude mugging operation. It would require thought and preparation, as well as networking and a certain amount of acting, including costumes and props.

First off, they would need a setup man, someone with accurate information about who the dealers were, where they kept their stash, how well they were armed, whether they were the type to put up a fight. He would get a third of the take. And Benny would need a partner, who would get another third. The idea would be to show up at a dealer's place pretending to be cops making a bust and steal everything in sight.

And they would need a good fence. Trying to peddle the merchandise themselves would be the one sure way to get caught.

Benny had no difficulty making the right contacts. He still had sources within the sheriff's office who would give him information for a price. At his painting job, which he now could look forward to quitting, one ex-con led to another, connections that spread throughout Anderson and into other counties. As his partner Benny selected Roice Littlefield (an alias), a con whom he had known at Brushy and who had a grudge against Trotter and was delighted with the idea of taking some of the action away from the sheriff. They agreed that they should not target any dealer known as a straight-up guy, honest within the terms of the criminal fraternity. They needed to keep loyalties intact for future jobs. The ideal victim would be someone in cahoots with the sheriff, or any known snitch. No respected Brushy alumnus would be hit.

As for the fences, they were everywhere. A certain Knoxville dealer in gold, silver, coins, and estate jewelry was one; a bartender at a Lake City veterans club was another. Both had plenty of cash available for instant payment, so the hot goods could be got rid of immediately.

Through Littlefield, Benny bought a gun—as a parolee, he could not have obtained one legally, and owning one put him in violation of parole, but that was not of paramount concern. A Smith & Wesson .38 special five-shot, with a four-inch barrel, it looked like something a plainclothes cop would carry. At Green Acres Flea Market, he bought a gold policeman's badge.

Gaining entrance to the dealer's house or apartment would be half the battle: it would not do to break the door down as in the drug raids depicted on television; someone might get hurt. To make Benny look more like a cop, Sherry trimmed his hair, giving him a conservative part on the left, and had him shave off his beard. She found him a sportsjacket that she altered to fit his broad shoulders and narrow waist, and she insisted that he wear a shirt and tie. She decided that the only thing he lacked for authenticity was a warrant.

Benny knew where the search and arrest warrant forms were kept in Sheriff Trotter's secretary's office. Sherry managed to make off with some while everyone was out to lunch. She filled one out with the name of their first target, entered "suspected possession of drugs for resale" on the proper line, and signed the name of a local judge. For extra effect she added the imprint of an old notary public's seal she had found at the flea market. No one would examine the imprint too closely. People who knew they were guilty tended to be cooperative.

"I reckon we're set for our first lick," Sherry said.

For Sherry, the scam was pure excitement. Even though she would not take part in the robbery itself, she felt as much a part of it as if she were actually going to be there. On the night itself she sent Benny off to work with a housewifely kiss, wished him luck, and told him to be careful. She waited in the apartment, smoking and pacing, trying to picture the action in her mind. She had driven Benny and Roice several times to check out the location, a small, isolated house on the outskirts of Briceville. There were no immediate neighbors; the place was ideal because of its obscurity and lack of outside lighting. The dealer, who was fairly small-time and sold mostly marijuana, lived there with his girlfriend. If his pickup was in the driveway, he was at home. If there were visitors, Benny and Roice were to drive around until any guests had left. The fewer people involved, the better.

Sherry jumped when she heard a noise at the door, but it was only the fellow who was letting them share his apartment. He was tight as a tick and quickly passed out on his bed.

The first thing she would do if this job turned out to be any kind of a success, Sherry promised herself, would be to put a deposit down on a house she had already picked out. How wonderful it would be to spend their first Christmas together in a place of their own. Her parents had still not accepted Benny, but they would come around once they understood what he was really like, so good with children, her soulmate. If nothing else won them over, his cooking would.

Out on Highway 116, about fifteen miles from Clinton, Benny and Roice pulled up a few yards from the dealer's house. There was his truck, with the girlfriend's Chevette parked on the lawn. A light burned inside.

Benny and Roice waited until the highway was deserted and made their move. As agreed beforehand, Benny knocked on the door. When the girlfriend answered, he showed his badge and asked if so-and-so lived there.

"We got a warrant here to search this place." He waved the form at her. The man came to the door and Benny repeated his speech. Roice was right behind him, ready for trouble with his gun.

But there was no trouble. They were no sooner inside than the man was trying to reach some sort of compromise.

"You trying to bribe an officer of the law?" Benny asked, just to gig him. "You want this to go down easy, you show us what you've got."

The man led Benny to a back bedroom. Meanwhile Roice noticed that the girl was wearing some pretty stones.

"You see that Biggin, my partner?" Roice asked her. "Let me give you a little hint. He's one mean son of a bitch. If he sees those rings of yourn, he'll take 'em off you. He can't get 'em easy, he'll chop off your fingers. Why don't you just give me 'em and I'll slip 'em into my pocket and give 'em back to you before we leave. That's a good girl."

When Benny finally returned in the early hours of the morning, Sherry knew at once from the smile on his baby face that everything had gone down as planned.

The dealer had swallowed their act cold, Benny told her, whispering so as not to wake their friend. The guy had practically begged them to take his stash. If only Sherry had been able to see how grateful he was when they didn't arrest him! Maybe by now he had figured out that they weren't even cops.

Benny showed Sherry the wad of bills that was his take. Some of it was cash from the dealer, but the reason they had taken so long was that they had gone directly to the fence in Lake City afterwards to get rid of the stuff. No problem there. They had waited around until the bar closed and gone home with the fence to put a value on the stuff and get paid. There had been several bags of grass and some jewelry, including rings the girlfriend had given Roice to hold for her, if you could believe that. It turned out Roice had a sense of humor.

Sherry counted the roll. Benny's take was just under five thousand, not a bad night's work. She gave him back two hundred and stored the rest in a shoebox under their bed. They had agreed that she would be the banker.

In bed Sherry made Benny tell her all over again everything that had happened. The only thing she regretted was that she hadn't been there. Next time, she was going to drive the getaway car. Armed robbery was some kick. There was nothing like it, was there?

"Not that I know of," Benny said.

During the following months Sherry and Benny expanded and refined their operation. Benny worked only when they ran out of money, about every five or six weeks, but they realized that the closer they were to home, the more they risked taking heat. In a system of trade-offs made possible by a widening network of contacts, they exchanged information with criminals in other counties. Someone over in Cumberland County would put the finger on a dealer in, say, Crossville; Benny would do a lick over there, paying the informant a piece of the take and, quid pro quo, tip him off to a job in Anderson, from which Benny could expect a piece. Little cheating was possible, because the informant knew more or less what the take was likely to be in his home area. Since law enforcement agencies were poorly coordinated from one county to another and were unlikely to hear or care about some ripped-off drug dealer anyway, the chief danger of the scam was retribution from offended dealers in one locale or another. The farther away Benny operated from home, the less vulnerable he was. That is to say, the less likely he was to end up in a ditch with his hands tied behind his back and his head blown off.

Sherry occasionally drove the getaway car. One of the first purchases she made with her new money was a 1980 Fiesta, replacing her '72 LTD. Deciding that she needed more zip hurrying home after a robbery, she switched to a Mustang, then traded that for a bright red '83 Dodge Charger, a car favored by bootleggers, moonshiners, and their offspring, stock car racers on the Southern circuit. To monitor the cops, she and Benny installed a police scanner, locating local frequencies from a code book sold at Radio Shack stores. They kept a battery-operated blue revolving light under the seat and attached it to the roof sometimes when making a bust.

Sherry devoted most of her energies to keeping Benny out of trouble, insisting that he stick to robbing illegals and rationing his cash so he would not be tempted to make some conspicuous purchase. None of the cars was expensive enough to raise an eyebrow; each was registered in her name. Drawing on her beautician's skill, she colored Benny's hair differently each time out, styled it variously, and used a theatrical makeup kit to give him scars, wens, wrinkles, bags under the eyes, or a hideous case of acne. Usually he shaved his beard and mustache, or Sherry had him keep sideburns or a goatee.

Worried about the gun, she bought an Army-issue steel waterproof ammunition box that held the .38 and boxes of bullets and buried it in the yard between robberies. She paid cash for everything. And there was ample cash. A typical lick netted five to fifteen thousand dollars. Benny's cut of one big job was thirty thousand.

She slipped up only once, neglecting to remove Benny's badge from a suit she took to the cleaners. She did not realize the oversight until the lady behind the counter handed her back the badge, enclosed in a plastic bag like lost change, when Sherry picked up the cleaning. "I was so worried," the lady said, "your husband would be furious if he thought you'd lost it." "He sure would have been," Sherry said. To herself she laughed to think that Benny would from then on be known at the cleaners as an undercover officer.

When things were slow, it was easy enough to pinpoint the major dealer in any town. It did not take any supersleuth. What did people think, that drugs were scarce? It amazed Sherry how obvious narcotics were in the life of every town, while everyone pretended that what mattered was high school football, the minimum wage, Jesus, trailer park rents, and the Dairy Queen. All you had to do was hang around the high school parking lot to see which kid was dealing dope. Probably he was fencing mom's cardigan from last night's break-in, too.

Benny and his partner would follow the kid and pretend to bust him—the blue light was useful for this. The kid would be scared shitless, and he would be quick to confess the name and address of his supplier in return for being set free. If the dealer turned out to be a nobody, the scam was to fake busting him and proceed up the ladder. By hook or by crook, eventually they arrived at the major dude. Nearly always, the head honcho in any town was not some weirdo pervert criminal à la Hollywood but a legitimate businessman, somebody with a phony front. Among the people from whom Benny confiscated drugs were a Chrysler dealer, a judge, a member of a school board, a furniture store owner who personally advertised bargains on BarcaLoungers on TV, the president of a local Lions Club, and a pediatrician.

To track these people, Benny and Sherry made use of police contacts, who could run checks on license plates, to identify the owners of cars and reduce the possibility of raiding the wrong house or staging a bust when guests or innocent relatives were at home. Interesting, wasn't it, Sherry thought, how easy it was to identify the entire structure of narcotics distribution in any town. Yet the police failed to make headway against the dealers, concentrating instead on busting some teenager for possession. It was enough to make you lose faith in our system of justice.

The one exception to Sherry's paying cash was when she used someone else's credit card. After she and Benny moved to a three-bedroom house in a modest section of Oak Ridge, Sherry struck up a friendship with someone from the local post office, engaging him in chat over the weather or the U.T. Vols. One day they got to talking about the way credit cards arrived through the mail. The issuing banks and companies used plain unmarked envelopes of various dull colors, as if they hoped to conceal something. But all you had to do was feel one to know that there was a card inside.

Sherry asked whether her friend wasn't ever tempted to steal a card and use it, to buy himself a new pair of shoes and socks. No, the friend said, he wouldn't care to take a risk like that, but he wouldn't be surprised if there were people who would—if a card got delivered to the wrong address, for instance. It would be almost like finding a sack of money. What a person did in those circumstances, it was anybody's guess.

Sherry began giving her friend ten or twenty dollars and, soon enough, the cards were misdelivered to her, three and four a month. Another foolproof scam, she figured.

The most desirable were cards issued for new accounts. These arrived accompanied by a welcoming letter assuring the recipient of his or her valued membership and, helpfully, specifying the credit limit, if any. Sherry understood that she could charge on one of these cards without the owner's knowing that it had been stolen until the bill came due. Some surprise.

With renewal cards, however, Sherry had to make sure that they had not been reported lost or stolen or were not over their credit limit. Her experience as a cashier and as an observant shopper taught her that the access numbers for Visa, MasterCard, or whatever were kept beside the phone next to the cash register. She would ask to use that phone, pretend to make a call, and memorize or copy down the number. From another phone she verified the card's validity, rapping out the lingo and code and reporting that Mrs. Whatsit's purchase of lingerie was for such-and-such an amount.

She was careful always to present the appropriate appearance. "I can hang with the best and I can hang with the worst," she liked to say. In some high-dollar department store at the Oak Ridge mall, she would wear a Rolex and diamonds from a recent robbery and act as if she had arrived in a limo, demanding service in an upscale accent and in general playing the bitch. Did the clerk ask for additional I.D.? Sherry knew the rules. "I don't have to show you my driver's license. I have never been so insulted in all my life. I been trading here for fifteen years and my mother before me." If things got nasty, all she had to do was turn on her heel and stomp out. She played on everyone's wish to avoid a fuss.

But trouble was rare. All she needed was plenty of nerve to see her through. Usually the clerk, lazy and therefore deserving of deception from Sherry's point of view, failed to bother to check the signature or even to read the name on the card. Sherry was able to use a man's card nearly as easily as a woman's. It helped to snivel and whine and paw the ground and say she hoped her husband would approve of whatever she was buying. Being abject, playing the cringing wife—no one was about to challenge that.

She never used a card for more than a day or two before tossing it into a Dumpster. Caution was key. Nor did she ever shoplift, which, like hanging paper (writing bad checks), was a rube's game, designed for people who were fixing to get caught. Sherry believed that the credit card game could last as long as she kept on playing it because she was so much smarter than the run-of-the-mill criminal and took such pains with her work. It was only when you thought you could never get caught that you started getting busted. Take advantage of stupid people, that was the ticket, and don't run with dumbbells.

What with helping dear, sweet Benny and doing her own thing, it was a wonderful life. Sherry took to teasing friends who were punching cash registers or peddling underwear or answering a phone or beating biscuits all the day long, "Whyn't you all get a *real* job that pays you some *real money?* You want to count pennies till you're senile? Fork over half your damn check to the damn government that's living high off the hog spending your damn money? Get you some sense. I could tell you how it is you could get you a right smart of money, but I ain't a-talking."

She wished she could tell the world how living illegal, as she called it, beat the tar out of punching a clock and your so-called Social Security. Let me be free was her theme song. Armed robbery was a kick and a hoot. By God, it was a natural high.

11

O N THE DOMESTIC FRONT, Benny and Sherry lived the life of any upwardly mobile couple. They stocked their house with television sets, VCRs, a four-speaker sound system, scores of tapes. Benny's preferences, grounded in his pre-Brushy days, ran toward basic rock, anthems of rebellion such as Led Zeppelin's eight-minute-long 1971 hit "Stairway to Heaven," with its counterpoint lyrical-pastoral acoustic guitar and savage, amplifed aggression. Another of his favorites was ZZ-Top's *The Eliminator* album, Texas-Southern rock with a whang of scumbag whimsy, as in "Pearl Necklace," a song that celebrated tit-fucking and ejaculation against a girl's neck.

Sherry shied from rock. Country was what moved her—Patsy Cline, Merle Haggard, Loretta Lynn, Conway Twitty, and younger singers such as Reba McEntire. Alone in the house, she might even play bluegrass, Flat and Scruggs—fiddle-and-banjo mountain music that Benny scorned as fuddy-duddy. Her preference for country went beyond the mournful melodies and tear-choked voices. When George Jones sang "Walk Through This World With Me" or The Hag recalled when Daddy played bass and Momma played fiddle and there was harmony everywhere, Sherry heard her own dreams; those were renditions of her own stories and wishes. Benny could not bear them. "Booger," he would say, "why do you keep on playing that stuff? It's too sad."

They united, however, on a devotion to fitness, riding around on

new ten-speed bikes and working out religiously at the Oak Ridge
Nautilus and Racquetball Club, where they joined other young pro-
fessionals and several officers from the Oak Ridge Police Department
as members. Benny introduced Sherry to a bodybuilding program. He
lifted for three solid hours four or five days a week. Sherry drew the
line at three days, and never on Sunday, but soon noticed the difference in her hard, flat belly, sculptured legs, arms that packed a wal-
lop. With the hearty meals Benny prepared and their mutual absti-
nence from alcohol, they were as impressive stripped as any couple
on a California beach. Sherry added glamour shots of a shirtless
Benny to her family albums.

They passed many an hour playing video games at one or another
of the amusement arcades in and around Oak Ridge. To Sherry, who
considered herself rather mature for this level of entertainment—
nearly all the other players were children and teenagers—Benny's fascination with shooting down planes or vaporizing enemy tanks on the
display screen was an aspect of boyish charm. He had never had
much of a childhood, she reasoned; nor had the video revolution penetrated Brushy Mountain, apart from the small black-and-white TV
sets in every cell. Playing with him was like having a son.

Not that she lacked her own girlish impulses. Nestling in Benny's
arms, she felt protected as never before; and when he brought her
breakfast in bed, as he often did, the aroma of his flapjacks and
bacon fried just so made her think that waiting all her life to be pam-
pered had been worth it. She had always loved dolls, and now she
was able to add at will to her collection, which ranged from Barbie
and Betsy Wetsy to porcelain-faced antiques.

It was an active life. Their house, while unpretentious, was large
enough to accomodate visits from the children of divorce and separa-
tion—Benny's second wife, whether through indifference or the per-
sistence of hope, held off filing against him. She permitted Dawn to
visit on alternate weekends, when she got acquainted with her half-
sister and, occasionally, Renee. Benny's ex-wife and nearly-ex had a
higher opinion of his "parenting" potential than did Billy Pelfrey, who
persisted in viewing Benny as an inferior kind of stepfather for Renee
and saw Sherry as an irresponsible mother. Sherry considered these
unfair judgments; she would never have given up custody of her
daughter had Billy not forced her to do so. She resented Billy's attitude toward Benny as typical of the prejudice against ex-convicts.

She did feel guilty about Renee. When she watched a mother bird in the tree in the yard bringing worms to her young, Sherry brooded about her maternal failures. She told herself that she had made her choice and would have to face up to the conflict of trying to be loyal to Renee and Benny at the same time. Life was more complicated for human beings than for birds.

When he cooked for them, showing the clearest possible evidence of his capacities as a family man, Benny won Sherry's relatives over. Her mom adored Benny's fried chicken and asked for the recipe, which he copied out for her—omitting, as he always did when granting a request for kitchen secrets, one key ingredient, so that the dish remained inimitable and everyone fretted over why his tasted so much better. At Christmas, Benny bought gifts for all, including Sherry's numerous nieces and nephews. Sherry described how Benny had selected each gift himself. He had gone wild, she said, at Toys "R" Us, racing up and down the aisles like a kid. It had been all she could do to drag him home to wrap the presents and keep him from messing with them. At Easter, Benny baked a ham with sweet potatoes, colored eggs, and like a giant bunny led children in the hunt. Sherry took pictures and pasted them into her album.

If E. L. and Louise wondered how Sherry and Benny could afford to be so generous and to live so comfortably on his supposed wages as a painter and hers as a part-time cashier, they did not pry.

When Sherry staggered into her parents' house one night in June 1983, weeping, with black eyes and deep bruises all over, E. L. and Louise decided that they had been right to mistrust Benny and urged Sherry to leave him immediately. She was lucky he hadn't killed her, a big brute like that.

The problem, Sherry explained when she was able to stop crying long enough to speak, was Benny's interest in other women. She had tried to believe him when he denied fooling around, had wanted so to believe him, but the signs were everywhere. What was she to think when she started to put his gym clothes into the washing machine and noticed that they had not been worn? "For what he'd been up to," Sherry said, "you don't need no jockstrap." She was sure she knew who the girl was this time, some jailbait teenager who'd been making eyes at him at the arcade. Sherry said that she ought to have gone after the girl, who was really to blame. She could understand

Benny; she could even forgive him, if only he'd tell the truth. He had been locked up so long, he was like a kid in a candy store. But he would have to learn to control himself. She was too jealous to accept it; she loved him too much. She confronted him, and he beat her up.

To tell the truth, she had done more than confront him. When he denied everything, giving her his "Who, me?" routine as he always did, even when she showed him his clean clothes, she saw red and hauled off and socked him right in the face. Not just a slap, either, but a sidewinder that would have dropped anyone else. He went wild. He threw her down on the floor and slammed his knees into her chest and beat on her face and banged her head against the floor. She was screaming so, she was surprised someone hadn't called the police. She was more frightened than anything else. Benny had told her some of the things he had done to people in prison. The second he stopped, she ran out the door and jumped into her car.

Sherry kept saying that it was her own fault that Benny had lost his temper. If she had not hit him first, he might never have beaten her up. They would have to work things out.

E. L. and Louise saw things differently. The next time, they told her, she might not live to tell the tale. But when Benny phoned, full of apologies, Sherry went home to him. He promised never to fool around again.

It was not long afterwards that Sherry began finding notes on the windshield of her car and receiving phone calls asking Benny to call a girl named Penny at a certain number. When Sherry phoned herself and asked if this was Penny speaking, the woman hung up.

Benny said that the caller and whoever was leaving the notes must be some nut. He did not know anyone named Penny. If you're going to do this to me, Sherry told him, can't you be a little less obvious about it? Can't you spare my feelings? Benny stonewalled.

I can't whup him, Sherry told herself, so I'll have to try something else. One day when Benny was at the health club, Sherry arranged for a male friend of hers to call this Penny. Benny had driven Sherry to work, the man told the girl, and would meet Penny at Jokers Arcade at two o'clock.

Accompanied by her friend and another man she had known since high school, Sherry drove to the arcade at the appointed hour and, telling her friends to wait in the car but to rescue her if trouble started, walked in and asked around for a girl named Penny.

"Are you Penny?" Sherry asked a tall blonde playing Pac-Man. A smaller, younger girl was beside her.

"Yeah," the tall one said, and introduced her sister.

"You know who I am?" Sherry asked.

"No."

"Well, I'm Benny Hodge's old lady. How do you like that?"

"I don't know no Benny Hodge."

"Oh, yeah? Then how come you been leaving notes for Benny on my car, bitch?"

When Penny told Sherry to go to hell, Sherry slapped her across the mouth. Penny's sister grabbed Sherry, Sherry hit her, too, and the three of them fell into a pushing and shoving and hair-pulling brawl. Sherry's friends rushed in to break up the fight with the help of the arcade manager.

That would have been that except that Penny and her sister, who was only sixteen, went to the police and swore out a complaint. A few days later, Sherry was arrested for disturbing the peace and assaulting Penny and a juvenile.

At the hearing, the judge listened to this story of jealous rivalry and asked who had struck the first blow. Sherry did not hesitate to admit that she had but defended herself. Here this woman had been trespassing on private property to leave notes and pestering a loving woman with phone calls. What was she supposed to do, sit back and take it and give up her man without a fight?

The judge must have been impressed with Sherry's candor. Noting that Penny stood at least five-feet-ten in her stocking feet, he remarked that Sherry must have had to do some leaping to land a punch. He dismissed the complaint, ordering the women to stay away from one another.

Benny said that he was so moved by Sherry's devotion and the lengths to which she would go to keep him that he had come away from this incident a chastened man. From now on, he would keep his hands to himself and his pecker in his pants, he promised.

But there were always other women, one after another. Sherry and Benny fought, made up, made violent passionate love, fought again, often physically, with Sherry naturally ending up black and blue from head to foot. Rather than upset her parents, she took refuge with friends after a beating. All of them urged her to leave Benny, but no, she said, she was not a quitter, and she had faith that he would reform. She was not the type to run off and abandon someone because he had a problem.

She often became depressed. Even the thrills of armed robbery began to pall. She contemplated going to see a marriage counselor or a psychiatrist. Then matters improved, until the next incident.

The friend whom Sherry sought out more than any other during these times of trouble was Pat Mason, who sold cars on a lot in Oak Ridge. Pat was a striking woman in her early thirties, slim and trim, with short, straight dark hair and a manner that gave off independent vibes. She was the only woman Sherry ever saw thumbing through copies of *Playboy* and *Penthouse* at the market magazine rack; occasionally she bought one and, unlike many of the men, did not appear the least embarrassed. Sherry could see that Pat Mason was the sort of person who took shit from nobody.

Sherry felt that Pat was someone she could trust. Of all her friends, Pat was the most adamant in urging her to leave Benny. Pat put the matter with characteristic bluntness: if Benny and Sherry stayed together, one of them would kill the other.

Sherry suspected that Pat was correct in her analysis and prediction. Maybe for one of them to die was the only way for their love to end.

When Benny began hanging out day after day, night after night at Frosty's service station, coming home grinning like a possum eating shit, Sherry did not believe for a minute that it was because of the ambiance or, as Benny insisted, that Frosty's had superior video machines. There had to be a girl involved. She concluded that it must be a certain redhead named Carla, who was pretty and just happened to be at Frosty's every time Sherry went there with Benny.

On a hunch one evening Sherry left work early and drove home to find Carla's car parked brazen as brass in the driveway. This is it, Sherry thought. Pat Mason was right. I am going to kill one or both of them or myself or maybe all three of us. She went quietly to the backyard, dug up the ammunition box, made sure the .38 was loaded, and entered the house through the back door.

She found them in the bed, the same bed she shared with Benny. They had not even bothered to turn out the light. They sat up. Blind with rage, Sherry pointed the gun at the bed, cocked it, walked toward them and shouted, "Prepare to meet your Maker, you sons of bitches!"

She was ready to fire. She didn't care which one she shot first.

But Carla leapt up in a flash and knocked the gun from Sherry's hand. It exploded as it hit the floor, the bullet smashing into the wall.

Sherry and Carla fought, falling down on the bed as Sherry tore at Carla's naked breasts and screamed that she would kill her and Benny next.

Benny seized both women by the hair and managed to separate them. Carla grabbed her clothes and left.

"Booger," Benny said. "Have you gone nuts?"

"I have," Sherry sobbed. "You done made me crazy!" She wept in his arms.

Benny promised never to see Carla again. To try to regain some dignity, Sherry turned up the stereo full blast with Tanya Tucker's "It Don't Mean a Thing to Me." Benny said he understood how Sherry felt. He was deeply sorry.

No longer confident of Benny's sincerity, Sherry began to think that he simply could not help himself, but that did not mean that she could bear to put up with his infidelities. One way or another, they would have to stop. She asked someone at Frosty's to tip her off the next time Benny was in there with Carla.

A few nights after the incident with the gun, Sherry came home to find the phone ringing. It was her informant from Frosty's. Benny and Carla were in there together. Sherry asked to have Carla come to the phone.

"Where's Benny?" Sherry asked.

"I don't know. Why are you asking me? Benny and me is through."

"Don't lie to me. I happen to know he's right down there with you." There was silence. "I think it's time you and me has a heart-to-heart talk. You get your ass over here, now."

Carla slammed down the phone. In a few minutes Benny came bursting in, demanding to know what Sherry's problem was. Couldn't a man spend a few hours with his friends without his woman making trouble?

"I'm not the one with a problem. You and Carla's got the problem. She is coming to this house tonight, and me and her's going to have a talk." She phoned Frosty's and told Carla that she had five minutes to get her rear end over there.

"You'd better not touch her," Benny warned.

"I ain't going to touch her," Sherry said. "I'm going to reason with her."

Carla arrived with two girlfriends in tow for protection. Benny arranged the seating. He placed himself in a chair between Sherry and Carla and directed Carla's friends to the couch. Sherry began the conversation.

"Carla, do you love Benny?"

"Well, yeah."

"Do you want to spend the rest of your life with him?"

"Well, I dunno."

"Then you sure don't love him very much. Benny, do you love her?"

"What do you mean, do I love her?"

"You know what I mean. Do you?"

Benny hesitated, looking at Carla, at Sherry, at the ceiling. Sherry pressed him.

"Well, yeah," Benny said, "I do love Carla."

"Okay," Sherry said. "You all see that door? You all get out of here till I have time to move my shit."

The women left. In front of Benny, Sherry telephoned Louise and asked her to come get her. "I'm leaving Benny," she said, and hung up.

Benny demanded that Sherry give him his share of their money. She fetched a wad from where she had it hidden in the children's room and threw it at him, the bills falling around the room. That was everything, Sherry said. She didn't want a dime. She had only kept it to keep him from spending it on Carla and the others. Benny was down on his knees, gathering up the money. He stuffed it into his pockets and stormed out.

Sherry phoned Louise again, who had not left her house, having assumed that it was just another fight and that Sherry would change her mind. No, Sherry said, this was it. She asked to borrow money for a plane ticket to New York, where one of her brothers was living. E. L. came on the phone. He agreed to give Sherry the money, but only enough for a one-way ticket. That was fine, Sherry said. She would not be coming back.

Sherry packed a bag, thinking of how much she loved Benny and how hopeless everything was. She resented him so much for treating her this way, after all that she had done, leaving her husband and child for him, trying to make a life. But she found herself feeling sorry for him, too. He could not help the way he was.

She wrote him a note:

Dear Benny,

I am gone forever. I wish it didn't have to be this way, but you have made your choice. We could not go on like we was. If you ever need a friend, I will be in New York City at my brother's. I hope you and her are happy.

Sherry

Louise drove her to the Knoxville airport and bought her a one-way, nonrefundable ticket to New York, by way of Atlanta. Kissing her good-bye and telling her to phone when she arrived, Louise told Sherry that this was the right thing to do and that she would pray for her.

The flight to Atlanta took less than an hour, but that was long enough for Sherry to weaken. What would she do in New York? She had never been out of Tennessee in her life. She had no money, no job waiting for her. If she had already shown herself to be less than the perfect mother by running off with Benny, what would Renee think of her now? By the time the plane touched down, she was telling herself that this time Benny might take her seriously. At least it would be a test of whether he really loved her. She could only know that by hearing his voice.

She called him from the Atlanta airport. He was at home, alone, he said, and miserable.

"You better come get me, Hodge-Podge."

Benny thought this impractical. He was sure that the airline would let her use her New York fare to come home. She should tell them it was an emergency, which it was, after all.

The airline was sympathetic, and Sherry phoned Benny back to tell him when to pick her up at Knoxville.

At Knoxville there were thunderstorms, the radar was out, and by the time Sherry landed, Benny was nowhere to be seen. She telephoned the house.

"Where're you at?" she asked him. "Couldn't you have waited? You coming to get me?"

"Take a limo. I'll pay when you get here."

They had a tearful reunion and made love all day.

12

THE NEXT TIME SHERRY CAUGHT BENNY WITH A GIRL—as usual, a teenager—she cornered him in the bathroom, aimed the gun at him, and squeezed the trigger, but nothing happened. She said that she was unable to locate the safety catch.

The next time, she fired and hit the headboard as he was lying in bed. He came at her with his butterfly knife. She screamed that she had not meant to hit him anyway, but he swiped at her and slashed her across the underside of the wrist. He drove her to the emergency room. The wound left a four-inch scar just above the heel of her right palm.

And the next time after that, she begged him to kill her, saying she could not live with his unfaithfulness and that life without him was not worth living. "Shoot me, shoot me!" she cried.

Benny got the gun, cocked it, and pointed it at her as she writhed sobbing on the floor.

"Don't do it here," she wailed. "You'll get caught. Ain't you got no kind of sense, Benny Hodge? You'd been caught a long time ago except for me. You want to kill me, do it right. Take me up to Buzzard's Bluff and plug me. I won't run, I swear it. Throw my body off the cliff. Nobody'll know."

Even at top speed in the Charger, it took Benny a good half hour to drive them, with the radio blasting to drown out her cries, up to Buzzard's Bluff, a favorite spot for lovers and hang-gliders. Sherry wept and muttered all the way that she had had enough of life, that it was time to end it all, with Benny snarling that he was happy to grant her wish because she was more of a pain in the ass than any man could bear.

The bluff—yellowish rock crowning Walden's Ridge—was deserted on that hot, hazy day, except for the turkey buzzards circling against thunderheads. The sheer drop was a good thousand feet. Spread out below were the valleys and hills and towns where Sherry had spent her entire life, the railway line and the river, the ribbon of I-40 stretching toward Knoxville, the towering twin chimneys of the Kingston Steam Plant; and over to the right across the narrow valley was the green dot of the Harriman Holiday Inn, where on her wedding night she had fought with Billy Pelfrey. Somewhere down there was Renee.

Sherry took it all in and turned to face Benny with her back against a tree near the edge.

"Shoot me now, honey," she said through sobs. "Just remember, I'll go to my grave loving you."

Benny took up a position some fifteen feet from her and raised the .38 with both hands, target-practice style.

"You ready? Say a prayer."

"I'm ready. Do it."

He fired. The first shot hit the ground two feet from her. She saw that the bullet made a furrow that ended inches from her foot. Benny aimed and fired again and again, four times in quick succession. The bullets kicked up gravel against her legs. After that, she closed her eyes and prayed to die quick.

She heard him emptying the cylinder and the spent shells hitting the ground and fresh bullets sliding in. The cylinder clicked shut.

Would he gun her down if she ran? Would he shoot her in the back if she tried to make it into the woods? *This time he is going to do it and everything will be over.*

The next shot cracked so loud, she was sure he had moved closer. Again. Three, four—rapid-fire, but still at her feet.

She opened her eyes to see him taking aim at her heart.

"You ready?" he shouted.

"I am. Do it. Please do it. I love you."

At the last split second he jerked the barrel down and hit the ground once more. Then he was sort of grinning at her with his ragged, discolored teeth. He so rarely smiled. He came to her with open arms.

"Come here, Booger," he said. "You are one damn fool. If that'd been me, you've hit my ass or my elbow, 'cause I'd've been moving!'"

The wind was terrific up there. They held each other and saw how beautiful everything was below.

Money was always short. So, right after Buzzard's Bluff, Sherry became a Wong. It was a practical rather than a sentimental decision. Benny and Sherry frequently ate dinner at a Chinese place in Oak Ridge. What with one thing and another, they fell into conversation with a waiter by the name of Wong who was an illegal immigrant, as he confided to them between courses. Wong was anxious to become an American. If the U.S. government sent him back to China, the Communists would throw him into jail and re-educate him to a standstill.

Wong wondered whether Benny and Sherry knew of some woman who would be willing to marry him, so that he could qualify for citizenship. He would require nothing of her other than her goodwill, and there would be something in the deal for her. He had managed to smuggle some gold bars out of China. His dream was to open his own restaurant some day (Szechuan); in the meanwhile, he would pay big to become an American.

Should they steal the fellow's gold outright, or should Sherry marry him? Wedlock seemed the safer, more profitable option. So it was that Sherry, in an Anderson County Courthouse ceremony, acquired her Chinese husband and surname. In return, Wong forked over close to fifty thousand dollars over the next several months and split for South Carolina. One of her friends asked Sherry whether she worried about getting caught. "The government's a diaper," Sherry said, "full of shit and always on your ass."

Why the government began to sniff her out, Sherry was unsure: their incoherent life, maybe a snitch, possibly a neighbor fed up with the late-night screaming, gunfire—whatever it was, one afternoon in 1983 a pair of Oak Ridge police officers showed up waving a search warrant. Renee was visiting that day. Benny answered the door.

"You Benny Holt?"

"No one here by that name."

"This one-twenty-seven Utah?"

"Yeah."

"Name don't matter, we got the right address. You better let us in."

Just then a local boy ran up to the porch holding a fistful of dollars. Sherry shooed him away.

"You don't owe me no damn money, hon," she said. "Go home to your mommy."

The boy scampered away. He would settle his debt for weed later.

To begin with, Benny and Sherry suspected that someone was trying to pull the phony-cop scam, but these officers were legit. They looked as if they were about to tear up the house; they didn't have to. They found a quarter-ounce of pot in a plastic bag taped underneath the bathroom sink and placed Benny and Sherry under arrest for intent to sell.

"You gonna put my mama in jail!" Renee burst into tears.

The officer, who said his name was Foust, got down on one knee to comfort her, saying that it was no big deal, she shouldn't worry, her mom would be out of jail in no time.

Officer Foust was correct. The case never went to trial. Sherry and Benny hired a lawyer who convinced the judge to dismiss the charges because of the improperly executed search warrant, which listed the wrong name for the suspect.

But it was a scare. A few weeks later they had a bigger one. Sherry's credit card ruse had worked so well for more than a year that she became careless and greedy, using cards to pick up spare change she did not need. In partnership with a girlfriend, she started swindling Howard's Discount Store out of four or five cartons of cigarettes a day, selling them to a beer joint at a discount from wholesale. The cashier became suspicious, kept track of the different names Sherry was signing, and one day stalled long enough to run a check. Sherry's friend managed to escape out the back as Sherry tried to act cool, telling the cashier to forget it, but by the time she reached the street she was aware of being followed by two Howard's employees. She ducked into Kroger's, spotted a fellow she knew, and quickly handed him her wallet, asking him to hold it for her.

A policeman was already after her, however, saw everything, arrested her, and retrieved the wallet, which held several cards, each bearing a different name.

At the station, who should be on duty but Detective Gene Foust, who asked Sherry what had inspired her to pay him another visit. She launched into the biggest, most elaborate lie she could invent. She knew nothing about those stolen cards, she said. A guy named Popeye had given her the wallet at Jefferson's Tavern. She had not even known that there were cards in it. She had beaten Popeye at a shuffleboard game, and he had simply handed her his wallet and left.

Detective Foust started to laugh. "Popeye?" he asked. "Popeye who?"

"I didn't know him by nothing but Popeye," Sherry said.

"If you think the fools around here will believe that," Foust said, "I'll let 'em believe it." He was laughing hard. "You're lying."

"No, I am not."

"You're the biggest liar I ever saw. A nice gal like you, why I bet you've never been in a place like Jefferson's Tavern. And you never met a guy named Popeye outside of the funny papers."

Sherry stuck to her story. She had to, now that she had told it, and she had the sense that Gene Foust rather admired her for her defiance. When the case went to trial, her attorney talked the judge into reducing the charge from grand theft to shoplifting, and she received two years' probation.

Detective Foust started dropping by the house to chat. Sherry and Benny were not sure what he wanted. He was friendly enough. Sherry liked him for the way he had treated Renee and for his sense of humor about her big lie, but it was obvious that he hoped for something from them. He had run against Sheriff Trotter in a previous election and was planning to challenge him again in 1984. Probably, Sherry believed, Foust was trying to turn them into informants so that he could make a couple of big busts and jack up his reputation. But she could not be sure that he was not also prepared to set them up and bust them, which would serve his political ambitions equally well.

Foust was a tough man to pin down. Physically he was Mr. In-Between, neither tall nor short, neither dark nor fair, with colorless thinning hair, enough overweight so that his features softened into the nondescript. He managed to be talkative, jovial, and blah all at once. He rattled on about cash changing hands all over the county from drug deals, without naming names or locations. When he indicated that on an evening in the near future a suitcase full of cash of an undetermined amount would be left in a doorway and could be exchanged for an empty suitcase and that there were foolproof, but unspecified, ways to launder money, Benny was all for pursuing the matter. Sherry convinced him to back off. Either Foust was letting them in on a deal or he was setting a trap, there was no way to know. If it was a setup, they would face a choice of jail or becoming full-time snitches. That was the way the system worked.

Because she thought it might do some good, Sherry did tell Detective Foust where the proceeds from the robbery of a prominent automobile dealer could be located. Her information proved accurate, and Foust was appreciative. Now you owe me one, Sherry thought.

Unfortunately her next slipup occurred over in Knox County, where Foust was in no position to help. She was working the credit card scam at a mall on the outskirts of Knoxville when her companion, the same woman who had escaped from Howard's Discount, was stupid enough to attempt to shoplift a leather jacket and was caught. This time it was Sherry who made it out the door—but the security officer recognized her from when they had been guards together at Brushy, followed her into another store, and tipped off the manager, who called the police as Sherry presented a phony Visa card.

Again she received two years' probation, the leniency this time the result of confusion over whether Mrs. Wong was actually the previously convicted Miss Sheets or was in fact a Mrs. Hodge. Sherry blamed herself for being so careless—she ought to have hightailed it out of that mall the minute her friend had been caught. But she also blamed her troubles with Benny, the sleepless nights, the fighting, the constant anxiety about his skirt-chasing and the way girls swarmed to him. A condition of her previous sentencing had been that she leave Anderson County and take Benny Hodge with her, but they were still on Utah Street six months later. "I'll get out when I'm good and ready," was her attitude. Now it seemed prudent to relocate, before Anderson authorities connected her to the Knox conviction. She also believed, or hoped, that fresh surroundings would encourage Benny to settle down.

Her idea was to find a house remote enough to be away from the constant gaze of the cops and to cut down on Benny's roamings. If she could discover a place big enough and nice enough, Benny might become more of a homebody.

She found her dream house in Roane County, deep in the hills near Harriman. Under the railroad bridge across the Emory River, a narrow road branched west, running along the south bank for five or six miles and ending in a dirt track. The houses along this seldom-traveled road to nowhere were few; one of those farthest from town was for rent, unfurnished. It sat on thirty-two acres of forest, up a curving driveway lined by a fieldstone wall, and it could not be seen from the road. For four hundred a month they would have privacy and space galore: three bedrooms upstairs; a living room with a stone fireplace all across one wall and a view of the river; a den with another fireplace and a downstairs bedroom with still another; a separate dining room; and surrounding woods perfect for burying firearms and money. Best of all, the lease included an option to buy. Sherry could imagine nesting there forever. She hoped her parents would think better of Benny when they saw what a wonderful provider he had become and would forgive him his violence and other peccadilloes such as wrecking a car registered in E. L.'s name and borrowing, without asking, one of E. L.'s guns, which unfortunately had turned up as evidence in an armed robbery committed by an unreliable friend. Poor E. L. had been distressed at having to identify the weapon as his and to profess ignorance of how it had escaped his possession.

As for decorating the house, Sherry had a vision of crystal and brass for the living room, where she installed brass sconces and candlesticks, crystal vases and bowls, and a crystal chandelier. A white velvet sectional couch curved eighteen feet around the fireplace. To her it was heaven, and nearly as difficult of access, off limits to everyone except during holidays.

She graced the dining room, where she insisted they take all their meals, with a brass and glass table and a glass-fronted oak hutch, in which she arranged her doll collection and stored her new china, crystal stemware, and silver. In the downstairs master bedroom she placed a king-size cherrywood four-poster bed for Benny and herself. The upstairs bedrooms were reserved for the children and other visitors. Renee now had her own room and four-poster canopied bed. As for the den, she conceived of it as Benny's playroom. There he could blast his rock and play Nintendo to his heart's content, undistracted by the temptations of teenage sirens. To further occupy him, Sherry bought Benny a powerful motorcycle and wrapped her arms around his waist as he tore up and down the river and into town.

In an event that Sherry hoped was a good omen and that gave her and Benny great satisfaction, Sheriff Trotter was arrested by the FBI in May 1984 and forced to resign from office. He and three other men were indicted on numerous drug conspiracy charges and were tried, convicted, and sentenced to from ten to fifteen years in prison. The FBI had infiltrated the sheriff's coterie and bugged him on numerous incriminating occasions, including a drug-financed excursion to the Stardust Hotel in Las Vegas, where Trotter unwound in his suite rolling joints and unveiled a scheme to use a fruit and vegetable stand on Highway 61 as a front for cocaine and other drug dealing as well as for prostitution. He and his cohorts also hatched plans to improve their methods of peddling evidence.

Trotter complained that law enforcement was not what it used to be. In the old days, he lamented, a sheriff could do absolutely anything he wanted and get away with it. Nowadays, he had better be careful. These and other recorded statements became the basis for one of the first indictments and convictions of ten East Tennessee sheriffs on narcotics charges during the next five years.

Count one against Trotter alone involved a hundred and nineteen separate overt illegal acts, including discussions about the importance of murdering people foolish enough to try to stand in the sheriff's way or to horn in on his business. Although still unsure about Gene Foust, Sherry and Benny rooted for him in the special election held to replace the fallen Trotter, hoping they might at least gain a sheriff who did not have Benny on his hit list. Foust lost, however, to the FBI agent who had exposed the previous administration.

Just as she and Benny were moving into their dream house, Sherry reached a point of desperation over his philanderings. No longer able to cope, in May 1984 she enrolled at the Ridgeview Psychiatric Center and Hospital for the first of twice weekly outpatient therapy sessions. She tried to convince Benny to accompany her or seek counseling himself; he told her that she was nuts and that if she cared to submit herself to the shrinks, she was on her own. He had had his bellyful of psychological counseling and testing in prison. And she had better watch what she said to the doctors, who were not to be trusted.

Ridgeview, also known as the Regional Mental Health Center of Oak Ridge, was a well-respected facility that accepted patients, or clients as they are sometimes known in the trade, from all economic levels and charged on the basis of their ability to pay. Sherry saw at least four different clinicians, including at least one woman therapist and one bona fide psychiatrist, regularly over the next four months and off and on for a year. It may be that they would have reached different conclusions about her had she been able to reveal that she was living on the proceeds from armed robbery and other shadowy acts but, as frank as she was in other respects, she described Benny only as a construction worker, herself as an unmarried housewife and part-time cashier.

"I'm an insanely jealous person," Sherry said when asked to identify her chief complaint; she added that she was also depressed because she feared that her ex-husband was turning their daughter against her. Her principal worry, however, was Benny, who had spent nine and a half years in prison for armed robbery but was "basically a good man." He had admitted to her, she claimed, that he had killed three men while in prison, but these homicides had been in self-defense. He had also beaten her and cut her during one of their arguments over other women, but he had given her the kind of love she had always wanted and had told her that she had taught him what true love really meant. On the other hand, she feared that he was going to kill her some day when she went into one of her jealous rages, or that she would kill him or herself.

The best part of their relationship was the sex, which for her was nearly always orgasmic. She had never had an orgasm with anyone else. She felt freer with Benny because she was sure that he loved her.

When a therapist asked Sherry why she thought she had had difficulty trusting other men, she volunteered that she believed that her problems had started with her real father, who had tried to rape her. She described how much she loved her sister and brother-in-law for raising her as their own but admitted that her relations with Louise were not as warm as they might have been. Louise was jealous of her; this had begun when Sherry was in high school.

Sherry said that she had had sex for the first time with a boy when she was fifteen. Her mistake had been in confessing this to E. L. He had interrogated her relentlessly and in detail and, she thought, had become aroused by what she described to him. Later he had tried to fondle her, she said. She told him to stop, and he did. She also thought that Louise had sensed what was going on, and E. L. had from that point on become distant and bitter toward Sherry, at the same time that Louise resented her. At twenty-one, she married Billy Pelfrey to spite Louise, knowing the marriage could not possibly work. It had been like saying, you want me gone, I'm gone. Now see what you've made me do.

"I only wanted their love," Sherry said, "and they took advantage of that. Benny loved me the way I wanted, then he screwed me over, too." He beat her, and she admitted having assaulted him and several of his girlfriends; but if he left her, she would lose all hope in life. She was frantic every time he was away from the house without her. She had begun leaving suicide notes lying around, hoping to shame him and inspire pity. She wished that she could crawl into someone's lap and cry.

Each of Sherry's sessions, perhaps forty-five or fifty hours in all, was on a one-on-one basis. All of her therapists agreed that she should leave Benny; none advised her how to accomplish this, other than to tell her that it was a decision she would have to reach on her own, that it would do no good for her to act merely on someone else's advice. Each discussed her attachment as neurotic and dangerous. As for a diagnosis of her psychological condition or specific steps that she might take to help herself, other than leaving Benny, none ventured to say. Months before she quit the sessions altogether, Sherry concluded that the therapists could not help her and that their only value was in letting her talk.

She was as frank with them as circumstances permitted. She described herself as angry and potentially violent from an early age, recalling an incident from the second grade when she broke the neck off a bottle and threatened two classmates who had been teasing her. Since she had already been convicted of it, she admitted the credit card scam. She portrayed herself as a person who did not become angry for trivial reasons but who when pushed could erupt. She would have gone into greater detail about her life with Benny, including the adrenalin rush she got from armed robbery, the pleasure she took in contriving disguises for him—how crime, like sex, made her happy. But when she asked whether the FBI or other government agencies could demand to see her files and question her therapists, she was told that absolute privacy could not be guaranteed. Under the law her sessions were privileged, but there were exceptions.

On their worksheets, which Sherry never saw, her therapists made notes and tried to categorize her and grade her progress, if any.

One marked her "Overall Severity of Condition" as "Fair," which was fourth on a scale of seven that descended from "Superior" down to "Very Poor" and "Grossly Impaired"; she was considered less than "Good" but better than "Poor." Another clinician remarked on her "casual attitude toward crime and violence," which was undoubtedly a reference to her bantering conversational manner rather than to her underlying feelings of erotic criminality, her intensely meticulous cleverness, or her deadly seriousness. When Sherry broke down and wept during a session, the subject was always either Benny's faithlessness or her guilt and frustration over Renee. She did not, or could not, reveal her emotional attachment to crime and violence themselves—put simply, that she enjoyed them both a lot.

All of her therapists took note of her jealous rages and suicidal tendencies; yet her "Community Living Skills" ranked "OK"; her "Support Systems" were deemed merely "Inadequate." "Long Range Goals" were defined as "Work through abandonment depression." "Problems to be Addressed" included "Rage eruptions—self-esteem—poor ability to trust—intense neediness of love & affection." Sherry might have been surprised to learn that she consistently received marks of "Fair" to "Good" on "Goal Progress."

The therapists were unanimous in considering Sherry of above-average intelligence but were uncertain as to how to label her according to the *DSM-III* (*Diagnostic and Statistical Manual of Mental Disorders,* third edition, of the American Psychiatric Association), the standard guidebook in the field. Her first therapist initially found her "non-psychotic" and with "good motivation" but suffering from "Antisocial Personality Disorder" (*DSM-III*, 301.70), a condition "in which there is a history of continuous and chronic antisocial behavior in which the rights of others are violated ...," in a pattern beginning before the age of fifteen. Some of the manifestations of the disorder were said to include "lack of ability to function as a responsible parent ... inability to maintain enduring attachment to a sexual partner ... irritability and aggressiveness as indicated by repeated fights or assaults ... impulsivity ... 'conning' others for personal profit ... recklessness ..." Because Sherry was, however, capable of long-lasting friendships and attachments and, also unlike the truly antisocial personality, did seem to feel guilt and remorse for some of her actions, this therapist crossed out that diagnosis and settled instead on the more restrictive "Conduct Disorder, Socialized Aggressive" (312.23).

The majority of her clinicians saw her as an example of "Border-line Personality Disorder" (301.83), characterized as a severe lack of a sense of integrated psychological identity, shielded by intensely active defense mechanisms, evident in Sherry's case in the form of wisecracking, joking, and making light of serious matters. In terms of this diagnosis, her "symbiotic ties to an exploitive relationship [and] terror at the thought of being alone," in the words of one of her therapists, reflected her lack of personality integration, which was the result of a "very emotionally deprived" infancy and childhood.

While she was unaware of these various and overlapping diagnoses, Sherry would not have been surprised by them and would have recognized something of herself in each of them. Her idea was that she already understood herself all too well, and that this self-knowledge, rather than inducing change, often made her want to die. She told her therapists, and Benny before them, that she believed that her troubles derived from her father's and others' betrayals; that she thought little of herself as a woman, had spent her life alternately trying to prove her worth or her worthlessness, considered herself a failure as a parent, and was at least dimly aware that she let Benny abuse her because it confirmed how little she valued herself. "I am the way I am," she would state to anyone who asked, "because no one ever expected me to be anything. But I take responsibility for what I do." That was her credo. She uttered it to herself daily and to others on request. She wondered, could a shrink know more?

She did not consider herself helpless. She knew she was a fighter and prayed that she was a survivor. She stood up to Benny, fought him toe to toe, and so far had lived to tell the tale. What she could not help was that he had the power to murder her soul and then to bring it back from the dead.

No one could tell her what to do about the feelings that swept over her when she tried to leave Benny and the ecstacy that she knew with him. It beat working at the Bi-Lo, that was for sure. She would die having had more than most women ever knew. True love came with a price she was willing to pay. That was the way she saw it.

13

L AKE CITY (POP. 2,335) WAS NOT ON A LAKE, the former Coal Creek having renamed itself when a dam was built during the Great Depression. Anyone exiting I-75 there in anticipation of aquatics had to negotiate a phalanx of tough, seedy bars billing themselves as private clubs, a misnomer coined to circumvent local booze laws. One of these dives was operated under license by the American Veterans, another by the Veterans of Foreign Wars, and one was where Benny's regular fence tended bar. The building, a flat-roofed cinderblock bunker, a rectangle with a concrete floor, had a parking lot that looked as if it had been under mortar attack and was often the site of punchouts, stabbings, shootings, drug deals, and hasty sex. A hangout for sleaze of all types, this bar was where, late in 1984, Benny Hodge first met Donald Terry Bartley, Roger Dale Epperson, and Carol Ann Keeney Ellis Malone.

Sherry avoided the place. That night she was at home wrapping presents, filling bowls with candies and nuts and potpourri, stringing lights and hanging balls in anticipation of what she believed would be the best Christmas ever. By New Year's everyone would have visited—her extended family, Renee, Benny's daughters, even Benny's mother. Some of them had yet to see the new house; Sherry worked to make it perfect. She envisioned the grown-ups relaxing before the fire, Benny busy in the kitchen, the children romping through snowy woods with Chrissy the chow and her puppies. The kids would inquire what had become of Benny's gorgeous Himalayan cat. Sherry debated whether to tell them that she had had to get rid of it because it loved him, hated her. As for Benny's mom, Eula Kate Sawyers, as she then called herself—or was it Burkhart, no one was sure—Sherry had managed to manipulate a kind of reconciliation between mother and son, although relations remained strained. Eula, who worked in a Morristown auto parts factory, would rehearse the hardships of her life, praise Benny's cooking, and probably show everyone the scrapbook she had kept of Benny's arrests, trials, and paroles, dating back to high school. Sherry called it the crapbook; at least it showed that Eula cared, after a fashion. Sherry was skeptical of Eula's maternal qualities. She believed that Eula visited mostly out of rivalry with her almost-daughter-in-law. You had to take what you could get; she was his mother.

On that starry December night Benny exchanged cocaine and assorted pills and jewelry for cash in an unlit corner of the parking lot. He was ready to hit the road when the fence, mentioning that Benny had said that he was in need of a new partner, suggested that there was someone inside whom he ought to meet.

In the bar the jukebox played the sad songs Benny tried to avoid. About twenty patrons, mostly male, stood or lounged about, many staring silently into drinks, one solemn pair playing pool. The atmosphere was gloomy as a Bible class.

The fence introduced Benny to a man standing at the bar, a sharp-featured little fellow with a trim dark beard and dark wavy hair cut to fall over his brow.

"Donnie Bartley, meet Biggin Hodge, the meanest son of a bitch in East Tennessee. Donnie here's from Harlan County up in Kentucky. You know what they say about Harlan. Don't say nothing about it! Ha!"

Benny, fresh from a workout and a job, was clean-shaven that night. Wearing sweats and athletic shoes, he hulked over the Kentuckian. His smile flashing, a middleweight with dark brown eyes darting back and forth, Bartley had the appearance of an imp of the perverse. His hand disappeared into Benny's, a key into a lock. He said how pleased he was to meet the man he'd heard so much about. Some of this courtliness may have been in deference to Benny's muscles, but Bartley specialized in polite first meetings.

"Hey, let's get down," he said, tossing his head in the direction of the toilet.

The men's room was equipped with the usual amenities—a seatless, encrusted bowl; a basin; phone numbers, reflections on life, and anatomical studies scratched onto the walls; and a battered coin-operated dispenser offering combs, condoms, and ProLong, an ointment guaranteed to "Satisfy Her Every Desire." It was a tight fit in there for the two of them. From the pocket of his windbreaker Bartley produced a vial, popped the black plastic cap, sprinked white powder into the webbing between his forefinger and his thumb, and held the mound of stuff under Benny's nose. To be sociable, Benny sucked up. He knew that that much would have little effect on him, would only level him out and then drop him down a notch, and that he would stop at one. He watched Bartley snuff up two hits.

Bartley brought a pitcher of beer to a corner table where they could talk, or where Benny could listen. He told Benny that he was doing some dealing, chicken feed really, and he was anxious to get into something bigger. Burglary was his game; he understood that Benny was looking for a partner. There was a friend of his, Roger Epperson, who had connections, major ones, and whom Benny should meet. Roger was supposed to be showing up that night with his Japanese squeeze. Benny nursed his glass, saying nothing.

Bartley said that he was living in a trailer over in Oliver Springs with his mother and sister and it was bugging him, he had to get a place of his own or hit the road. Up in Kentucky back in January he had been given five years on a burglary rap. It was his fifth conviction and he had figured that this was it, two or three years inside at the minimum, but he had been able to make a deal. They let him go on the condition that he leave Kentucky and not come back. Pretty funny, wasn't it?

"I'm such a bad dude, they figure, let some other state have me. I figure, hey, I'll go visit my mom and sister in Tennessee. I'll take that deal anytime, right? So here I am. But this place is locked up, man. I mean, I'm getting by, but I need more action. You got to meet Roger. He should be here. Excuse me a minute."

Bartley headed for the men's room again. He was still in there when a big, amorphous man wearing a Western-cut leather jacket and cowboy boots, trailed by a tiny Oriental woman, entered and ordered drinks at the bar. Benny assumed this was Epperson and watched as another man walked slowly up to the girlfriend and said something to her. She turned aside. Epperson, in a snarl that silenced everything but the jukebox, told the man to go fuck himself and get out.

"I ain't moving," the man said. "Let's see you throw me out. Why don't you clear out and take this slanty-eyed snitch with you."

Bartley was emerging from the men's room as Epperson reached inside his jacket and jerked a .45 semiautomatic pistol from his belt, pumped it, and pointed it at the chest of the other man. People scrambled for cover. The woman hid behind Epperson; Bartley retreated into the toilet. Only Benny stayed put. *Crack! Crack!* Epperson fired two rapid rounds into the ceiling. In that confined space the noise was terrific, reverberated, hung in the air. Benny did not flinch. He stayed in his chair in the corner, impassive, as if watching a video.

Epperson stood over his opponent, spat on him, and smashed the toe of his boot into the man's ribs and kicked him in the butt as he started crawling toward the door. Epperson moved after him, but the woman, her arms around him below his waist and her head against the small of his back, held onto him and told him to let the man go, he would never show his face in there again. Epperson put away his gun and downed his whiskey and ordered a double.

Bartley poked his head out for a view. He let out a rebel yell and hurried over to embrace Epperson, and led him and the woman over to meet Benny.

Carol Ellis, as she was introduced, was then twenty-seven, the daughter of Anderson County Commissioner Jack Keeney, an Air Force veteran who had met Carol's mother, Toshiko, a seamstress, when he was stationed in Japan. Like Benny, Carol was a talented cook, but of a more sophisticated kind, specializing in whole-grain breads and complicated pastries. For a while she had run her own catering business but had let that slide as her associations with drug dealers expanded. She had a four-year-old daughter by her ex-husband, a TVA employee; but her way of life was ill suited to motherhood, so her parents cared for the child. What had gone wrong with their daughter, who was so bright and pretty and full of imagination and who had finished two years at a community college before dropping out, Jack and Toshiko Keeney had no idea. They could only blame drugs.

Carol had just recently taken up with Roger Epperson, who was a friend of her previous attachment, Terry Phillips, a dealer now in Brushy after a series of busts in which Carol had also been implicated. The most notorious of these, involving the seizure of supposedly a million dollars' worth of amphetamines and barbiturates at the Norris Resort Motel, had ended up becoming a key factor in the demise of Sheriff Trotter, when the evidence disappeared for several weeks, only to reappear magically just in time for the trial. "I couldn't find the drugs," the sheriff had said, "but that doesn't mean they didn't exist." Because the chain of custody of the evidence had been broken and, possibly coincidentally, the deputy in charge of the drugs had suddenly dropped dead, the judge dismissed charges of possession with intent to resell against Carol and Phillips. The judge convicted them both, however, of robbing a drugstore to obtain the drugs in the first place. Phillips received a total of six years for this and other charges of jail escape, burglary, and assault with intent to kill; Carol pled guilty to petty larceny and was given a year's suspended sentence.

The leniency came with a price. Carol agreed to go undercover for the state police as a drug informant. She was issued a new identity, including a driver's license identifying her as Carol Malone. Many people suspected that she had cooperated in Phillips's convictions, although she denied having done so. That was what the argument that had just occurred in the bar had been all about, Epperson explained: he was not about to let anyone call Carol a snitch. She had pled guilty, as anyone would to get off; that was all there was to it. As for her working undercover, that was a joke. She pacified the cops with bullshit from time to time and used her phony driver's license to cash checks.

Benny was aware of the Norris Resort drug case because it had been highly publicized, Sherry had read about it in the papers, and it had helped to bring down Trotter. Benny also thought he remembered a certain kind of bread that somebody used to supply to the county jail, although he had never met Carol before.

"Was that your dark rye bread at the Clinton jail?" he asked her. "That was great bread."

It was hers, Carol said. She had not baked any in a while. At the moment what she really needed and wanted was something else. She headed for the ladies' room.

Benny was favorably impressed with Donnie, Roger, and Carol. They agreed to do business together after the holidays.

Sherry was not pleased by Benny's account of his new associates; and when he brought Donnie Bartley home to dinner one evening, she took Benny aside and told him that he was making a big mistake, hanging with trash. He had already told her that Carol was an informant, or had been. Once a snitch, always a snitch. And what about Bartley? Hadn't he copped a plea in Kentucky to get off? It didn't

take a genius to figure out that he must have ratted on his friends—
that was the only way somebody like him, with previous convictions,
ever beat a rap. You could tell just from looking at him and listening
to his bullshit, the scummy little weasel. Snitches hung together,
didn't Benny know that? The next thing you knew, she and Benny
would be doing time while the others walked. Her opinion did not
change the next time she met Bartley.

"I'm telling you that Bartley is no good. My grandmother always
said, if you want to buy a pig, look it over twice. If you don't like it
the second time, let it go."

One morning Benny brought Sherry breakfast in bed—hotcakes,
fried eggs, sliced tomatoes, sausage, Karo syrup, biscuits, and white
gravy dotted with pepper. She started in again about Bartley; Benny
insisted she was wrong. Nor was it any of her business. It was one
thing to get after him about his women. Now she was jealous of his
male friends, too. What did she want him to do, stay home and cook?
She was behaving like a typical bitch, trying to fence him in.

"Women are like dogs," Benny said. "They crawl into bed with
you and the next thing you know, they's inching over and over, and
you're on the floor."

"Oh, yeah?" Sherry said. "You treat me like a woman, I'll treat
you like a king."

Meeting Roger and Carol did not reassure her. Roger's handshake put
Sherry off: Sherry told Benny it wasn't really a hand at all, more like a
shinbone, or a cock with cartilage in it. And he would not look her in
the eye. Epperson spoke of doing one big lick that would put everyone on Easy Street, and he acted as if he had the authority to pull
rank on everyone.

They often dropped by the house unannounced. So much for a
quiet life between jobs. Sherry still attended therapy sessions; she
wanted to convey to the doctors these latest assaults on her sanity;
but she could not risk incriminating Benny and herself as they sank in
deeper with this collection of drugged-out misfits who telephoned at
all hours and descended on the house. She demanded to Benny that
he break with them; he told her to shut up or get smacked. Sherry felt
hemmed in. The only person she trusted enough to confide in, Pat
Mason, had moved to Florida. There seemed to be nowhere to turn.

Donnie collapsed from hepatitis after the New Year and sacked
out at Benny and Sherry's so as not to be a burden on his mother and

sister in their cramped trailer. Benny made pots of soup; Carol delivered bread; momentarily Sherry caught herself feeling sorry for Bartley. He talked about his parents' divorce, how he had had to go down to the Harlan County courthouse as a kid to collect his father's mandated child support payments, how he had labored for five and a half years in the underground mines, how life had dealt him blow after blow.

The stronger Donnie became, the less impressed Sherry was with his whining. She had had her fill of sob stories in her time and had numerous relatives who could tell worse. When Bartley began asking her to telephone various women for him and began bragging that he got more nookie in a month than most men dreamed of in a lifetime, Sherry learned to despise him. If there was one thing she hated, it was a creep who thought he was God's gift to women. She exploded when he said that he knew she was dying to go to bed with him.

"You pea-headed little nut," she told him as she brought him orange juice. "You put one paw on me and Benny Hodge will bust your head in like a melon."

Donnie lingered on at the house after his recovery was well advanced and he was able to begin helping out on burglaries. One girlfriend, then another moved in and out, sharing his bed and drugs. His ex-wife and six-year-old daughter visited. Sherry set deadlines for his departure but, pleading weakness, by the beginning of May Bartley was entering his third month as a nonpaying guest.

The way Benny looked up to Roger Epperson troubled Sherry. Number one, she hated to see Benny following anyone. He seemed to receive some sort of a lift, tagging after Roger. Did Roger's big, soft, slow, lumpy, deep-voiced self-assurance hypnotize Benny? Was it because Roger's parents were rich, or so he said, flush with property and money? Did the attraction derive from the idea of someone from a well-off family who chose a life of crime of his own free will and who had spent years at it without once, except for a couple of arrests, seeing the inside of a slammer? Did Carol, with her equally respectable background, also impress Benny by her devotion to Roger?

None of these reasons added up, because Sherry understood that Benny was oblivious to Roger's and Carol's origins and past lives. He did not think that way, did not ask questions, was as incurious about the past as he was indifferent to the future, living for the moment.

The problem was that beneath his muscles he thought next to nothing of himself—and was therefore an easy mark for an arrogant bullshit artist like Roger. Benny was like a kid doing push-ups at the command of a football coach, never asking why.

In prison, where only brawn and silence counted and where you survived by following the code, Benny could endure, even prosper. In the free world, he had to be led. Would it be by Sherry or by Roger, that was the question.

In Sherry's view, Roger and Carol both had screws loose and had fried their brains so often that neither could distinguish shit from Shinola. Carol was living on a moonbeam. Often during her druggie monologues, directed at no one in particular, she talked about Patty Hearst and identified with her as if she, too, were some kidnapped heiress rampaging through the underworld with a drugged-up gang. Roger thought himself a big-time gangster; Donnie had the mentality of an untrustworthy slave.

Let things play themselves out, Sherry decided. What happens, happens. Hang on, something big might go down, you never knew.

The boys' work together began with an insurance scam. Jim Millaway (an alias) owned a gold, silver, and jewelry shop in Knoxville. Millaway, in turn, was close to a big-time mall developer who had a cash flow problem. The developer's young third wife was bananas for diamonds and sapphires. When the couple was off sailing in the Caribbean, Millaway arranged for Roger, Benny, and Donnie to rob the developer's house. The gang took a percentage of the goods, Millaway fenced them, and the developer collected the insurance. Everybody was happy, except the bride.

They did other jobs for Millaway. The way Roger explained it, only the insured people took any real risk. Sherry pointed out, to no effect, that if the person who was insured were caught, he or she might easily be induced to name Millaway, who could then be induced to name the actual burglars—who, if things worked out as they usually did, would end up taking the rap. But Sherry's was a lonely voice.

One evening at the house, Roger talked of the opportunities awaiting them if only they would set their sights high enough. They were just getting started together; they needed to range more widely and hit a greater variety of targets. On the dining room table he spread out several calling cards he had collected from inquisitive FBI and IRS agents. It was a cinch to make these cards into official-looking IDs, Roger explained, bearing their own photographs and fake names.

"Snapper Hall," Donnie said. That was his favorite alias. A snapper was the brakeman on an underground coal car; that had been Donnie's job in the mines. Roger suggested that it did not seem appropriate for a government agent.

"Shane Hall," Benny suggested. He identified with the solitary blond gunman played by Alan Ladd.

"Cool," Roger said. "'Come back, Shane.' Saw that on TV." He did a line of coke.

All they would have to do was to cut out the agents' actual names and substitute the phony ones, using a camera and a copying machine. The Knoxville fence could provide at least one FBI badge. With this kind of ID, they could gain easy entrance to any home or business. They would not even have to confine themselves to robbing illegals. The whole goddamned United States of America was a target.

"You keep on dreaming, Straw Boss," Sherry said, "and you'll get us all arrested in a New York second."

Sherry had nicknamed Roger "Straw Boss" the first time she heard him talking big. She meant by it a phony, a blowhard, someone like a foreman's assistant with no authority but a loud mouth—a man of straw. Roger hated the name, whether or not he fully grasped the degree of the insult, but it stuck.

She bored in: "Me and Benny's went two damn years without us getting caught, doing what we been doing. Why change it? You all is fools not sticking to illegals."

"We listen to you," Roger said, "we'll be doing dipshit ripoffs till we're ninety."

"You live to be ninety, I'll bake you a cake, and I don't bake. Keep on a-talking."

"Bug off, Sherry," Carol said. "You're just being aggressive because you're lacking in self-esteem."

"You defending Straw Boss again? I reckon he needs a woman to protect him."

Carol showed her loyalty to Roger by responding with her own big idea, a scheme that had been proposed to her the last time she had been arrested. When Terry Phillips and Carol were being held at the Clinton jail on the Norris Resort drug charges, Tim Schultz, Sheriff Trotter's chief deputy and the very man who had had the decency to drop dead before the case came to trial, approached her about doing a job for him. The plan, which had died with Schultz, involved crossing the Kentucky border to pull off a robbery up there.

The story Carol told was known to many besides her. It was widely rumored in those parts that there was a miser dwelling in the mountains of Kentucky. An old man was supposedly hoarding a pile of cash in his house. No one knew how much, but it was said to be substantial. The man was so feeble, the story went, that there would be no difficulty, if only you could get inside the house and escape without being seen.

The hitch was, this miser had an alarm system that was hooked into the police station less than a mile away. So many people knew about the money that the old man would have been robbed years before, except for that alarm and the smallness of the town, where everybody knew everybody and neighbors watched out for one another. And so far no one had been able to secure cooperation from the local cops or the Kentucky State Police.

Roger had known about the old man long before Carol had ever heard about him and had been talking about robbing him for years. Roger, born and raised in Perry, the next-door county, was in frequent contact with his home grounds and was certain the rumors were true. According to a friend of his, the miser was a doctor who at one time in the seventies had arranged to have some high-value coal stripped from land he owned. There came a day when he agreed to purchase a bulldozer for fifty thousand dollars; he said he would go to the bank to withdraw the cash. In less than an hour, he returned with the money in a sack, a collection of fifties and hundreds, and handed it over. The joke was, it was Thanksgiving Day. Everybody knew the banks were closed. And what did that tell you, except that he must have been keeping the cash at home? And there were other telltale indications.

Roger said that he planned to look into the matter further. He was beginning to see a way to do the job. He had good contacts up there. He would devise an airtight plan of attack and they would all clean up, if somebody else didn't get to the old man first.

Sherry hoped somebody would.

14

Early in May, Roger, Benny, and Donnie decided to drive up to Kentucky to see about robbing the doctor and other job possibilities. Roger took the wheel of his 1978 Thunderbird, black with a white vinyl top, his destination an obscure spot in the southeast corner of the Commonwealth, down near the Virginia border. Choosing a route that was roundabout but the fastest, he picked up I-75 at Lake City, traveled north over mountains to cross the border at Jellico, and continued through rolling cattle farm country past Corbin to London, where he turned east along the Daniel Boone Parkway into the heart of the rugged Eastern Kentucky mountains—a journey from straightaways to twisting ups and downs, from open skies to shadows.

A few miles east of the Daniel Boone National Forest, he left the parkway to turn south at Hazard, a town that could boast of a Wal-Mart, a two-story McDonald's, a liquor store, La Citadelle ("Kentucky's Most Magnificent Mountaintop Motel"), and the sinking Holiday Inn. Roger did not stop to visit with his family, who he knew would not have been pleased to meet his new companions, nor even to see him. From Hazard, Highway 15 snaked past the Viper turnoff, running alongside isolated houses and trailers with their narrow patches of corn and tobacco, and paralleled the CSX tracks past abandoned and active underground and strip mines—with their heaps of coal, called tipples, their gob piles and clusters of bulldozers, backhoes, towering power shovels, and heavy trucks loading up

and lumbering onto the road showering clumps of mud. After bridg-
ing over Carr Fork Lake and Irishman Creek, the highway crossed
into Letcher County near the village of Isom, where a sign pointed to
the Mountain Motor Speedway, a dirt oval where on Saturday nights
NASCAR hopefuls thrilled as many as three thousand highlanders
and irritated the residents of Race Track Hollow, who complained
that the roar of engines and crowds kept them awake until three
o'clock on Sunday mornings. From Isom it was another eight miles to
Whitesburg, the county seat, a brick-faced town remarkable for its
cleanliness and enterprise. Roger, Benny, and Donnie had no business
there.

They had come some two hundred miles and had about another
twenty minutes to go. They could have taken any of several more
direct routes, but these were tortuous roads much of the way, and
two of them would have meant cutting directly across Harlan County,
where Bartley could easily have been recognized and arrested, or
pumped full of lead, or all of those.

From Whitesburg Roger drove along the Virginia border east on
119, then branched off northeast through the twists of an obscure
secondary road, paved but splashed with mud and not much wider
than a pair of buggies. On all sides the woods grew thick, the hills
rose and steamed with damp. As spring advanced, thunderstorms
came nearly every afternoon to the mountains, and floods were a
threat to isolated houses and villages. People stared at them from the
porches of occasional shacks and from the few cars and pickups that
passed. A story often told in those mountains captured why traveling
back roads was a jittery business. There once was an old man living
in a hollow who lay in bed all day staring out a window through a
rearview mirror salvaged from some wrecked car. He sprawled there,
a finger crooked through the handle of a moonshine jug, watching.
When he heard the noise of an unfamiliar engine or spotted a
stranger on foot, he grabbed his shotgun, shoved it through the window, and opened fire. It passed the time, he said, between Christmas
and the Fourth of July.

Donnie asked Roger if he knew where he was going. The road
seemed to be headed nowhere, twisting back on itself, confounding
any sense of direction. They ought to have put Kentucky plates on the
T-bird. At least they had guns. Donnie did some coke. "Man, where
the fuck *are* we?"

Roger told Donnie to shut up. This was home territory for Roger. He had worked in the vicinity stripping coal, scheming to steal trucks. They were halfway between Whitesburg and Jenkins, was where they were.

They passed through Seco, not much more than a grocery store with a pair of gas pumps but once the headquarters of the South East Coal Company, hence the acronym. Roger made a sharp left onto another narrow road. Suddenly they were in Neon, what was left of it.

A new pinkish-brick bank building, its freestanding sign embedded in petunias, contrasted with the other structures along Main Street—a Super 10 variety store, a Radio Shack outlet, a GE appliance shop, a storefront library, all housed in crumbling brick buildings two and three stories high, images from the Great Depression. Many windows were broken or boarded up. At the intersection, ankle deep in muddy water from a recent flood, Roger turned right, passed over railroad tracks, and was in Fleming. Sometimes called Fleming-Neon, the two dingy towns, with a combined population of under two thousand, shared a post office and police and fire departments. In all of Kentucky there was not a more forlorn place.

Many years ago, the towns had known prosperity. Fleming, named after an Elkhorn Coal Corporation executive, started as a company town, built more or less overnight in 1912 when the Louisville & Nashville Railroad reached that point. It consisted mostly of a line of rickety two-story wooden duplexes stretching all the way to McRoberts, some three miles up the road. These housed two miners' families, with each allotted half the front porch and covered rear stoop. As long as the men and boys could work, a family could stay; death or permanent disability meant eviction. Lured by steady wages, mountaineers abandoned their log cabins and their independence, which, once lost, could never be recovered. They found themselves better clothed, housed, and fed, for a while, but at an unimagined price.

To guarantee subservience, the corporation issued scrip against future wages, requiring workers to purchase groceries, coal for heat and cooking, and everything else from their employer. This tyranny forced miners into perpetual debt, as Tennessee Ernie Ford sang in "Sixteen Tons," with its line about owing your soul to the company store. The stranglehold on goods and services gave birth to Neon—

like Argon and Krypton, named after the "noble gases"—a merchandising center that sprang up at the end of the L & N tracks as an alternative to Elkhorn Coal's monopoly. There miners could pay cash for goods at competitive prices and enjoy the forbidden pleasures of liquor and bordellos.

When the price of coal plummeted in 1928, however, both towns sank with it and declined further through the Depression, until World War II brought a new boom that lasted until the late forties. Just after the war, old-timers recalled, Neon was still a bustling, rip-roaring place, where a carton of cigarettes could buy you an hour with a woman. Except for the boomlet of the seventies, it had been going down the tubes ever since, along with Fleming, where the curse of company scrip gave way to food stamps and welfare. The Appalachian balladeer Jean Ritchie mourned the plight of Neon and Fleming when she sang, "The L & N Doesn't Stop Here Anymore."

It was along that line of miners' shacks in Fleming that Roger Epperson searched for the doctor's house. The old duplexes still stood, peeling and rotting, many of them empty, most occupied by old folks or a single struggling family. Here and there the hopeless gazed out from porches strewn with broken furniture, rusting washing machines and refrigerators, bottles and cans. Tires and trash littered the ground. A few of the desolate were blacks, descendants of railroad workers brought up from the Deep South a hundred years ago, John Henrys who had wailed,

> Cocaine done drove me crazy,
> Morphine done kill'd my baby,
> An' I ain't a-goin' to be treated thisaway!

The majority of the tenants were the remnants of white miners' families, people weakened by economic collapse and welfare checks. Cynical, indifferent, and defeated, they lolled and wasted away. The idea that a miser hoarding anything more valuable than bottle caps might live among them seemed incredible.

But beyond the scruffy field of Fleming-Neon High, around a bend in the narrow road, sat a house unique in the town. Roger slowed as he passed it—one story, ranch-style, sturdily built of thin slices of sandy-colored Crab Orchard stone, with a low-pitched shingled roof and white trim. It was immaculate and had no litter anywhere around it, an island of order in that backwater.

"That's it," Roger said. "That's the doctor's."

The house extended from a two-car garage, past a bay window and three dwarf evergreens in square stone planters, a white front door recessed under a porch supported by a pair of wrought-iron posts, and ended in a wing partly concealed by a trimmed hedge. A low wall of matching stone fronted the road and framed the driveway with stout square posts topped by big glass globes. Bland and severe, geometric and antiseptic, it held dominion over slovenly surroundings. On either side of it, the old shacks stood.

Roger continued up the road about a quarter-mile to pause at the doctor's clinic, a wooden shack set back in a graveled lot. No sign announced its function; only the heavy wire mesh across the windows hinted that there might be something worth stealing inside, but thieves in the know had hit it numerous times. So simple, so modest, the clinic evoked the hard life as the house did not. It was so evocative of depression that location scouts had chosen it for scenes in *Coal Miner's Daughter*, the 1980 movie biography of Loretta Lynn, filmed in Letcher County with locals hired as extras.

Roger circled the parking lot in front of the clinic past pickups and cars, some battered and others new and bright, and headed back down the road. He slowed again at the doctor's house, but the big T-bird, with its Tennessee tags, was too obvious to allow for a thorough, professional reconnaissance. They would return, Roger said, when the time was right. They would work out a plan, and they would need a different car.

The boys lingered for days in the mountains. Roger was at home. With the idea of finding a car likely for FBI or IRS agents, he and Benny visited an auction one evening, leaving Donnie with a girl he had met in a Hazard bar. Cars were Roger's family's business; he knew these auctions well. One took place Thursday nights off Highway 80 near London, the center of the used car trade for Eastern Kentucky. In a grassy field full of automobiles—shined up, the tires Armor-Alled, odometers optimistic—a canny breed of men roamed and haggled. It was no different from the horse fairs of another century. Knowing many of the dealers since childhood, Roger mingled with them, Benny silently following. No one rushed up to greet Roger. A few returned his hellos. Bobby Morris, from Gray Hawk over in Jackson County, was more or less friendly.

Bobby Morris's father had traded with Roger's father for decades.

How *was* his daddy, Roger inquired of Bobby, and did Ed Morris still carry a big fat roll of bills? Old Ed Morris, he'd always had enough on him to buy a Cadillac, Roger said in a jocular way. No, Bobby Morris replied, his father had been sick and didn't fool much with cars anymore. His mom and dad stuck pretty close to home these days.

Roger did not buy a car that night. He and Benny and Donnie spent the next week visiting Roger's friends at Isom, where they took in a race at the speedway, and in Hazard, Viper, Vicco, Delphia, and Cumberland, where Donnie also had contacts. Cumberland (pop. 3,172) was just over the Letcher line into Harlan County, about twenty miles from the Virginia border. Donnie decided that it was worth sneaking that far into Harlan because of some information they had to check out. With all of the dope they had been scoring—Benny had brought a set of weights with him and usually worked out while the others snorted, smoked, and drank—they were low on funds and decided they ought to try to do at least one lick before heading back to Tennessee. Cumberland was a place to pick up accurate, inside scuttlebutt because it was the center of gang activity in the area. Men from there ranged into several states, pulling jobs and distributing narcotics, sometimes managing operations of surprising sophistication. It was a gang from Cumberland that had masterminded the burglary of a South Carolina art museum, making off with a Frederic Remington bronze and other works.

Cumberland was also close to Linefork, on the Letcher border, where, Roger had been told by friends in Tennessee, a fence lived whose house was supposed to be a veritable warehouse of hot goods. A Cumberland contact expanded on the rumor and helped plan the job. The only problem was supposed to be a night watchman.

Around midnight on May 13, 1985, Roger, Benny, and Donnie drove to an isolated house near Linefork. They had already cased the place by daylight and conceived of a plan to make entrance easy. The blue light atop the T-bird threw the watchman off guard. Donnie and Benny ran up the drive with guns drawn, took the watchman's gun, tied him up, and warned him to keep quiet or be dead. Roger, who had been waiting in the car for fear of being recognized, followed them into the house. They roused a husband and wife and their small son, tied them up, and ransacked the house.

It was less than they had hoped. They emptied every drawer, even checked out the refrigerator—and ended up with about four thousand dollars in cash and a number of rifles, shotguns, and pistols. They headed south on 160 through the town of Appalachia, west through Virginia and down to Knoxville, and were home before dawn.

If the victim was actually a fence, he did not behave as if he had anything to hide, because he immediately reported the crime to the police. The watchman stated that the men had at first identified themselves as federal agents, whether IRS or FBI he could not say; nor could he describe their car.

Benny withheld from Sherry any details of the adventure in Kentucky. She knew only that they had done some minor job and that money was running short.

As if resigning herself to a new phase in her life, Sherry had formally discharged herself from the Ridgeview psychiatric clinic while Benny was away. On May 12 she attended a final session. Her clinician on that occasion, a man with a Ph.D. in psychology, noted that Sherry, who gave her last name as Hodge, was terminating treatment of her own volition, for "reasons unknown." His "Final Formulation" was that the patient was "very emotionally deprived," unable to break with a harmful relationship, was suffering "terror at the thought of being alone," and was "impulsive and self-destructive." "Followup Plans" included only "will await further patient contact."

When the boys announced that they were heading across state lines again, targeting the Memorial Day weekend for a robbery in Rome, Georgia, Sherry, ever determined to make the best of things, decided that they might as well have some holiday fun along the way. Some of her happiest times with Benny had been spent visiting various tourist attractions around Tennessee, especially Gatlinburg, a resort on the banks of the Little Pigeon River, at the entrance to the Great Smoky Mountains National Park, where they rode quaint, brightly colored trolleys, shopped for handicrafts, and where even Benny had to admit that the country music was great. They had taken Renee and Benny's daughters there several times. Looking at a map, she saw that Rome was only some fifty miles above Atlanta and Six Flags Over Georgia, a vast amusement park that several of her friends and relatives had raved about. She persuaded everyone that a Sunday spent at Six Flags would make a festive prelude to the robbery, set for Monday.

This particular job was arranged in cahoots with a pair of brothers from Ooltewah, a suburb of Chattanooga near I-75 and the Georgia border, about seventy-five miles north of Rome. The target was a reputed drug dealer whom the Ooltewah boys had been checking out and following around. They knew his car; they figured that the man would likely be at home on Memorial Day at his house in rural Floyd County, a few miles outside of Rome—a city of thirty thousand souls built on seven hills and notable for its city hall statue of the Capitoline wolf and her sucklings, Romulus and Remus, a gift from Benito Mussolini in 1929. Roger and the others decided that this would be a good opportunity to run a full-scale test of their federal agents scam. They elected to pose as IRS agents, since drug dealers were always paranoid about unpaid taxes on illegitimate income.

May 26 was a sunny Sunday at Six Flags, perfect for the whitewater rafting adventure, the triple-loop roller coaster, banter with a strolling Bugs Bunny and Porky Pig, and several rides on Sherry's favorite, the Octopus, with her and Carol snapping pictures to immortalize the occasion. They gorged on hot dogs and cotton candy; they had so much fun that for a few hours Sherry was able to cast her anxieties aside and giggle like a kid. She showed great form in knocking over six milk bottles with a softball, winning a cuddly stuffed pink buffalo she named Big Ben.

Donnie had a new girlfriend along, a seventeen-year-old from Oliver Springs whom he had met through his sister. She was Rebecca Jane Hannah, and she had first been attracted to Donnie when, early that May, she had seen him riding a motorcycle on a visit to his mother and sister's trailer. Her birthday had been on Friday, so the outing at Six Flags was a belated celebration for her. Sherry disliked her immediately, thinking there was something both snotty and stupid about her and ridiculing her when she said proudly that she was related to a governor of Tennessee, without saying which one. Sherry suggested it must have been Ray Blanton, who had gone to jail in 1979 for selling pardons.

Rebecca was not told about Monday's plans. They sent her home in her own car Sunday night, while the rest of them stayed at the Ooltewah brothers' house. The next evening Sherry and Carol prepared to wait as the men took off, Roger driving his T-bird with one of the brothers, the other brother in his green Dodge with Benny and Donnie as passengers. Donnie and Benny, who would do the talking, wore suits; Sherry had done her best to make them fit their roles, trimming their hair short and slicking it down, ironing their white shirts. She noted how convincing Benny looked with his muscles hidden by the jacket she had tailored to hang loosely on him.

But she was nervous. It was more than the usual adrenaline. She was not confident of the brothers' intelligence. As the evening wore on and she watched the clock and fidgeted, she felt like socking Carol, who was driving her batty with chatter—how everyone needed to discover the inner child within herself; how parents could be toxic to their children; something about a female guru in the West who believed that it was all right to murder your husband because you would have a new one in the next life anyway. "Can't you cool it, Chop, you scatterbrained rumdum?" Sherry pleaded, turning up the volume on the TV. By ten o'clock Carol was Patty Hearst again. Sherry hugged her buffalo and tried to think positively.

15

AT ABOUT NINE O'CLOCK THAT EVENING they found the address in a well-lit subdivision beyond the Rome city limits. Except for bright street lamps, everything looked good. Only one car was in the driveway. Roger switched on the blue police light and stuck it onto the roof of the T-bird. Donnie and Benny piled out of the Dodge and hustled up to the front door and banged on it, Benny shouting, "Open up! This is the IRS!"

A man opened the door a crack. "IRS," Benny said, flashing his badge—as did Donnie, but as briefly as possible, as his was merely a toy made of tin. When the man hesitated, Benny wedged his foot in the door and, drawing his gun, forced his way in, with Donnie following. "You better be real peaceful," Benny said. "We're here to collect back taxes." Donnie signaled for the others to come on in as the man protested that he did not owe any taxes. Two teenage girls and an older woman clung together on a couch.

"Tie 'em up," Roger ordered as he burst in with the brothers. Benny handcuffed the man. The girls and the woman submitted to being tied with rope and gagged with duct tape. Benny demanded that the man show him his stash of drugs and any cash he had in the house. The man insisted that he had nothing and that there must be some mistake. Roger looked at the Ooltewah boys. "Bullshit," one of them said. "It's got to be him. He's lying."

It was a modest tract house that betrayed no sign of wealth. They went from room to room turning over beds, emptying drawers, hurl-ing clothes from closets and found—nothing. No cocaine, no cash, not so much as a joint. Was it under the house? Buried in the yard? They demanded, threatened—the man pleaded that he had nothing to hide and begged them not to hurt his mother and and daughters.

"A fuckup," Roger said at last. "Take what you can and get out of here."

They threw jewelry, a few firearms, bank certificates, odds and ends, even a marble-topped table into the trunk of the T-bird. They wrapped the man in tape, sealed his mouth, and were on the way out when one of the girls began to writhe and squeal. Taking pity, an Ooltewah brother stripped off her gag. She begged him to loosen slightly the rope around her wrists. He did so and fled.

Within minutes the girl wriggled free and untied the others. Discover-ing that the telephone lines had been cut, she drove her father to a service station and helped him phone the police. He described a big black and white Thunderbird.

A trooper based in Rome was on patrol in Chattooga County when he received the all points bulletin. Almost immediately he spot-ted what looked like the rear lights of a T-bird up ahead. Drawing close enough to make out a Tennessee tag, he followed as the car turned from Highway 100 onto 114, slowed down, and headed toward a Pay and Tote store.

In the Dodge, Benny and Donnie argued with their driver about whether the victim had cleared out his stash because his family was visiting for the holiday or whether, as seemed more likely, he was not a dealer at all. Could they have invaded the wrong house? It was entirely possible; the police made that mistake frequently. Turning onto 114, the driver pulled over to the side of the road to wait when he saw through his rearview mirror that the T-bird was stopping at a convenience store.

"What are you doing?" Benny asked. "Look at that! Keep mov-ing!"

A police cruiser bounced into the store's parking lot and slid to a stop beside the T-bird. Under the bright lights a trooper emerged with his gun drawn.

*   *   *

The trooper confronted Roger and his companion and asked for permission to search the trunk. Roger refused. Holding his gun on the suspects, the trooper radioed for help; backup officers arrived in minutes, and a sheriff's deputy brought a warrant.

Yet another trooper drove up accompanying the victim, who identified the T-bird and its occupants and the stolen goods in the trunk—everything except two pairs of Bermuda shorts he said did not belong to him. Searching these, officers discovered keys, small change, and two men's wallets.

The Dodge was equipped with a fuzzbuster on the dash, but they kept to the speed limit because they quickly realized that getting stopped would finish them. Benny and Donnie knew that they had left their wallets, including driver's licenses, in Roger's trunk. They had worn shorts to Six Flags, the better to enjoy the weather and the whitewater adventure and other rides. When they had changed into suits Monday afternoon, they had tossed their casual clothes into the trunk and had forgotten about them until now. They knew it may have been a fatal carelessness. The police would already have their names, addresses, heights, weights, the colors of their eyes, even their photographs.

From a service station outside Chattanooga Benny telephoned Sherry and told her to leave the Ooltewah house immediately and go to a coffee shop down the street to wait for them. Roger had been busted. They would have to start running.

Sherry and Carol had barely made it to the coffee shop when the Dodge pulled up and they jumped in. Sherry, who prided herself on never panicking under stress—"I'll have a nervous breakdown later" was one of her mottoes—grasped the seriousness of the situation when she heard about the wallets and, screaming at Carol to shut up or get clobbered, told the Ooltewah brother to drive straight to her Harriman house. It was a gamble, because the address was on Benny's license, but she knew that it would take the police at least a few hours to organize a search across state lines; she would have to improvise something from Harriman—what this might be, she had no idea as yet. She asked where the Dodge had been parked during the robbery and figured it must not have been identified, or they would already have been stopped.

It took nearly an hour and a half to reach Harriman; it was now past midnight. Sherry told Carol to go to her house in Clinton and pretend she had been asleep all evening if the cops showed up. They would have to decide later what to do about bailing Roger out. For now, the important thing was to take Benny and Donnie somewhere. Their only other option was to turn themselves in. Since this would mean at least a twenty-year sentence for both of them, it was not an attractive alternative. After being warned to keep his mouth shut, the brother headed back to Ooltewah, saying he had relatives who would hide him.

Sherry knew that the most important thing was to get Benny and Donnie away from the house and off the road. She drove them to a motel in Kingston, only ten minutes away, the nearest town east on I-40, a well-to-do bedroom community for Knoxville and one of the least likely places for the cops to look for fugitives. She registered for them, keeping them out of sight, using the name Wong and entering a false tag number for the Charger, wishing she were driving a car more anonymous than the bright red speed machine. In the room she gave the boys changes of clothes and took their suits. Kissing Benny good-bye and telling him not to worry, she would think of something, she hurried back to Harriman, tossing the suits into a Dumpster along the way.

She worried about tomorrow. The FBI would soon be after them. They had impersonated federal officers, and they had crossed state lines. Everything she had feared would result from Roger's hot-air recklessness and Benny's subservience was coming down.

When she reached the house, she telephoned the motel. They were safe. She tried to calm Benny down, saying she loved him and would stick by him no matter what.

"I love you, too, Booger," Benny said.

Sherry wandered around, touching the possessions she and Benny had acquired together and wondering what to do. She was filled with dread, sensing that it was now only a matter of time before her hopes for a normal life with him were over forever. Or maybe not. Maybe they could go on the run and disappear. People did that, didn't they?

She walked out the back door and into the woods and, pacing off the distance from a certain tree, unearthed by moonlight a jar of money, a couple of thousand stored for an emergency. There were other jars buried here and there; no sense taking it all now—if she were caught on the run, the less cash she had with her, the better.

Lying on the big bed, she took deep breaths, trying to hold her anxiety in check. What she knew she was going to do, had to do, brought agony. It was not that she was hesitating to help Benny. What did stand by your man mean if not that? But her dad was ill, his lungs deteriorating. What if he needed her while she was running and she couldn't go to him? What if she couldn't see or speak to him before he died? She felt she was betraying him.

And there was Renee, who had come to accept Benny, more or less. How long would it be before she saw her daughter again? What would Renee think when and if she found out that her mother was helping Benny run from the FBI? And what if she were watching TV one night and saw that her mother had been arrested with the likes of Donnie and Roger? Or killed in a shoot-out?

Near dawn Sherry fell asleep and dreamed that she was alone, wandering across some featureless white plain, an arctic waste, calling Renee's name and hearing nothing but the wind. When she awoke, she remembered that she had had this dream before, only not so vividly, and she had the feeling that she would be dreaming it again. She had the impulse to telephone Renee, catch her before she was off to school, tell her good-bye for now. Tell her some lie or other.

Instead she phoned Benny and told him to get ready. She would bring him and Donnie their toothbrushes and shaving things and some other clothes. Benny asked her not to forget his weights. There was no sense in letting himself get out of shape. He might need all his strength.

BANDITS POSE AS IRS

read the banner headline in the *Rome News-Tribune* that morning. The story gave details of the robbery, said that two of five suspects were already in custody, and was accompanied by a photograph of the T-bird, identified as "car used in robbery." The next day a story reported that officers had gone to Tennessee to search for three other men wanted in connection with the armed robbery: "Floyd County police officials believe the men will go to an area near Knoxville."

On Thursday, May 30, a third suspect, identified as a thirty-nine-year-old resident of Ooltewah, Tennessee, and a "cousin" of one of the men already in custody, turned himself in to authorities in Rome. Family members, understanding that he was a fugitive, had convinced him to surrender. Newspaper and television reports announced that FBI and IRS agents had joined in the search for the remaining two suspects, who were believed still to be hiding out in the Knoxville area.

By then Sherry was convinced that it was only a matter of time before Benny was caught, and she discussed with him the possible advantages of turning himself in. He was adamant, however, and she could easily sympathize with his point of view. He would rather die, he said, than go back to prison. In a telephone conversation with him—she was now moving him and Donnie to a different motel every night— she told him that she would remain loyal to him forever and would try to help him to the end.

"They won't take me alive," Benny said.

"I'll die with you," Sherry said. "We'll shoot it out with the cops if they get us. I love you forever."

In the meantime she did her best to help her outlaw escape. She contacted him only from pay phones, worried that the FBI would surely have her home line tapped. She was certain that agents were following her, hoping she would lead them to Benny. They had not come to the house, but they must have known about her by then. Driving around during the day, she could tell that she was being followed.

But the FBI was no match for her, Sherry convinced herself. She counted on their believing that one dumb broad would never be clever enough to elude them, and she doubted that they would bother watching her twenty-four hours a day. She moved Donnie and Benny only late at night, taking every precaution. For an hour or so she would run preliminary, pointless errands here and there, parking in well-lighted lots and scrutinizing everything that moved when she did. If she strongly suspected she was being tailed, she drove home, waited with the lights out, and crept down to the road on foot through trees to make sure no one was waiting for her. She enjoyed the game.

But after a few days of this, she decided to confront the FBI head on and con them out of wasting their resources on her. She telephoned Gene Foust and asked him to set up an interview for her with an FBI agent, telling Foust that she knew that she was being followed because Benny was on the run, that she did not know where Benny was, and that it was time to get the Feds off her back. Foust agreed to help, asking no questions. Sherry relied on her belief that, like most local police officers, Foust resented the FBI for its arrogance, its reluctance to share information, and its interference with local practice and custom. It was the FBI that had nailed Trotter and other sheriffs and that posed a constant threat to local autonomy. Foust, Sherry calculated, would stay neutral, at least, in her present difficulties.

She met with Foust and Special Agent Burl Cloninger in a room at the Oak Ridge P.D. Cloninger, graying and avuncular, more casual and friendly than Sherry's standard concept of the FBI, thanked her for coming forward. He assured her that the Bureau was interested only in Benny Hodge and Donnie Bartley, not in her—a statement Sherry pretended to accept at face value. Seizing an opportunity to appear cooperative, she pointed to a wanted poster depicting Benny that was tacked to a bulletin board behind Foust. That photograph looked nothing like Hodge, she said.

"You all could run right up against him and not arrest him, if you was to have that there picture in mind," she said. The photo showed Benny with a scraggly beard, unkempt as he had never been since being with her. It must have come from Brushy and was ridiculously out of date. "Benny don't look like no criminal, I can tell you that much, if you wants to know. Benny's handsome and real clean-cut."

She told Cloninger how distressed she was at the disappearance of her boyfriend, whom she deeply loved and had been trying to help stay straight. Unfortunately, her relationship with Benny was a rocky one and on May 27, the last day she had seen him, they had had an argument over money. Earlier that day they had worked out together at the Racquet Club. After the argument at home, he had telephoned someone, she did not know whom. Then he had taken a few clothes and left. He did not take the car, so he must have met someone. As he stormed out, he warned her that if she so much as looked out the window, he would kill her.

At this, Sherry burst into tears and, to illustrate the tragedy of her situation, she displayed to Cloninger the knife wound that Benny had inflicted on her right wrist. Avoiding Foust's eyes, for fear of faltering or even laughing, she said that she and Benny had often fought violently, after which he sometimes left for brief periods. She had expected him to return as usual this time, until she learned from the

TV that he was on the run. She now believed that he was not coming back to her because he did not want her involved in his present diffi- culties. In spite of everything, she believed that Benny loved her. Agent Cloninger offered her a Kleenex.

Where did she think Benny might be hiding, Cloninger wanted to know. Through fresh tears Sherry said she hoped Mr. Cloninger understood that, because she loved Benny so much, she could not be expected to help in his arrest. She had no idea where he was. Maybe he had gone to his first wife and daughter or his mother in Morris- town; maybe he was with his second wife and daughter in Knoxville. Sherry supplied the names and addresses of all these women.

She added that Benny had spent so many years in prison that he had often said that he would rather "blow his brains out" than go to jail. She expected that he would not be taken without a fight. He had with him, she believed, a .38 pistol with a four-inch barrel but no automatic weapons, as far as she knew. Benny did not especially like guns.

She volunteered that he was a weight lifter who did not drink or use hard drugs but smoked marijuana occasionally as well as about a pack and a half of Camels a day. He had left a Kawasaki 900 motorcy- cle at her house. Because she was broke, she had sold the bike for eight hundred dollars and was now living on that. She had been working for a gold and jewelry shop whose owner had recently been arrested for dealing in drugs and stolen property. Fortunately, she had quit that job because she had worried about having her own proba- tion revoked.

As for Bartley, Sherry admitted knowing him casually, said she disliked him, and described his Honda 500 turbo bike, red and silver, that she believed he kept at his sister's trailer in Oliver Springs. She named the sister and supplied her telephone number.

Sherry was proud of her performance before Cloninger, who had seemed downright sympathetic and had thanked her for her coopera- tion. She believed that she had sprinkled her monologue with just the right convincing mixture of specific fact and bullshit, giving both more and less than she had been asked, playing the verbal shell game she knew so well. From what she could tell, it had worked, because she was no longer aware of anyone following her. About what Foust may have said to the FBI about her and whether she could continue to trust him, she was less sure—but in that she had little choice and had to rely on instinct.

Two days after the interview, however, an acquaintance who worked at the federal building in Knoxville relayed a message that the FBI was about to close in on Benny and Donnie that very night. Sherry immediately telephoned a motel in Crossville.

"I'm coming," she said. "Be ready. Just get in the car and don't ask no questions. Everything'll be okay."

16

I
T WAS SHERRY'S POLICY always to hide the boys at a motel that was close to an interstate, in case of the need for a fast getaway and because these were generally crowded and more conducive to anonymity. The one at Crossville, some thirty-five miles west of Harriman, was near the I-40 exit. Believing it might be a mistake this time to wait for nightfall, she arrived there in midafternoon, circled the parking lot twice to check for cops, paid the bill in cash, and kept the motor running as Benny and Donnie climbed in.

"What's the big rush this time?" Benny asked.

"I got a tip. The Feds might be on to you. I got to get you out of this area."

"Where we going?"

"Haven't thought of that yet."

She did not decide whether to turn west or east until reaching I-40 and, simply because it came first, headed up the east on-ramp. In less than a mile the traffic began to thicken and slow; it soon crawled to a halt. Up ahead they could see flashing red lights.

"Goddamn it!" Donnie said. "An accident! We'll never get out of here! Turn around!"

"You crazy?" Sherry said. "Turn around where? You want them to think I'm drunk? Keep your lid on. They'll think you escaped from the loony bin."

A patrol car coming the other way crossed over the median and joined the head of the double line of traffic; two more police cars passed on the shoulder to the right.

"I'm running!" Bartley said and started climbing over the front seat to get at the door. With a mighty stiff-arm Benny sent him crashing back and told him to calm down or he'd break his neck. It was just a big accident, was all it was. They'd get through.

Sherry turned up the radio and began singing along. Then she fell silent. They were close enough now to see that there had been no accident.

It was a roadblock. Standing on the highway, police were looking into every car and checking licenses.

They were all too scared to speak, even Bartley, who pressed himself into a corner of the rear seat. When he tried to hide on the floor, Benny pulled him up by the shirt and Sherry told him for God's sake to sit up and try to act normal. The cops would see him down there, and it would all be over for sure. "Just don't let out a peep, can you?"

It seemed to take forever to reach the head of the line. Benny slowly removed the .38 from his gym bag and placed it under his seat. Finally Sherry rolled down her window and, switching off the radio, gave the officer a smile and asked what the matter was. Somebody rob a bank?

The officer looked in and asked to see Sherry's license. He examined it. Then he said:

"Sorry to detain you, Mrs. Wong. You're right. Somebody did rob a bank, in Crossville. They won't get far."

"Well, good luck to you all," Sherry said. "C'ain't have no criminals running around, Lord knows. Times is bad enough."

They held their breaths until the roadblock was well behind them, and then they let out whoops and hollers and yip-yip-yips and shouted hallelujahs.

"You are one cool-headed bitch," Bartley said. "God*damn!*"

"Don't you forget it, numbskull."

Deciding that the entire Harriman–Oak Ridge–Knoxville area was too hot, Sherry drove to Gatlinburg, seventy-five miles distant, and deposited the boys at the Homestead House motel in a room with a view of the Smokies and a kitchen. She stocked the refrigerator with food and drink and told them they could expect to stay put for a couple of days. The cops would be unlikely to look for them at a resort, but they should take no chances. They should not leave the room except maybe to take a quick swim in the pool while they let the maid clean up, so as not to arouse suspicions. She told Donnie, who was worried about running short of coke, that Roger would rejoin them soon. As she left, she hung the "Do Not Disturb" sign on the door-knob.

Inwardly Sherry was eaten up with anxiety. She spent the next forty-eight hours on desperate errands. Closing up her house, she distributed her furniture and other belongings among various relatives and tried, and failed, to convince her mom and dad that she was doing the right thing by helping Benny. Like everyone else in East Tennessee, they knew that he was on the run. They begged Sherry to give him up; she said she could not, he was her one true love, she could not desert him now. But where would she go? What would she do? Sherry said that she did not know what would happen to her, but she had made a commitment and would stick by it. Her old room was waiting for her, E. L. and Louise told her, if only she would come home. She left her doll collection and other belongings with them, said she would be back one day, and asked them to pray for her.

As for Renee, Sherry told her only that it was time for Mommy to take a holiday. She would not be gone long. Renee cried when Sherry kissed the child good-bye.

Getting Roger out of jail required some doing, but Sherry managed it, midway through the first week in June. Because Roger was unable to tell Carol where he had buried money that could finance his seventy-thousand-dollar bail, Sherry gave some of her jewelry to a Chattanooga bondsman as down payment on the required ten percent, securing his release along with the Thunderbird. Because Roger had never been convicted of a felony, the judge accepted his promise to return the car as evidence for the trial.

It was time for a powwow at Gatlinburg. Sherry, Carol, and Roger gathered with Donnie and Benny in the motel room to map strategy. Although he was technically free for the time being, Roger knew that the evidence against him in Rome was overwhelming; he had no intention of standing trial and was as committed to escape as the others. To Sherry's dismay, despite the Rome fiasco and other proof of his incompetence, Epperson at once assumed again his role as Straw Boss. What was worse, Benny and Donnie listened to him

with childlike attention, hanging on his every word and telling Sherry
to keep her mouth shut. She may have issued warnings that had
proved correct. She may have saved their necks by hiding them. She
may have been the one person shrewd and brave enough to have gotten them past a roadblock and to have squirreled them away where
they were safe for now—but she was still a woman and ought to
know her place. When Benny threatened to cream her if she kept
interrupting Roger as he held forth on the future, she bolted from the
room, jumped in her car, and took off for home, convinced at last that
her parents were right.

But on the road she knew that her heart could not let her abandon her Biggin. Why am I so crazy lonely over you, she asked herself.
"I just went to get you all some beer," she said when she returned,
knowing she would never leave him again.

Kentucky was the answer, Roger said. He had endless contacts up
there, and they would be better off out of Tennessee.

"You said I needed a vacation," Carol said. "You promised you'd
take me to Florida."

"Chop," Sherry said, "what you need is a brain transplant."

"We'll go anywhere we want," Roger said, "after we knock off
that doctor."

On June 7, the five of them headed for Kentucky in the Thunderbird.
Sherry left her Charger with her parents, telling them not to object
when the repo man came for it. She figured that her car was too well
known to the FBI, too much associated with Benny, and that it was
not worth worrying about the payments while on the run. She gam-
bled that the police would not be looking for the T-bird, since Roger
was legally out on bond and the police would assume that he would
be smart enough to stay clear of his fugitive companions. In Roger's
case, the way Sherry saw it, it was less a matter of outsmarting the
cops than of his being more of an idiot than anyone could imagine.
She was permitting herself to be drawn along in the wake of Roger's
decisions because all she cared about now was to be with Benny
when whatever happened happened. Agitated one minute and emotionally wrung out the next, she felt that she had finally lost control of
her life and had no choice but to surrender to events. If that was what
standing by your man meant, so be it.

There was hardly enough room for the five of them in the car.

With all their suitcases and belongings, including Benny's weights, they decided to rent a U-Haul trailer. They set off looking for all the world like a family that had pulled up stakes. On the way north they stopped off at the veterans' bar in Lake City so Roger could negotiate with the fence for marijuana and cocaine and various weapons and ammunition—an arsenal that included high-powered rifles, pistols of various calibers, and a .45 caliber Mini-Mac 10 handheld machine gun that Roger said was a favorite of international dope smugglers, as lethal a weapon as money could buy. Let the FBI come after them. They would be ready.

For once, Sherry managed to keep her opinions to herself, but beneath her uncharacteristic silence she began to wonder whether Roger was not only stupid but stark raving mad. It was all a game to him, cops and robbers. As a kid he had probably played Junior G-Man. Now he was pretending to be Al Capone.

They stopped that evening at a motel in Corbin, twelve miles south of London on I-75. After a dinner of prime rib, they sat around smoking dope and Roger revealed his latest brainstorm. They needed to buy time, he said, to pull a job or two first, because they were running low on cash. They would have to buy a different car. Then they could close in on the doctor over in Fleming-Neon. The big job would have to be planned down to the least detail; there could be no screwups this time.

They would get off the road, away from the pressures of the hunt, to stay in a place where the cops would never think to look for them. Now that he was back in home territory, ideas were coming to him thick and fast. What they would do was to hide out in the woods for a spell. He knew just the spot.

"You mean camp out?" Sherry asked, emerging from a dopey reverie. She was onto her second joint, double what she normally permitted herself. "You mean sleep on the ground? Straw Boss, I ain't no damn heifer. I didn't make this trip to drop dead of pneumonia."

The weather was mild, Roger said. They would secure some equipment. He had been in the Navy, and he knew what bivouacking meant and what survival meant. Do what he advised, and everyone would be fine. Weak sisters were invited to decamp pronto.

Donnie complained that he was the only one without a girlfriend along. He was no outdoorsman; it would be no fun out there in the woods alone, without a warm body against him. He spent the next couple of hours on the phone to various females, including his ex-wife and Rebecca Hannah. He told them to hang tight, lover boy would be sending for them. They were in for one romantic holiday.

In the morning Roger drove them along a back road that skirted a section of the Daniel Boone National Forest. This was not the mountains but a hilly terrain of piney woods, rivers, and glimpses of broad lakes through the green. Daniel Boone had passed through there on his way north from the Cumberland Gap; it had been the site of Kentucky's bloodiest Indian wars. A heavily visited recreation spot during the height of the summer, it was nearly deserted early in June.

After a few miles they came on a man and two boys, stripped to the waist and pouring sweat, and a woman working in a vegetable garden beside a creek. Donnie and Benny recognized the man as Harold "Sky" Clontz, an old friend of Roger's whom they had met on their previous Kentucky foray in May. Clontz did not appear over-joyed to see them. He paused in his digging, leaning on his hoe, eyeing them. Roger got out to speak to him as the boys and the woman continued turning over the earth in silence.

Roger said that Clontz would help them. You could always count on old Sky. He had asked no questions. They waited for Clontz at his log house up the road.

Clontz proved hospitable enough. He gave them moonshine, pouring the clear liquid from jars. When Roger asked him if he was having any trouble from the FBI, he said no, but that the FBI might be having some. They were trying to nail him for interstate transportation of stolen property and were coming up empty. He loaned the gang a tent big enough for the five of them.

Sherry and Carol drove into London to buy sleeping bags, air mattresses, a Coleman stove and lantern, frying pan, coffeepot, cups and plates, and other provisions from a list Benny wrote out. Together, with the boys lying low, they registered at the entrance to the Holly Bay campground, paying a fee for the 8th through the 10th. Carol signed in as Carol Malone.

They picked out a campsite on the shore of Laurel River Lake—idyllic, a vacationer's dream, the only sounds birdsong, the wind in the pines, and the lapping of the waters, a fantasy in blues and greens. Occasionally the sound of an ax cracked through the air, or a car starting up; there were a few other campers here and there, nowhere close.

That night they roasted wieners and marshmallows and smoked dope. Roger, Carol, and Donnie did a few lines while Sherry watched Benny work out in moonlight on a weight bench borrowed from Clontz. She played her newest tape on the T-bird's deck, the Allman Brothers' "Midnight Rider," a hardassed redneck beat invading the night.

Except for the occasional shower and one big storm, a rolling black blizzard that sent them to huddle in the car, it was like that for several nights and days. They extended their registration through the 16th. Benny managed a version of his beef stew; Carol, the resourceful earth muffin, produced bread from an oven of heaped stones. They swam in the lake, showered in stalls provided—a more wholesome display of vigor could not have been found at a Scout Jamboree, except for the dope and sex.

And constantly they schemed. Roger summoned a Knoxville fence who supposedly would set up jobs but who proved more interested in camping than robbery. He was sent packing after two days. Donnie's ex-wife, pregnant and not in the mood for outdoor living, arrived and quickly departed. Another of his women came and went. At night the occasional grunt and cry escaped the tent to mingle with an owl's hoots, but the mood was more somber than passionate. Scoring cash was on their minds.

When the men left the campsite, they did so before the ranger's hut opened or after it had shut for the evening. They set off talking of raiding a dope dealer or a fence or, one night, of swooping down on a high-stakes poker game that Roger knew of in the mountains. Each time, they returned empty-handed. There was talk of robbing the house of the mother of TV's Bionic Man, Lee Majors, who supposedly owned property in the area, but this, too, came to nothing.

Tempers shortened. Roger grew especially irascible, cuffing Carol around and complaining of having too much responsibility for the general welfare. When Benny made squirrel chili—the bounty of target practice—Sherry refused it, calling it trash food. The chef sulked. They could not nest there forever, Sherry said, living off the land and Straw Boss's horseshit. If they had to camp out, Carol whined, why not on the white sands of Florida?

Sunday, June 16th, 1985, was Father's Day. At about seven o'clock that evening, Roger, Donnie, and Benny drove to Clontz's house.

They found Harold sitting on a log drinking beer with a few men who had been cutting pine posts that day. Roger asked to borrow Harold's 1975 blue and white Chevy van, saying Harold could use the T-bird if he needed to go somewhere. They wanted the van for a few hours, that was all. Harold said he wasn't going anywhere and gestured toward the cases of beer stacked up. He said the keys were in the van.

At about eleven-thirty that night up in Jackson County, some forty miles northeast of Laurel River Lake, two young men in a pickup were driving home on a two-lane blacktop road. This was rolling farm country, towns and villages few and far between. Frankie Baldwin and Mike Riley had spent the evening at the Hilltop drive-in movie. Heading toward Annville, they crested a hill and were passing through the village of Gray Hawk when all of a sudden a van pulled out of a driveway directly in front of them.

Baldwin slammed on his brakes, fishtailing and coming within inches of slamming into the rear of the van—which lumbered ahead, slowly picking up speed, then quickly veered right onto a side road as Baldwin leaned on his horn.

Baldwin and Riley marveled at the close call and cursed whoever was the idiot driving that van. What had the guy been thinking, and whose van was it, anyhow? They agreed that it had been black or dark blue and white or silver but could not settle on the make. A strange vehicle was rare in those parts. It had lurched onto the road from the driveway of Ed and Bessie Morris's house—they were certain of that: the driveway ran between the Morris place and the gas station and post office the family owned. Frankie Baldwin had known the Morrises all his life; his father had been in the car business with Ed. Why would those old folks be having late-night visitors, and on Father's Day of all Sundays? None of their children owned a van, Frankie thought. It didn't make sense.

Sherry was awake by the fire when the boys returned well past midnight. They had money, Benny's take was over a thousand, but they did not seem very happy about it. Donnie was snorting coke like a fiend. Benny refused to talk; he walked to the water's edge and threw stone after stone into the lake. Roger said that now that they had some money, they would leave tomorrow.

* * *

(*Left*) Lester Burns, "the people's lawyer," and his custom-made bus, Somerset, Kentucky, 1982 (note diamond rings). (*Courtesy Lester Burns and Lexington Herald-Leader.*)

(*Below*) Brushy Mountain State Prison, East Tennessee, where Sherry met Benny. (*Courtesy Chris Cawood.*)

Benny Hodge displays his muscles, 1984. (*Courtesy Sherry Sheets.*)

Benny Hodge, chief cook at Anderson County jail, prepares Christmas dinner, 1982. (*Courtesy Clinton Courier-News.*)

(*Left*) Benny, Donnie Bartley (rear), and Sherry ride the roller coaster at Six Flags Over Georgia, May 26, 1985, before a robbery. (*Courtesy Sherry Sheets.*)

Miners' shacks, built 1912, line the road from Fleming-Neon to McRoberts, 1991. (*Courtesy Chris Cawood.*)

Main Street, Fleming-Neon, 1991. (*Courtesy Chris Cawood.*)

(*Left*) Dr. Roscoe J. Acker's clinic, Fleming-Neon, 1991. His house is just down the road. (*Courtesy Chris Cawood.*)

(*Above*) Dr. Acker's house, Fleming-Neon, where Tammy Acker was murdered in 1985 and $1.9 million in cash was stolen. (*Courtesy Chris Cawood.*)

Tammy Dee Acker, 1962-1985.(*Courtesy Whitesburg Mountain Eagle.*)

(*Below*) Benny being searched, Laurel County jail, 1987. Officials expected an escape attempt. (*Courtesy Alice Cornett.*)

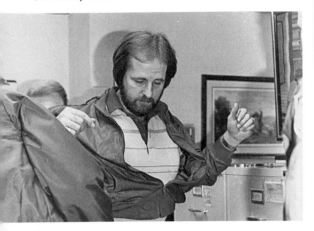

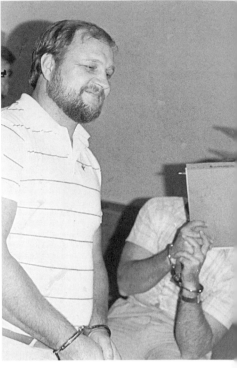

(*Above*) Clowning around at the Laurel County jail: Roger Epperson (left) and Benny Hodge (hiding face), 1987, during their trial for the Gray Hawk murders. (*Courtesy Alice Cornett.*)

(*Left*) Roger Epperson, Laurel County jail, 1987, on trial for the murders of Ed and Bessie Morris. (*Courtesy Alice Cornett.*)

ROGER DALE EPPERSON   BENNY LEE HODGE   DONALD TERRY BARTL

Mug shots, Orange County, Florida, jail, August 1985: the end of a long, deadly crime spree. (*Courtesy Kentucky State Police.*)

Lt. Danny Webb, commander, KSP post, Hazard, Kentucky, 1991. His contacts helped crack the case. (*Courtesy Suzanne O'Brien.*)

Sherry Sheets Hodge (left) and Carol Keeney Epperson await the verdict, Letcher County Courthouse, during the Acker trial, 1986. (*Courtesy Whitesburg Mountain Eagle.*)

The Acker trial dominates the news.

(*Right*) James Wiley Craft, Commonwealth's Attorney, Letcher County Courthouse, 1991. He prosecuted the Acker and Morris murder-robberies. (*Courtesy Suzanne O'Brien.*)

Circuit Judge F. Byrd Hogg in chambers, Letcher County Courthouse, 1991. He presided at the Acker trial. (*Courtesy Suzanne O'Brien.*)

Tawny Rose Acker and Dr. Roscoe J. Acker watch the trial, Letcher County Courthouse, 1986. (*Courtesy Lexington Herald-Leader.*)

Donald Terry Bartley testifies for the prosecution, Letcher County Courthouse, 1986. (*Courtesy Whitesburg Mountain Eagle.*)

(*Left*) Lester Burns, indicted, confronts the media: "I will sail from this court on the ship of truth." Lexington Federal Courthouse, 1987. (*Courtesy Alice Cornett.*)

(*Below*) Benny and Sherry pledge eternal love before the death sentence is pronounced, Letcher County jail, 1986. They had a suicide pact. (*Courtesy Whitesburg Mountain Eagle.*)

Bobby Morris, Jerry Morris, and James Wiley Craft (*right*), Laurel County Courthouse, 1987. (*Courtesy Alice Cornett.*)

(*Below and right*) Sherry, hand-cuffed and in tears, led away after her reunion with Benny, Laurel County jail, 1987. She would not see him for three years. (*Courtesy Alice Cornett.*)

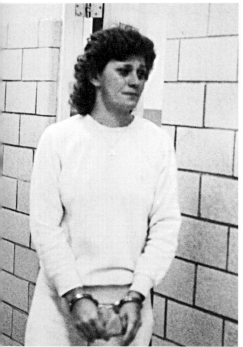

(*Below*) Sherry Sheets at work at Rockwood Sportswear, Tennessee, 1991, sewing a jacket. (*Courtesy Suzanne O'Brien.*)

(*Above*) Sherry Sheets Hodge doing time at Lexington Federal Correctional Institution, 1989. (*Courtesy Sherry Sheets.*)

On Monday morning Jerry Morris, who at forty was the youngest of four children, went to check on his parents before going off to work at the family's used car lot. His father was sixty-three and had lost fifteen pounds over the past three weeks, suffering from what the doctors called walking pneumonia; his mother was sixty-nine, had had cancer, and was not strong, although she still cooked three meals a day and ironed his father's shirts and did her quilting. Jerry's daily routine was to pay an early call on his oldest brother, Bobby, who ran the family gas station and post office, before making sure that their parents next door were all right.

That morning, which was bright and turning warm, Bobby told Jerry that he had heard something peculiar the night before. He had gone out back, it must have been around eleven o'clock or so, to get a breath of fresh air and look at the stars. It was such a beautiful night, he had never seen such a sky, not a cloud in it, the stars so bright they seemed to hang there close enough to touch. He had heard something odd—four or five popping noises that sounded like firecrackers. It must have been somebody getting ready for the Fourth of July. The noises had sounded as if they were coming from the direction of their parents' house—but that could not have been, unless there had been kids roaming around.

Jerry had better see to Mom and Dad, Bobby said. By that time of the morning, nearly half past eight, you could usually see Bessie Morris through the glass of the sun porch, cooking breakfast in her bathrobe. But she had not even opened the kitchen door yet. Bobby hoped his father had not taken a turn for the worse, the poor old guy.

Jerry strolled over from the gas station, whistling through the morning air, which was fresh with the smell of newly mown grass. He was about to knock on the outside door to the sun porch when, to his surprise, he saw that it was open a crack—strange, because his mother fretted about burglars, even though Gray Hawk, with only a hundred or so souls living in it, had not known any sort of crime for years and years. He entered.

It was many months before Jerry could bear to talk about what happened next. Even then, he could hardly get the words out:

"The light was on in the sun room, what we call the sun room, it's got glass, an enclosed room, but the kitchen door hadn't been opened and a lot of times Mother and Daddy would get up and eat in their nightclothes, you know, but when that kitchen door was opened you knowed it was all right to go in and I waited till about twenty or twenty-five minutes after eight and it had never opened up and I told my brother Bobby, I said Bobby I am going to go over and check on them because I've got to go to work and so I walked over to the sun room and I always when I got hold of the kitchen door I would always say 'Mother, it's Jerry, don't let me scare you.' Well I got hold of the door and I said 'Mother, don't let me—'" Jerry had to pause for a while, he was crying so hard.

"And I saw Daddy's feet laying on the kitchen floor—they were tied up. Then I stepped on in and he laid on the floor all tied up and looked like his face was—oh, Lord." He had to stop again. "So I knew from looking he was dead, the blood and his face and all, but I got down over him and sort of shook him like you would shake a baby, you know, and I laid my hand on him and I thought Lord where is Mommy at and where Daddy was laying you could see down the hall to the bedroom." He had to pause and take a breath. "So I run down the hall to the bedroom and there was Mother laid across the foot of the bed, her hands been tied up and her feet was tied up, they was blood all over and I knew she was dead, too, but I got down over Mother and I thought Lord, Lord, how am I going to tell Bobby and the next thing I knew I was outside, and then I hollered at Bobby, I said Lord God help me somebody has killed Mommy and Daddy and Bobby run over there and I thought Lord keep him from seeing them and I got hold of him and after that I really don't know what happened."

They abandoned the campsite in a hurry that morning. They left the equipment by the lake, hitched up the trailer, and on the way out of the forest asked Harold Clontz to retrieve his tent and to save the stuff that was theirs, they would be back eventually to pick it up.

For once Roger did not seem to know what to do or where to go. He drove north on I-75, turned around and headed back into London, kept going on to Corbin, turned around again, exited at London, and instructed Carol to check them into the Ramada Inn. They occupied three rooms.

They gathered over pizza that night in Roger and Carol's room. He was not forgetting the doctor, Roger said, but it would be wise to get out of Kentucky for the time being. He had been on the phone to a friend in Florida; everything was set for them there. Carol seemed delighted.

Sherry asked no questions, believing that she was better off not knowing what had happened to send them running again, glad at least to be sleeping in a bed. Not that she thought that she would learn much if she asked. Benny included, the men were treating her as no better than a camp follower; for now, she accepted that role. She telephoned Renee and told her that Mom was enjoying her holiday and would be home soon.

Investigators from the Kentucky State Police were in Gray Hawk by nine o'clock and found that Ed and Bessie Morris had been shot to death. The bedroom where Mrs. Morris lay had been turned upside down, drawers emptied, clothes strewn everywhere. On the floor beside the bed officers found an open Bible, its pages sprinkled with pressed four-leaf clovers. More clovers dotted the carpet, some of them soaked with blood. His mother had had cancer in one eye, Bobby Morris said, "but she could find every four-leaf clover there was."

Mr. Morris lay with his pockets turned out. His father usually kept a fair amount of cash on hand, Bobby said, enough to buy a used car and to cash checks for neighbors when the banks were closed. Ed Morris had loved to trade. You could often find him at the weekly auto auctions around London.

Investigators photographed and videotaped the bodies and the entire house inside and out. Both victims had been tied with electrical wire, Bessie Morris with a cord ripped from an alarm clock that was stopped at ten forty-three. The gunman or gunmen had tried to muffle the sounds of the shots: a pillow with a large, singed hole in it covered Ed Morris's head; another holed pillow lay propped against Bessie. In all, five bullets of two different calibers were recovered: two in the crawlspace under the kitchen floor, one in the box springs of the bed, one in Ed Morris's head, and one in Bessie's left breast.

At the autopsies, which were given highest priority and performed at the University of Kentucky Medical Center in Lexington under the supervision of Associate Chief Medical Examiner and Professor of Pathology Dr. John C. Hunsacker III, it was determined that Ed Morris had been severely beaten before being shot twice, one bullet grazing his forehead, nicking a kitchen cabinet and penetrating the floor, the other lodging at the base of his skull. The top of his right ear was blown off where the fatal bullet had entered. A pistol's muzzle had caused two fractures of the skull before death.

Someone had jammed a wool man's sock into Ed Morris's mouth and tied a stocking airtight around his head and face, blocking his nasal passages; he would have suffocated to death had a bullet not done the job first. The amount of blood escaped from the wound through his ear showed that his heart had been pumping when he was shot. The bullet found in his head was thirty-eight caliber, fired from either a .38 special or a .357 Magnum pistol, the ammunition for these weapons being interchangeable. The two bullets found under the house beneath the body had come from a different gun: they were nine-millimeter slugs.

Bessie Morris had been shot twice in the back, once with the same .38 special that had killed her husband, once with the same nine-millimeter gun that had fired the two bullets through the kitchen floor. Either shot would have been fatal; which had been fired first could not be determined. One had entered near the spine, passed through the lung, and exited just above the nipple of the left breast, then passed through the bed, hitting the carpet and bouncing back up into the springs; the other had gone through the spine, the aorta, the sac around the heart, and the heart itself, penetrating the front ribs before coming to rest in the breast. She had been lying on her stomach across the bed when she was shot.

Unless one person had used two different guns on both victims, an unlikely hypothesis, both had been shot by two separate gunmen. Why such overkill had been thought necessary was not apparent; perhaps the killers enjoyed their work or for obscure reasons felt it advisable to share the guilt. The old couple—Mrs. Morris toothless and one-eyed, her husband of forty-eight years grown feeble from illness—could hardly have offered much resistance.

Bobby Morris told the police that his father had kept a .38 pistol on top of the refrigerator; what make it had been, Bobby could not recall, but it was missing. Whether it had been one of the two murder weapons—both of which had probably been manufactured by Smith & Wesson, as forensic analysis of the rifling on the bullets indicated—was anyone's guess. It seemed more likely that the killers, who were experienced enough criminals not to believe in leaving witnesses, would dispose of the murder weapons and keep the stolen gun, if any—but that much was guesswork. As for the possible identity of the gunmen, no one had a guess.

*   *   *

On Tuesday, June 18, leaving the others at the Ramada Inn, Roger and Carol made the rounds of several car lots. At Earl Bowles's place on Main Street in London they spotted something that looked to them like the sort of vehicle the FBI might favor, a dark blue 1978 Oldsmobile Delta 88 four-door sedan, as staid and anonymous a car as they could find, and one fitted with the all-important Kentucky plates. Roger peeled off twenty-four hundred-dollar bills; Carol signed the invoice as Malone.

With Carol following, Roger drove the T-bird north to Mount Vernon and left it with a couple whom he had known for many years and felt he could trust. He asked them not to tell anyone that they had seen him.

That afternoon they slapped four new tires on the Olds and headed south. They stopped in Lake City to fence some jewelry and score some dope and at Carol's house in Clinton, which was owned by her father, to leave some belongings. They dropped the trailer in Atlanta and sped on to Florida.

The double funeral drew nearly every member of the church and friends of Ed and Bessie Morris from all over Eastern Kentucky. Among the mourners, none seemed more grief-stricken than one of the honorary pallbearers, who dabbed at his tears throughout the service. He had driven over from Hazard with his wife, his daughter, his sister, and two of his three sons. His name was Eb Epperson, and he had called Ed Morris the best friend he had in the world. Of "Bug" Epperson's immediate family, only his eldest child, Roger, was not in attendance.

17

ROGER'S FLORIDA RESOURCES WERE CLUSTERED in the Daytona Beach area, most of them former Kentuckians; Carol had once been close to a Clinton businessman and dope dealer who was now a resident of West Palm Beach; Sherry's friend Pat Mason was living in Hallandale, a suburb of Miami, working for an automobile broker— so they were not without contacts that far from home. During the drive down, Roger announced that the general plan of operations would be to establish headquarters around Daytona for the time being, to do a few jobs to build up some capital, finally to close in on the Letcher County doc, and to leave the country.

He had in mind fleeing to Bimini, an island less than fifty miles from Miami that Roger said had no extradition treaty with the U.S. While the others were not precisely sure what extradition meant, and were not aware that Roger was mistaken about the absence of a treaty, they found his scheme seductive. They would buy a fast boat like the ones featured on "Miami Vice" and run dope into the coast and live it up lolling in the sun wearing pastel clothes and sipping rum.

In the meanwhile they checked into the Sands Motel on the beach in Daytona. Neither Sherry nor Benny had ever seen the ocean before; they spent their first afternoon frolicking in the surf, Benny showing off his muscles and thirty-inch waist, Sherry demure in a one-piece she bought down the street. When the others joined them,

Carol turned heads in a white bikini that complemented her tawny skin and black hair. Sherry caught Benny staring and told him that if he didn't watch himself, she would kill him.

Roger had the habit of hiding money in his athletic shoes, which he left on the sand while he went in for a swim. Puppylike, Donnie romped in after him, presenting a complex and colorful picture in bathing trunks, his body adorned with nine tattoos—including a star on his right wrist, a duck with the word "love" superimposed on his left upper arm, "Donnie" on his upper right back, and a spider and a butterfly on his right calf. Sherry called him Sandwich Board. When Carol decided she wanted a drink, she took Roger's money from his shoe and picked her sexy way up to the motel.

Roger and Donnie left the water before Carol returned. Drying himself off, Roger bent down to check inside his shoes. He shook one and then the other and began yelling at Bartley, accusing him of stealing and threatening to twist his head off. Sherry told him to leave Donnie alone.

"Dragon Lady kyped your roll. She went to buy a drink, is all."

"Is that right? She did that? Well, that is going to be one sorry bitch."

When Carol came back with her margarita, she handed Roger the change. He told her through clenched teeth to put down her drink, they were going in the water. She did not want to go in, Carol said. It was late and getting cool. They were the only people left on the beach.

"Put that shit down. We're going in the water."

Carol obeyed. Roger took her by the hand and led her roughly into the surf. The slope of the sand was gradual. He pulled her out farther until the waves were breaking against her breasts and into her face and she had to keep hopping not to drink in saltwater. The others watched her trying to get free of him, flailing with one arm, thrashing like a gaffed fish. Roger's shoulders were still above the water.

He let go of her hand suddenly and grabbed her with both hands around her throat. His screaming—"Bitch! Fucking lying bitch!"—drifted in to the beach over the noise of the surf. He shoved her under and yanked her up by the throat above his head, screaming into her face, and pushed her under, again and again, jerking her up and plunging her down as if she were no more than a kitten.

By the time Sherry and Donnie and Benny could struggle through the waves to reach them and pry Roger loose and carry Carol to the beach, she was turning blue and passing out. Sherry rolled her onto her stomach and pounded on her back. Seawater trickled from her mouth. She began to breathe, cough, at last to cry.

"She'll never do that again," Roger said. "Nobody takes my money."

By morning the marks of Roger's fingers were visible on her throat. He advised her to get some sun.

It took them a few days to locate a suitable apartment. One night the others talked Sherry into accompanying them to a nightclub a few blocks from the Sands. She put aside her aversion to clubs and bars, lured by the promise of live country music. She had never heard of the band or the singer, but maybe they would cheer her up. Looking at herself in the mirror, she thought she had aged ten years in the past month.

It was called Castaways: bamboo and wicker tables and chairs on different levels around the dance floor and stage, red and green running lights, the walls and ceiling draped with fishing nets, waitresses in coconut-shell bras. The band was adequate, the singer a pert brunette from Nashville, or so she claimed, doing okay versions of classic Patsy Cline. The only thing that bugged Sherry was their waitress, a blonde flirt who rang a cowbell hung around her neck every time Benny gave her a tip and bent way over scooping up the money so Benny could gawk at her coconuts. Every waitress had to wear a cowbell, and they were clanging all over the room. It drove Sherry nuts. She broke training to order a double strawberry daquiri, then another and another.

At tables pushed together behind them sat a large party, four or five couples, including a mother and two daughters and a man who looked like Willie Nelson, wearing a T-shirt and jeans, a red bandana around his head, an earring, and braids. Donnie, always a menace on his own, started chatting up one of the daughters, even asking her to dance, right in front of her date, who told him to bug off. Trying to head off trouble, Sherry led Donnie onto the dance floor and did her best to wear him out, but he was so coked up he could have done the Cotton-eyed Joe to Miami.

When they returned to the table Roger and Carol—she had been mixing cocaine and Valium all day—had managed to get into an argument with the party behind them. It was at the shouting stage. One of the women called Roger a hick and a bum and a big slob. He smashed the neck of his beer bottle against the edge of the table and jabbed the jagged thing through the air, snarling and demanding who was ready to get cut first. Carol told the woman not to talk to Roger like that. The woman sprang forward and dumped Carol over in her chair and started stomping on her with high heels. Another woman fell on Carol and tore at her blouse.

"You take Chop on one at a time or forget it!" Sherry shouted. She grabbed both women by the hair and yanked them up. One of them called Sherry a bitch. Sherry shoved her back and Benny slapped the woman's face.

It was a free-for-all after that, glasses and bottles flying, women clawing at each other, men wrestling and tumbling on the floor, tables overturned. The band struck up "The Star-Spangled Banner" to no effect. In the middle of it all Sherry heard the waitress screaming that someone had stolen her cowbell. "You did it! You've got my cowbell! Give it back!" She came at Sherry.

"Here's your cowbell," Sherry said, and busted her right in the chops. She cratered.

"Benny!" Sherry shouted. "Donnie! This ain't good sense! We got to get out of here!"

They made it through the door before the cops arrived and ran flat-out to the motel. In the room they laughed and broke out more beer and dope. Except for Carol, who was hurting all over, no one was injured.

"Me and Benny was the only ones throwed a punch," Sherry said. "The rest of you all never swung a lick. I tell you one dang thing, it's a hell of a way to act when we's on the run!"

In their room Sherry and Benny undressed each other and she told him how proud she was that he had slapped that dogfaced woman for calling her a bitch. He said he'd do anything for his Booger.

"Right smart, you will. Do it all night."

They found the perfect accommodations for themselves in Ormond Beach, just north of Daytona. It was one of forty condos in a compound grandly named the Garden of New Britain, clustered around a swimming pool and tennis courts, behind a high fence off Chipping-wood Lane. This was on the ocean side of the Intracoastal Waterway, a block and a half from Highway A1A and the beach. Theirs was Number 55. Like all the others, it was painted white with gray wood trim and a sloping red roof, semidetached, two stories, nestled amid attractive landscaping that included lawns and red and yellow hibiscus and palm trees. They could enjoy three bedrooms and a living room, all completely furnished, and a kitchen with built-in appliances and stocked with dishes and pots and pans. The downstairs bedroom, claimed by Benny and Sherry, had sliding glass doors that opened onto a small yard; the upstairs bedrooms came with balconies ideal for sunbathing in the nude.

Even with the Garden of New Britain's reasonable rent, six hundred a month, it was time to replenish their supply of cash. They began by faking busts of high school students in the tried-and-true method of tracing local dealers; Roger pinpointed other scores through contacts made at two nearby bars, the Pelican Lounge in Daytona and The Barn. Sherry complained that the addicts among them drained off too much of the communal nest egg. Nearly every day, a man driving a taxi dropped by to deliver drugs. While the others got stoned, Benny and Sherry ran and worked out on the beach.

Donnie became hard to handle. His habit had become voracious, up to three and four grams of coke a day and nearly constant marijuana. The stuff would run low, they would have to do another job—and these were penny-ante scores, comparatively speaking. Donnie also spent plenty on women. He was hitting the bars four nights out of five, bringing a different girl home with him every time, bragging and jiving. Sherry considered him deranged, a sex fiend who apparently had to prove himself nightly, and she never knew what might be hanging around the kitchen in the morning, slurping coffee or throwing up in the sink. Going to the beach and swimming in the pool were great, but Sherry was getting her fill of the Sunshine State sooner than she would have thought.

When the boys left on an excursion to Knoxville to do some jobs the fence there had finally set up for them, a reunion with Pat Mason proved an enjoyable break. Sherry and Carol flew to Miami. Pat, tan and looking fit and on top of the world driving a new Mercedes—on loan from her boss—and accompanied by a stunning woman, drove everyone to Fort Lauderdale to celebrate the Fourth of July. That evening they were on their way to the beach to watch the fireworks, cruising the Lauderdale strip in bumper-to-bumper traffic, feeling free and wild away from the men. A single guy pulled up beside them in a convertible and gave them the eye. Sherry, who had had a couple of beers and a joint, lowered the window and began talking to him, saying that there was one girl in their car that thought he was the cutest thing she'd ever seen, and that if he guessed which one of them she was, she'd jump into his car with him. The guy pointed to Carol.

"Go ahead, Chop," Sherry said. "I dare you."

Carol hesitated; Sherry double-dared her. Carol was out the door just as the traffic started to move. She ran to the convertible, which was barely creeping ahead, vaulted in beside the startled driver, gave him a kiss, and jumped out to hurry back. Horns honked up and down the line.

"You see?" Sherry teased her. "You might've could've run off with that boy. See what you'll do when Straw Boss ain't a-looking? He'd kill you if he knew. Poor Chop, you ain't nothing but a slave to love, Lord help you."

The boys returned on the sixth. Their trip to Tennessee had been only moderately successful, but by the middle of the next week there seemed to be plenty of money to go around again. Sherry was not asking any questions. When she telephoned a friend in Knoxville, however, just to pass the time, saying that she was on a Florida vacation without being more specific than that, she ended up with an earful.

That was a coincidence that Sherry was in Florida, the friend said. Was she anywhere near Palm Beach? Not that she knew of, Sherry said. She had never been near the place. Well, the friend said, the Knoxville paper had a story that morning about Moon Mullins. Did Sherry remember him? No, Sherry said, but she had heard of him, Carol's old pal. What was up?

"He's dead. They think he was murdered. It says right here, murdered in his house at West Palm Beach. Says he might've known the person, or else he left his door unlocked. 'No signs of forced entry,' the paper says."

"Read me that," Sherry said, her mind awhirl.

Paul "Moon" Mullins, a former Clinton and Knoxville businessman, had been found dead, "an obvious homicide victim." His house had been ransacked and several items of jewelry had been taken. His body had been discovered on Tuesday evening by a neighbor. Mullins had been tied to a chair and apparently strangled. Rumors were that one finger, on which Mullins was said to have worn a large diamond ring, had been severed, but the police refused to confirm this detail.

A Kentucky native who had also been involved in the coal business, Mullins had developed several shopping centers and had founded Mullins Carpet and Upholstery, a store now operated by his ex-wife. "He started out on a shoestring and made it," Dimples Mullins was quoted as saying.

Shoestrings aside, Sherry knew that Moon Mullins had been a fairly big-time dope dealer. He had suffered from narcolepsy, a condition that caused him to fall asleep suddenly, and Carol had at one time been his caretaker, as someone had phrased it, driving him around and performing other services for him. Roger knew about that. Mullins's name had cropped up several times in conversation since they had come to Florida—something about his Las Vegas connections. He was supposed to have been rolling in dough.

"I guess you never know when your time is up," Sherry said. "I got to go now."

Better not to speculate, Sherry decided. The important thing was that Benny would never strangle anyone, let alone cut off a finger to get at some damn ring. It would take a real sicko hombre to do something like that.

Whoever had killed Moon Mullins, it had not been Benny. That was what mattered, Sherry told herself. And as for Mullins, from what she understood, it would be a small funeral.

"We got to get that dude a full-time woman," Sherry said to Benny one day. Donnie's escapades had become intolerable. He was playing Don Juan twenty-four hours a day, whether he had to pay for it or not. When he wasn't picking them up at night, he was after women on the beach during the day. He and Roger bought remote-control model cars, big ones that you could send out a hundred yards or more. Donnie would direct one over the sand to where some girl lay sunning herself, make it bump into her, and call it back. The girl would follow the machine with her eyes until she saw Donnie grinning at her. What an introduction. Sometimes he'd attach a note: "Put your bra in this car and meet the man of your dreams," or "Ride me on the highway to heaven."

Sherry did not know which was more disgusting, Donnie or the inexhaustible number of dimwit women willing to play with him. To her, he had the sex appeal of a chimpanzee. A neighbor had complained about the late-night shoutings and carryings-on; the manager had been by to see them. And with all the dope he had been consuming, he could not be trusted not to shoot off his mouth. There wasn't a better way to have a prostitution or a narcotics charge against you dropped than to tip off the cops to some thieving addict.

Sherry suggested to him that he import his ex-wife to Florida. But when Donnie telephoned the ex, he blabbed that they would soon set sail for Bimini and she, still pregnant, declined the offer, worried about whether there were doctors on the island. Sherry got on the line to try to convince her: "If they has babies, I reckon they has doctors. They ain't cannibals out there." But the woman would not be persuaded.

When Sherry overheard Donnie sweet-talking Rebecca Hannah on the phone one afternoon, she got another idea. Bartley was hooked on Rebecca; that had been obvious since Six Flags. Sherry did not think Becky was as pretty as Donnie thought she was, or as *she* thought she was—"beef to the heels like a Tennessee heifer," was Sherry's analysis—but she did have a pretty sort of a dishface and, in Sherry's view, cared about a good time and a fast dollar. Sherry asked Benny to sound Donnie out about bringing Becky down. It might be the one way to calm his hormones, or to channel them.

"Bro," Benny said to Donnie at the pool. Benny had taken to calling him that lately because, Benny said, "Donnie walks, talks, acts, and fucks like a nigger." "Bro," Benny said to him, "how'd you like to have some full-time butt?"

Donnie was for it. He knew Becky was nuts for him, he said. She had been hanging around his sister, exercising with her every damn day just to have the excuse to talk about him. She was polishing his motorcycle, from what he had heard.

As it happened, Carol's daughter's fifth birthday was the eighteenth. Carol could see her child, Sherry would visit with Renee, and they would bring back Becky Hannah with them. Sherry was uneasy about leaving Benny on his own for a few days—as far as she knew, he had been faithful to her for more than two months—but she could not pass up the chance to see Renee and her parents.

On July 18 Rebecca Hannah met Sherry and Carol at the Knoxville airport and drove them in her Datsun sports car to a pizza parlor on Kingston Pike, where Carol's father, mother, and daughter joined them to celebrate. Show Biz Pizza, which featured balloons and popcorn and an actual clown and relentless repetitions of "Happy Birthday," was designed to entertain and placate a child whose parents' work schedule, style of life, or other commitments rendered more demanding observances, such as a party at home, inconvenient. It was extra-special day care, where clashing cymbals and fake calliope toots made conversation avoidable.

After that Becky drove Sherry and Carol to Harriman, where they took Renee out to dinner. They spent the night at the same Kingston motel where Sherry had first hidden Benny and Donnie after the retreat from Rome.

They left early the next morning for Kentucky, taking advantage of Becky's car, which was presumably unknown to the police, so Sherry and Carol could retrieve belongings left with Harold Clontz and the Mt. Vernon couple. They were lunching on corn dogs at a drive-in restaurant near London when two men, one wearing a sports jacket and the other casual clothes, approached the car from either side and displayed FBI badges.

"Let me do the talking," Sherry said under her breath. She was in the passenger seat, Carol in the rear.

Sherry showed her license.

"Are you also known as Sherry Hodge?" an agent asked. Sherry said yes but that Wong was her true, legal name, because she was married to but separated from a Chinese. She had lived with Benny Hodge until recently and had from time to time assumed his name. They had shared a house on Route 5 in Harriman, but she was now living with her parents and did not know where Hodge had gone.

The agent showed her photographs of Benny and Donnie; she identified both of them. She knew that they were fugitives and that assisting them could lead to charges against her.

It would probably be a good idea to take a full statement from her, the agent said. Would the ladies agree to follow him to the local KSP post, where they could conduct an interview in more private surroundings? Of course, Sherry said. To tell the truth, she had begun to hope that the FBI would find Benny, if they could capture him without hurting him. The strain of not knowing where he was had begun to take its toll on her.

On the short drive to the station Sherry wondered aloud how the FBI had found them. They must have been following Becky after all, knowing of her connection to Bartley. Becky had been present with Donnie's sister when the FBI had questioned Sharon about her brother's whereabouts. Or had the manager of the Kingston motel recognized the name Wong from Sherry's previous registration and tipped off the FBI? It had probably been a mistake to have stayed there again.

Four FBI agents took turns asking Sherry questions at the London KSP post, a modern glass structure on an island at the juncture of I-75 and Highway 80. They isolated her in a room away from Becky and Carol, in whom they displayed less interest.

Sherry spoke of how she had met Benny at Brushy. She said that she loved him with all her heart and was lost without him. She repeated word for word what she had told Agent Cloninger in Gene Foust's presence—the fight on May 27, her speculation that Benny might have gone to his mother or to one of his wives, his professed determination to kill himself rather than return to prison. Her purpose in being in Kentucky now, she said through tears, was to try to contact acquaintances of Benny's in a desperate attempt to locate him. She had persuaded Becky and Carol to come with her because she was afraid.

Where had Sherry spent the previous night? With her parents, Sherry responded. The agents suggested that they had information that conflicted with that idea. Perhaps she would care to correct herself? No, Sherry said. Whoever claimed that she had not been at her parents' house was a liar.

She volunteered that she had a "close personal friend" with the Oak Ridge Police Department whom she would contact if and when Benny chose to surrender. She trusted this friend and believed he would not hurt Benny. If Benny ended up dead, maybe killing himself, she did not wish to be responsible. The honest truth was, she said, she was as anxious to find him as the FBI was. If he did contact her, she would try to talk him into giving himself up.

The agents let the women go; they drove back to Tennessee. From

what Sherry could determine, the FBI had believed her, except possibly about where she had spent the previous night—but it would not
be unusual for someone to try to conceal having stayed in a motel
close to her hometown. For safety's sake she slept that night with her
parents, fending off their questions and trying to ignore their warnings that she was ruining her life for a lost cause. She told them nothing about where she had been and said only that she would be returning to Benny and would stay in touch. Her father was wheezing so
heavily that she could not sleep, thinking of the anxiety she was causing him and wondering if she would ever see him again.

The next day she had Becky drive her to Lake City, where Sherry
confronted the fence and demanded money from him that she said he
owed Benny. The fence responded by pulling a gun and threatening to
blow her head off. Sherry instructed Becky to head straight to the
Lake City Police Department, where Sherry telephoned Burl
Cloninger and said that she was terrified. She was being stalked by
one of Benny's acquaintences, who was threatening her over some
money Benny supposedly owed. She had never seen nor heard of the
man before in her life.

What was she to do, being hounded by the FBI and now some
crazed gunman? Was there some way she could be given police protection? She should relax, Cloninger told her. If she was not harbor-
ing Benny, did not know where he was, and did not owe money to
criminals herself, she had nothing to worry about. He would be grateful if she stayed in touch. She said she certainly would. It was a tough
world out there.

The women took three days to travel to Ormond Beach, driving only
at night. Sherry was confident that they were not being followed.
Even the FBI had to sleep, and they had better things to do than to
trail women around the country.

Becky Hannah was delighted with the accomodations at the
condo and spent hours each day running and walking on the beach,
enjoying her first experience of the ocean. Sherry was pleased to see
that Becky's presence had the desired effect on Donnie, who was
after her day and night. "Those two is going to croak of heart
attacks," Sherry predicted.

Soon the men plunged into preparations for what Roger began
referring to as the million-dollar lick. It was just a phrase, Sherry sus-

pected, typical of Roger's bullshit. They would probably be better off robbing one bank and getting out. The target Roger had chosen was no secret: he studied a map of Kentucky and marked in a booklet obtained from Radio Shack the police frequencies for the Eastern Kentucky region. Sherry bought Benny a nondescript summer suit, altered it for him as she always had, and asked few questions.

Early on Sunday morning, August 4th, she kissed her outlaw good-bye and asked him to be back by Friday, which was his thirty-fourth birthday. Benny said he would make every effort.

18

THEY DROVE THE OLDS STRAIGHT THROUGH from Ormond Beach to Hazard, where Donnie and Benny registered at the Mountain View Motel as Snapper and Shane Hall. They timed the journey at nearly fourteen hours.

On Monday they made a quick run to Fleming-Neon, checking on the route and the doctor's house. Returning through Whitesburg, Roger stopped at Maloney's department store, which specialized in automotive and sporting supplies, to buy a box of Remington .45 automatic shells. That evening they drove to Viper, a village hidden in a hollow about eight miles south of Hazard, to pay a call on Sonny Spencer, whom Roger had known since they had been kids together. Sonny, Roger said, was blessed with a special talent, of which they could make very good use.

Sonny Spencer had not seen Roger for more than a year and a half. A wiry, taciturn fellow, Sonny had been in jail during that time; he greeted his old pal with something short of effusiveness. He led the men into his kitchen and offered them beer. He did not have any dope, he said; he was trying to stay clean on probation. He had managed to get hold of a bulldozer to do some stripping on the land he had inherited and was planning to rely on that and on the odd jobs he could pick up as a carpenter. He was just thanking his stars to be out of prison. Actually he had Lester Burns to thank. He would have been inside for twice as long, and convicted on other charges, if it hadn't been for Lester.

Roger agreed that Lester indeed was a wizard, a friend to the needy if there ever was one, and recalled a couple of Lester's more spectacular performances. Donnie said that he had heard his mother talk about Lester Burns, who was supposed to be the smartest lawyer in Kentucky and the richest.

They had in mind a job, Roger said, that would set the mouths of even the likes of Lester Burns to watering. What was more, they were prepared to let Sonny Spencer in on it. All he would have to do was open a certain safe.

He was not interested, Spencer said. He could not take the risk. The cops were watching him. Lieutenant Danny Webb from the KSP post over in Hazard knew his every move. It was like living in a gold-fish bowl.

Donnie removed some cocaine from his jacket and began cutting it on the kitchen table. When he had three neat lines, he offered one to Spencer, who declined. Donnie sniffed up two through a rolled-up dollar bill and Roger did the other one.

It was nothing that complicated, Roger said. He had absolutely reliable information that a certain person over in Letcher County, way at God's end of nowhere, had recently purchased one of those home safes. And Roger himself knew for a fact and had known for years that this man kept a truckload of money at home. If anyone could open that safe lickety-split, it was Sonny Spencer.

He was out of practice, Spencer said. He had no idea whether he could open it, the mechanisms changed all the time, and if it was a new one, he might not be able to crack it.

"Your mother's ass you couldn't. What if I told you this safe's got a million bucks in it?"

Spencer whistled but said he was still not interested. He asked Roger not to talk about it anymore. He did not want to know more than he had already heard. He wished them the best of luck, but it was very important to him to keep his nose clean at the present time.

Maybe Sonny would like some help stripping that coal, Roger said. Where was the field? Just over the next hill, Spencer said. No, he did not need any additional men. It was a small operation.

"You might find you could use some help," Roger said.

They checked out of the Mountain View Tuesday morning and drove over to Fleming-Neon for another look-see. Roger's information was that the old man lived in the house alone, his wife having died a year ago. Rolling past at a crawl, they noticed for the first time

a siren horn attached to the house beside the front door. The trick
would have to be to play their FBI routine well enough for the doctor
to open the door voluntarily to let them in. Any sort of scuffle might
be noticed from the road or heard by neighbors out on their porches
on a warm summer's evening, and the doctor might easily trip his
alarm.

They continued on past the clinic. A patient was entering; others
were waiting in their cars. It looked like a land-office business. Supposedly the doc was there every day without fail, until around five. It
had been in the clinic that Roger's friend Roe Adkins had received the
fifty thousand in cash in a garbage bag from the old man, seven or
eight years ago. Adkins never tired of telling the story.

Donnie asked what made Roger think that the doc still had that
kind of money lying around. Maybe it had been a chance thing,
because the banks had been closed that day.

Why did Donnie think the doc had bought a safe only a few
weeks ago? Roger asked sarcastically. To keep his choppers in? To
store his underwear? Besides, there were other indications nobody
needed to know about. Donnie and Benny should just listen to him,
follow orders, and get rich. Hadn't he been right about the other
Letcher County job and about Gray Hawk? What they needed to do
now was to convince Sonny to help them open the safe. It would save
precious time and could be crucial. Once they were inside the house,
they would need to get out fast.

It was one of those hot, wet afternoons when it had rained so much
and so regularly in the mountains, for days and days, that with the
sun shining briefly here and there, water condensed, sending great
plumes of mist into the air. This fog, this mist, was not a continuous
thing, not a blanket as in the lowlands, but a scattering of rising
smokelike columns forever moving and shifting among the verdant
hills and hollows and mountaintops, as if ascending from mysterious
conflagrations underground. It lent to the already shadowy landscape
an atmosphere of silvery, eerie unease.

That afternoon Sonny Spencer leaned against his bright yellow
450 bulldozer, watching one of his two hired men operate a backhoe
while the other shoveled coal that was slick with wet into a ten-ton
truck. Suddenly, over the noise of the engine and the scraping of the
claws of the scoop, he heard his name shouted from far away, echoing

through the hollow. He turned to see three figures on the ridge, silhou-
etted through the mist. The black barrel of a shotgun or a rifle pro-
truded over the shoulder of one of the men. They began to descend the
side of the hill. As they drew closer, Spencer recognized Roger Epperson and his sidekicks Bartley and Hodge. Bartley carried a rifle in the
crook of one arm; in his other hand he dangled a big pistol.

The engine stopped. Spencer saw that Hodge was cradling a
machine gun in his arms. The fellow working the backhoe jumped to
the ground. The other hired man was already running. They jack-rab-
bitted into the woods. Spencer stayed put, leaning against the bulldozer, sending a stream of tobacco juice splatting against a heap of
coal. Epperson and his buddies approached.

Roger, unarmed from what Spencer could see, was smiling.
"Thought you'd need some help," he said. "Show you how it's done. I
am one mean son of a bitch with a dozer."

He climbed behind the wheel and brought the engine to life and
began working levers like a pro. The great caterpillar treads moved
into the pit. Roger rocked the machine back and forth, dropping the
blade to send it smashing and splintering the blossom of coal.

"Damn good, ain't he?" Bartley shouted. "Fucking-A he is."
Roger kept at it for what must have been ten or fifteen minutes.

All at once Benny, yawping like some fanatic Arab, pointed the
Mini Mac at the clouds and sent a full twenty-round clip streaming
into the air. He jammed a fresh clip in and filled the air again with fire
and lead. With a third clip he sprayed the woods, the big slugs
thwacking trees, splintering off chunks of bark. Birds wheeled, disappearing into the mist. Donnie, down on one knee now, fired one shot
at a time at birds and trees with his Ruger .44 mag semiautomatic
carbine, one-two-three-four-five, reloading, firing again. The bulldozer, the machine gun, the rifle—then a pistol's reports as Donnie
fired his .357 Magnum and sent chips of coal skipping along the lip
of the pit—it was louder and crazier than a hundred thousand Bap-
tists at an Elvis concert. Sonny Spencer threw up his hands and
screamed: "Hey! What the hell! I got neighbors! What the fuck do
you guys want?"

Roger switched off the engine of the bulldozer and climbed
down. Benny and Donnie held their fire.

"We just want to reason with you," Roger said, sidling over and
throwing an arm around Spencer. "We want to show you how much

we care about you, and we want to do you a favor. Hey, man, what you so goddamned worried about, huh? We ain't about to leave no kind of witnesses."

Spencer did not budge. He did not want in on any deal. No job was worth it to him now, not for any amount of money. He wished they would leave. They were fucking him up. He was in violation of parole merely being around people with weapons. And this was no place to take target practice. There were neighbors. Somebody would hear the shots and call the police, and then where would they all be?

"Sonny," Roger asked, "what do you plan to do with the rest of your life? Break your ass on a gob pile? I bet you never even seen the ocean."

"I can live without it. I reckon I'll work for the rest of my life. Seems good to me."

"You could be sitting on a beach stoned out of your mind."

"Working for a living sure does beat the penitentiary. Hell, you all can nail my nuts to that tree if you has a mind to. I ain't afraid to die, no way. Ain't no job worth no jail time, no way."

"I wouldn't never hurt you," Roger said, getting into his face. "Sonny, you my old buddy. I just feel sorry for you, is all. Looks like you'll be loading coal till they drop you into the grave."

They left Sonny and went to score some dope from a man living up a hollow near Leatherwood and checked into a motel near there. On Wednesday they cased the doctor's house once more, drove around to visit and score cocaine and pot. On Highway 15 near Hazard a dark blue, almost purple Porsche tore past them going in the other direction, and Roger said he recognized it. The car belonged to one of the doctor's two daughters, who both drove Porsches, or so he had been told. The younger one was supposed to be in college, but she might still be home for the summer. If she was, it could be a problem.

There were other potential difficulties, but if they were going to hit the doc, they agreed, it would have to be tomorrow, or they would have to head back to Florida having gained nothing. They were out of money, with barely enough left for a motel and the gas to get home. They worried about the getaway. They had decided that the best route was through Whitesburg because it was the quickest way to the main highways from Fleming-Neon. Once they reached the Daniel Boone Parkway, there were two tollbooths between Hazard and London that might be tricky; but if they made it to I-75 they ought to be home free.

Among them, only Bartley remained hesitant. He could not imagine that a doctor would be so stupid as to keep a lot of cash in his house. Trust him, Roger said. The money was there. Benny added that tomorrow had to be the day for the job, because the day after was his birthday, and he had promised Sherry he'd be back for it.

At a motel in Whitesburg that evening they spread out all their equipment on the floor, exactly as if they were planning a military operation. Roger gave everyone a rank: he was the general, Benny the captain, and Donnie the sergeant. When Donnie objected to his low rank, Roger told him that anybody who stood only five-feet-seven didn't deserve to be an officer, and besides, he was the youngest. If he didn't shut up and follow orders, Roger said, he would bust him to private. His assignment as of now was to take inventory.

Donnie called out their gear item by item: guns and ammo; suits, shirts, and plain ties for Bartley and Hodge; badges and IDs the general had fashioned from cards FBI agents had left with him when they had interviewed him at the Rome jail; thin brown gloves they planned to don after gaining entrance; a piece of plain white paper with "Federal Bureau of Investigation" photocopied across the top; two-way Motorola portable radios and battery testers; a black attaché case that looked official and would be used to carry the money.

"Dr. Roscoe J. Acker," Roger said. "That's his name. Make sure you got it straight. You better write it down."

They were up early on Thursday morning, the 8th. With time to kill, they drove around Whitesburg as it came to life on a day that promised to be warm and humid; at nine o'clock it was already eighty degrees. Benny and Donnie decided it had been a mistake to have put on their suits, since they would not be heading for Fleming-Neon until late that afternoon. They would have to find somewhere to stay cool and relax until then.

For no particular reason they pulled into a small shopping center, the Whitesburg Plaza, and got out to look around, to kill time. The Rite Aid drugstore was just opening up, and they strolled in and began to browse. The pharmacist was reading a newspaper, his elbows on the counter. A young woman was unlocking the cash register. Benny asked her where the film was kept, she pointed down an aisle, and he pretended to examine some rolls. Donnie purchased a package of breath mints, and they left.

They spent the day at Sonny Spencer's house, Benny and Donnie switching into casual clothes to stay cool in the air conditioning. At around half past six, after having failed once again to persuade Sonny to join them, they headed out.

Donnie drove to Fleming-Neon, following Roger's directions because, as often as they had driven there, it remained an elusive place. As they entered Neon, Roger, who was wearing jeans and a polo shirt and had not shaved in three or four days, squeezed down onto the floor in the back. It was now close to seven o'clock.

Donnie pulled into Dr. Acker's driveway. The garage door was closed, so there was no way of telling who, if anyone, was at home. Donnie and Benny got out, leaving Roger on the floor clutching a two-way radio; the other transmitter-receiver was in the attaché case, which Donnie carried. Benny took the lead and pushed the doorbell, using a ballpoint pen so as not to leave prints.

From a speaker built into the wall beside the alarm siren, a woman's voice asked who was there.

"This is Agent Shanker of the FBI," Benny said. "I'm here with my partner Agent Todd. We're looking for a Dr. Roscoe J. Acker, ma'am, if you please. We'd like to ask him a few questions. It's a matter regarding someone else."

"My father's still at his office," the woman's voice said. "He's at his clinic. I don't know when he'll be home. You can talk to him there, if you like."

"Oh, no, ma'am," Benny said. "We wouldn't want to disturb him at work. We've been driving up from Georgia and we're pretty tired. We'll just find a motel and wash up and come back later."

"That will be fine," the voice said. "He should be back by seven."

In the car they determined that the woman had to be one of Dr. Acker's daughters. Donnie worried that she would call her father at his clinic and that he would check with the FBI to verify their identities, but Roger said that was unlikely. People always said they were going to be that cautious, but they rarely were. If the girl did call Acker, he would probably be too nervous to do anything, especially if, as Roger suspected, the doc was hiding money from the government. He would probably be thinking he was glad it was the FBI and not the IRS.

Donnie turned around up at McRoberts and headed back toward Fleming, past shack after ramshackle shack, past the clinic again. On his knees, Roger peeked over the front seat. As they approached the doctor's house he instructed Donnie to turn left onto a narrow dirt track that climbed the hill opposite. Two hundred feet or so up, he told Donnie to get as close to the edge as he could and to stop under a tree.

It was the perfect place from which to monitor the house while they waited for Dr. Acker to show up. Their position was at an angle to the front door, which was across the two-lane highway some fifty feet beneath them. They were perched on the side of what the locals called Haymond Hill, on a road that had been cut to an abandoned strip-mining operation and was now a shortcut to the tiny settlement of Haymond a couple of miles away. The hill was so thick with trees and brush and the ubiquitous kudzu vine that no one was likely to notice them up there. Benny removed a pair of binoculars from the glove compartment; they took turns at keeping watch or, as Roger termed it, aerial surveillance.

After half an hour there was still no sign of the doctor. Donnie announced that he absolutely had to take a pee and, removing his jacket, got out of the car to relieve himself. Benny also stood up to stretch. Just as Donnie was finishing, they heard a car coming from below. Donnie and Benny climbed back in and shut the door as the car slowly passed with inches to spare. There were two men in it, the passenger slumped to one side holding a beer can.

By eight o'clock they were feeling thirsty. They backed down through the fading light, entering the highway behind a police car that slowed as it passed the doctor's house, then veered left across the road into a parking space at the Edge of Town Market, a small store. Donnie followed. As the driver got out, they noted that he was wearing chinos with his shirttail hanging out, obviously off duty. Donnie went into the market to buy pop.

They resumed their perch, slightly lower down this time. At about ten minutes before nine a car's headlights approached from above through the near-dark. Only a driver's head was visible through the rear window.

It was just after nine when Roger spotted a solitary figure on foot passing under a streetlamp at the bridge that spanned the creek between the doctor's house and the clinic beyond. As headlights swept along the highway, Roger made out an old man, slightly stooped, dark-suited, a small creature who turned into the Acker driveway and approached the front door to insert a key.

"Zero hour," Roger said.

Roger and Benny had been snorting coke off and on all day; Benny had done a line during the vigil. Now all three took one final jolt. Donnie let the car roll back down, switched on the lights, and crossed over to the driveway.

Again it was the woman's voice on the intercom. Benny apologized for the late hour, identified himself and his partner once more, and asked if by chance Dr. Acker had returned as yet; otherwise they would come back at a more convenient time. It was all right, the woman said, her father would be out in a minute.

Dr. Acker opened the door halfway and came out to shake hands when Benny and Donnie displayed their badges. He said he was happy to cooperate with the FBI, any time—but he did not invite them in. Closing the door behind him, he gestured toward garden furniture on the porch and suggested that the men make themselves comfortable in the warm evening air. Benny sat on a recliner, Donnie and the doctor in straight chairs.

They were investigating a man named Roe Adkins, Benny said. Did the doctor know him? He did, the doctor said, but he had not had any dealings with him for several years. He had once been in the coal business with Roe Adkins, it must have been back in the seventies, when it seemed as if everybody was in coal. Adkins had dropped out, but there were no hard feelings. He had nothing against him.

Stalling for time to try to figure out how to coax Dr. Acker into letting them into the house, Benny, pretending to be cautious about revealing confidential information, suggested that the Bureau had gathered quite a bit of incriminating material on Adkins and would soon be moving to have him indicted for fraud, illegal coal mining, and various other interstate offenses. It was important to verify who was and who was not involved in these crimes because the Bureau was in the process of lining up witnesses.

Benny spoke with clarity and precision, as he was capable of doing when the occasion demanded. Donnie chimed in from time to time but for the most part let Benny carry the ball. Meanwhile, huddled on the floor of the Olds, Roger heard the rise and fall of voices through the air.

Would Dr. Acker be prepared to sign a statement to the effect that he had no present dealings with Roe Adkins and had not done any business with him for several years? Of course he would, Dr. Acker said. He would make out a statement right then and there.

"The light's pretty dim," Benny said. "Is there somewhere we could go that has better light?"

"We can go over to my office. I can sit at my desk."

"We don't need to waste that much of your time."

"All right. Come into the kitchen."

They followed Dr. Acker into the house. From somewhere down the hall they could hear the strains of a piano, some light, romantic melody, unaccompanied. Donnie closed the door behind them. In the kitchen, which was to the right of the front hall, Donnie removed from the briefcase the official-looking sheet of paper and placed it on the table. Dr. Acker sat down and began to write.

"We'll need a witness," Benny said. "Is there someone who can act as a witness to this?"

"My daughter can. That's her, playing. Tammy," he called, "Tammy, can you come in here?" The music stopped.

Tammy Acker came from her bedroom down the hall and into the kitchen. She was twenty-three and tiny, just over five feet, wearing a blue tank top and matching shorts. With her bright hazel-green eyes and her shining dark-brown hair that touched her shoulders, she was poised between girlhood and maturity—small-featured, full-figured, radiant, beautiful. She went to her father and balanced on one foot to kiss his cheek as he sat at the table.

Donnie grabbed her from behind as Benny snatched a revolver from his shoulder holster and poked the muzzle at Dr. Acker's head. Tammy screamed. Donnie covered her mouth with his hand and warned her to shut up or else.

"Where's the safe?" Benny demanded, crumpling up the sheet of paper and stuffing it into his pocket.

"I don't have one," Dr. Acker said.

"Get her out of here," Benny said. "Tie her up."

Donnie slung Tammy over his hip and carried her back to her bedroom. It was a large room, decorated with girlish mementoes—a purple-and-white PIRATES pennant on the wall above the upright piano; a poster of Prince, the rock star, above the fireplace; dozens of records and tapes stacked beneath the stereo. As Donnie dropped her to the floor and began tying her up with anything he could find—scarves, a sheet ripped from her bed—Tammy pleaded, "Please don't hurt my dad! Please don't! He's suffered so much! My mother's just died and it almost killed him!"

"Don't you worry none, honey. Ain't nobody going to be hurt. You just lie here and it'll be all over in a few minutes and we'll be gone." He gagged her tight.

Donnie returned to the kitchen, where Benny had the doctor on the floor with the gun to his head, and he told Donnie to tie the old man up. As Donnie did so, Benny kept demanding the location of the safe, but Dr. Acker refused to say.

Donnie removed the radio from the briefcase: "General, this is Sergeant. Come in, General."

"Sergeant, this is General. I hear you." Roger had stayed out of sight for fear that the doctor might recognize him and spoil the FBI ruse. He had not actually met Dr. Acker, but he had spent so much time in the area working with Roe Adkins and others that there was no sense taking chances.

They decided to search for the safe rather than trying to beat its whereabouts out of the doctor, whom they would need to tell them the combination; he was too frail, it appeared, to withstand much punishment. Benny removed Dr. Acker's eyeglasses and threw a sheet over his head as Roger entered and, saying nothing, distributed the gloves for everyone to put on.

They decided on the bedrooms first. That was where most people kept a safe. Donnie took Tammy's room. In minutes he made chaos out of order, tearing the place apart in a frenzy, emptying the closets, overturning boxes of new clothes that had been stacked in a corner. There were so many clothes, and so many of them brand new, that it was obviously a rich girl's room, and the opulence made Donnie salivate. Contemptuously he tossed a bikini top across the nape of her neck as she lay facedown on the carpet. Along with the Rolex and a gold bracelet he had already removed from her wrists, he slipped a black pearl necklace into his pocket.

He had gone through every drawer, sent shoes and handbags flying from shelves, when from the room across the hall he heard a shout.

"Sergeant!"

They had discovered the safe at the back of a closet in the doctor's bedroom. It was about three feet high and eighteen inches deep, solid steel, bolted to the floor. They considered trying to shoot it open but doubted that would work and worried about the noise. They would have to get the doctor to tell them the combination.

Dr. Acker capitulated. Donnie wrote the numbers down on a pad from the kitchen counter and they returned to the bedroom to try the lock.

Benny went through the combination as Donnie scoured the rest of the house and piled valuables, including numerous rifles, pistols, and shotguns, in a heap by the front door.

Benny failed to crack the safe; Roger had a go at it. No luck.

Back to the kitchen. Roger kicked the doctor in the ribs as Benny accused Dr. Acker of having lied. Dr. Acker swore that the numbers were correct.

Benny untied him, helped him to his feet, gave him back his glasses, and led him by the elbow down the hall. The three of them watched as Dr. Acker, sweat dripping off his chin and nose, having to pause to wipe his glasses, hands trembling, the gun at his head, knelt before the safe and spun the dial back and forth. Finally the tumblers clicked.

"It's open," the doctor said.

"Then open it," Benny said.

Dr. Acker plunged the handle downward and swung open the door. Simultaneously the three onlookers emitted noises of appreciation.

"Holy shit!" Donnie squealed. "Holy fucking shit! It's plumb full!"

The safe was stuffed with cash. It was stacked from bottom nearly to top with bills, most of them neatly wrapped, some of them loose.

"All right, boys," Dr. Acker said. "You've hit the jackpot, leave some for me."

19

At ELEVEN-THIRTY THAT NIGHT the dispatcher at the Fleming-Neon police station received a telephone call. Over the wire came the halting voice of an old man:

"This … is … Dr. Acker. I've been robbed.… My daughter …"

"Dr. Acker? Hello?"

The dispatcher reached Officer Cobran Phillips, who was sitting in his squad car at the Chevron station, chatting through the window with Tom Haynes, an Emergency Medical Technician who was manning the fire department ambulance that night.

"Dr. Acker's house," Phillips told Haynes, who said he would follow right along.

Within five minutes Officer Phillips was knocking on Dr. Acker's door. He knocked several times, he banged with his fist, he rang the bell, but there was no answer, and the door was locked. He could hear the siren of the approaching ambulance and was about to radio for additional help when the door of the house opened and Dr. Acker stood there, staggering, grabbing hold of the doorframe.

The doctor's face was smeared with blood; blood trickled from his nose and mouth. An orange appliance of some sort, a soldering or a curling iron, dangled from around his neck.

"Tammy … Tammy …" Dr. Acker mumbled, blinking his bloody eyes, coughing up blood. Officer Phillips helped him loosen the electrical cord.

"Where is she? Doc? Where's Tammy?"

"In here. Back there," he motioned, and stepped to one side.

Phillips ran down the hall. He entered Tammy's bedroom.

He nearly stumbled over her. She lay on her side on the floor, her body parallel to her bed, her head nearly touching a wicker chest on which a lamp stood lit. The glare showed everything, more than enough—the room a shambles, clothes everywhere, shoes, hangars, open handbags, dresser drawers pulled out, boxes thrown about, the bed stripped. And Tammy. She was covered with so much blood, the surrounding carpet drenched with blood and urine, that Phillips had to force himself to look. Her knees drawn up, her bare legs bound with a bloody sheet, her hands tied behind her back, her mouth gagged with a blue scarf, her eyes wide open, she looked like a human sacrifice. Sticking out of her back was the handle of a knife that had been plunged in up to the hilt—and this was not the only wound. Her bloodsoaked shirt back showed many other two- or three-inch nearly vertical tears above, below, and on either side of the knife.

Phillips bent down to take her pulse at her throat. He felt none. That close to her, he understood the savagery of the attack and was nearly overcome by horror and terror.

He hurried out to radio for the state police and the coroner as Tom Haynes arrived in the ambulance.

"Too late," Phillips said. "Tammy Acker's been stabbed to death. You won't believe it. You might better check on the doc. He's alive somehow."

Dr. Acker, who was seventy-seven, began to recover when policemen walked him over to the next-door neighbors, who helped him off with his clothes and into a shower. His assailants had tried and failed to strangle him; he had passed out and it was difficult to guess how long he had lain there before crawling to the phone. As the hours he kept at his work attested, he was a vigorous man who clung to life.

After reaching the police dispatcher, he had managed to telephone his older daughter, his one remaining close family member. Tawny Rose Acker, who lived in Lexington, was now on her way to the scene. Washing and tidying himself, Dr. Acker drew on strengths that had his neighbors and everyone else amazed.

Numerous local and state officials arrived within the hour. Kentucky State Police Lieutenant Danny Webb, who had been asleep at home, was there by midnight along with KSP detectives Lon Maggard and Frank Fleming. While Fleming, whose special interest was physical evidence, took Polaroid photographs, Lt. Webb made the unusual decision to telephone the KSP Crime Laboratory in Frankfort, some two hundred miles away, to ask that a team of experts be sent immediately to Fleming-Neon. Webb decided that the brutality and magnitude of the crime, which involved a prominent local citizen, required the most sophisticated analysis the Commonwealth could provide. He ordered that nothing but the body itself be touched until the team from the lab arrived.

James Wiley Craft, the Commonwealth's Attorney, who had a policy of trying to view a major crime scene as soon as possible after the event, stood mesmerized before the body. There must have been fifteen people in the house, but they were padding about so quietly, talking in whispers from shock and respect, that the silence, Craft thought, was as disturbing as the wrecked bedroom and the body. The sharp smells of urine and blood, the sight of her pitiful little curled-up form, the shredded soaked shirt, the soaked blue shorts—Craft struggled with nausea and outrage. James Wiley, as he was popularly known, knew the Ackers well. A brief look was all he could take—he hurried into the night air and, standing in the driveway, told Danny Webb that anyone who could see what some son of a bitch had done to Tammy and not believe in the death penalty must be some fucking raving idiot. How could any human being subject another to such *indignity!* My God, my God, Craft kept muttering as he wandered toward the road trying to catch his breath.

When David Polis, the coroner, who also had known Tammy well and remembered the family's grief at the mother's death such a short few months before, saw the body, he nearly passed out. Frank Fleming stood beside him and steadied him. Polis knew that it was going to be his job to get Tammy into a body bag and into his hearse for transportation to Pikeville, where the autopsy would be performed. What were they going to do about that knife that was sticking out of her? Polis whispered to Fleming. Polis's family owned the Banks Funeral Home; he had had more experience with embalming than with crime scenes, being fairly new at this job and never having dealt with anything so grotesque as this. And it was not just a body, it was Tammy, wonderful Tammy. "God help us all," he said, and began reciting the Lord's Prayer.

The knife handle looked to be five or six inches long. What was he to do? Put poor Tammy on her face in the car? Try to slip a bag over that thing? He looked at Fleming. "What do we do?" Fleming said he would telephone the county pathologist for advice.

Fleming reported to Polis that the doctor said the knife had to be removed, now. Fleming offered his handkerchief, to protect fingerprints that might be on the handle. He held out the cloth, but Polis stood there immobile, hands at his sides, staring at the ceiling. He could not act.

Frank Fleming, not sure that it was proper but sensing that someone had to do it, forced himself into the room and planted his feet on either side of Tammy's folded legs. He wondered how much strength this would take. His hands shook as if palsied. He wrapped his right hand with the handkerchief and made himself seize the handle. He took a breath through his mouth and began to pull. After a slight tug to release the point, which was stuck in the floor, the blade started coming out. It was easier than he had feared. It was like pulling a knife slowly through water, except that he felt bone and cartilage passing along the blade, causing it to tremble slightly. The blade was much bigger than he had imagined, a steel triangle some ten inches long, razor-sharp and pointed. The thing looked as if it could go through a wall. He held it up for Polis to see, but the coroner had gone into the hall and had his back turned.

Fleming, as methodically as he could, bagged the weapon and brought it to Danny Webb, who told him to label it and place it on the kitchen table. Fleming did so. Then he hurried outside and to the highway, vomited, and buried his mouth in the crook of his arm to stifle the sobs.

At ten minutes to one that morning, Detective Lon Maggard went next door to see if Dr. Acker was able to make a statement. Maggard found the doctor sitting up in a chair, wrapped in a blanket, in shock but not clinically so: he appeared to be lucid. He agreed to try to recount the evening's terror, sipping at a cup of coffee as he talked.

"About nine P.M.," Dr. Acker began, "the doorbell rang. And Tammy answered the intercom. They said they were two men from the FBI and wanted to talk to me about Roe Adkins." Dr. Acker's speech bore traces of his native Boston. He had come to Appalachia as a young physician more than forty years before. He described a husky man, about six feet tall, with blond hair and a mustache, who showed him a badge:

"He asked me if I would write him a statement about Roe Adkins.

I told them I knew Roe about eight or ten years ago, that we were going to mine some coal together but he dropped out.... We walked into the kitchen and the blond-haired one pulled what looked like a snub-nose thirty-eight. The other one, who was short, about five-eight and a slender build with black hair, was also dressed very nice in a suit, he grabbed Tammy and took her into the other room. The tall one was holding the gun and told me to do what he told me and no one would get hurt. He was dressed in a dark suit, I think."

Dr. Acker described being tied up and hearing the men ransacking the house for about thirty minutes. He told of giving them the combination to the safe and seeing one of them write it down.

"They could not open it and came and untied me and took me to the safe and made me open it. After this, they took me back to the kitchen and tied me and gagged me again. They put the rope around my neck and tightened it up and I passed out.

"I think it was about eleven o'clock when I came to. After a while I got loose and I couldn't find my glasses. I yelled for Tammy and started looking for her. I found her in the other room."

Here Dr. Acker had to pause to compose himself. He continued:

"She had a sheet over her head and was tied up with her hands behind her lying on the floor. I went to her and bent down and removed the sheet and started to talk to her. I started to roll her over and untie her and I saw the kitchen knife in her back. I felt for a pulse and she had none. I called the sheriff's office."

Dr. Acker's account squared with the condition of the house and the body. What he referred to as rope was obviously the cord from the Windmere curling iron Officer Phillips had noticed hanging from the doctor's neck; he had been bound with neckties and gagged with a T-shirt, wet with his own blood and other fluids that had come from his nose and mouth, that he had dropped on the kitchen floor after regaining consciousness.

When Lt. Webb heard that the killers had posed as FBI agents, he connected the crimes with another that had occurred earlier that summer at a house on the Letcher–Harlan county line. The previous victims, who as Webb recalled had not been physically harmed, had also said that the thieves had identified themselves as government agents of some kind.

It was now nearing two A.M. Webb telephoned the supervisor of the FBI office in London, Special Agent Rod Kincaid, who was at home asleep in Somerset, to the west in Pulaski County. Kincaid remembered the earlier case, and not only that one. The FBI had been searching for months, Kincaid said, for suspects who had been posing as FBI or IRS agents. The Bureau already had warrants on file for at least two men, as Kincaid recalled, charged with unlawful flight to avoid prosecution in a case involving Georgia or possibly Tennessee. He would get back to Webb with the details.

At four-thirty that morning the laboratory crew from Frankfort arrived and began to process the house. Dr. Acker identified firearms and other objects left by the door as his but said that at least two or three pistols, including a pearl-handled .45 automatic, as well as Tammy's Rolex, bracelet, and a black pearl necklace, were missing. As for the stolen cash, he estimated it as between four and five hundred thousand dollars, some of it in old bills, in mixed denominations of twenties, fifties, and hundreds. He was a frugal man, he said, and had saved back a few thousand each year from his practice. Although he did have bank accounts and had once been part-owner of a Whitesburg bank, he had been through the Great Depression and knew enough not to believe that his money was absolutely safe in anyone else's hands. He had purchased the safe recently; before that he had kept his money in a trunk on the back porch.

Among all the clothes and other items piled and scattered throughout the house, Dr. Acker said that only one object did not belong to him or his daughter. This was a black attaché case. He believed that he had seen one of the men, possibly the short one, carrying it into the house.

When a Frankfort investigator opened the briefcase, he found that it contained only two items, an empty plastic baggie of the type with a resealable top and a plastic card with the call letters and radio frequency numbers "WSKZ-106, Chattanooga" embossed on it that might indicate a Tennessee link to the crimes. These were carefully wrapped along with the briefcase to be taken to the lab for processing.

In continuing to talk to Dr. Acker and to try to comfort him, impossible as that seemed, Lt. Webb learned that Tammy had been home that night only by chance. She had stopped by to see her father and to pick up a few of her possessions before returning to classes at the University of Kentucky, where she was a junior and a member of a sorority. She was such a wonderful girl, the doctor said, and had been so devoted to him. When her mother had died, Tammy had left the university in the middle of the semester and had taken the rest of the year off to care for him and nurse him through his grief. If only she had come to see him a day earlier or a day later ...

With children of his own, Danny Webb could scarcely bear to hear the doctor talk and weep. When, later that morning, the lieutenant walked over to the clinic to check for possible signs of a break-in there, he found that Dr. Acker's office was decorated with memorabilia of Tammy, including photographs of her playing nurse for her father as a child and a childlike drawing of a man wearing a surgical gown and a stethoscope. The picture was inscribed "M.D. Stands for My Dad. Tammy."

By mid-morning Special Agent Kincaid had brought the resources of the FBI into the case and had relayed the identities of two suspects, Benny Lee Hodge and Donald Terry Bartley, to Lt. Webb. Physical descriptions of them matched those given by Dr. Acker of the large and the small man. Dr. Acker now said that he believed he may have seen a third, large man standing near the safe in the bedroom but had not gotten a look at his face. Unlike the others, the third man had not been wearing a suit. When composite drawings, made by Detective Fleming based on Dr. Acker's descriptions, matched photographs of Hodge and Bartley supplied by the FBI, Agent Kincaid instructed the FBI office in Louisville to issue the following teletype:

015 KYFBILSOO 080985

ALL KENTUCKY, WEST VIRGINIA, OHIO, INDIANA, TENNESSEE, AND NORTH CAROLINA STATIONS.

B O L O 1983 GREY DATSUN 200SX TN LIC 13772W AND 1978 BLACK THUNDERBIRD WITH HALF VINYL, SILVER ROOF, TN LIC 3L4X78 POSSIBLY DRIVEN BY DONALD TERRY BARTLEY, W/M, DOB 081858, 5′8″, 160 LBS, DARK BROWN HAIR AND EYES, AND/OR SECOND SUBJECT BENNY LEE HODGE, W/M DOB 080951, 6′, 210 LBS, BROWN HAIR BLUE EYES POSSIBLY WEARING FULL FACE BEARD AND MUSTACHE. SUBJECTS MAY BE TRAVELING WITH CAROL ELLIS, W/F, DOB 102357, 5′2″, 126 LBS, BROWN HAIR, GREEN EYES AND REBECCA HANNAH, W/F, DOB 052468, 5′3″, 135 LBS, BLONDE HAIR, BLUE-GREEN EYES. SUBJECTS DONALD TERRY

BARTLEY AND BENNY HODGE CURRENTLY WANTED BY FBI. WAR-
RANTS ON FILE FOR UNLAWFUL FLIGHT TO AVOID PROSECUTION
FOR ARMED ROBBERY. SUBJECTS ARE ALSO SUSPECTS IN RESI-
DENTIAL ARMED ROBBERY AND HOMICIDE WHICH OCCURRED
22:30 HRS 8/8/85 AT WHITESBURG, KY. PERPETRATORS OF HOMI-
CIDE GAINED ENTRANCE RESIDENCE BY FALSELY IDENTIFYING
THEMSELVES AS FBI AGENTS. IF LOCATED HOLD CAR AND OCCU-
PANTS FOR FBI LOUISVILLE. ALL SUBJECTS ARMED AND
EXTREMELY DANGEROUS AS THEY ARE KNOWN TO HAVE AUTO-
MATIC WEAPONS, ARE ESCAPE RISKS, AND ARE SUICIDAL.

Subsequent bulletins issued shortly by the FBI and the KSP cor-
rected Carol's race designation from "W" to "O" and added her
maiden name and the Malone alias. Soon Roger Epperson's name and
description, which had been left off the original bulletin only because
he was technically not a fugitive but out on bail, were added when a
victim of the Harlan–Letcher robbery of May 13 identified him from
a photograph. The KSP and the FBI considered it significant that
both Bartley and Epperson were natives of counties bordering
Letcher. One of the first questions Danny Webb had asked himself
when he learned that the killers were strangers to Dr. Acker, who
knew everyone in Fleming-Neon and had treated most of the local
population, was why and how on earth outsiders would have known
enough to pick out a victim in such an obscure, godforsaken place? If
they were natives after all, it made more sense.

As for the Datsun 200SX mentioned in the bulletins, this was
Rebecca Hannah's car, as observed by Agent Cloninger in Tennessee
and in July by the agents who had interviewed her, Carol, and
"SHERRY L. WONG, nee SHEETS, also known as SHERRY L.
HODGE," as she was identified on records of that interview. A
description of Sherry and her various names was added to the bulletins when the FBI confirmed that she had fled the Harriman area.

As inclusive as the teletypes soon became, they were not sent to
Florida, as that state was neither adjacent to Kentucky nor known to
be associated in any way with any of the suspects. By one o'clock on
Friday afternoon, Donnie, Roger, and Benny had already reached the
Ormond Beach condominium.

Somewhere between Knoxville and Chattanooga, they had realized that they had left the briefcase behind. Having discovered that the case was too small to hold all that money, they had stuffed the cash into three pillowcases and fled when the telephone had begun to ring, not even bothering with the heap of valuables by the door, except for a few pistols and pieces of jewelry. Speeding away, monitoring police calls on their scanner, they had every reason to assume that both Tammy and her father were dead—the girl obviously, the old man because he had stopped breathing and lost control of himself. Safe in the traffic flow on I-75, they panicked and stopped to check the trunk when Donnie admitted that he was afraid he had forgotten the briefcase.

But they concluded that they had nothing to worry about. The briefcase was empty, they were sure, and Donnie had touched only the handle. His gloves would have wiped off any prints there.

Except for stops for gas and snacks, they continued on straight through, switching to I-16 east at Macon, hitting I-95 south at Savannah, passing through Jacksonville, past St. Augustine and into Ormond Beach. In the shelter of the condo's garage, they removed the pillowcases and weapons from the trunk and carried everything inside—home from the hunt, swaggering and triumphant.

The women were waiting. They began jumping up and down as first Roger, then Benny, then Donnie let the money whoosh from the pillowcases onto the living room carpet. Like a victorious team, they embraced. "We did it! We did it!" they shouted, hugging and kissing and falling down to toss the cash into the air and roll in it. Sherry was in ecstacy—until, lying on the floor with her cheek resting on bills that were scattered like so much Monopoly money, opening and closing her eyes to make sure she wasn't dreaming, she noticed Donnie Bartley's dirty shoes. They looked as if they were crusted with dried blood.

The sight gave her pause. But this was hardly the time to ask impudent questions.

Delirious, yahooing, gone loco with joy, they played like children on the floor, bathing in cold cash—until Sherry heard the doorbell and told everyone to shut the fuck up. She peeked out a window. It was the condominium manager! Carol had called him to come fix the refrigerator. Sherry ran to her bedroom for a blanket and rushed back to throw it over the money.

She opened the door and ushered the manager into the kitchen. If he was curious about that lumpy blanket on the living room floor, he gave no indication.

"Sounds like party time," the man said as he fiddled with the ice-maker.

"My husband's birthday," Sherry said, nattering on about how she was going to put up streamers and balloons and how much fun every-one was having in Florida with the sun and the water and some of the best pizza you could find anywhere and the whole life-style was so neat. On his way out the manager wished Benny a happy birthday and asked everyone to try to keep the noise under control.

When Sherry finished decorating, Carol served the chocolate cake she had baked for Benny. The taxi man arrived with a delivery of cocaine. It was the best birthday he had ever had, Benny said, the best of all time.

Late that afternoon they lugged the loot up to Roger and Carol's bedroom—just in case the manager or somebody else came to call—and began to count it. The money was in denominations of twenties, fifties, and hundreds. With the cash in a great heap and in growing piles on the carpet, the room was a hothouse of greenbacks. They could smell the stuff, a dank, sour stink like loose mulch. The wrapped stacks labeled "Bank of Whitesburg" that contained an even five thousand each in crisp new bills were easy to calculate, but it took forever to sort random denominations and total them up. Some of the currency was faded, so old that some of the bills did not even have "In God We Trust" on them. Some stuck together and, speckled with mildew, gave off an especially pungent whang.

Sherry played bookkeeper. Around nine o'clock, she told every-one to stop sorting. She had an announcement to make.

"I want you all to know," she said, "that we have reached one mil-lion dollars."

"Holy fucking shit!" Roger said. "We ain't even halfway there!"

It was like halftime at the Orange Bowl. They cheered and hugged each other. They threw bills around. Donnie popped cham-pagne and sprayed everyone. Roger drove Carol into a corner and yanked at her pants.

"Don't stop now," Sherry said. "Let's see what we really got."

After another hour the men lay on the floor and watched as the women kept counting. Close to midnight, staggered, deranged by the booty, they quit as Sherry announced one million six hundred thousand. Big piles remained. Sherry said that she wasn't sure that they hadn't counted some twice, but she could swear there was close to two million, all told.

"My daddy would shit in his pants," Roger said.

"Why don't you call him up and tell him the good news?" Sherry said.

They divided what was left into what seemed like three equal parts. Of the grand total, somewhere between a million-nine and two million, the men awarded the women three thousand dollars apiece to do with as they wished.

"I guess that's my counter's fee," Sherry said. "Let's head down, Biggin."

In bed with their take, Benny and Sherry held one another and whispered love pledges. Sherry asked about what she had seen on Donnie's shoes. Benny confided that, unfortunately, someone had had to die during the job. There was nothing to worry about. They had left no witnesses.

Blood, death, her mistrust of everyone, most of all the mound of cash made Sherry's heart run wild with desire and hate.

"We ought to kill them all," she said into Benny's ear. "We ought to kill every one of them, right now. Do it quiet."

"Booger, what are you talking? Kill who?"

"Kill Donnie and Roger and Carol and the dumbbell. Kill them in the beds, now." She ground her teeth and threw a leg over Benny and pressed against him. "Hodge-Podge, they ain't no good, you know that. Lowdown snitches. We takes our money and all the money and we could run to California, don't you see? Forget this island shit. We could mix in with them students at U.S.C., like I seen them on TV, honey. You look just like them students. I could, too. Kill 'em! Kill 'em, now!"

"Naw," Benny said, "not after all we been through together," and he touched her with indifferent fingers.

20

By THE TIME ROGER, BENNY, AND DONNIE HAD ARRIVED back in
Ormond Beach to celebrate that Friday, the autopsy on the body of
Tammy Acker was already complete.

Dr. George F. Buckley began his examination at nine A.M. that Friday at Methodist Hospital in Pikeville, with Frank Fleming among
those in attendance. The murder weapon, a butcher knife measuring
ten inches from the point to the hilt, three inches across at the base of
the stainless-steel blade, was already under examination at the Frankfort lab. Dr. Buckley, observing a ligature mark around her throat,
determined that Tammy had also been choked, apparently with a
stocking, before succumbing to the stab wounds. He estimated the
time of death at ten P.M., meaning that Dr. Acker, who presumably
had been choked nearly to death at about the same time, must have
lain unconscious for nearly an hour before reviving.

Eleven separate stab wounds, most measuring between two and
three centimeters in length, lacerated the right side of her upper back.
Some of these were relatively superficial, suggesting that the killer
had hacked at her before finding a passage through the back rib cage.
The two largest wounds passed completely through her chest cavity,
with the knife's point exiting through her right breast and sticking
into the floor, as Frank Fleming had felt. She could have bled to death
from several of the wounds, but Dr. Buckley concluded that Tammy
had actually died of the two deepest ones, both of which had ripped

through her right lung. One thrust passed through her liver on its downward course; lack of bleeding there suggested that by the time this wound was inflicted, she was already dead. She had stood no chance of survival against a man wielding so formidable a weapon. Dr. Buckley measured her body at five feet one and weighed it at just under a hundred and ten pounds.

WHERE THE BLOOD FLOWS PURPLE read a sign posted at the Fleming-Neon city limits in tribute to the diehard enthusiasm of fans of the local high school athletic teams, whose colors were purple and white and who played as the Purple Pirates. Tammy, who had been a leader of the pep squad and whose mother had helped to drill the marching band, had been famous for her fierce loyalty to Fleming-Neon High, where she had been a top student, excelling in music as well as in academic subjects, and had been one of the most popular girls in her class. In tribute to her affections, at her funeral at the First Church of God she lay in an open coffin dressed in the purple leotard of her cheerleading days.

The church overflowed with some four hundred of her classmates, teachers, school administrators, and many of Dr. Acker's patients, friends, and business associates. He sat with his older daughter and Steve Reynolds, the boy from Pound Gap who had hoped to marry Tammy.

The music included a tape of "Purple Rain." Friends remembered how Tammy had flown all the way to Detroit for a concert to see in the flesh the epicene, purple-clad phenomenon Prince, whose multi-platinum album and autobiographical movie *Purple Rain* had sent millions of girls swaying with the chorus of "ooh-ooh-oohs" and flicking their Bics.

The music had a powerful effect. It was so unlike typical funeral music that it intensified the grief of everyone, reminding them how full of life, how exuberant a young woman Tammy Acker had been, as ready to dance and sing and have a good time as she was devoted to her parents, her studies, and her school. This was the girl who had taken a whole year off from college just to nurse her father through his grief at the loss of his wife of thirty years. Dr. Acker, whose display of strength on the night of the murder had been drawn from the instincts of a physician used to blood and death, seemed ready for death himself this day—frail, broken, clinging to Tawny. Incredibly, he had missed but one day at work at his clinic, although his patients came only to grieve with him. At the gravesite Dr. Acker sank to his knees in the clay and wept uncontrollably through the prayers. People standing near him heard him muttering "my darling, my darling, my darling." It was dreadful.

"You can't understand what this does to us," a man from Neon said to a trooper from Whitesburg. "Dr. Acker is everything to us. He's all we have. He's given his life to us. That girl, she was such a lovely thing! Poor, poor Tammy! We loved her. We love him. Who would do this? Why?"

Those who had seen it could not forget Tammy's mangled body. Lieutenant Webb, a fifteen-year veteran of the KSP, had dealt with bodies that had been burned, clubbed, mutilated, decapitated; he told everyone that nothing in the scores of homicides he had investigated equalled the savagery of this. Sickened as he was by them, he examined the photographs of the corpse again and again. Why had she been stabbed *eleven* times? That all of the wounds were within inches of one another on the same side of her back indicated a single frenzied killer, a maniac thrusting and thrusting with unimaginable fury. The ligature mark around her neck was something of a puzzle. Would he have tried one method, then switched to another? Or had the mark been made by the way she was gagged?

Nearly always, such violence against women accompanied rape. Yet neither the autopsy nor any other evidence thus far discovered betrayed any sign of sexual assault. The initial motive, obviously, had been robbery. If premeditated, the elimination of witnesses had not been carefully planned. The butcher knife came from the Acker kitchen—a weapon of convenience seized on the spur of the moment, like the curling iron. How could they have done such a hideously thorough job on Tammy and yet have failed to kill a nearly eighty-year-old man?

Danny Webb was commander of the Hazard KSP post, a two-story office building and communications center on Highway 15 near the Daniel Boone Parkway exit. Webb was well known as the kind of cop who considered himself one of the community rather than above it or against it. A native of Whitesburg, where he had lived all his life, he knew Eastern Kentucky the way cops who walked a beat used to know a neighborhood. And he loved it—the mountains, the changeable weather, the music, the stories, the characters who made his way of life fascinating. He also loved detective work and the mysteries of the criminal mind. Somewhat to his wife's annoyance, off-duty he was always watching crime stories on TV and renting videotapes of crime movies, especially those based on fact. He estimated that he had seen the film of Truman Capote's *In Cold Blood* at least ten times, and he was ready to watch it again.

Lanky, loose-jointed, with spaniel eyes set in a long, dark-complected face, Danny Webb prided himself on understanding intimately the people he was paid to protect and the outlaws who tried to outsmart him or outgun him. An affable, joking, folksy manner was one of his assets. It was hard not to consider him your friend when he sat down to chew the fat—maybe putting you at your ease by telling the story about the time he and Frank Fleming had gone down to New Orleans to interview a suspect and how this fellow had been with a Bourbon Street stripper and what had happened after that— and he *was* your friend, as long as you were cooperative. If you tried to clam up, he might throw an arm around you, bring his mouth close to your ear, mention your wife and kids, and remind you about that marijuana stash he knew you had hidden somewhere, or maybe that burglary charge lying dormant that could still be brought, if he chose to revive it. Throughout the region, Danny Webb was a familiar figure, loved by many and respected for his honesty and integrity, and feared by some for his shrewdness and dogged pursuit of facts.

"I don't own a fancy car or live in a big house," he liked to say. "I'm just a country boy, with a wife and kids I love. But the one thing I do have that's worth more to me than all the gold in Fort Knox is my reputation."

That was why when Tawny Rose Acker, Tammy's older sister, approached him the day after the crimes and told him that she and her father were about to hire a private detective, Danny Webb took offense. He tried not to show it, but he was insulted, maybe even a little hurt. And he was alarmed.

Because Tawny Acker was someone to be reckoned with. Some called her feisty. Some good old boys called her a bitch. To Danny Webb, Tawny was an independent woman who, especially in the present situation, could cause a whole lot of trouble. Unlike her murdered sister, Tawny had never been regarded as the epitome of sweet girlishness. Tawny had not lived at home since the age of sixteen. A graduate of the University of Kentucky, where she had been a journalism major, she continued to live in Lexington, applying her writing and editing talents to university publications. Although it was hardly exceptional for ambitious young people to move away from the mountains, some of the locals resented her and considered her a snob. The owners and publishers of the *Whitesburg Mountain Eagle* recalled that when Tawny had worked there briefly one summer as an intern, she had been delivered to the paper each morning by her mother in a Cadillac and had quit one day when she was asked to sweep the floor.

Like her sister, Tawny was exceptionally attractive, but her beauty was of a more aggressive kind. With her long, sharp fingernails and her teased blonde hair, Tawny would have looked at home on Rodeo Drive. Danny Webb, however, far from being hostile to her, respected her as a sophisticate. When she told the lieutenant that she intended to bring in a PI, clearly indicating that Webb and his men were not up to the job, he was inclined to tell her to go fuck off but, realizing the strain she was under, and being himself an admirer and, as it had turned out, a protector of her father, he forgave what might in other circumstances have been interpreted as arrogance. Her irritation was even admirable. Not only had her sister been stabbed to death, but her inheritance had disappeared. She was distraught. Why should she tolerate anything but the best?

"I am going to hire the outstanding detective in the state and in the country," Tawny Acker said.

They were standing beside Webb's cruiser in the driveway of the Acker house, which was cordoned off with crime-scene tape. "I'm not going to take the chance of having this investigation end up going nowhere."

Biting his tongue, Webb conveyed his sympathies. He explained, however, that an investigation such as this one depended on intimate knowledge of the territory. Somebody coming in from the outside, nosing around, interfering with witnesses—that would be the worst possible thing to happen now.

"I've got every confidence we'll solve this thing," he told her. "I think I'm a pretty good detective, and so are my men."

"How do I know that?"

"Well, if you don't think we're any good, how about the FBI? They've got a fair reputation, it seems like. Look, give us a chance. If it looks like we're not getting anywhere, I wouldn't blame you if you did whatever you want."

Tawny Acker agreed to hold off for the time being. In the meanwhile she was going to hire guards, off-duty policemen, or whatever it took to give her and her father twenty-four hour protection. After all, he was the only living witness, and she was a prime target for kidnapping. Webb said that he would do his best to protect her and the doctor but that he had no objections to extra help with that.

Webb had not enjoyed having to point to the FBI to mollify her; it seemed demeaning to his officers and himself; but it was true, this had quickly become an FBI matter. Rod Kincaid had already provided names and descriptions of suspects. Webb's relations with Kincaid were cordial and cooperative, far more so than was usually the case between local authorities and the Bureau. The two men frequently worked together as a team, different though they were in style. Webb liked to kid that the restrained, methodical, precise Kincaid's idea of a celebratory blowout after solving a case and obtaining convictions was to splurge on *two* Big Macs. On his part, Kincaid trusted Webb so completely that he readily shared information with him that he normally had to conceal from indiscreet or corrupt officers, notably sheriffs. Kincaid told everyone, including fellow FBI agents, that Danny Webb was the kind of cop that others wished they were.

Within forty-eight hours of the crimes, Danny Webb's extensive contacts and the trust with which he was regarded by the community began to pay off as a number of local residents came forward with information that looked promising. One of the first was Jesse Spicer, a garage owner from Neon, who telephoned the lieutenant and told him that he had seen a suspicious-looking car parked near the Acker house on the night of the murder.

Spicer met Trooper Larry Carroll at the Acker house and led him across the highway and some hundred yards up the dirt road that cut through to Haymond. He had been driving someone over to Haymond that evening, Spicer said, a fellow who had had too much to drink. There had still been plenty of light when he saw the strange car.

"As I come up Haymond Hill it was a blue General Motors product, about a 1980 Chevrolet Caprice or Impala, light blue in color, and was very clean. It was so clean that it appeared like it was just washed or waxed. The two front doors were open and gentlemen were standing in the open doorways. There was a gentleman sitting in the backseat on the driver's side."

Spicer described the standing men as having been dressed in suits. One was tall and sort of blond, with an athletic build, the other shorter and darker. The man in the rear seat "had everyday clothes on. It appeared he hadn't shaved in three or four days. Like he had worked outside or something, dark hair, not neat. He looked out of place with the other two fellows. Never seen the two guys, but I've seen somebody resembles the guy in the backseat. But I can't remember wherever. The main thing that struck me was the guy in the backseat. He was out of place with the other two."

An hour or so later, coming back down on the return trip, Spicer said, he passed the car again, only it was slightly farther down the hill.

Spicer's account matched others. One man said he had seen a 1978 or 1980 blue Chevrolet sedan with three laughing men in it at McRoberts the afternoon of the murder. The men had been wearing suits. Two Fleming residents recalled seeing a blue or gray car parked in Dr. Acker's driveway between nine and ten o'clock on Thursday evening, while a man wearing a suit stood by the front door as it opened. Both witnesses had thought this "strange." A clerk at the Edge of Town Market gave a similar description of the men and recalled the car as blue or silver, possibly an Impala. And Debbie Benge, a clerk at the Rite Aid drugstore in Whitesburg, described how three strange men had entered the store as she was opening Thursday morning. One had asked for film, without showing any intention of buying some; another had asked how long it took to drive to Neon. Two were in suits, the third in casual clothes. They had driven away in "a big blue car."

An interview with Steve Reynolds provided indications of how someone could have known about Dr. Acker's money. Describing himself as Tammy's fiancé, Reynolds, who was twenty-one, said that he could not imagine anyone wanting to kill her. Everybody had liked her; she was "so good to everyone." She had been frightened of living alone in Lexington but felt at ease in her hometown. If only she had not come home to visit her father on that one evening!

Reynolds was suspicious of a handyman who had a key to the Acker house. Money had started missing after this fellow was employed there. One day Reynolds caught the man in the garage with a stack of fifty-dollar bills sticking out of his pocket. He had pulled his shirt down over the money. At that time, Dr. Acker was keeping his cash in an old trunk that was not even locked. He had the alarm system but evidently had trusted anyone he let work inside the house. It was Reynolds's "hunch" that Dr. Acker had bought the safe because of this incident.

An interview with the handyman produced nothing substantial. He had obviously not been one of the intruders and gave no indication of being the type of person to make elaborate plans for a break-in. He may have shot his mouth off about the cash, but that the doc had money appeared to have been relatively common knowledge, or was at least suspected, around Fleming-Neon.

The man Danny Webb most wanted to talk to could not be located until Sunday, August 11, when Webb finally found Roe Adkins at home in Isom and interviewed him there. He had taken a trip to Lexington on Tuesday, August 6, Adkins told the lieutenant, staying at the Continental Inn with a friend, Tid Adams. It had been strictly for pleasure. On Friday they were still drunk and decided to stop at the Abner Motel in Stanton instead of driving on home.

He had learned of Tammy Acker's murder on Friday, when his mother called his daughter about it, and he had happened to reach his daughter that afternoon.

"You called her from the Abner Motel, even though you were too drunk to drive?"

"I like to keep in touch," Adkins said.

"So you were gone from Tuesday till Saturday?"

"You can check on it."

Webb knew Adkins, had had occasion to speak to him many times over the years, gathering evidence on various charges. That Adkins would decide to travel to Lexington to get drunk in the middle of the week, that particular week, when his name was being used to gain entrance to a house was interesting. The hotel records would probably give him an airtight alibi.

Webb asked him how long he had known Roger Epperson. For about two years, Adkins estimated. He had met Roger through Sonny Spencer of Viper. At that time, "there was a seam of coal to be mined," and he and Tid Adams, Spencer, and Roger Epperson had combined to do the job. They had gone broke on the operation and had parted ways. Adkins said that he had had no contact with Epperson since that time. It was true, however, that Epperson knew of Dr. Acker's former business dealings with Adkins. And yes, Epperson would have known about Dr. Acker's money. Adkins had told Epperson about the doc. He had told many people the story of how Dr. Acker had produced a bundle of cash one Thanksgiving Day. But the Acker riches were common knowledge. It was a crying shame what had happened, but the doc had been a sitting duck, you could say.

Leaving Adkins, Lt. Webb decided that a Sunday drive over to the Epperson family house near Hazard was in order. He assumed that the Eppersons would be expecting him, since their eldest's name was by then all over the newspapers and the airwaves. He knew the family well and had had friendly relations with them, particularly the father. This time he was not sure what sort of a reception to expect.

It was hostile. Mildred Epperson, flanked by her two younger sons, came to the door and told the lieutenant to leave them alone. They were not about to permit him to harass them just because of some rumors. The sons were silent, cold-eyed.

Webb persisted. When was the last time they had seen Roger? Did they know where he was? They had neither seen nor heard from him in years, Mrs. Epperson said, and asked Webb to please leave.

Eventually Eb Epperson agreed to come out and talk to the lieutenant on the front porch. Webb was as soft as he could be. He said he knew how painful this was, but he had a job to do. How long had it been since Roger had come around?

"*I don't have a son named Roger,*" Eb Epperson blurted—and suddenly he burst into tears, covering his face with his hands as he sobbed and sobbed.

"You don't understand ..." he managed to choke out. "I just buried my best friend, the other week. This ... it's too much. I am real upset," and he continued crying.

"Who was that?" Webb asked. "Bug, who was it you buried?"

For a moment he did not answer, struggling to contain himself. Then he said:

"Ed Morris. Him and me ..." and he turned and went back into the house.

By the time Danny Webb was down the porch steps, the links had joined in his mind. He felt like a child who, tinkering with a chemistry set, ignites an explosion that scalds and alters everything.

Jackson County was not one of those for which he had direct responsibility, but he knew about the double homicide in Gray Hawk, because it had occurred close to his territory and remained unsolved. Ed and Bessie Morris ... Ed Morris's turning out to have been Eb Epperson's best friend ... Roger Epperson ... Tammy Acker ... a father who disowns his son ... the uncontrollable tears. Probably without intending to do so—and without providing anything that would stand up in court or even be admissible as evidence—Eb Epperson had connected Roger to the Gray Hawk killings. It was the first link to any suspect there. As significant as his emotional outburst was, what Eb had *not* said seemed to Webb also telling. There had been no pro forma parental denial of a son's guilt—only the expression of grief and frustration over the murder of a friend, as well as what came across as shame.

Webb sat in his cruiser for a minute or so, letting everything sink in, feeling the pieces slide together. The more he thought about these fragments in relation to one another, the more they became part of one big, bloody, probably still-unfinished picture. The Gray Hawk killings were now one incident in a spree of at least four over three months' time. Webb had no further doubt.

All at once his chest tightened. Roger and the others may already have killed again, and most certainly would, the longer they were loose.

But where were they?

He raced to his office to call Rod Kincaid.

21

WHERE THEY WERE BY THEN WAS IN HALLANDALE and elsewhere in and around Miami enjoying their spoils and feeling on top of the world. That Sunday afternoon, as Danny Webb experienced revelations, the gang roamed shopping malls like kids on some dream of a spree, scarfing up forty thousand dollars' worth of doodads at one jewelry store alone. Roger bought cluster and solitaire diamond rings for himself and a three-karat number for Carol; Donnie traded Tammy Acker's bracelet for another; Sherry bought Benny a gold lion's head pendant with diamonds for eyes and a big diamond stuck in its mouth, to match the ring she had already given him because his birth sign was Leo. She imagined how he would get all silly when he found it under the Christmas tree or maybe a coconut palm on the island where they would be living happily ever after—she made every effort to hope.

As the others shopped on, Roger drove through thick heat down to the Miami waterfront to negotiate for a ninety-six-thousand-dollar cigarette boat to take them to Bimini. He inquired about false passports for everyone except Sherry, who, for just such a contingency as this, had carried a bona-fide one since her days as Mr. Wong's bride. Fake documents would cost maybe twenty-five thousand apiece—but what did it matter? They were up to their armpits in cash and, as any fool could tell you, money made money.

To jump-start a life, or to end one, there was no place like South

Florida. Aside from its polyglot population—Cubans and Central and South Americans fleeing Communism and other tyrannies; Italians and Jews down from the Northeast to retire in the sun; blacks drawn from the rural South; Anglos who had been there for generations and some who had not; always the tourists, lines of them boarding and leaving cruise ships—what gave South Florida its distinctive hum was crime. For the bottom-feeders as for the high-rollers, for the desperate and the unscrupulous on every level, it had been a sizzling crap-shoot for at least fifty years, since Meyer Lansky established the beachhead of an international syndicate on the Broward–Dade county line in 1936. For Eastern Kentuckians and East Tennesseans like Roger and his pals, it was where you went to gamble on the future. It meant no more chicken-fried steak, bring on the prime rib and the butterfly shrimp and the daquiris; no more up-a-hollow Mountain Motor Speedway, this was the fast lane. Glitzy, tacky, sexy, hot, it meant the promises of tangerine and aqua nights. Dope-heads, dealers, smugglers, pimps, whores, hitmen, cons—you could find them anywhere, but here the bitterness of nonentities fed on dreams as broad as the Atlantic, as seductive as the Caribbean.

That evening the gang entertained Pat Mason and her friend at the Shangri-la restaurant in Plantation, west of Ft. Lauderdale. From the moment they had arrived at her apartment driving an English sports car and a pricey conversion van, it was apparent that they were not broke. Within an hour Roger forked over thirteen thousand plus for a gold Toyota MR2—faster than a Ferrari from a standing start, it was said—that Pat happened to have in her inventory as sales manager at Autoputer. Roger fetched the cash from his car but permitted Carol to hand Pat the stack of bills. It was the third automobile he had bought in the past twelve hours, and he wasn't even warmed up yet.

The day before, on Saturday morning up at Ormond Beach, only Sherry had shown concern about getting rid of evidence and keeping track of the money and trying to stay cool. She asked the others to help her gather up the Bank of Whitesburg wrappers scattered all over the condo. She deposited these, the badges and fake FBI IDs, Donnie's bloodstained suede hush puppies, and his and Benny's dress shirts and ties, which she cut into shreds, in various Dumpsters up and down Atlantic Avenue. She left their suits at a dry cleaner's, with no intention of ever picking them up, and took Carol and Becky to an office-supply store in Daytona to purchase what she called pilot's cases (map cases or salesman's sample cases) for the cash. Carol and Becky fancied leather ones; Sherry settled for vinyl. Each was equipped with a lock; for fear that the others would forget the combinations, Sherry wrote the numbers down.

That afternoon Roger drove the Olds to Terry Taylor Ford in Daytona, where a ruby-red 1985 Triumph TVR convertible had been sitting on the lot catching his eye since July. Carrying an attaché case and the pilot's case, he approached a salesman and asked to take a test drive. The salesman, who introduced himself as Bob Loturco, invited Roger into his office and told him that the asking price was twenty thousand. He would be getting a great deal, Loturco said, because the car was technically used, but it had only sixty-five hundred miles on it. Custom-built. What a beauty. Terms could be arranged.

"No problem," Roger said. "If I like it, I'll pay cash," and he patted the cases. "Might need more than one. Looking for a van. Got anything?"

Aroused, Loturco said he had several possibilities. He could work out some super prices, with more than one car involved, especially if this was a strictly cash arrangement.

"I had some business deals come through," Roger said.

"Great," Loturco said. "Many of our customers pay cash."

Roger sensed accurately that he had chosen a salesman who would not be overly scrupulous about the source of a cash payment. Had he known that Robert Loturco had spent fourteen years behind bars in Michigan for armed robbery, Roger would have been even more confident. From a crook's point of view, that was one of the great things about Florida: if you wanted to find someone sympathetic to your needs, the odds were always in your favor. Another customer had already put a deposit on the Triumph, Loturco said; but with cash, something could be worked out.

Roger drove the car around the block and returned ready to buy. Closing the door to the office, Roger opened both cases and let Loturco gape at the bundles of greenbacks and a chrome-plated .45 semiautomatic resting atop the bills. He paid nineteen thousand for the sports car and fourteen thousand six hundred for a 1984 Dodge van.

At first Roger listed the buyer of the TVR as Carol Malone and that of the van as Dale Epperson, then asked that a Ron Dykes of Daytona be named as the purchaser of both vehicles. He indicated that he might be interested in additional transportation: he was leaving town for a few days but would be back in touch. Advising that his associates would retrieve the van and the Olds, he took off in the Triumph with the top down.

There actually was a person named Ron Dykes, a fellow in the drywalling (Sheetrock) business whom Roger had talked to at the Pelican Lounge about going into business together. Telephoning Dykes from the condo, Roger told him that the time was right to start a new company, which they would call Hang Rite. He would have his lawyers and accountants in Miami set things up. In the meanwhile Dykes, whose own van had broken down, should pick up the Olds at Terry Taylor Ford and feel free to drive it for the time being.

That night the gang headed down the coast. When Roger bought the MR2 for Carol, Sherry ventured to inquire whether he wasn't acting sort of impulsive. But he was too drunk and stoned to listen or care. On Monday, August 12, he paid Pat Mason another eleven thousand-plus for a 1985 Dodge van that he said his partner in the drywalling business would pick up later that week. He gave Mason another two thousand to install a mobile phone and engage an answering service.

The trouble with the other van, Roger said, was that the sound system in it was lousy. He decided that the men should make a run back up to Ormond Beach to get a new one installed and to close up the condo. Sherry accused them of wanting to do nothing more than party away from their women and warned that they were taking too much of a chance going back; but they shouted her down, and she agreed to wait for them with Carol and Becky in Miami. They were about to leave when Donnie discovered that he had left his case of money under the bed at the Tiki Motel in Hallandale. At this, Sherry managed to convince everyone to let her, the only one with a clear head, take charge of most of the rest of the cash, lest they lose it or spend it. Sheepish for once, they agreed to trust her. "You so cool," Donnie said, "you ain't even human."

On her own, Sherry deposited the three pilot's cases in a locker at a Hallandale ministorage located behind the Ramada Inn. She told no one of the location, keeping the key in her jeans, and did not mention that she had skimmed about twelve thousand from Roger and Carol's share—fair payment for services rendered, she figured, and for putting up with their aggravation.

At Hollywood, just north of Hallandale, the Triumph broke down and had to be towed to a garage, where no one could make it work.

"Fucking English," Roger said, climbing into the van for the rest of the trip. "From now on I'm buying American, or Jap."

He did not wait long. On the outskirts of Daytona he spotted a 1963 Corvette parked at a body shop. "That's it," he said. "That baby's been waiting for me." He still had the attaché case full of cash. The car needed some work, so he put eleven thousand down and agreed to pay the six-thousand-dollar balance when he picked it up.

It must have been just about the time that Donnie remembered that he had left his money under a bed that, a thousand miles or so away in Kentucky, investigators at the laboratory in Frankfort discovered the importance of something else he had forgotten. The lab technicians had been working day and night since Friday, processing hundreds of fingerprints taken from the Acker house. None had matched those of any of the three suspects; the murder weapon had yielded no prints at all. The technicians had paid special attention to the black attaché case supposedly left behind, but had found nothing on it, nor on the plastic card found inside.

A new "superglue" technique, however, finally yielded two promising prints from the plastic baggie inside the briefcase. Comparison with the prints on record of the suspects determined that those from the baggie matched the right thumb and right ring finger of Donald Terry Bartley.

"Not that we had any doubts," Lt. Webb commented when he examined the prints, "but it was real thoughtful of those fellows to leave us some solid evidence, wasn't it? Now all we got to do is find the bastards." He informed Rod Kincaid; the FBI issued arrest warrants and in its internal memos and bulletins gave the case the code name ACKMUR.

As head of the London FBI station, a suite of offices in a bank building on Main Street—six agents and a secretary-receptionist who sat behind bulletproof glass and a steel door—Kincaid's responsibility was for all of Eastern Kentucky, which made him one of the busiest agents in the country. It was he who organized undercover and other operations against the endless succession of corrupt sheriffs and interstate theft and narcotics rings and various fugitives who used the mountains as hideouts and strongholds. Throughout the Bureau, as within the IRS and the Bureau of Alcohol, Tobacco and Firearms and the Drug Enforcement Agency, it was agreed that being a federal agent in the mountains of Kentucky and East Tennessee was about as hairy a job as you could find. You did not win any popularity contests.

As different as Special Agent Kincaid was in personality from Lt. Webb—more methodical than instinctive; more restrained than ebullient; inclined to build a case piece by piece rather than to act on a hunch—he was also an Eastern Kentucky native and knew the area equally well, if through conscientious study more than through spontaneous personal contacts. Nor was there anything of the country boy about Wilburn R. Kincaid, the name under which his home phone number was listed in the Somerset public directory. Informants often rang Danny Webb at home; hardly anyone connected Rod Kincaid with Wilburn R., and few would have thought that a major FBI agent would have a listed home number anyway. Kincaid liked it that way; he tried to keep his work as separate as possible from his home life. His wife had her own work, teaching mentally and physically handicapped children; the Kincaids' own three children were still in school, the youngest preparing to enter the University of Louisville. With a B.A. in English literature from Eastern Kentucky University, Kincaid himself could easily have gone undercover as an English professor. About five-ten, with sandy, wavy hair and bright blue eyes, he spoke deliberately, precisely, in an orotund baritone, with no regional accent and with an absence of local idiom. His favorite spare-time reading was H. L. Mencken's three-volume *The American Language*. Making notes at his desk, he might have been preparing for a Mark Twain seminar, except for the loaded shotgun propped in a corner.

On Tuesday morning, August 13, Kincaid sat behind his desk studying the bill of sale for a 1978 blue Oldsmobile Delta 88 four-door sedan. The price was twenty-four hundred dollars, "cash on delivery." The receipt was dated June 18, 1985, and the buyer's signature was Carol Malone. Mrs. Quanita W. Bowles, owner of Earl Bowles Used Cars, had telephoned Kincaid's office earlier that morning to volunteer that Roger Epperson, whom she had known for some time through his father, had come to her lot earlier that summer and had bought the Olds. He had been driving a Thunderbird and had been accompanied by an Oriental woman, who had signed the receipt.

As Kincaid noted how closely the Olds matched descriptions of the car involved in ACKMUR and that the date of the receipt was within two days of the Gray Hawk killings, giving credence to Danny Webb's connection of the crimes, he took a call from another woman who wished to volunteer information about Epperson. She was reluctant to give her name, because she said that if her husband knew that she was talking to the FBI, he would beat her. She was telephoning from a pay phone.

Kincaid asked the woman if she would meet him at the London KSP post. She said that she would be there in half an hour.

The woman arrived looking frightened. She said that the only reason she was coming forward was that she feared that if she had information and concealed it, she could be prosecuted; but she didn't know whether to be more afraid of the FBI or of her husband, who would be glad of an excuse to whip her. Kincaid, introducing himself and the assistant commander of the KSP post, assured her that her identity would be kept secret.

Haltingly she revealed that she knew where a car belonging to Roger Epperson was. It was a Thunderbird. Epperson had left it behind several weeks before and had driven away in a blue four-door car.

"Did he say where he was going?" Kincaid asked.

"I didn't talk to him. I just seen it, is all."

Kincaid suspected that fear of her husband was causing the woman to hold back. He suggested to her that she might have heard a rumor about where Epperson was headed. If he had bought a different car, he must have been planning to drive somewhere. Had she heard anything? Even secondhand gossip would do.

"Florida," the woman said. "I heard they was going to Florida."

Kincaid dispatched two other agents to find the T-bird and obtain permission to search it. He alerted all Florida FBI stations to be on the lookout for an Olds with Kentucky plates and for the fugitives: the woman had not been able to say where in Florida they might have been headed, and they might no longer be there, but it was a start.

As Kincaid dictated a full account, known in the Bureau as a "302" report, of the interview, he received word that the T-bird had been found in Mt. Vernon and that a search of the glove compartment had yielded an "insurance due" notice dated June 17, addressed to Roger Dale Epperson at Lake City, Tennessee; and a resumé and personal data sheet on Carol Keeney Ellis of Clinton, Tennessee.

Kincaid put in a call to Danny Webb.

* * *

At that moment Lt. Webb was in a trailer home at Delphia, in the southeast corner of Perry County, interviewing Tom McDowell, whom Webb guessed Roger Epperson may have had reason to visit during the days before the Acker murder. The lieutenant's hunch proved correct. Tom McDowell acknowledged that Epperson and two other men, one about six feet and stocky, the other small and dark, had driven up to the trailer the previous week in a big blue car that had clothes hanging in the back. Epperson had told him that they had just driven up from Florida, where they had been in contact with McDowell's brother, Travis, in the Daytona Beach area.

"Is that right," Danny Webb said. "You wouldn't have a phone number for Travis, would you, Tom?"

McDowell said that his brother was a musician who played five or six instruments and moved around a lot from gig to gig. His mother might know where he was. She was also in Florida.

Webb telephoned Mrs. McDowell, who said that her son Travis was working a construction job at the Holiday Inn in Orlando. The lieutenant reached the manager of the inn and asked to speak to a worker named Travis McDowell. It took about five minutes for Travis to come to the phone. The lieutenant began with pleasantries, how he was up visiting Tom, was the weather great in Florida.

"Tell me something, Travis. We know you've seen old Roger Epperson down there, around Daytona, wasn't it?"

Travis did not answer. Webb pressed him, in a fairly friendly way. Travis finally admitted that he had run into Epperson at the Pelican Lounge and at Castaways, where Travis had been sitting in with the band. He had also been to a party at a place in Ormond Beach that Roger had rented.

"Where was that?"

"Chipwood. Chippinwood. Something. It's near the beach."

"Who was at that party?"

"There was a man there everyone called Ben. This guy showed me a weapon looked like a damn machine gun. Roger showed me all this police stuff he had. There was a Oriental girl there."

"So Roger's got this place and he hangs around the Pelican Lounge?"

"Yeah."

"Travis, I want you to do me a favor. Are you heading back to Daytona anytime soon?"

"Tomorrow. This here job's about done."

"When you get back to Daytona, will you not say anything about talking to me when you run into those guys, and will you call the FBI office in Daytona?"

He agreed.

Lt. Webb telephoned Rod Kincaid from the Hazard post and told him about this hot new lead. Webb said that he could not guarantee that Travis McDowell would contact the Bureau, but he thought he would.

"We can't take a chance and we can't wait," Kincaid said. "We're going to move right now."

As soon as he was off the phone with Lt. Webb, Kincaid contacted Special Agent Bill Fluherty, a seventeen-year FBI veteran who from 1979 through 1984 had been in charge of security for the Attorney General of the United States and for the Director of the FBI. Fluherty was now supervisor of the Jacksonville office, headquarters for northern and central Florida. Kincaid explained how ACKMUR had broken open in the past few minutes, thanks to Danny Webb.

Fluherty agreed that Travis McDowell should be approached without delay. Fluherty said he would also alert the satellite office in Daytona and begin organizing plans for the arrests.

It was an extremely delicate prospect. The fugitives were known to have automatic weapons, were said to be suicidal, and would have nothing to lose. How to capture them without getting agents killed and endangering civilians—that would be the challenge.

But the first priority was to decide on the quickest, most effective way to bring in Travis McDowell and to impress on him the gravity of the situation. They needed to take him from Orlando to Daytona before he had a chance to get cold feet or perhaps become confused about his loyalties and tip off his friend. Travis himself was no crook, according to Danny Webb, but the bonds between these Kentucky mountain boys ought not to be discounted. Travis's misfortune was in the company he had been keeping. Sooner or later, as Webb liked to say, if you climb in with the hogs, you're going to get dirty.

"How about a helicopter?" Kincaid suggested. "It's quick, and it ought to have the effect of reinforcing his perspective."

"I was thinking the same thing," Fluherty said.

22

WAITING IN MIAMI FOR BENNY AND ROGER and Donnie to return, the women were getting antsy. They had nothing to do but shop, and Sherry especially was tiring of that, never having been one to care that much for jewelry anyway. When the men had not returned by dinnertime on Tuesday, she telephoned Benny at the Ormond Beach condo and told him he had better get out of there fast. What was he waiting for? Benny tried to explain that Roger had a number of things to take care of. The stereo for the van would not be ready until tomorrow. Roger was driving a Cadillac this car salesman was loaning him until the Triumph was fixed. Donnie was feeling left out, with all the cars being bought and none for him, so Roger had advanced him sixteen thou for a slightly used Datsun 300 ZX, gray, a really sharp little machine. Benny would take over the van when it was ready. And, oh yes, Roger had bought a classic 'Vette but it wasn't on the road yet, so he was thinking of buying a newer Corvette, maybe a brand-new one that he could count on to actually run. They would be down in Miami in a day or so. Everything was cool.

"Roger is nuts," Sherry said. "How much coke are they on? I want you to get out of there. I want us to get out of here, together."

"Booger, stop bugging me, will you? You just afraid we're going to party all night."

"I'm nobody's fool."

What Benny did not tell her was that Roger had phoned Roe

Adkins in Kentucky and had learned that the old doctor had survived and that there were warrants out. There was no reason to panic, Roger assured Benny and Donnie; no one knew where they were.

On Wednesday morning Sherry telephoned Gene Foust at the Oak Ridge P.D. to ask whether he knew anything about the status of the FBI's search for Benny and Donnie. They had been on the run now for more than two months; the Feds must be getting pretty frustrated.

"I don't know how frustrated they are," Foust said, "but I'd say they're putting out a lot of effort. Haven't you heard? There's warrants out for Benny and his buddies. For murder. What the hell have they done? Where in hell are you?"

Sherry hung up and dialed the condo. No one answered. She kept trying into the night, hoping Benny and the others were on their way back to Miami. She gave up and tried to sleep and rang again early Thursday morning. Benny answered, but she could barely hear him, there was so much noise in the background. Partying.

"Benny! What's going on? Are you crazy? They've got warrants for you all! You got to leave! Don't you know they's bound to find you?"

Benny hung up. Sherry called Pat Mason. "I'm leaving Benny," Sherry said. What she did not say was that she had a premonition that Benny was about to be arrested, probably killed, because he had been insisting for weeks that they would never take him alive.

The truth was that Benny and the others had been acting even more recklessly than Sherry could imagine. The party had begun Wednesday afternoon over drinks at the Pelican Lounge. Roger was in a frenzy of largesse. He decided to buy the Pelican Lounge, settled with the owner on a price of fifty thousand, and took five thousand out of his briefcase right then and there and plunked the bills down on the bar as an advance. Quite a crowd piled in, swollen by Roger's generosity. He bought rounds of drinks and offered lines of coke. Men in tank tops, women in bikinis—the place was like Daytona at spring break. Donnie poured beer over a girl's T-shirt and she happily pulled it up to display her breasts. Hands plunged into pants, girls dropped to their knees. Bob Loturco, celebrating his take from all the cars his new benefactor had bought, was there with his wife, assuring Roger that he could find him a new Corvette over at Jon Hall Chevrolet. Several old Kentucky pals of Roger's crowded in. Roger loaned one of them five thousand in cash, out of the goodness of his heart, and paid another fifteen hundred for his gold bracelet. The fellow selling the bracelet was from Perry County. His name was Travis McDowell.

On Tuesday afternoon, when the FBI helicopter descended into the parking lot of the Holiday Inn at Orlando, Travis McDowell was speechless. It wasn't until they were up in the air whirring off toward Daytona that he began to get the picture. The agents weren't interested merely in interviewing him. They wanted his help. They wanted him to show them exactly where Roger Epperson was living and to lead them to Epperson and his pals.

Travis was reluctant to cooperate. It seemed too much like being an informer, something Travis had never been and never wanted to be. But he felt trapped. When Agent Fluherty, who was six-feet-seven and two hundred and fifty fat-free pounds and talked slowly and distinctly and looked clean through you with the steady, cold eyes of a man whose favorite recreation was hunting, explained how Roger and the others had stabbed a young woman up in Letcher County eleven times through the back with a butcher knife and nearly strangled her father to death, Travis wavered. And when Fluherty counseled, fatherly but firm, that what Travis would be doing was not really informing but rather helping to save innocent lives by speeding up the arrest process and enabling the FBI to organize a plan that would protect innocent people like him, Travis saw matters in a different light and capitulated. He just could not find a way to argue with Bill Fluherty.

From the FBI office in Daytona, McDowell directed Fluherty and Special Agent Chuck Boling north on Atlantic Avenue to Ormond Beach, around a few corners to the Garden of New Britain and No. 55 Chippingwood Lane. The agents then drove Travis back to Daytona and dropped him off at the Treasure Island Inn, across the boulevard from the Pelican Lounge. Travis promised to hang around with Epperson and the others when, as he was sure they would, they came in for cocktails. Other agents would be keeping track of him, Fluherty assured him, and he had no reason to be frightened.

That evening Fluherty and Boling paid a discreet call on the manager of the condo complex, sizing him up to judge whether he would be cooperative and could be trusted. What about the people living in the condo that was kitty-corner across the driveway from No. 55? Would they be willing to stay in a hotel for a day or two, so that agents could watch 55 from their upstairs window? It would probably also be a good idea to evacuate Epperson's next-door neighbors. They would be happy to go, the manager said. They had complained several times about the noise in 55 and visitors appearing at odd hours.

Back at the Daytona office—like those in most medium-sized cities, it was located on the top floor of a bank—Fluherty calculated that fourteen agents would be needed for the operation and summoned several down from Jacksonville. He targeted the condo as the prospective site of the arrest: there would be relatively few civilians around, and it was the likely place to catch the fugitives in possession of evidence. Using maps and making drawings of the New Britain complex, Fluherty and Boling devised a battle strategy. To the residents of the complex, it was a retreat from traffic and crowds, and its enclosed layout, with only a single entrance from the street, offered a sense of security. To the FBI, it had become a fortress to be liberated as efficiently and bloodlessly as possible.

Four agents would keep No. 55 under surveillance from the vacated condo across the way. Ten others, under Boling's command, would form a SWAT (Special Weapons and Tactics) team, using the beach at the end of Cardinal Drive, about a quarter-mile away, as a staging area. At Fluherty's radio signal, the SWAT team would move in. Here the lone entryway to the complex was key: some SWAT members would seal that off. Others would deploy at No. 55 and outside the perimeter of the complex, to prevent escape over the fence. Fluherty and the other members of the surveillance squad would make the actual arrests. Such a large show of force would, Fluherty hoped, discourage Epperson and the others from trying to resist.

Talking to Travis McDowell and, by phone, to Rod Kincaid, and observing the fugitives as they roamed around Daytona and Ormond Beach partying and flashing money during the next twenty-four hours, Fluherty concluded that Epperson was the leader of the trio. Hodge was the muscle man and probably the most dangerous. Bartley seemed to be a hanger-on sort of a twerp. Ideally, they would get to Epperson first, and the others, with no one to lead them, would surrender. That was the hope, anyway.

*   *   *

Before dawn on the morning of Thursday, August 15, Bill Fluherty and three other agents, one of them a woman, watched from the upstairs window of the borrowed condo as Epperson, Hodge, Bartley, and other revelers arrived in various cars and entered No. 55. There were more than a dozen people, Travis McDowell among them, coming to continue the partying that had begun at the Pelican Lounge.

Rock music and shouting drifted out into the hot, wet night. There were too many people in there to risk making the arrests now, Fluherty said, and besides, the plan was to maneuver in daylight, to be sure of the targets. He would not order the SWAT team to begin staging until some of the guests, at least, had left. Whenever Epperson, Bartley, and Hodge were sleeping it off—that might be the moment.

When, by ten o'clock that morning, only one male guest had left and music was still blasting, Fluherty telephoned the manager and asked him to go to No. 55 to ask Epperson to shut the party down. That worked, people began to leave; but unfortunately one of them was Epperson, who drove away with a middle-aged woman. Agents followed them to a Chevy dealer's in Daytona and reported over the radio that, after more than an hour, Epperson had driven off alone in a new red Corvette that he had apparently just purchased. They would be tailing him.

At about two, Hodge and Bartley left, Hodge driving a black and gray Dodge van, Bartley in a gray Datsun 300 ZX. They would be back, Fluherty said. They had taken no extra suitcases with them and had not been in a hurry. Even cokeheads had to sleep eventually.

Fluherty rehearsed various contingencies. He ordered the SWAT team to begin staging, and he asked the manager to put up a sign to say that the swimming pool was closed for cleaning. Fortunately, it was too hot for anyone to be out on the tennis courts.

Hodge and Bartley returned at about five that afternoon. All we need now is Epperson, Fluherty said. He calculated that it would take the SWAT team less than two minutes to arrive, once signaled. Local police were on the alert to stop traffic on Atlantic Avenue so that the team, with their M16 rifles and protective equipment, could cross the busy boulevard unimpeded in three unmarked cars.

At ten past six, Fluherty watched as Hodge, shirtless in jeans, carrying several hangers hung with clothes, came out the front door and began walking toward the van, which was parked in an alleyway beside the condos across from 55; the van's rear end was pointed toward the street. Just then the automatic garage door at 55 was raised up and Bartley appeared, also carrying clothes, and walked toward the Datsun, parked directly in front of the garage.

"This is it," Fluherty said. "Move up *now!*" he radioed Chuck Boling with the SWAT team—but Fluherty instantaneously decided that he could not wait for them to arrive. Bartley and Hodge might be leaving for good. An impulse born of the instincts of a seasoned hunter flashed through his mind. You cannot hit all the birds at once. Pick off one or two quick as you can and worry about the rest of the flock later. He saw Hodge take hold of the door handle of the van.

Fluherty raced downstairs and through the back door, jumped into his car, and jammed the key into the ignition. Squealing rubber, he streaked past the tennis courts into the street, past the fence surrounding the complex, and screeched to a stop inside the entryway just in time to block the van as it was backing out.

With no time for thought, improvising all the way, relying on training and instinct, Fluherty jerked his steering wheel to the left as he skidded, leaving his car at an angle, so that as he blocked the van, he could get out with the car between him and gunfire—he hoped not from a machine gun. Drawing his pistol, he leapt out and ran thirty feet to protection around the corner of a building, where he had a clear view and a clean shot at the driver's side of the van, about thirty-five feet away. He had only his pistol. Neither Hodge nor Bartley had been carrying weapons—with Hodge stripped to the waist, that was another good reason to abandon the battle plan and move fast—but there was no telling what guns Hodge had in that van.

Fluherty could not see through the van's tinted glass. He wondered whether Hodge might try to roll out the passenger side and counted on other agents to catch up to the action quickly. For now, it was one-on-one.

"FBI!" Fluherty shouted. "Hodge! You're under arrest! Come out with your hands up!"

After a short pause, Fluherty saw the door open a crack. A hand slowly emerged. A gold watch and a big ring glittered in the sun. The fingers took hold of the rain gutter. Then there was no movement, only the glint of gold and jewels. For fifteen to twenty seconds, there was silence, broken by distant shouts.

Fluherty did not dare move forward. He was wearing a protective vest, but his head was bare, and he knew he presented a big target. Foremost in his mind was that Hodge had supposedly vowed never to be caught alive and was now probably trying to figure out how to get hold of his gun, if one wasn't already gripped in his right hand.

"FBI!" Fluherty repeated. "You're surrounded! Come out with your hands on your head!"

At last, very slowly, Hodge climbed down and out of the van and placed his hands on his head. With his bare, golden upper body, the gold chain around his neck and all the hardwear on his wrists and fingers and all those muscles shining with sweat, the sun lighting up his dark blond hair, he might have been an awe-inspiring sight to someone other than Bill Fluherty—who hurried over, shoved Hodge around to brace him against the van, and handcuffed him. As he clicked the cuffs shut, Fluherty glanced into the van and saw a chrome-plated, pearl-handled .45 semiautomatic pistol resting on the console between the driver's and the passenger's seats. In that brief interval before surrender, Hodge must have been trying to decide whether to live, or to die trying to kill once more.

Other agents now rushed up to help. Finally able to look around, Fluherty saw that the SWAT team was deploying around No. 55.

"Did you get Donnie?" Hodge asked.

"I don't know. Is there anyone else in the condo? Are there weapons in there?"

"If Donnie's not inside, there's no one else. I think there's guns in the van. Can I have my wallet? It's on the dash. There's a lot of money in it and I don't want to leave it in the van."

Fluherty reached in to pick up the wallet, which was so stuffed with bills that it could not be folded in half. Did he really have to explain to Hodge that this was evidence and could not politely be handed back? Among all the vagaries of the criminal mentality Fluherty had observed over many years, the sense of utter unreality was constant. He recited to Hodge the Miranda formula, looking into his eyes and wondering what he understood, since he appeared to comprehend so little of anything. A moment before he and Hodge had been a hair's breadth from shooting it out and possibly killing each other. Barechested, Hodge would have stood little chance. Now he was worried about his money. For what? Fluherty's anxiety gave way to disgust.

Chuck Boling trotted over to relay that SWAT members had caught Bartley as he ran and tried to scramble over the fence. He had surrendered meekly.

Fluherty patted down Hodge's jeans and in the right rear pocket felt a slender, hard object. He removed a six-inch butterfly knife with dragon designs on the case. He opened it; the surgical steel blade gleamed. As he shoved him into an Ormond Beach squad car, Hodge glowered back over his shoulder: "That's not my knife. You did not take that off of me."

I didn't? Fluherty said to himself. Funny you're so sensitive about a knife.

Less than half an hour later, Chuck Boling watched as agents and local police forced a red Corvette to the curb on Atlantic Avenue about three miles south of the condo. Monitored by a police airplane, Epperson's new car had been trailed after it had left the Castaways parking lot.

Epperson refused permission to search the Corvette. It did not belong to him, he said. It was the property of a guy who had loaned it to him that afternoon. There were papers to prove that the owner was named Travis McDowell.

At the Ormond Beach cell where he was held before being transferred with Bartley and Hodge to Orlando, Epperson continued to refuse to sign a "Permission to Search" form, repeating that the Corvette and its contents belonged to Travis McDowell, with the exception of a leather briefcase stashed behind the seat. He would like that returned to him. It contained personal papers.

The police kept the condo sealed off through the night, with two FBI agents on guard. The next day, after warrants were issued and Letcher County Assistant Commonwealth's Attorney Mike Caudill arrived with two KSP troopers to join Fluherty, Boling, five other agents, and an Ormond Beach police lieutenant, a search was made and an inventory compiled. The place looked as if it had been in the process of being vacated, but evidence remained.

One item caught everyone's eye at once. On the coffee table in the living room sat a vase holding two dozen red roses, tagged with a card addressed to Roger Epperson from Bob Loturco of Terry Taylor Ford, "in grateful acknowledgement of your valued patronage."

The hapless Loturco, however, had already been fired. On his way to negotiate for the Corvette, he had been the first guest to leave that morning; his wife had accompanied Roger to the Chevrolet lot. Loturco was sacked, not for accepting cash of dubious origin, but for committing a Ford salesman's unpardonable sin, encouraging and assisting a customer in the purchase of a Chevy.

Items less sentimental than the flowers included a police scanner, a 9-mm shell found in an ashtray, a map of Kentucky, a police radio-frequency booklet with Kentucky codes marked, currency wrappers from the Bank of Whitesburg, and more than seventy-five thousand dollars in cash. Bill Fluherty discovered one fifty-dollar bill at the bottom of a bed in an upstairs room.

Searches of the various cars yielded drug paraphernalia, small amounts of cocaine and marijuana, a two-way radio, a brown cotton glove, knives, and guns. A homemade garotte, consisting of a rubberized cord knotted at both ends, led Fluherty to request a check of recent Florida homicides to see whether any involving strangulation remained unsolved. The Moon Mullins murder quickly stood out because of the victim's Tennessee background and the information that his house showed no sign of forced entry, which suggested the possible use of fake IDs. The victim's occupation made solving this case less than urgent, but Epperson, Bartley, and Hodge became top suspects.

Roger had indeed listed Travis McDowell as the purchaser of the '85 Corvette, for twenty-seven thousand. Since the owner of the 300 ZX and the conversion van was recorded as Ron Dykes, the FBI quickly located him, the Oldsmobile, and the second Dodge van. Dykes's account of how he had unwittingly become an overnight automobile freak led the FBI to Autoputer and Pat Mason who, admitting that she knew Sherry but professing ignorance of the group's sources of income, added the MR2 to a list that now totaled an expenditure of about a hundred and eleven thousand dollars in six days. Adding this to the cash found at the condo, cash and the down payment receipt for the Pelican Lounge discovered in Roger's briefcase, and twelve thousand in Benny's wallet, investigators could account for about two hundred and eighty-seven thousand dollars—more than half the amount stolen, according to Dr. Acker's estimate.

Becky Hannah had left her 200 SX parked in the condo garage. It had a faulty throttle spring, she told Agent Burl Cloninger when he found her, back in the bosom of her family in Tennessee, eager, she said, to begin her senior year in high school. She provided an account, filled with innocence and bewilderment, of her experiences with Donnie Bartley and his pals, saying that she had no idea where they got their money but had worried that they might have robbed someone. The woman she knew as Booger, or Sherry, had put her on a plane from Miami as soon as news of the arrests became known.

When Mike Caudill came down from Kentucky to interview her, he asked her to describe the personalities of the three men with whom she had been associated, or vacationing, or however she had spent her summer. Becky replied in a dreamy voice that Benny had been like a big brother to her. He reminded her a lot of her own brother:

"Benny does have a temper, I guess, but that's another thing that reminds me of my brother. And Donnie is—I've never met anyone like him before."

"How is that?"

"He's extremely sweet to me. This is how they are to me. I've just never met anyone like him before."

"And Roger?"

"I don't know. He's sort of quiet and to himself."

Becky's Tennessee drawl enhanced the impression of scenes from a girl's holiday heaven. Caudill, an earnest, hard-working fellow, dark-haired and chunky, was annoyed. Hoping to jolt Becky into some sense of reality, he reminded her of what these kindly fellows had actually done, describing the mayhem at the Acker house, with emphasis on the butcher knife. "Your friend Bartley's fingerprints were found on the scene. We have a witness. The doctor himself has identified both Bartley and Hodge as being there. Another eyewitness saw all three of them together in the area." Was Becky under some illusion that she owed something to these people, that she should protect them?

"They absolutely did do it. They absolutely committed a horrible crime. They are very brutal men, and it's not the first time that they did it." Caudill did not mention Ed and Bessie Morris; he was guessing that Becky Hannah might know or suspect something about the Gray Hawk killings, or that he might jolt her into making connections in her mind. If she did, she gave no sign. From what he could tell, he may as well have been addressing a houseplant.

She was worried about her car, Becky said. She understood that her Datsun was impounded and sitting out in the hot Florida sun. Someone had told her that a window was broken and sealed with orange tape. She hoped that the tape would not melt onto the paint. Could she have her keys? Mike Caudill gave up.

When Lester Burns descended on Orlando to represent Roger Epperson, Detective Frank Fleming was privately delighted. He did not think that even Lester Burns had much of a chance of getting Epperson off, not with the way the case was developing; but Lester was bound to make things more interesting, certainly more entertaining. Like most mountain people on either side of the law, Fleming admired Lester Burns for having come so far from such humble origins, and he appreciated the humor and the shrewdness Lester brought to everything he did. With Lester on the scene, it would be a different case, because Lester's effect was like cayenne pepper. Fleming now assumed that it would take weeks of maneuvering to get Epperson extradited back to Kentucky.

To Fleming's surprise, when he ran into Burns at the Orlando jail, Lester revealed that he was waiving extradition for his client and that Fleming and Lon Maggard could take Epperson home in a matter of days. At dinner at their hotel on August 22, Lester confirmed that extradition would quickly be allowed, although Hodge and Bartley, still without attorneys, continued to refuse it.

Fleming and Maggard had thought that they had come down to Florida only to gather evidence and otherwise assist Mike Caudill in dealing with local authorities and the FBI. They were more than willing to take Epperson home with them, but they had only Fleming's Chevy Impala cruiser, which was equipped with neither the special restraining devices nor a screen separating front and back seats as required by KSP regulations for the transportation of dangerous criminals over long distances.

Fleming knew Roger Epperson. He remembered having arrested him years before on auto theft and other charges, knew his parents and his brothers fairly well, and saw no reason why two armed Kentucky boys could not handle another unarmed fellow from the mountains. They were all about the same age and size, but Roger was out of shape from a strenuous style of life. By telephone, Danny Webb decided to waive the regulations, agreeing that it was not worth the cost to send another car and that they might as well haul Epperson back while they had the chance.

They headed for home on Saturday morning, August 24. Frank drove with Lon Maggard beside him, Roger in the middle of the back seat, handcuffed behind his back but otherwise unrestrained. Right from the word go he talked a blue streak, offering suggestions on the fastest route and agreeably entering into conversation about the narcotics trade—how much a mule received for carrying drugs from Florida or Tennessee up to Cincinnati, how much a kilo of this or that brought in various markets, what the markup was from drug grower to dealer, from importer to customer. It was a regular education, Frank thought, even if half of what Roger said might be bullshit. Epperson talked so big, he was the kind of guy who had to have an answer to whatever question, and he had a personal anecdote or two to embellish every point, always with himself as the smart dude, the one who pulled something off when everyone else went down. He reminded Frank of a second-rate Lester Burns, except not as funny or as likeable. He could understand why Roger had hired Lester, who was maybe the only man Epperson had ever met who could out-horseshit Roger and who actually made money at it.

A stranger in that car would have found it hard to believe that these cops and this criminal were adversaries, the talk flowed so easily, so matter-of-factly among the mountaineers who had grown up together knowing the same people up the same hollows speaking the same lilting, snappy lingo. Somewhere in central Georgia, Roger, leaning forward to thrust his head over the seat between the troopers, complained that the handcuffs were cutting into his wrists and stopping his circulation. They hurt so bad. He hated to complain, but they were killing him.

What the hell, Frank thought. He ain't going nowhere. He told Maggard that it would be all right to take off the cuffs. Roger twisted around and Maggard reached back to unlock them.

"I sure am obliged," Roger said.

"You want to jump out at ninety or a hundred miles an hour," Frank said, "go right ahead. If you live, we'll shoot you."

What he would really like, Roger said, was a pen and some paper so he could write a letter to his girlfriend. He wanted to tell her that the cops were treating him fine. He knew she'd be worried.

Fleming and Maggard watched from time to time out of the corners of their eyes as Roger scribbled, then tore up a couple of sheets, tossed them on the floor, and started over. I guess he wants to get whatever he has to say down right, Fleming thought.

Late that afternoon they stopped for dinner at a restaurant off the highway in Atlanta. Fleming and Maggard, in street clothes, did not feel like putting on their jackets, it was so hot; but neither did they want to barge into the restaurant wearing exposed shoulder holsters and service revolvers. They left their guns in the car and, in shirt sleeves, walked casually with Roger, who was wearing jeans and a polo shirt, into the dining room. Only Maggard among them carried any sort of weapon, a small pistol in a holster strapped to his ankle.

All three ordered big steaks and iced tea. It was not that Fleming was growing to like Roger, far from it, but he now felt he knew him well enough to be certain that he would not try to run under these cir- cumstances. A kind of rapport had been established. If Roger did try to run, Fleming was sure he could catch him and would not hesitate to punish him.

Their corner table permitted conversation. They reminisced about old crimes—rackets, scams, coal schemes. Having listened to him and studied him for hours, Fleming found it difficult to imagine Roger actually stabbing Tammy Acker. Which of the three had killed her was the question that haunted Fleming more vividly and persis- tently than any other, because he could not forget the sensation of removing that butcher knife. As the one who had pulled it out, he felt a peculiar link to whoever had plunged it in—a bond that joined cop to killer at right hands.

Fleming decided to take advantage of the friendly atmosphere to ask what had been making him wake up in a sweat every night for two weeks.

"Roger," he began in his blunt, cheerful way between bites, thrusting out his square jaw and cocking his head as he narrowed his eyes, "which one of you all stabbed Tammy?" With his fingertips he touched Roger's bare forearm. "You ain't under oath, buddy. I'm not recording this. Just between us, off the record, who did it?"

"I never did nothing wrong," Roger said, and he looked Fleming in the eye, something Frank had noticed he usually avoided. "Donnie Bartley. Bartley done it."

"Why? Why like that?"

"He went nuts after she wouldn't do what he asked."

"What was that? What wouldn't she do?"

"Give him a blow job. She wouldn't come across. He wasn't real happy about that."

"So he went crazy?"

"He didn't have far to go."

"You want to make that official? It might go better for you if you did."

"Sure," Roger said. "I'll take a deal. Here's what it is. If I talk, I walk."

"I don't think we'll go for that one," Fleming laughed. "Let's have us some of that strawberry shortcake."

That night they booked Epperson into the Knott County jail, from which he was scheduled to be moved to the state penitentiary at La Grange, near Louisville, where security was tighter. After bidding Roger farewell and saying they'd be seeing him again before too long, Fleming opened the buck of his cruiser and gathered up the pieces of paper Epperson had dropped there. "Dear Carol," one of them began, and went on as if describing a Sunday drive. On another sheet Roger had been calculating large numbers. Fleming saved these for evidence, doubtful that they would prove anything.

When Fleming told Danny Webb what Roger had said, the lieutenant was skeptical. Epperson, Webb pointed out, was facing the chair and had every reason to blame someone else. If Bartley had wanted sex with the girl, why hadn't he raped her? The evidence showed that they had been in too much of a hurry to think about sex. The next thing you knew, Bartley would accuse Hodge, and Hodge would blame Epperson, or whatever. Who had done what mattered less than that they were all legally equally guilty, just for being there for the reasons they had been.

It still mattered to him, Fleming said, which one had done that to Tammy. The more he thought about it, the more it made sense. It was a little guy's crime, the act of a squirt pissed off because he had been rejected. When Danny Webb finally saw Donnie Bartley in the flesh, the lieutenant would understand.

"I believe what Roger said," Fleming insisted as Webb continued to try to talk him out of jumping to conclusions. "You had to have been there. I believe he was telling the truth."

The important thing, Webb reminded him, was that they were building such a tight case against all three of them. Even Lester Burns was going to have one hell of a time trying to figure out how to plead this one. And new indictments would be coming down soon in the Morris murders and in the robbery back in May. Lester Burns had telephoned from Florida saying that he was bringing back a large cash fee. Where *that* money was coming from was another good question, but you could be sure that Lester had himself covered.

Webb recalled having run into Lester a few weeks ago over at Jerry's Restaurant in Somerset, before the Acker murder. Old Lester had been table-hopping, working the crowd as if he were running for governor again, coming over to flatter the lieutenant and his family. He had gone on about his loyalties to the KSP and reminded Webb that he would take care of any trooper's legal problems for a dollar.

"The way I hear Lester's been hitting the bottle lately," Danny Webb laughed, "I figure a dollar might be about right."

23

By THE AFTERNOON OF AUGUST 27, when Lester Burns returned to Somerset with the gym bag full of money in the trunk of Houston Griffin's car, his anxiety had reached such an acute state that whiskey no longer calmed it, was only fueling it. Somewhere near Atlanta he had become possessed by the fear that Griff might run off with the money, had ordered the caravan to a halt, switched cars, and ridden the rest of the way in Griff's LTD, leaving Lillian Davis to continue on her own.

His bad hip was paining him; he had fantasies of being stopped by the KSP and arrested; he was less and less sure of the wisdom of having accepted this case, which was daily revealing itself as more grisly, more complex, and more difficult; he had not been able to discover anything likeable or redeeming about Roger Epperson or either of his cohorts, nothing to persuade himself or a potential jury that these murderous thugs deserved mercy; and he no longer was confident that being upfront about the money he received would be enough to persuade anyone that he had no idea it was part of the stolen cash. A strong inner voice told him that his best course would be to head for the nearest KSP post and turn in the money, claiming that he had been shamefully misled by his client, whom he could no longer in conscience represent.

But the familiarity of home territory soothed his nerves and restored some of his confidence. The closer they came to Burnside, the little town just south of Somerset where his office stood on Highway 27 overlooking Lake Cumberland, the more Lester strengthened his resolve to keep the money and find his way toward getting his hands on more of it. He had the suspicion that before too long Sherry Wong and Donnie Bartley's relatives would be contacting him for help in securing other attorneys. There were opportunities ripe for the picking, more than a million bucks still out there.

Everywhere he looked around Somerset and Burnside reminded Lester of his power and prosperity: his house beside the Eagle's Nest fairways, his farm that increased in acreage every year as he acquired the farms bordering it, his commercial and agricultural and mining properties all over the place, others on which he was ready to pounce. Unlike the mountains, it was a booming area, owing mainly to tourism and the houseboat-building industry that brought year-round employment. Lester was such a major presence there that many people believed that Burnside had been named after him; nor did he choose to disillusion them, although he knew that the name honored a Civil War general renowned for his whiskers, later called sideburns.

It was great to be home safe and sound, Lester proclaimed as Griff drove past new fast food joints and motels and boat factories and automobile dealerships, in the most progressive and beautiful spot in Kentucky, where the fish were biting and the cattle were fat and they had the best country ham and his bank account was full and people understood what it meant to work hard for a decent living.

"Pull off here," he instructed as they approached Max Flynn Motors. "I want to give these boys a little something to cheer them up and fill their sleep with iridescent dreams."

He retrieved the gym bag and, with Griff following like a mastiff, sashayed into the office where Max Flynn himself was sitting with one of his salesmen.

"Look at this, boys," Lester said as he unzipped the bag and plopped it open on Max's desk. "Feast your eyes. I bet you never saw so much cash in your life. There's ninety-two thousand in there. I got it from a client in Florida. Not bad for a day's work, wouldn't you say?"

He grabbed a stack of bills and gesticulated as he crowed about his good fortune and asked how car sales were going. He might be interested in a new one himself. The Rolls-Royce was in the shop again. "Worst car I've ever had."

From Max Flynn's Lester took Griff to dinner at the 7 Gables Motel restaurant, where he showed the money off to everyone, bewildering a pair of white-haired Ohio tourists to whom for good measure he offered "the best deal in Kentucky" on a houseboat.

Griff departed for Okeechobee the next morning, without having acquired the promised Black Angus bull. By ten o'clock Lester, the money bag cradled in his arms, was in the passenger seat of Sheriff John Mar Adams's cruiser, on his way to the Citizens National Bank on Courthouse Square in Somerset. Lester, who had known Sheriff Adams for thirty years, since their days together at the KSP Academy, asked the sheriff to accompany him to deposit cash received from a client whose cohorts were ruthless cutthroats and would stop at nothing to abscond with it.

In a private office at the bank Lester deposited the ninety-two thousand dollars, most of it in fifties, into his checking account, assuming that the bank would quickly report the transaction to the IRS, as it did. He also withdrew some twenty thousand in the form of a cashier's check made out to the IRS, saying that he believed in paying his taxes not only on time but ahead of time.

Outside he thanked Sheriff Adams for his assistance and said that he might soon be needing help again.

The last thing Sherry Wong wanted to do was to turn to Lester Burns for help. If Lester found Sherry the most human of the gang members, the sympathy was not mutual. Lester appeared to her an outrageous, bizarre, and patently untrustworthy character. His behavior during that week in Orlando seemed little short of lunatic, even as she observed how easily he won over Carol and Donnie Bartley's mother and sister. A jury might fall for him. Not Sherry. Yet on Saturday, September 1, only two weeks after Benny's arrest, Sherry found herself being driven by Carol up Highway 27 into Kentucky and on toward Lester's farm, with Donnie's sister, Sharon Wilson, in the backseat. They were on their way to a meeting with the living legend himself. Sherry was depressed.

And desperate. Attempts to find an attorney for Benny, first in Florida and then in Knoxville, had failed. Lawyers either gave her the brush-off or insisted that she be able to prove that her money came from legitimate sources. She was making attempts to launder Benny's share, but there had not been time enough to accomplish that while

Benny languished in Florida. Lester Burns had already obtained a Kentucky lawyer for Donnie, one Lester could work well with, so he said, and indicating that he had another in mind for Hodge, if required. What Sherry began to fear was that Lester and Bartley's attorney would cook up a deal between themselves, maybe naming Benny as the killer and getting that pair of snitches light sentences. She had to act, now, and she hoped that cooperating with Lester might preclude getting screwed by him. She disliked him, she feared him, she distrusted him—and here she was being driven in one of Lester's cars, no less—not the Rolls; an Oldsmobile—to pay court to him and to beg his handpicked pal to take Benny's case.

It was dark by the time they reached the farm, several miles out-side of Somerset on Slate Branch Road. A bumpy dirt track led them through fields where Sherry could barely make out cattle grazing, past an outbuilding or two, over a low hill and down toward the barn and the big stone house. To Sherry's shock, their headlights suddenly illuminated a squad car. A deputy climbed out and shone his flash-light on them.

"Don't panic," Carol said. "Lester told me the sheriffs would be here. He uses them for guards. He owns the county."

The deputy told the women to go around to the back of the house. They found Lester with a drink in his hand. He stood up to greet the ladies and introduced one man as a friend, another as his accountant, and a third as Dale Mitchell, the attorney whom Sherry was to consider hiring. Lester offered drinks and said how sorry he was that they had arrived after dark, when all they could see of Lake Cumberland down below was a path of moonlight on the water.

"What a pity," Lester went on. "I insist that before you leave tomorrow, Sherry, and I'm so delighted to have you here, you'll drive over to see Cumberland Falls. There's nothing like them. A young lady fell over them just last week, poor thing, and killed herself. Very dangerous, and very beautiful."

"Let's get down to business," Sherry said.

"Getting and spending," Lester said, "it's the way of the world, alas. You and Dale can talk privately in the kitchen, if you like. The attorney–client privilege, I'm a great believer in it. You'd be well advised to put everything into Dale Mitchell's hands, is my advice. He and I go way back together. We practiced together for years. Dale's a dandy lawyer, let me tell you."

"He better be," Sherry said, and went inside with Mitchell, a graying, regular-featured man in his early forties. They were gone about ten or fifteen minutes. When they came out, Sherry did not look pleased. Mitchell was somber.

"Did you two get everything worked out?" Lester inquired. "Did you plight your troth?"

"Carol, drive me home," Sherry said. "I'm heading out."

"What's the trouble, my dear?" Lester followed and touched her shoulder as she reached the steps. "You all hung up on some technicality? We can work that out."

"You want to call it that. Your buddy here asked me for three hundred and fifty thousand dollars. Plus expenses! I ain't got that kind of money."

"You're saying no to him?" Lester jumped in front of her, spreading his arms and inching toward her until he bumped up against her. "You're saying no to the one man who stands between Benny Hodge and the rope? I mean the chair. What kind of a woman are you?"

Sherry backed away. Lester inched toward her as she said that she was no fool and repeated that she did not have that kind of money.

"*The hell you don't!*" Lester boomed out, and he twirled around, a dervish in python cowboy boots, flailing his arms. The whiskey flew out of his glass, drenching the accountant. Lester emitted a yelp that was somewhere between a rebel yell and a stuck pig's squeals. His eyes bugged out. "Why—" he rendered the word in several syllables, drawing it out through three octaves—"you *selfish* little bitch! You moneygrubbing no good goddamned ornery little Tennessee hog-calling pennypinching low-class idiot! You Judas! I have seen many a scheming heartless bitch in my time and you beat them all by a country mile! Don't you see what you're doing?" He screamed into her impassive face. "What good is all that money going to do you when they march Benny Hodge into that dark and dank horrible room and pull the switch? Have you seen a man die by electrocution, young lady? Have you smelt the awful stench of sizzling human flesh? Are you going to spend the money on his funeral? You mean to say you're running out on that poor boy? What kind of a love is it that abandons a loved one in his hour of greatest need? I thought so! I knew you were going to run! I could see it in your cold eyes! Heartless! Heedless! Indifferent! Callous! Monstrous! A predator! You'd lead a lamb to slaughter! Treachery, thy name is *woman!*"

Lester's diatribe, which ran a full two minutes, accompanied by kicks and thrusts and the rolling of eyeballs, ended as he hurled his glass over the railing, dropped to his knees, flung his arms wide, and cried out to the moon, "Oh, Lord God in heaven, if You are listening, hear the prayers of a man who asks Your bountiful mercy for this poor, pitiful female child, who knows not what she does, and for her beloved, who will soon be with Thee, or in hell! If Epperson walks and Hodge fries, she'll have only herself to blame!" And he wept.

Sherry, who had stood gaping throughout the performance like everyone else, not moving a muscle, watched Lester struggle to his feet, rubbing his hip.

"That is the damndest fit I ever seen pitched," she said at last. "Lester Burns, you're hired."

"What about Mitchell?" Lester asked, suddenly gone soft and plaintive with the voice of a puppy. "What about this sincere, brilliant man who wants to help you and get paid enough to do a decent job?"

"I'll have to ask Benny. I'll have to consult with him." She walked to the car.

Lester and Dale Mitchell thought they had lost Sherry that night but the next day she telephoned and said that if Mitchell were willing to negotiate, she would meet with him at the McDonald's in Oneida, Tennessee, on the border, about halfway between Harriman and Somerset. At that meeting, which took place on Tuesday, she agreed to pay Mitchell a hundred and fifty thousand upfront in cash and to sign over to him a house she claimed to have bought in Florida that was worth another hundred thousand. Lester, who had coached Mitchell in the art of asking high and settling for less, thought this acceptable, although he doubted the value or the existence of the house. The plan was for Sherry to return to the farm on the evening of Friday, September 7, to turn over the cash.

"We'll be here," Lester said. "And we'll have plenty of protection. I don't trust any of them." He continued paying sheriff's deputies a hundred dollars each per twelve-hour shift, round the clock.

In the meantime he had to drive over to Whitesburg to get Carol out of the Letcher County jail. He had not fulfilled the promise he had made—there had not been time, he insisted—to detectives in Florida to turn Carol over for questioning when she reached Kentucky. The KSP issued a warrant for her arrest, charging her with facilitation of a crime, citing the bill of sale she had signed back in

June for the Olds used in the Acker murder. When, on September 3, information reached the KSP that she had been staying at the Somerset Holiday Inn and was in the process of checking out, a pair of local policemen were dispatched to pick her up. They arrested her, against her frantic protests, at the reception desk and took her to the Somerset Police Department, where she was permitted to telephone her attorney. She could only leave a message at his office, however, because at the time he was overseeing a cattle-worming operation at his farm. KSP troopers arrived to take Carol to the Letcher County jail.

Lester did not hear about the arrest until that evening, when Sheriff Adams visited the farm. Lester immediately wondered about Carol's car, the MR2. Discovering that it was still parked at the Holiday Inn, he prevailed upon the sheriff to have the car towed to the farm, telling Adams that the MR2 belonged to him.

Lester knew that he would have to turn the MR2 over to the KSP, but he found that it could not be driven, because Carol had been arrested with her keys. He summoned a locksmith, who punched out the trunk lock in order to make a key from it, only to figure out that the trunk and ignition keys were different. When Lester finally had the car delivered to the Hazard KSP post, the trunk lock remained missing.

Lester had begun to find Carol a pain in the neck. "She drives me nuts," he told everyone. "She won't let me alone. I've hidden behind trees to get away from her. She thinks she's Patty Hearst. The woman is nutty as a pet coon."

On the day of Sherry's scheduled return with the money for Mitchell, Lester passed the time by attending a land auction near Cumberland Falls. He adored these events, their challenge, the stylish patter of the auctioneer, the secretive hand signals and the furtive, mumbled exchanges among men, most of them older than himself, with hats pulled down over sunburned faces, who formed dark conspiratorial knots here and there on the green field. In that part of the South, all land was sold at auction on the spot, a custom derived from Britain and Ireland. Lester was the shrewdest of players and the most garrulous, badgering people, kidding them, distracting them, complaining of being canoodled and hornswoggled, stalking off in a snit and plunging back in just in time to bid once more. His was the winning bid that day, nearly half a million dollars for several hundred acres. He wrote out a check for the sixty-eight-thousand-dollar down payment.

Sherry was supposed to show up at ten-thirty that night. The same four men as before waited for her at the farmhouse, inside this time, as fog was rolling in from the lake and autumn was in the air. Flush with his latest acquisition, Lester recounted the day's triumph and poured down the bourbon with his pal, a small farmer deeply in his debt, with Mitchell and the accountant staying sober. Around nine, Lester sent the deputy on guard to town for chicken.

Eleven o'clock. No Sherry. Was she lost in the fog? Lester wondered. Mitchell grew pessimistic and went home, to see his parents, he said. He could be reached if Sherry showed. Lester fell asleep.

About three o'clock that morning, Lester and his two remaining companions were preparing to leave the farm. They were climbing into the accountant's car and telling the deputy that he could go home when they saw headlights approaching through the fog. Lester hurried back inside to phone Mitchell, who lived only ten minutes away, as Sherry drove up in a new Bronco she had purchased. She was accompanied by two men wearing sidearms.

She walked into the house carrying a cardboard stereo box and introduced her escorts as a detective with the Oak Ridge police and his friend. She sat holding the box, waiting for Dale Mitchell to return. Even Lester, who had drunk himself sober, had no conversation but kept his eyes on the box.

When Mitchell returned, he and Sherry went into the kitchen and closed the door.

"Here's the money," she said, handing over the box. "A hundred and fifty thousand. I didn't count it bill for bill. If it's not all there, tell me and I'll make it up. If I overpaid you, you can give it back to me. I wouldn't spend it all in one place, if I was you."

Mitchell took the box. He said he would count the money later.

"Okay," Sherry said. "Now give me a receipt."

"A receipt? I'd rather not do that. I, ah …"

"What if you go down the road and have an accident and get yourself killed? I'd have no proof I paid you."

Mitchell continued to balk. Sherry insisted, threatening to take the money back. Mitchell gave in. On a yellow legal pad he wrote that he had received the amount from her as an attorney's fee. He dated it, signed it, and handed it to her. She slipped it into her jeans.

After Sherry and her bodyguards departed, Lester and Mitchell drove to Lester's law office. There in a waiting room Mitchell handed Lester fifteen five-thousand-dollar stacks of new one-hundred-dollar bills. Half his fee, Mitchell said, as he and Lester had agreed, an even split of seventy-five thousand.

Sherry had not been lost in any fog that night. Fearing ambush, she had deliberately delayed her arrival to catch the others off guard. Back home in her parents' house—a new one E. L. and Louise had just moved into—she read over the receipt from Mitchell in the early-morning light.

In the privacy of her bedroom she contemplated her doll collection. Choosing a fat little baby doll wearing a jumpsuit and wrapped in a tiny blue blanket, she undressed it and pried open a plastic hatch on its back. She removed the batteries, stuffed the folded receipt into the hole, replaced the batteries, and snapped the hatch closed. Dressed and rewrapped in its blanket, the doll whimpered as she returned it to its place on the shelf.

Because she figured that the FBI must have her parents' line tapped, Sherry provided Dale Mitchell with a code to use when he telephoned. When Sherry said "one," "two," or "three," the numbers indicated various pay phones at which the lawyer could reach her within a certain number of minutes. It was over one of these phones that Mitchell asked her to return the receipt.

"Don't worry about it," she told him. "I'll tear it up."

Mitchell soon flew to Miami to check out the house he was to receive as part of his fee. He had it appraised and learned that it was worth no more than sixty thousand. He also discovered that she had rented it, with only an option to buy, and was not in any position to sign it over.

Sherry agreed to pay Mitchell more money. She did so with a series of at least a dozen five-thousand-dollar cashier's checks, listing the payer as any one of several names she made up or borrowed from her or Benny's relatives, including his mother.

By mid-September, the FBI already had reasons to suspect that the total take from the Acker robbery was considerably more than Dr. Acker had been able to estimate. And late that month, when an event occurred involving someone closely linked to Sherry Sheets and the rest of the gang, Rod Kincaid became convinced that more than a million dollars must have been stolen. He also began to worry that recovering it might prove very difficult.

On September 24, Pat Mason flew to Las Vegas and checked into the Frontier Hotel. Waiting for her room to be made ready, she started playing the slots. She dropped sixty dollars at one machine, stopped to eat a cheeseburger, and began at another. Within minutes, three sevens came up.

The machine started to vibrate. Bells sounded. Lights flashed. Other players gathered round. "JACKPOT! JACKPOT!" The words blinked on and off across the video screen. No coins poured forth. Instead a long number printed out beneath "YOU HAVE WON." The total was beyond any one-armed bandit's capacity to hold.

The casino manager rushed up. Pat Mason had won one million, twenty-three thousand, six hundred and thirty-six dollars and sixty-two cents. She was very happy.

The FBI was not. Agents with a special interest in this unusual stroke of good fortune visited the Frontier the next day. This particular machine, the hotel's management told them, had never paid off before. It was brand new, with only sixteen hours on it. The odds against this payoff had been, well, nearly incalculable. But that was Vegas. You never knew.

What the agents did know was that the standard Vegas fee for laundering money was forty percent. In this instance, however, they could find nothing, apart from the winner's unsavory associations, to indicate that the good luck had been anything other than that.

For the next week or so, Pat Mason was a celebrity. She was the second-biggest slot-machine winner in Las Vegas history. According to Florida newspapers, Ms. Mason had foretold her astonishing success before leaving for Nevada.

"She told me the day she left that she'd win a million," Marvin Friedman, her boss at Autoputer, informed the *South Broward Sentinel.* "I just couldn't believe it when she called me and told me that she actually did it." What a fantastic thing to happen to a forty-five-year-old single woman from a small town in Tennessee. At the car brokerage she had been making no more than a thousand a week.

"I had a feeling," Pat Mason confided to the *Miami Herald.* "It's hard to explain."

24

FRUSTRATED AS HE WAS BY THE APPARENT MYSTERIES of Pat Mason's good fortune, Rod Kincaid was not entirely pessimistic about the Bureau's chances of tracing and recovering a large amount of what remained missing of the stolen Acker money. By late September and through the end of the year, he was spending many hours alone in his London office making notes while listening to certain intriguing tape recordings.

The principal voice on these tapes was male and distinctly Eastern Kentuckian. It crooned, bellowed, blustered, murmured, and cackled, caressing words and phrases as if they were the hollows and undulations of a woman's body. So commanding and cajoling and in its own way majestic was this voice that if the language it uttered had been anything other than specifically American, one could easily have assumed it to be that of a prince or king, describing the conquest of territories and the splendor of his own domain during some long-gone feudal era. Stories, jests, attacks, enumerations of riches, the voice traversed the plains of human experience. Often Kincaid reversed the tape and ran it again to hear that voice spin a yarn once more.

Kincaid made sure he was alone when playing these tapes because he frequently found himself bursting into guffaws and emitting inarticulate noises of appreciation that had nothing to do with his role as an agent and could have been misunderstood by some humorless colleague as unseemly enthusiasm for a crook. Something about the voice made its scheming malice as seductive as its wit, its wickedness as compelling as its humanity. The sound of it was not merely regional: it *was* Eastern Kentucky, the authentic thing manipulated by an artist of the vernacular who was as precise with timing and as attuned to nuance as some great fiddler. What irony, that Lester Burns might do himself in by means of the very instrument he had perfected. "Why, Lester," Kincaid thought. "You scallywag!"

Because it was Lester Burns's voice that Kincaid had managed secretly to record: Lester boasting and bragging and confiding and revealing one thing and another about his control of the Acker money and other, unrelated goings-on. It was an explosion of disclosure.

Hearing Lester spill bean after bean as if his glands excreted sodium pentothal, Kincaid marveled at the manic candor of this man who had the reputation of being the canniest lawyer in Kentucky. Whatever on earth he thought he was doing, Lester Burns seemed compelled to confess. Something had come over him. It was not only the tapes. Only the other night, Kincaid heard from a reliable source, Lester had taken several friends to dinner at a Burnside restaurant and, having ravished the buffet, had dropped to his knees, wept, pressed a napkin to his brow, extended his hands palms up, and begged forgiveness—nobody knew for what, presumably not merely for gluttony. It was the whiskey talking, his friends had said. Kincaid had many reasons to believe that this thirst for absolution derived from other sins.

Two undercover agents posing as good old boys out to make fast bucks were recording Lester at his farm, at the 7 Gables restaurant, and elsewhere as he bragged about his fee and conspired with Dr. Billy Davis—Lillian's husband—and the agents to defraud an insurance company of over a million dollars. The men working undercover were Robert W. Comer, who had agreed to his new career in 1983 after being confronted with various kinds of fraud he had committed in the coal fields and three and a half million dollars in unreported illegal income, and H. E. McNeal, who was actually a Virginia state trooper and a Special Deputy United States Marshal on loan to the FBI. Comer had known Lester for some fifteen years and, believing that Lester had cheated him in a coal deal years before, was glad of the chance to get even; McNeal, who was going under the name of Harry McBride, was the one who wore the concealed recorder. The two would get Lester talking—the easiest part of their assignment—until a tape ran out, then meet regular agents at the Fish and Creek Recreation Area near Cumberland Falls to summarize the conversation, receive a fresh tape, and return to record more.

Comer and McNeal were part of Project Leviticus, a multistate operation designed to expose criminal activity in the Appalachian coal fields. In Kentucky, Project Leviticus's targets included numerous law enforcement officials, judges, lawyers, and businessmen in an investigation of public corruption, drug dealing, influence peddling, and fraud. Comer and McNeal had been hanging around Lester for months, visiting him in Okeechobee as well as sticking close to him at home. Theirs was essentially a sting operation: they had already tried and failed to suck Lester into cocaine and marijuana distribution schemes in which other Kentuckians were involved. They had failed at that because Lester refused to have anything to do with drugs and told them they were crazy to mess with narcotics. But they had persuaded him to bite on the insurance scam, in which McNeal pretended to have suffered head injuries in a truck on which Comer carried the insurance. They pushed the truck over a cliff and Dr. Billy Davis built up a phony medical file on McNeal, coaching him on how to fool a CAT scan that the insurance adjustor would accept. Lester was to draw up the papers and file the suit against the company. On one of the tapes, Rod Kincaid heard Lester talk about back dating a lease to his farmhouse in Comer's and McNeal's names so that they could establish Kentucky residence and avoid filing the suit in Federal court, where Lester would be less in control. He also heard Lester ask the agents to stay away from the farm on certain nights early in September when, Lester said, he was expecting an important visitor from Tennessee. He did not say who this visitor was, but Kincaid had a fairly good idea.

It was only by chance that, because of Project Leviticus, Kincaid through Comer and McNeal was able to stumble onto revelations about the ACKMUR money. He listened to Lester confide that he was hiding an Oriental girl from the law and that she was an incorrigible dopehead and flibbertigibbet who was running off her mouth and throwing money around like Kleenex and would get herself killed and cause innocent clients—Comer and McNeal reported that Lester winked as he said this—to be convicted. He heard Lester brag that his fee was as much as four hundred thousand, that he had driven a rental car six thousand miles from Florida to Canada and back to avoid being traced with the money, and that part of his fee was a 1963 Corvette that he had stashed in his Okeechobee garage.

It was from Comer and McNeal that Kincaid learned that Lester was using sheriff's deputies to guard his farm and his Eagle's Nest house and that Sheriff John Mar Adams of Pulaski County was a frequent visitor to the farm. One by one, warning them that to talk about the interview would be a serious breach of their duties as law enforcement officers, Kincaid grilled the deputies, including the one who had been sent out for chicken on the night of September 7. That deputy described the arrival of a woman and two men in a dark car early on the morning of the 8th and recalled that Lester Burns and attorney Dale Mitchell were in a jubilant mood afterwards and had tipped the deputy an extra hundred dollars. Eventually Kincaid interviewed Sheriff Adams himself, who described Lester Burns as "different" from other local attorneys, mentioned his long friendship, and admitted that Lester could possibly have been using him. The sheriff, who said his records were sketchy, agreed to try to provide an accounting of how much Burns had paid his deputies.

It was remarkable, Kincaid thought, how thoroughly Lester had been taken in by Comer and McNeal. As a resident of Somerset himself, Kincaid was well aware of Lester's reputation as a man on whom supposedly nothing was lost, in or out of the courtroom. Obviously Lester's judgment was slipping, whether through whiskey or hubris or both; perhaps his years of outsmarting everyone else had finally begun to wear him down. It was particularly amusing to hear him advise Comer like a wise uncle to take out more insurance on a Lincoln Continental that was actually government property that had been seized in a Virginia drug raid. The question now was when to bring the inevitable indictments. These had to be coordinated with the rest of Project Leviticus, and it would be a shame to stop Lester talking when every day he was revealing more about ACKMUR.

Lester's New Year's resolutions for 1986 included cutting down on his drinking, losing weight, and having his hip replaced so that he would be fit for the Acker trial, set for the first week in June. Early in March he went under the knife and emerged from the anesthetic to find himself with a new hip and troubles potentially more serious than any others he had faced in his life.

On March 14, a federal grand jury in Lexington indicted more than a dozen Kentuckians as the result of investigations carried out under Project Leviticus. Among the accused were a judge, a sheriff, a former KSP commissioner, and Lester Burns, who among seventeen other counts was indicted for conspiring with Dr. Billy Davis to bilk an insurance company on the basis of the accident faked by Comer and McNeal. Publicly Lester issued a statement pooh-poohing the indictments as nothing more than an attempt to ruin him by law enforcement officials angered by his courtroom successes over the years.

Privately he was as appalled by his own stupidity as he was nervous about the charges, which together carried maximum penalties of something like ninety years in prison. How could he have been such an idiot, he told family and friends, as to have been taken in by Robert Comer, who he knew was a crook but for whom he had felt compassion because Comer had supposedly suffered a heart attack and could not pay additional medical bills incurred by the illness of his little boy? The record would show, Lester insisted, that he himself was to profit exactly *zero* from the insurance suit, for which he was acting as the attorney only out of common decency and Christian charity.

As for the rest of the counts, they were bunk. The ones connecting him to dope deals were not only nonsense, they were insulting, slanderous, and libelous; and they were grounds for a multimillion-dollar harassment suit against the government.

Without saying so, Lester was also worried by what he knew he had told Comer and McNeal about the Acker money. Not only had he revealed his knowledge that his fee was part of the stolen money, he had exaggerated the amount—more than doubled it, as he recalled—and talked about everyone's need for "a washing machine." And all along he had thought that he was merely impressing in his usual hyperbolic fashion a couple of backwoods bozos down on their luck.

"Imagine being an FBI agent," Lester said. "What a disgraceful way to earn a living!"

Although, so far, nothing had been disclosed from the Comer–McNeal tapes concerning the Acker money, Lester fretted about that possibility and strove to fashion a defense of his indiscretions. Perhaps the government planned to wait to see how the trial was progressing and would move against him if he appeared able to get Epperson off. Was there still time to give the money back, to defend Epperson for a dollar or withdraw? He concluded that that would amount to resigning his license to practice law.

Suspicions about his fee surfaced sooner than he had thought they would, and from sources other than the tapes. POLICE THINK LAWYER MAY HAVE WASHED ACKER MONEY, reported the *Whitesburg Mountain Eagle* on May 7, under the masthead bearing a drawing of an eagle in flight and the paper's motto, IT SCREAMS! The *Eagle* credited the scoop to the *Louisville Courier-Journal,* the biggest paper in the state, which had run a Sunday story accompanied by a photograph of Carol's MR2 with the trunk lock punched out. According to both papers, it was the condition of that car, which Burns had turned over to police after Carol's arrest last September, that led police to believe that the lawyer had jimmied the trunk to retrieve money Carol had hidden there.

Lester, in Florida recovering from surgery, was "unavailable for comment." This incident, the Whitesburg paper said, "marks the second time this year that Burns has been implicated in wrongdoings."

Commonwealth's Attorney James Wiley Craft stated that he did not expect current investigations of Lester Burns to delay the start of the trial of the three men accused of murdering Tammy Dee Acker of Fleming-Neon. The bar association had already issued an opinion saying that Burns, like anyone else, was innocent until proven guilty. Circuit Judge F. Byrd Hogg, who would preside at the Acker trial, was mindful of the danger of a mistrial because of Burns's situation and had summoned Roger Epperson to inquire formally of him, on the record, whether he wished to fire his attorney and hire another or be represented by a public defender. Epperson had said unequivocally that he believed in Burns's innocence and chose to continue with him. That, Judge Hogg ruled, obviated any possible conflict. Jury selection would begin as scheduled during the first week in June.

Down in Okeechobee, Lester was indignant. If the police actually thought that he had taken money out of the trunk of that car, did they believe that he would be such an idiot as to drive it to the KSP post with the lock missing?

For the past several months, Epperson, Bartley, and Hodge had been housed in various facilities around the state. Pulling various strings he referred to as "just sheer politics," Lester had arranged for his client to stay in the Pulaski County jail some of that time, so attorney and client could consult more easily. Carol, free on bail from her criminal facilitation charges, visited Roger almost daily there—and caused Lester more headaches. Once, on his way to see his client, Lester found Carol in the waiting room wrapping something into a sheet. Lester was alarmed. He did not know what she was doing, Lester told her; she might be wrapping a present of pipe tobacco or talcum powder for her beloved that had nothing to do with the knotted sheets found recently in Roger's cell. It would doubtless be farfetched to imagine that she planned to tie her sheet to one of Roger's so he could pull them in through the cell window. Lester knew she was too sensible to try to play a game like that. But he did wish to remind her that there was a commode in the next room. If she felt the urge to make use of that convenience, she should feel free to do so.

By February all three defendants had been moved to the Laurel County jail, in London, to await transportation to the Letcher County jail for the trial. It was at the Laurel County Courthouse that month that Carol married Roger and Becky Hannah married Donnie Bartley. While these pledges of faith had an uplifting effect on the prisoners' morale, the exchanges of vows meant that under Kentucky's strict marital exclusion statute, the wives could not be compelled to testify against their husbands.

Sherry also married Benny, but she had to wait until her divorce from Mr. Wong was final. The delay gave her time to devise a more complex and in a sense traditional ceremony. Remaining convinced that, whatever else he had done, Benny had not murdered Tammy Acker, Sherry was intent on having her marriage blessed by God as well as recognized by the state for practical purposes. She wanted a church wedding. How to arrange this required ingenuity. The authorities declined to permit Benny to leave his cell.

Sherry gathered with E. L. and Louise and other members of her family at the Baptist church her parents attended in Harriman. Technically and legally, the marriage took place on April 8 in Roane County, Tennessee; electronically and metaphysically, however, it occurred simultaneously in Kentucky at the Laurel County jail, where Benny recited his vows over the telephone to the minister, who pronounced Benny and Sherry husband and wife although the groom was invisible to him. There was no reception.

Sherry began commuting to Whitesburg when Benny and Roger were transferred there early in May, with Bartley remaining in London—for security reasons, officials said. The new Mrs. Epperson was also in Whitesburg, and the brides did their best to provide domestic comforts for their men, delivering fast food to supplement the jailhouse fare, television sets, VCRs and tapes, and other amenities to their cells. As a honeymoon spot it was no Niagara, but Sherry found the jailer a humane sort of fellow.

Within a week of Epperson and Hodge's removal to Letcher, Rod Kincaid received a telephone call from John Bowling, the Laurel County jailer. With his office only two blocks away, Kincaid knew Bowling well. At some three hundred and fifty pounds, Big John was beloved for his cheerful approach to his duties, reknowned for stringing thousands of colored lights around the jailhouse each Christmas and playing carols in his office day and night from Thanksgiving through the New Year. He was a shy fellow, afflicted with a serious stammer; his phone call to Kincaid on the morning of May 8 lasted the better part of twenty minutes, although what he had to say was as simple as it was dramatic.

He was with Donnie Bartley's mother, Big John Bowling said, and Bartley himself, who was saying that he wanted to make a statement about the Acker case and related matters. Bowling, who kept one of Rod Kincaid's cards pinned to the jailer's office bulletin board, was telling Bartley that, if he really did have something important to say, he ought to speak to the agent, who was a man everyone knew as a straight shooter. Big John was contacting Kincaid on the prisoner's behalf.

He would have to talk to the U.S. Attorney's office, Kincaid said, and to Letcher County officials prior to any interview. He spoke briefly to Bartley's mother, Louise Farley, telling her the same thing. She insisted that her son wished to talk to no one except the FBI.

The next morning, Kincaid and another agent met with Bartley's mother and father, Donald Terry Bartley, Sr., at the jail; the parents were upset about Donnie's legal representation. They complained that Donnie felt that his attorney, O. Curtis Davis (no relation to Dr. Billy Davis), to whom they had been referred by Lester Burns, was misrepresenting the facts to his client and sharing confidential information with the other attorneys in the case. Donnie would no sooner tell his lawyer something, his parents claimed, than it would be repeated to him through Epperson, who must have heard it from Burns.

Their son had decided to fire O. Curtis Davis and accept a court-appointed lawyer: they were out of funds, and they figured they would be better off anyway with a lawyer who wasn't in it for the money. In the meanwhile, Donnie wished to make a statement. He was prepared to tell everything he knew. Kincaid advised the parents that he was not in a position to make either promises or threats. He understood that Bartley was acting entirely of his own volition. They should inform their son of this and see whether he still wished to talk.

An hour later Bartley was ready. Aware of the possible significance of what was about to take place, Kincaid took extra precautions to make sure that Donnie understood his rights so that his confession, if that was what it proved to be, gave no appearance of having been coerced or extracted through promises of leniency. He had Donnie read an "Interrogation, Advice of Rights" form out loud, read it aloud to him himself, and had him sign it. He also wrote out by hand a statement for Bartley to sign saying that he was acting entirely voluntarily and summarizing the circumstances through which he had contacted the FBI. Kincaid instructed an accompanying agent to keep a detailed log of these precautions as well as of everything that occurred during the interview, down to cups of coffee and cigarettes.

The interview took place in Big John Bowling's office. Bartley began with an account of his first meetings with Benny Hodge and Roger Epperson. He went on to describe the botched Rome, Georgia, job of nearly a year before, implicating the brothers from Ooltewah, recounting the fiasco, the methods of forging fake IRS and FBI IDs, and the reason he and Hodge had become fugitives.

Except for the occasional intrusion to encourage Bartley to try to keep the narrative as chronological as possible—the sequence of facts was as important as the facts themselves—Kincaid remained as passive as he could, like a priest in the confessional. The idea was to stay silent so as to encourage the sinner to fill the dead air. Even after years of experience, Kincaid found that the toughest part of the job for him was to control his emotions, to remain a blank when the subject revealed lurid details and even reveled in them, as killers often did, smirking and congratulating themselves. The challenge for the agent was to stifle the urge to throttle the subject or throw up. Kincaid's principal pleasure in his job was the painstaking piecing together of evidence. Years of hearing firsthand accounts of horror stories had failed to numb his reactions to them and were the main reason he looked forward to retirement.

His composure was tested when Bartley reached the Jackson County killings of Ed and Bessie Morris. Donnie's account of these events was matter-of-fact, as if he assumed that the police already knew more about Gray Hawk than they actually did. Where the gang had camped out; how they had borrowed a van from Harold Clontz; how Roger had known the victims—it all came out in logical order. Bartley recalled how Epperson had shaken the old man's hand before entering the house with Hodge.

At this point, however, Bartley's account became less specific because, he said, he had remained in the van as the lookout, hearing four or five shots ring out but not witnessing the actual killings. Afterwards they had burned clothing worn during the robbery and killings and had thrown the cleaned and disassembled guns into a river somewhere in Levi Jackson State Park. The robbery had netted some jewelry and about four thousand dollars in cash.

"So you don't know how the killings were done or who killed which victim?" Kincaid asked calmly.

Back at the Laurel Lake campground, Bartley said, Benny Hodge had described the murders to him. Roger had clubbed the old man on the head with a gun, with the gun going off twice; Benny had finished the job by firing his gun through a pillow into the man's head. Benny then went into the bedroom to find that Roger had already shot the woman with a 9-mm pistol. When Benny said, "She's still moving," Roger shot her again, and she was dead. Benny had carried a .38 into the house. When he came out he had two .38s with him. They had disposed of all three weapons.

They had left for Florida a day or two after that, where the condominium became headquarters for the remainder of the summer until their arrest.

"Did you commit any serious crimes in Florida?" Kincaid asked.

Bartley stated that the next big job was the Moon Mullins robbery. Carol Epperson had known Moon Mullins in Tennessee and knew where he was living in the Fort Lauderdale area. Bartley, Epperson, and Hodge used FBI cards on this occasion to gain entrance to Mullins's house, saying that they were looking for Terry Phillips, a mutual acquaintance of Carol's and Mullins's. Hodge pointed a .44 Magnum at Mullins and Bartley tied him up; but when Epperson came in, he said, "This one is mine." Epperson asked Bartley to bring a knife from the kitchen. Roger wanted to cut Mullins's throat, but when Bartley handed him the knife, Roger said, "It wouldn't cut hot butter."

Bartley and Hodge watched as Epperson choked Mullins with an extension cord and finished strangling him with a pair of pantyhose tied around his neck, a technique Roger said he had learned in Vietnam. He appeared to enjoy strangling Mullins. There was no blood, as far as Bartley could remember.

This robbery amounted to about ten thousand in cash, plus some cocaine.

Kincaid suggested a coffee break. Bartley left to go to the bathroom. Kincaid tried to evaluate Bartley's credibility. Obviously his motivation in confessing at the eleventh hour had to do with his hope of escaping the death penalty. Except for his claiming that he had been conveniently outside during the Morris murders—not an implausible circumstance, since it was likely that someone would have had to play lookout, and it had to have been either Bartley or Hodge, because Roger was the one who knew the victims on what one could call a friendly basis—everything he had said so far squared more or less with the known evidence. Much of the rest could be checked out. On the whole, Kincaid believed, Bartley must be telling the truth. As so often happened, the threat of the death penalty was proving useful.

As for Bartley's manner and tone of voice, they were not those of a typical psychopathic killer. He looked Kincaid in the eye, for the most part, and seemed to be making a genuine effort to remember details. He was agitated, smoking cigarette after cigarette, if not remorseful. And he could not have been coached by his attorney, since he was no longer on speaking terms with him. Everything depended on what he was about to say about what had happened in Dr. Acker's house that night, because that trial was imminent, and other convictions hinged on it.

As Kincaid had expected, Bartley did not deny that he had been inside Dr. Acker's house. How could he, when his fingerprint had been found there? His account of how he and Hodge had gained entrance squared with the doctor's recollections that night and in a later deposition. That Bartley had summoned Epperson with a "handy-talkie" radio was new information corroborated by physical evidence found in Florida.

Bartley admitted having carried Tammy Acker back to her room and tying her up. He had not, however, harmed her, he insisted. When he left her, she was alive and well.

Bartley described how they had forced the doctor at gunpoint to open the safe and had stuffed the money into pillowcases. With the doctor tied up again, Epperson told Bartley, "This one is yours." The message was that, as Bartley had not participated in killing the Morrises, he had to kill the doctor so that he would be in as deep as the others and they could not rat on one another.

Bartley said that he began choking Dr. Acker with the cord from a curling iron, but the cord pulled up around the doctor's mouth. Exasperated, Epperson jerked it down around the victim's throat, saying, "Now do it right, dumbass." At this point, the telephone started ringing, they became frightened, gathered up the pillowcases, and left.

Kincaid asked about the girl.

Bartley said that before he had started choking Dr. Acker, Benny Hodge had said, "I'll take care of the girl." Epperson had handed, tossed, or thrown—Bartley could not be sure of the exact gesture—a knife to Hodge. The knife had come from a kitchen drawer. He saw Hodge walk back toward the bedroom where the girl was tied up, but he had not been present when Hodge stabbed her.

In the getaway car Hodge told Bartley that he knew the girl was dead because he felt the knife "go all the way to the floor." Epperson had stated that he was sure the doctor was dead because he had seen his face turn blue. Bartley told Kincaid that he had not known whether Dr. Acker was dead or not but that he had hoped he was still alive.

When he, Epperson, Hodge, Becky, Sherry, and Carol had counted the money, they found that it amounted to one million nine hundred thousand dollars. Bartley believed that Sherry Hodge, who became the banker because she was "the smartest," had ended up with more than her and Benny's share and had invested some of it in a house for her parents, a steak house, and an automobile dealership and possibly other properties through Pat Mason. Mason would not admit this, Bartley claimed, because she was Sherry's friend.

Bartley provided details of one other crime, the robbery of the family on the Harlan–Letcher line earlier that same summer. He also warned that Epperson and Hodge were trying to escape from the Letcher County jail and were bribing somebody to make this possible. The interview concluded near five o'clock, having lasted more than three hours.

At the FBI office, Kincaid telephoned Letcher County authorities to let them know the gist of what Bartley had said. Then he dictated a summary based on notes of what he had heard and sat back to weigh the truth of it. The window of his office looked out over London's Main Street toward the peaceful-looking countryside, where a few lights were coming on as it grew darker. Only a few miles from there, the gang had camped out before the Morris murders. Kincaid rehearsed Bartley's long narrative, for the most part stunning in its detail, down to the version of events at Dr. Acker's house. Had Hodge actually done the stabbing? Any one of the three men could have done it. But Kincaid concluded that Bartley was the least likely, because from a criminal point of view, he was weak. He had failed to kill the doctor; he had run from arrest like a scared rabbit; he had become the first to crack.

What if Bartley were lying about being the one to have botched the job on Dr. Acker? Could Epperson have been the one who failed at that task? Most unlikely. From what Kincaid had gathered, Carol's previous relationship with Moon Mullins gave Roger a motive for strangling the drug dealer, and Epperson had managed that job with grim efficiency. As for Hodge, surely someone of his physical strength could not have failed to have strangled an old man. The hypothesis that Bartley had chickened out of killing the doctor or perhaps, as Bartley would prefer to have everyone believe, had not really wanted to kill him, but had also stabbed Tammy Acker eleven times was absurd. If you believed Bartley was the one who had attempted to murder the doctor, you could not believe that Bartley killed Tammy.

Kincaid compared Bartley's demeanor during the interview with that of the many other copouts he had witnessed during nearly twenty years with the Bureau. He believed that by this time he knew when he was being conned. Probably, he concluded, he would never be absolutely certain about who had stabbed Tammy. His gut feeling, however, made him think that yes, Bartley should be believed. Benny Hodge had done it.

25

AT ELEVEN O'CLOCK ON THE NIGHT OF MAY 9, only a few hours after Bartley had unburdened himself, Danny Webb climbed the stairs to the second floor of the Letcher County Courthouse, a two-story glass-and-steel structure in the center of Whitesburg, and told the jailer to open up the cellblock. The lieutenant was accompanied by five troopers, a deputy U.S. marshal, and James Wiley Craft.

The search party found Epperson and Hodge in their cells but not suffering. Benny was chatting on a portable phone that he quickly clicked off. Epperson was watching a cop show. The cells looked like the aftermath of a teenage house party—littered with boxes from local pizza and chicken restaurants, peanuts, cheese dip, chips and crackers and other goodies. Each cell contained a TV, a VCR, video-tapes, and audio recorders and tapes. Carpets covered the floors.

Webb and his men uncovered several items hidden inside the VCRs and taped under beds: four pieces of hacksaw blades, two jeweler's strings capable of cutting through steel bars, a spoon with its handle sharpened to a fine point, and a makeshift key fashioned from a bucket handle that, when tried on the cellblock door, opened it.

At a press conference the next morning, James Wiley Craft stated that as Commonwealth's Attorney his responsibilities did not extend to running the jail, but conditions there spoke for themselves. He was asking the grand jury to investigate how Epperson and Hodge had received the contraband items and whether jail personnel might be involved. He said that he believed that visitors—he did not say who they might be—had smuggled in the hacksaw blades and jeweler's strings inside the VCRs. Possibly they had been delivered by unwitting local rental outfits with the saws already hidden in them, since the prisoners appeared to have been ordering the machines by specific serial numbers. Craft also believed that Epperson and Hodge had been communicating with the third defendant by means of audiotapes carried back and forth by visitors from Whitesburg to London.

"They were just like motel rooms," Craft said, "only smaller. Very pleasant. Maybe we should rent them out to tourists."

In response to a question from a *Mountain Eagle* reporter, Craft said that he was not at liberty to disclose the source of the information that had led to the raid, other than that it had resulted from a tip supplied by the FBI.

The *Mountain Eagle*—which came out every Wednesday, had a circulation of eight thousand (five times the population of Whitesburg), and had won more national honors, including the John Peter Zenger and Elijah P. Lovejoy awards, than any other small-town paper in America—published a six-by-four inch photograph of the hacksaw blades and other devices, devoting its entire front page to the story in its issue of May 14. By that date, the Acker trial was the single biggest story across the state now that the Derby had been run. The *Courier-Journal,* the *Lexington Herald-Leader,* and many other papers, as well as the wire services and television stations, sent reporters and photographers to Whitesburg for the duration, filling motels as far away as Hazard and Pikeville. The story—a miser and his beautiful daughter in their mountain fastness, rapacious invaders from afar—had the qualities of a nightmarish fairy tale. When it became known that girlfriends, too, may have been involved in the crimes, few reporters could resist analogies to Bonnie and Clyde. And there was Lester Burns, who was always news and had been for thirty years, now more than ever with the indictments and other suspicions hanging over him. But with all the reporters on hand, some with rich and powerful resources behind them, the *Mountain Eagle* consistently provided the most thorough coverage and, time and again, scooped everyone else. When James Wiley Craft released the transcript of Donnie Bartley's second confession, the *Eagle* printed it in its entirety, all six thousand words of it. It made sensational reading.

This confession was recorded three days after the first, untaped statement Bartley had made to Rod Kincaid. Assistant Commonwealth's Attorney Mike Caudill asked the questions, with Danny Webb and Frank Fleming in attendance, at the Laurel County jail. The interview lasted only half an hour, because it concerned only events directly related to the Acker trial.

Bartley told the same story that he had given Kincaid, with the key, or at least the most sensational, element being that Benny Hodge had done the stabbing. He was more detailed about where he thought much of the money had gone, saying that he and the others had left more than a hundred thousand dollars with Pat Mason and that he believed that Mason's Las Vegas miracle was part of a laundering scheme: "I think it was a setup, where she won that money." He had been in jail, however, and admitted he knew nothing about Mason's possible role for sure. He also said that Epperson had told him that Lester Burns had received some four hundred thousand of the money, plus the '63 Corvette.

The *Eagle* asked Lester to comment. "Bartley is a young man trying to save his hide," Lester said. "I think you could find a great amount of his statement in a barnyard. And testimony by an alleged accessory to a crime is totally unreliable." Was there anything Bartley had said that might be correct? "His name was correct," Lester replied, adding, "I'll tell you this. Bartley may be the murderer."

What the *Eagle* did not print, because even with all of its inside sources the paper was not informed of it, was that there was disagreement between Caudill and Webb on the one hand and Frank Fleming on the other as to whether Bartley should be believed. Caudill and Webb agreed with Rod Kincaid that Bartley was credible. Fleming, who remained unshaken in his belief that Epperson had told the truth off the record during the drive from Florida months before, thought Bartley was lying about who had done the stabbing. "Besides," Fleming argued, "show me a killing like that and nine times out of ten it's a little guy who did it. It's just what an insecure pint-sized coked-up little runt would do under the circumstances if a girl refused him. Hodge is a big old stud. He might kill a woman, but not like that. He's got nothing to prove. Bartley is out to save his own ass, is all. He's copped out before. He's a snitch and a chickenshit, is all he is. He couldn't kill anybody in cold blood, but he could go berserk. He was on coke. He's a pipsqueak and a liar."

Danny Webb, with Mike Caudill concurring, said that there was no more reason to believe Epperson than Bartley. As for Hodge, his size and strength alone were the strongest argument that he had stabbed Tammy. Didn't Frank remember? The knife's point had gone through the body, out the breast, through the carpet, and into the floor. *That was a stone floor!* That part of the Acker house must have been built on the foundation of one of the old miner's duplexes. The floor beneath the carpet was like cobblestone, actually stones laid together and filled in with mud for mortar. The knife had been jammed between stones and into that hardened mud. Nobody but a tremendously strong man could have done that. It had to have been Hodge.

The number of wounds, all of which could have been inflicted in under a minute, could be explained by the panic they were in to get out of there. The telephone had rung. Hodge was trying to make sure he did the job right, like the good criminal he was. Bartley had botched his, just as he did when he left the briefcase. Bartley did nothing right.

"It doesn't matter what I think," Fleming said. "What a jury believes is what matters. But I'm not convinced."

Word came to Rod Kincaid that Benny Hodge, reacting to Bartley's allegations when they were made public, was ready to talk in return for leniency. Kincaid refused the overture, saying he would not be a party to any deal with the man he believed was the killer.

For Sherry the news that Bartley had fingered Benny and would do so at the trial was crushing. She took little satisfaction in remembering that she had warned Benny from the start not to have anything to do with him. Staying by herself in a motel near the jail, she was not surprised when she read in the *Mountain Eagle* that Bartley's confession had surprised few people in Harlan who had known him since childhood. What old acquaintances revealed about Donnie only confirmed to Sherry what she believed she had always instinctively known. Some old-timers interviewed around the Harlan County Courthouse claimed that they had predicted that Bartley would tell authorities that he had taken part in the crime but did not commit the murder: "We were all saying that Donnie would say he did some of it, and that he didn't have a thing to do with the rest of it."

Bartley was remembered as a boy who was a charmer but could

not stay out of trouble. A high school classmate recalled that Donnie had been in trouble since his first day in school: "Everybody knew that if they got into a fight with him, he had a knife." Confessing to crimes was nothing new with him. In the seventies he had taken advantage of plea-bargaining agreements by implicating co-defendants in other cases. In 1983 he had been one of five men indicted on several burglary charges. Pleading guilty, he had claimed that his only role had been to stand watch, while others testified that it had been he who had done the planning and the actual breaking and entering.

"He always gets to telling that someone else did something," someone identified as "a long-time Harlan County courtroom observer" said. "It makes you wonder, doesn't it?"

"I've never known Donald Bartley to tell the truth," the classmate said. "You name it and I think the boy's done it."

A deputy circuit court clerk remembered Bartley as a little boy, coming in to pick up his mother's child support check. "He was the sweetest and most polite person," she recalled, "and good looking, too. I almost cried the first time he got in trouble." When he was testifying in the burglary trial, he had remembered her and said, "'Hello, you look so nice.' He handed me that same line, just like nothing in the world had ever happened. And he was just as pretty as he ever was, too."

Pretty Boy, Sherry thought bitterly.

Once the trial began, on Monday, June 2, she was forbidden to enter the courtroom because she was under subpoena as a witness, barred from hearing others' testimony, although she had every intention of refusing to testify and had notified the court that she would cite the marital exclusion rule and, if necessary, take the Fifth. She considered being kept outside a cruel ploy on the part of James Wiley Craft, who everyone said fully lived up to his name, to influence the jury into thinking that Benny Hodge was so evil that not even his wife would stand by him. She could only visit Benny in the jail, under strict observation, since certain implements had been discovered in his cell. She tried to comfort him, but Benny was despondent. He was sure the FBI had put Bartley up to his statement and was doing everything it could to see him fry.

When Rod Kincaid approached Sherry on the courthouse steps and urged her to testify fully and truthfully, implying, she thought, that things might go easier for her if she did, she told him to go to hell. She was not going to betray her man; she was out to save him, any way she could.

She thought she found a possible avenue when Ben Gish, who was covering the trial for the *Mountain Eagle* and with whom she had had several off-the-record conversations, asked her formally for permission to do an interview with her. She liked Ben, the son of Tom and Pat Gish, owners and publishers of the *Eagle;* he seemed like a down-to-earth, good-hearted young man; he was friendly to her when everyone else, as soon as they found out she was married to Hodge, shunned her like the plague, which confirmed her lifelong belief that most people were hypocritical jerks. Ben treated her like a lady and a human being. Like a true gent, he even picked up the check when he found her sitting alone at the Courthouse Café, biding her time and feeling so anxious and blue. Sometimes they talked about music; like Benny, Ben Gish preferred classic rock, and he worked part-time as a radio disk jockey, playing oldies; Sherry listened to his show.

She decided to grant his request and to tell the world her side of the story. She knew that members of the jury weren't supposed to read the papers, but she figured some of them must cheat.

They did the interview sitting outside near the courthouse park-ing lot, where the six cars that were evidence in the case were impounded.

"If Benny was a murderer," she began, "he would already have killed me. I've given him every opportunity. What really hurts me about Bartley is that we were so good to him and I helped him get over hepatitis and kick his cocaine habit. Bartley's more likely to have done that murder than Benny is. I know of at least two times that Benny had kept Donnie from killing someone." She described the incidents, one in which Donnie had pointed a gun at a man after hit-ting him over the head with a poker, the other in which Donnie had threatened to kill his own sister. She provided vivid and elaborate details. Donnie was a liar through and through. He had even lied about her buying her parents a house with the Acker money. Her father had borrowed that money from his credit union.

Her husband, Sherry said, was a man who walked away from trouble: "I don't know of anyone who ever met Benny that didn't like him. He's never even spanked his daughters, or mine." He was the world's best father and a man who lived for his family and his body-building.

Sherry said that she had often made Benny mad enough to want to kill her and hit her and that, instead of becoming violent, he had left home each time and rented a motel room. She spoke of her happiness with him, of a trip to Six Flags Over Georgia and other outings with the kids. This trial was taking its toll on her daughter and on Benny's children, who couldn't understand why they couldn't see their daddy and touch him. She was having a rough time herself, reduced to supporting herself by cutting the hair on dead bodies in mortuaries. The FBI had told her that she would be arrested after the trial was over.

"If loving Benny's a crime, they can lock me up and throw away the key." She was being treated poorly by the FBI and the state police, but she wished to thank Letcher County Jailer Frank Tackitt, who had been especially nice to her and Benny.

The *Eagle* printed the long interview, in which Sherry came across as the devoted wife of a misunderstood victim, on the front page. She read it aloud to Benny, who was thrilled by it but doubted it would do much good. More and more every day, he was convinced he was going to get the death penalty.

Sherry told him, as she had so many times, that life without him would not be worth living. If he were condemned to death, which she was praying every day would not happen, she would kill herself. She knew where she could get some cyanide pills. She suggested that they make a twin-suicide pact. She would bring the pills into the courtroom if he ended up sentenced to the chair. The instant the sentence was pronounced, she would rush up, and they would take the pills and die in each other's arms.

Benny agreed.

Whitesburg was the prettiest town in Eastern Kentucky and also the most sophisticated and progressive. In addition to its weekly newspaper, it was home to Appalshop, an arts center housed in large studios of contemporary design that broadcast over its own radio station and produced documentary films, traditional and current music recordings, television programs, and original plays performed by an ensemble troupe that traveled throughout the nation. On one of his CBS television programs, Charles Kuralt correctly described Whitesburg as the cultural capital of Appalachia. The town was also home to Harry M. Caudill, the writer and lawyer whose *Night Comes to the*

Cumberlands and other books were widely acclaimed and had had a powerful effect on Robert F. Kennedy, among other government and academic figures. Many of Whitesburg's citizens lived there by choice, some moving back, like the publishers of the *Mountain Eagle,* after successful lives elsewhere, or staying on after discovering it, like the Yale graduates who owned the Courthouse Café, where they served health-conscious dishes that tasted more like California than Kentucky.

But if Whitesburg differed from, say, Fleming-Neon, it was still an isolated mountain town, where the biggest event of the year might be a high school football game or the Fourth of July celebration and most of its citizens worked in the coal industry, when they could. When reporters started pouring in and Lester Burns drove up to the courthouse in his gigantic plush law office on wheels to plug his computers into the 220-volt line and begin putting on his jurisprudential Wild West show, the town became captivated by the trial that had the whole state talking and was predicted to last from three to four weeks. The atmosphere, Ben Gish said, was like a circus. You never knew what bizarre act was going to perform next.

After Lester's entrance, the most dramatic turn was executed by Pat Mason, "the millionaire witness," as the press called her, who arrived driving a new white Cadillac Eldorado convertible with the numbers "7 7 7" on the Florida plates and embossed in black above the door handles. Her jet-black hair cropped short, she emerged from the car wearing an all-white pantsuit and flourishing a white walking stick topped with gold.

Her statement, revealing no more than her sales of two cars to Roger Epperson, was stipulated into evidence, with Lester and Dale Mitchell reserving the right to call her to the stand at a later time. She declined to be interviewed.

26

Lester Burns stayed with his entourage and Dale Mitchell at La Citadelle—"this beautiful motel, on the apex of a forest-clad mountain, is Kentucky's contribution to relaxation, recreation and the gallant hospitality of the fabled mountain country"—throughout the trial. His only complaint about the accomodations, the most sumptuous in that part of the world, was that he had trouble getting his bus up the steep climb. He descended the thirty or so miles to Whitesburg each morning, favoring the press with a choice quote or two as he alighted to enter the courthouse.

Resplendent in yellow rattlesnake boots, several diamond rings, and enough gold to tempt Cortez, his effect enhanced by his being on crutches and confiding to reporters that he was in pain from severed ligaments and tendons slow to heal, Lester began his defense work with a flurry of preliminary motions. Epperson and Hodge were pleading not guilty. Lester wanted the trial moved out of Letcher County because there had been so much publicity that it would be impossible to select an unbiased jury. Circuit Judge F. Byrd Hogg denied this, saying that he read newspapers himself and took them *"cum grano salus,"* as anyone with any common sense did, and that, at any rate, Whitesburg was not Fleming-Neon, where the crimes had occurred. If prospective jurors from Fleming-Neon felt they could not be fair, they would be dismissed. The judge did not believe that "the Supreme Court thinks that we have to go to the moon to try a case like this one."

Lester also asked for a delay. It was the second day of June; James Wiley Craft had turned over the transcript of Donald Bartley's statement to the defense only on May 28, explaining disingenuously, Lester sneered, that it had taken that long to have it typed. There was not time enough for the defense to adjust to this major development. Judge Hogg denied that one, too. He denied all but the most trivial motions Lester and Dale Mitchell introduced. (As Bartley would now plead guilty, he had been granted a separate trial, and would be appearing later as a witness at this one; his new court-appointed attorney did not participate in these procedures.)

Judge Hogg also lectured Lester. He told him that he knew him by reputation and would not tolerate in his courtroom the kinds of disruptive behavior for which the attorney was famous. Blatant appeals to emotion might be acceptable elsewhere, but not here.

"Yes, Your Honor," Lester replied softly.

F. Byrd Hogg was a tough law and order jurist who was never afraid to speak his mind. Danny Webb liked to say privately that he always felt better when Judge Hogg was on the bench because then the scales of justice tipped ever so slightly to the prosecution's side. Others enjoyed speculating that the character called Boss Hogg in the television series "The Dukes of Hazzard," which was set in highly fictionalized Kentucky mountains, was modeled after him. It was true that, like the boss, the judge was a small, stout man who talked in a loud voice in a rich highlands accent. Unlike Boss Hogg, however, Judge Hogg never wore a white suit with matching Stetson and was not in any sense the boss of anything other than his courtroom.

A Republican in a heavily Democratic area who displayed photographs of Presidents Dwight Eisenhower and, defiantly, Richard Nixon on the wall behind the desk in his chambers, Byrd Hogg had been elected and reelected despite strong opposition from the United Mine Workers, the most powerful political force in the county. People appreciated his warm, unpretentious personality and knew that behind his folksy manner there was a first-class legal mind. His rulings were hardly ever reversed by a higher court.

His physical appearance may have encouraged his forthrightness. In World War II he had participated in the D-Day landings as an infantryman and in Germany was hit in the face by enemy shrapnel. His nose, or what was left of it, and the right side of his upper lip bore the scars of those wounds: he liked to joke that the Army must have assigned an apprentice plastic surgeon to him, figuring his face hadn't been much to begin with. He had learned to deal with life as with his disfigurement, as if to say, "Here I am. If you don't like it, too bad." His opinions could be downright startling, on and off the bench.

A visitor to his chambers was likely to be treated to vivid statements on the virtues of the death penalty as retributive justice. To illustrate, the judge spread out on his desk his collection of gruesome photographs of homicide victims, bodies mutilated and burned and hacked to bits, while commenting on each in hideous detail. He would ask whether whoever had done this or that ghastly thing to another human being didn't deserve to be put to death. What right did such a person have to be housed, clothed, and fed by society for the rest of his natural life? What about the victims? He planned to write a book advocating the death penalty, illustrating the text with these photographs, to which he would add those of Tammy Acker, after the trial. That would give the misguided lamebrains who whined about cruel and unusual punishment a thing or two to think about.

Judge Hogg frequently volunteered that, after years on the bench, he did not believe in the jury system. He was stuck with it and would abide by it, but it no longer worked. Standards had fallen so low in American schools that the average person was too ignorant to be trusted with important decisions. In avuncular tones punctuated by gruff laughter, he explained why jurors were becoming more inadequate every day. Most of them were befuddled by legal arguments and judges' instructions; hardly any of them were capable of understanding the scientific evidence that was such an important part of homicide prosecutions nowadays and would grow more complex in the future. Was anyone prepared to tell him that the typical numbskull sitting on a jury, who had an attention span about as long as a breakfast cereal commercial and had never read a book in his life and didn't know a pathologist from a pickax, was equipped to evaluate medical testimony, let alone decipher psychiatric folderol?

Judge Hogg indulged certain tastes that might have been considered eccentric in more refined sections of the nation. He chewed tobacco on the bench, spitting into a paper cup or a brass spittoon. It was not that Byrd Hogg was unaware that this practice was elsewhere regarded as unsanitary and uncouth. The judge liked to say that he believed he was as well-informed as the savages wearing silk suits in

New York or loincloths in Los Angeles. He watched satellite TV. He was current with the Yale, Harvard, and other law reviews, read the *Wall Street Journal* every morning, and occasionally perused the *New York Times*. He was aware that chewing on the bench was not as common on the U.S. Supreme Court as it once had been; neither were brilliant opinions much in fashion. Nor was he unaware that reporters from Lexington, Louisville, and other far-flung metropolises delighted in portraying mountain folk as barbarians. Like his Texan relations, who had named a pair of daughters Ima and Ura, Judge Hogg simply didn't give a damn what outsiders thought. What was America about but freedom, and what were the mountains if not one of the last places where you could be what you wanted to be?

His chambers, crowded with memorabilia and family pictures, were down the hall from the jail, just off his courtroom on the second floor of the courthouse. On most days he had the jailhouse cook fix him his lunch. His favorite meal, in which he indulged once a week, was boiled hog's head. His eyes danced with anticipation as he recited the recipe for what his English ancestors had called brawny. Plunge one entire hog's head, boned and quartered, into a pressure cooker. Add cabbage, carrots, garlic, salt, and pepper to taste. Boil an hour; drain and serve. The judge sometimes wandered over to the jail kitchen to oversee the preparation of this dish, which he consumed at his desk while meditating points of law. In his opinion the ears were the tastiest, but the snout—as the French would agree, calling it *museau de porc* and adding white wine and shallots—was succulent, too. In appreciation, exulting in this pungent break from legal tedium, the judge had been known to imitate the gobble of the wild turkey.

It may have been Judge Hogg's admonitions to him; it may have been the sight of that pugnacious face, the unvarnished manner, the brusquely confident way in which Byrd Hogg overruled objections and denied defense motions; it may have been the knowledge that, for once, he was sparring with a man who knew the law as thoroughly as he himself did; perhaps the mere sight of that gritty, chunky man with his granite-gray hair brushed straight back and his chaw was enough to give Lester Burns pause. It could have been the indictments hanging over his head—whatever, by the second day of the trial, as everyone noticed, Lester had shed his jewelry. He still wore boots and Western shirt, jacket and tie, but his fingers were bare of diamonds and only his watch and belt buckle shone gold. For Lester, the getup was homespun, and his mien was grave.

He was still on crutches, but without the jewelry they conveyed less gallantry than humility. One mischievous trooper, hoping to break Lester's composure and trick him into a nimble move that would prove that he was faking, surreptitiously removed a rubber tip as Lester sat at the defense table. When Lester struggled to his feet and noticed that the crutch had been tampered with, he looked around and plaintively asked, "Who would do this to me?" That afternoon he told reporters that "in a murder trial like this, there are no winners, no matter what the verdict. It is a painful experience for everyone."

His manner toward Dr. Acker, who was the first prosecution witness, was deferential. Somber and subdued, leaving the pro forma objections for Dale Mitchell to raise, Lester sat as Craft led the doctor step by step through that August night. Craft had already established the foundations of his case with a dramatic opening statement. His voice was a resonant baritone that carried no trace of regional accent; in the old days of radio, he could have been the announcer of some action-packed mystery or adventure series. The defense denounced Craft's language and tone as inflammatory but offered no opening responsive account, reserving any alternative scenario until completion of the Commonwealth's presentation of evidence. This was a tactic that had precedent but left Craft's words hanging in the air and raised the unspoken question, what plausible defense could there be for Epperson and Hodge?

James Wiley Craft was nowhere as histrionic as Lester Burns, but was in his own way as strong a personality. Danny Webb thought Craft the most effective prosecutor in Eastern Kentucky. In his private practice, Craft's reputation extended beyond the mountains, and other lawyers avoided tangling with him; he was thorough and could get nasty. He was one of several successful siblings of parents who had not been educated beyond the eighth grade but had stressed reading and education to their children. James Wiley had a brother who was a professor of comparative literature at the University of Chicago.

In trying to recite what he recalled of the sequence of robbery and murder, Dr. Acker spoke in the high, thin voice of a man of his years.

His Bostonian inflections had the effect of objectifying his story and elevating it, as if he too had died and were signaling from a distant galaxy. His voice quavered once, when he had trouble remembering what day of the week it had been, and he said, "Time matters so little, now that Tammy is gone." Mitchell's objection to this sounded callous.

In a dark suit, starched white shirt, and tie, his face almost as fleshless as a bird's foot, Dr. Acker sat in the witness box facing the jury, which at that point in the proceedings consisted of eleven men and three women. In Kentucky the final panel of twelve is not selected until almost the end of the trial as the jury is about to retire to deliberate, when the court clerk draws the names of alternates by lot. In this courtroom, as in some others in Kentucky, depending on the shape of the room and the choice of the architect, the jury box sat directly below and in front of the bench and witness stand, rather than off to the side as is the usual configuration. This design, which gave the jury front and center seats, three rows deep, involved them much more closely in the action, permitting them to look at a witness straight in the face and allowing the lawyers to perform close to and in front of them at all times. The defense and prosecution tables were off to either side. Spectators sat beside and behind the jury box, on benches that remained filled throughout this trial.

Lester, sitting beside Epperson, let Mitchell conduct almost all of the cross-examination of the doctor. Short of being abusive, but not far short of it, Mitchell did not hold back. It was true, the doctor admitted, that he had had some difficulty in picking out Hodge's photo from the display the police had shown him several days after the murder. This was because he had experienced blurred vision after the choking he had received, which had caused his eyes to hemorrhage. He had also suffered a heart attack during the assault. But he had no doubt that the blond-haired man sitting there today was one of the two who had first entered the house and tied him up. The other, darker man was not in the courtroom, but he could identify him, also, with absolute certainty. A third, big man had also been in the house, but he had not seen that one's face.

Mitchell attempted to undermine Dr. Acker on the basis of the amount of money kept in his house. In emphasizing this, Mitchell tried to provide what a successful defense ought to have, an alternative version of events. Since there was no doubt that the defendants

had been in the house, might there not be a motive other than robbery for their visit? Collusion, perhaps? This strategy was, while not
directly accusing him of crookedness, to imply something shady
about the doctor and to insinuate that whoever had come to rob him
that night did so because of unspecified illegitimate connections
between the thieves and their victim. If this approach would not
exonerate the defendants, it yet might sway the jury toward leniency.
Why, Mitchell asked, had the doctor told the police that half a million
dollars or less had been stolen, when the figure turned out to be
closer to two million?

He had been surprised by that huge figure, Dr. Acker said. He did
not count his money; he just earned it. Until her death from cancer,
his wife, Dee, had managed the household expenses. He gave her the
money from his practice, she paid the bills, and they saved the rest.

"You're saying you saved five hundred thousand dollars from grocery money, is that what you're saying?"

"I'm saying I probably saved a great deal more," Dr. Acker
replied steadily. It was true that, many years ago, he had owned an
interest in a bank, but the bank was many miles away from his home
and practice. For thirty or forty years, he and his wife had simply
stored their money in an old trunk. Three or four months before the
robbery, he had bought a safe. He used banks as seldom as possible.
He did have a business account, for processing checks.

A few years ago, noticing that some of the money was getting
moldy and mildewed, he had taken it to the Bank of Whitesburg to
exchange it for new bills in clean wrappers. Everyone knew him.
There had been no questions. The tellers had simply given him new
bills for old. He had not counted it; he had no idea how much had
been involved in this transaction. He trusted people.

"We were never extravagant, and we saved considerable money.
But I don't know how much."

Mitchell tried to imply that the intruders had actually had permission to enter and to linger; to insinuate that some or all of the money
had been owed to these men, who had come to collect it, by force if
necessary.

Why then had Hodge and Bartley bothered to pose as FBI agents,
if the doctor knew their true purpose? One would assume the jury
would be aware of this contradiction, but James Wiley Craft decided
to underline it. On redirect examination, over Mitchell's strenuous

objections and demands for a mistrial, Craft asked whether any of the money had been owed to Bartley, Hodge, or Epperson.

"Not one red penny!" Dr. Acker snapped.

"And did these intruders have any permission to enter or remain in your house that night?"

More defense objections.

"Did you hear the question, doctor?" Craft asked.

"Yes, I heard it," Dr. Acker replied vehemently. "And they never had any permission at any time—any one of them—to remain in my home, no more than they had permission to kill Tammy, throttle me and take my money!"

Mitchell objected and asked for a mistrial.

"Same objection. Admonish the witness to answer the question only," Lester said.

"The jury will not consider that," Judge Hogg agreed.

But Dr. Acker's outburst remained on the jurors' minds and in the consciousness of everyone.

When it was his turn to cross-examine, Lester took a different tack. He hobbled over to the stand, less an adversary than a supplicant.

"Dr. Acker," he began, "my name is Lester Burns, and I'm hard of hearing, and I'll move over."

"I beg your pardon?" Dr. Acker asked.

"I'm hard of hearing and I'll move over close beside you, if you don't mind, sir."

"That would be perfectly all right."

Had the jury not been sitting so near and able to view at such close range what followed, the subsequent colloquy would have been lost on them. Lester, balancing on his crutches, arching forward and downward toward the witness box as if gripping a trapeze, spoke into the doctor's ear.

"I have very few questions to ask you, doctor," Lester said in a voice that trailed off, then ascended like the smoke from a funeral pyre. "If you do not understand them, please ask me to repeat them. Because I'm not trying to pull any tricks."

Lester paused. Dr. Acker nodded as if to say, "I trust you."

"I understood from your testimony that the first time something was put around your neck that it did not render you unconscious or insensible?" No, he had not lost consciousness then, Dr. Acker said; he had heard everything, as he had already told the jury.

"It did not affect your mental faculties at all, did it?"

"No."

"And you told the jury what you heard?"

"That's right."

"Dr. Acker, thank you, sir, but that's all I have at this time."

The dialogue had lasted less than a minute—Lester spent longer making his way to and from the witness box. There was more point to it than was just then apparent, Lester knew, but for the moment the impression was that he was primarily conveying his sympathies.

Lester had concluded that attacking Dr. Acker was counterproductive. The wiser course was the reverse, to concede the doctor's credibility, to avoid appearing no better than the men who had already turned an old man's final years to tragedy, and to make use of what the doctor had already said to undermine the credibility of Donald Bartley, who would repeat conversations Dr. Acker never heard.

To defend Epperson while being himself involved in aspects of the gang's crimes was proving to be extraordinarily difficult for Lester. He was constantly aware of the web of deceit in which he had entangled himself that threatened his own freedom and career. After so much scheming and subterfuge, he longed to tell the truth without compromising his client and himself. He could not see how.

Alone in his room after picking at dinner in the Skyline Room and watching the dying of the day through tinted windows, he contemplated the mess he was in. That afternoon in court a Fleming-Neon policeman had described what it was like being the first person on the scene, encountering Dr. Acker bloody-faced in the doorway, nearly stumbling over Tammy's body as it lay on a heap of her blood-soaked clothes, seeing the butcher knife and her wrecked room. During a break Lester had approached James Wiley Craft in the narrow corridor outside the Commonwealth Attorney's office.

"What a tragedy," Lester had mumbled. "James Wiley, I been thinking. What if I gave back my fee?"

Craft arched one dark eyebrow above his glasses, touched his thick mustache, and disappeared into his office.

Had Craft heard or understood him? Even if he had, *he doesn't take me seriously!* Lester thought in frustration. *There must be some way I can give that money back!* He could think of none.

The only course was to defend his client and deal with personal difficulties afterwards. Other than making every conceivable motion and objection in an attempt to catch Judge Hogg in reversible error, the most promising strategy appeared to be to go after Donald Bartley when he took the stand as the government's star witness. Tactics aside, Lester believed that Bartley was lying. It was always a plus as a lawyer when you thought the government was trying to pull something and you could believe in what you were saying, no matter the guilt or innocence of your client. Lester's reasoning was the same as Frank Fleming's: Bartley, not Hodge, was the type to kill a woman in that way and was fingering Hodge only to save himself.

Lester had not had the stomach to try to impugn Dr. Acker to begin with. A small-town doctor was nearly invulnerable to criticism, and Lester avoided blaming victims for crimes. Many people who had been through the Great Depression distrusted banks; there were mattresses stuffed with cash all over Kentucky, although none perhaps with two million dollars. Although he had not seen the actual returns, information had come to Lester that Dr. Acker paid taxes each year on a reported six-figure income and was not in trouble with the IRS. If he was guilty of imprudence, perhaps even of arrogance, in assuming that an alarm system was enough to protect his family and his cash, his popularity in Fleming-Neon could easily have induced a false sense of security, even after his clinic had been burglarized. He would suffer during whatever years he had left for his negligence; no jury was going to blame him beyond that.

Born in Boston in 1908, Roscoe Jacob Acker received his medical degree from the College of Physicians and Surgeons there in 1943 and began practicing in the coal fields after the war at a time when the United Mine Workers offered young physicians as much as thirty thousand dollars a year as an inducement to come to Appalachia. (A doctor starting out then could normally expect to make less than half that amount.) Beginning in Charleston, West Virginia, by the mid-fifties Dr. Acker had established his private practice and a small hospital in Fleming-Neon. As the region declined economically, people recalled, Dr. Acker often accepted chickens and eggs for fees, until the establishment of the Medicare and Medicaid programs in 1964.

He was always at or near the top of all doctors in the state in amounts claimed from Medicaid, usually well over a hundred thousand dollars annually. This was not surprising, given the proportion of his patients on relief. He had been suspended from the program in

1969–70 and was indicted, accused of billing for doctor–patient visits that had not taken place; but a judge dismissed the charges, and Dr. Acker gained immediate reinstatement. That had been a merely unfortunate episode, most people believed, caused by a mean-spirited bureaucracy. Lester saw no point in bringing it up and doubted that it would be admissible anyway, surely not with Judge Hogg on the bench.

If some people, and there were a few, thought that the idea that Tawny and Tammy had owned Porsches was offensive when many of the people of Fleming-Neon were lucky to have shoes, most of his patients begrudged him and his family nothing. They saw him as a distinguished Eastern gentleman, whose favorite recreation was grouse hunting, who graced their community with his nobility, weighing so lightly what he gave in long hours of personal attention. Lester speculated that Dr. Acker had increased his wealth dramatically through the coal business in the seventies, as the incident involving Roe Adkins and the bulldozer suggested. But to take the attitude that he did not deserve his riches, let alone that he deserved to have had his daughter murdered, was to adopt the criminal mentality that assumed that wealth belonged to whoever could grab it, by whatever means.

To break Bartley down, that was the only way to save Epperson and Hodge from the chair, perhaps to cause a mistrial. If the prosecution based its case on a lie, Lester believed, it deserved to fail. He intended to hound Bartley into revealing himself as a murdering, sniveling rat.

27

FRANK FLEMING, DR. GEORGE BUCKLEY, Jesse Spicer, Roe Adkins, Sonny Spencer, Robert Loturco, Tom and Travis McDowell, a clerk from a Whitesburg drugstore, the laboratory technician who had lifted Donald Bartley's print—one after another they took the stand to tell the story Craft and Caudill constructed scene by scene. Bit by bit the physical evidence mounted up, money, weapons, receipts, drug paraphernalia, jewelry. When Dr. Buckley used the butcher knife, still caked with Tammy's blood, as a pointer, Lester objected and the doctor apologized. But there was the knife.

Dale Mitchell tried to get Dr. Buckley, who in his testimony emphasized that it must have taken tremendous force to penetrate Tammy's entire body, to admit that speed was also a key factor, that weight and force were only factors in speed, and that an adrenaline (cocaine) rush could increase strength. Buckley conceded these arguments to an extent but was insistent that a large man rather than a small one was likely to have done the stabbing. The issue of the knife's actually penetrating the stone floor—an added consideration so important to Danny Webb's belief that Benny must have done it—could not be considered at the trial, since the knife had been removed before it could be photographed sticking between those stones. Probably it could not have been photographed in its original position, since Tammy had been on top of the point. Webb felt that most reasonable people, if informed of this extra evidence, would concede that a true muscle man must have done it.

Travis McDowell added further drama when, obviously nervous, he said that an unidentified voice on the phone had threatened him if he testified. Without revealing his role in leading the FBI to Epperson, Travis described a druggy party at the condominium with the defendants and denied that he was the actual buyer of the '85 Corvette: "Why would I need a Corvette when I'm already driving a Porsche?" Bill Fluherty told of the arrests, emphasizing how Hodge had hesitated before leaving the van and had denied owning the butterfly knife. Chuck Boling outlined the SWAT team's role and Epperson's arrest.

Fluherty and Boling were housed at a country club in the mountains near Jenkins as they waited to testify. They played a few rounds of golf at the otherwise deserted course and wondered if the club actually had any members, it was such an incongruous emblem of leisure amid poverty. The mountains thick with trees, bright green with the birth of summer; the rivers and lakes; the grungy towns and trailer homes surrounded by trash; the long, bony faces of unemployed mountaineers; the sunken, dark, blank eyes of so many of the women; here and there the attractive house, children bouncing with energy—it was surreal. To drive to Whitesburg, such a contrast with its cleanliness and bustle, its wooden signs saying BIRD SANCTUARY and DUCK-XING, they had to pass through a black tunnel carved out of a mine shaft.

In the courtroom Boling kept thinking that he was a day's drive from Florida but a century away. The characters, the whole quaint scene made him recall the Scopes Monkey Trial testing Tennessee's anti-evolution laws in 1925—but, far from scorning the anachronisms, Boling liked them. The people, especially the judge, were so, well, *human.* They might seem rough, but they held up well against the oily breed Boling knew from Florida. He had expected a lynch-mob atmosphere; instead he found the people matter-of-fact, impressed perhaps by Lester Burns's entrances and exits and by the cars and money involved in the case but otherwise calm. When James Wiley Craft introduced into evidence the heaps of cash agents had found in the condo, in Hodge's wallet, and in Epperson's car—some hundred and sixty thousand—Judge Hogg instructed his bailiff to dump the bills in a basket to pass around to the jurors. "Let them take a good look," the judge said, grinning. "They'll never get that close to that much money again in their lives." As for Burns, Boling thought that the attorney could have made another fortune in Holly-wood. Boling was not aware that several people in that courtroom, including the Assistant Commonwealth's Attorney, had played roles in *Coal Miner's Daughter*. Mike Caudill had met the challenge of act-ing tanked-up on moonshine inside Dr. Acker's clinic.

Relations between government and defense attorneys, fairly civil up to that point, turned sour during the third and final week of the trial. On Monday, June 16, a surprise witness appeared for the prose-cution. In a tense in-chambers conference, Lester and Mitchell com-plained that although they had known the gist of what this witness would testify, having been given a copy of his handwritten statement on May 28, they had not known his name until a few days ago. Mike Caudill said that it had been necessary to conceal the witness's name to protect him until he was brought from Florida to Kentucky. How could they have been expected to investigate this witness, the defense argued, without knowing his identity? Judge Hogg ruled for the pros-ecution. Lawrence Anthony Smith took the stand.

Smith testified that he had been an inmate at the Orange County jail in Orlando when Benny Hodge was brought there and placed in an adjacent cell. Hodge, Smith claimed, had almost immediately begun talking about the crimes for which he had been arrested. Among other details, Hodge had bragged about stabbing Tammy Acker "several times"—possibly thirteen. Smith also said that Hodge had described piling the money from the robbery on top of his bed at the condominium and making love on it with his girlfriend.

Lester believed Smith to be a liar, a typical inmate trying to get his own sentence reduced by disclosing, in this instance fabricating, information supposedly learned from another inmate. Whether authorities had put Smith up to his testimony, or whether he had made up his story from reading the newspapers or listening to another inmate—possibly Bartley?—Lester could not figure out. But, to begin with, the idea that a man such as Benny Hodge, who had survived nine years at Brushy Mountain, knew well the consequences of blabbing to other inmates, and was by nature so closemouthed that he would hardly talk to his own lawyer—that such a man would begin shooting off his mouth the moment he was arrested was pre-posterous.

Lester was unconvinced by Smith's written statement for addi-tional reasons. Smith had originally spoken to two FBI agents on

August 30, 1985, while he and Hodge were still in the jail together. His written statement, however, was not witnessed and notarized until September 27. To Lester, as to Dale Mitchell, the statement looked fake: the syntax was fairly regular and grammatical, but there were numerous misspellings ("durning," "outher," "docktor," "togeather," and so on) of simple words, while words commonly misspelled by the semiliterate were correct ("proceeded," "officials," "committed"). Some of the information seemed overspecified. Would Hodge conceivably have given this man Pat Mason's phone number? Would Smith have remembered it to write it down a month later?

Lester let Mitchell hammer away at the curious misspellings, the time elapsed between Smith's first contact with the FBI and the notarizing of the statement, and the matter of the phone number. Smith testified that he had jotted notes down on an envelope, from which the statement had been composed later. Unable to make much headway with this line of questioning, Mitchell began to introduce material relating to Smith's long arrest record. Smith denied having been convicted of distributing dangerous drugs to a minor. Craft accused Mitchell of distorting Smith's record.

"Your Honor, please," Lester interjected. "That gentleman, Mr. Smith, said he had never hurt anybody. If giving dangerous drugs to a minor doesn't hurt anybody, then what does?"

"The record doesn't say that," Craft nearly shouted.

"Well, I can read it!" Lester shot back. "That's what I read, and I want to hear this man in chambers!"

"That's fine with me!" Craft said.

"And I'll loan you my glasses," Lester said, taking off his reading spectacles and holding them out.

In chambers, the defense attorneys had to back down. Smith's record was full of arrests, but most of the charges had been dismissed or reduced to misdemeanors. Judge Hogg ruled that it was enough that the witness had admitted to having been convicted of a felony.

"I want an apology from Mr. Burns," Craft said.

"You owe me one and I owe you one," Lester said, without indicating what Craft's offense may have been, "so we're even."

Back in court, Lester took over the cross-examination and asked whether the handwriting at the top left-hand corner of the first page of Smith's statement was his own—the part indicating the date and time. Smith said he had written it.

"Have you been in the United States Army?" Lester asked him.

"No."

"Have you been a policeman?"

"No."

"How did you happen to write out '2300' hours? Most folks would have put that as 11:00 P.M."

"In the jail where I was confined that's how they referred to time."

When Lester showed Smith the page, the witness admitted he had not written out the time and the date. That was someone else's handwriting.

"Why didn't you tell the jury that when I first asked you?" Lester asked and, addressing the jury, added in an exasperated aside, "He wouldn't tell the truth if you kept him here all day."

After the furious objections this remark brought from Craft, Lester continued to do what he could to portray Smith as a liar. Asking the witness to repeat his name, Lester asked:

"Didn't you like the name your Mommy and Daddy gave you?"

"That was the name they gave me."

"Do you know a Steven Tim Stokes?"

"Yes, I do."

"Who is he?"

"That's the name I used when I ran away from home."

"You were sixteen when you hit the road?"

"Fifteen."

"You got as far as the jail. Now, I want you to tell the ladies and gentlemen of the jury when and why you decided to change your name to John Gibbs."

"That was another time when I was arrested."

"Why don't you tell them why you got tired of John Gibbs, Tim Steven Stokes, Lawrence Anthony Smith and Tony Smith, and changed your name to Kenneth Moron and Kenneth Michael Moron?" Lester put heavy stress on the first syllable of the last name. Smith admitted that it was another of his aliases.

"Well," Lester sighed, "here is Kenneth *Moron*. You liked Moron a lot, didn't you? When did you decide to change your name to Tony Sparks? Can you think of any other names you've changed to?"

"No, I believe you've gotten them all."

"That's enough. I have no further questions, Your Honor."

* * *

The question of whether Sherry Hodge and Carol Epperson would be called as witnesses was not settled until after Smith left the stand, when Judge Hogg ruled that spousal immunity and the Fifth Amendment precluded their being called; they were then permitted to observe the rest of the trial as spectators. From what she learned about Smith's testimony, Sherry was incensed. Benny insisted he had never met Smith in his life, she told Ben Gish and others who would listen. And Smith's allegation that Benny had told of making love on the pile of money was pure crap. Why, the only money the FBI had found in any of the beds had been a fifty-dollar bill, and that was in Roger and Carol's. If people got their kicks listening to that sort of garbage, let them.

Sherry was in court to hear Rebecca Hannah Bartley, who waived spousal immunity, say that everyone in the gang had been on drugs, except for Sherry, who was pleased by that statement but by nothing else in Becky's testimony. She was there to tell the truth, Becky insisted, as Mitchell and Lester tried to portray her as a woman out to save herself and her husband at the expense of the other defendants. There were some inconsistencies between this testimony and Becky's earlier statements to the FBI and to Mike Caudill. She had been frightened when first interviewed, Becky said, and not under oath. Now she admitted seeing all that money dumped out on the floor and helping to shred and dispose of the clothing after the murder and robbery. She had not been promised immunity, she insisted, but she acknowledged hoping that her testimony would help her and her husband. Donnie had told her when they had first met about having been an informant for the police, but she claimed to know nothing about his history of turning state's evidence in other cases. When Mitchell tried to get her to admit having seen blood on one of Donnie's shoes after the Acker murder—information that presumably came to Mitchell from his client, Hodge—she denied this.

Lester treated Becky with a degree of gentleness and courtesy. She had just turned eighteen; she came across as nothing more than a misguided kid; she was not charged with anything. He decided to hold his fire, knowing that Epperson's and Hodge's lives depended on whether Bartley could be made to crack.

Clean-shaven, boyish, polite, dressed in jacket and open shirt, Donnie Bartley took the stand the next morning, June 17. His future, while not bright, was at least assured. His lawyer, Ned Pillersdorf of Lexington, who was being paid by the state, had succeeded in securing from the government a promise that, in return for his testimony, Bartley would not face the death penalty. Beyond that, there were no deals.

James Wiley Craft's strategy was clear from the start when, after asking Bartley his name, he inquired of the witness his weight and height. He had gained about twenty pounds since his arrest, Bartley said; he now weighed about one-sixty-eight.

"Would you care," Craft asked him, "to step out of the witness box, out in front of His Honor here, and take your coat off?"

Judge Hogg overruled the defense objections to this disrobing, and Bartley stood before the jury in his shirtsleeves, a healthy-looking specimen but a small, slight one. Craft let the witness display himself without comment, but the unstated hypothesis was obvious. Could a little man such as this one have been able to inflict such terrible damage on Tammy Acker? Could he have run a knife all the way through her at least twice, and penetrated deep within her organs more often than that? The unvoiced answer was meant to be no, the killer must have been a big powerful man, a weightlifter, Benny Hodge.

Lester and Mitchell had anticipated this strategy when they had asked Rebecca Hannah Bartley whether it wasn't true that her husband also lifted weights. She had admitted as much but downplayed it, saying that Donnie had only occasionally worked out with Benny, who was the serious lifter. Becky had also said that when she had told Mike Caudill, during her first interview with him, that Benny Hodge had a "sweet" personality and had been "like a big brother" to her, she had been confused, unreliable, trying to protect everyone, and not under oath.

Donnie's and Benny's relative strengths aside, Lester was convinced that either one of them was capable of having inflicted the wounds on Tammy Acker. From what Lester understood of the forensic aspects of the matter, the strength of whoever was flailing away with that knife was, if not irrelevant, not the determining factor in relation to the depth of the wounds. Technically, it was the *speed* of the knife as it was plunged downward that determined the degree of penetration—the speed together with the kinetic response of the tissue, which when hit set up a ripple effect that actually eased penetration rather than resisting it. As to the speed itself, the principle of physics involved was known to most baseball fans: the speed of the bat as it meets the ball means more than the strength of the hitter in determining how far the ball will go; the batter must be strong enough to sweep the bat and to follow through after the hit; but a small player with fast hands will hit the ball farther than a big player with slow hands. Of course, a big player with fast hands will hit the ball farther than a small player.

Lester had the option of bringing in a forensic pathologist to testify, as Lester privately phrased the matter, that "a child could have done it." But would the jury comprehend this sort of technical argument? Even if they did, might it not prove counterproductive, coming across as nit-picking and a trivializing of Tammy's death? At most it proved only that Bartley could have done the stabbing, not that he actually had done it. The risk of further alienating the jury did not seem worth it.

Bartley admitted under Craft's questioning that he had been the one to carry Tammy back to her bedroom and tie her up. As for how it was decided who would kill her, Bartley quoted Epperson as having said to Benny, "Which one do you want, Brother?" and quoted Benny as having replied, "I'll take the girl." Benny then went to the bedroom, Bartley said.

Bartley described how the telephone had rung as he was trying to strangle Dr. Acker. At that point Benny, Bartley claimed, ran in from the bedroom saying, "She's not dead." Craft asked Bartley to repeat this.

"He said, 'She's not dead.' Then Roger walked away from me ... and pulled out a drawer and tossed Benny the knife. By that time, Roger said, 'The doctor is dead.' I looked at him myself. Benny came out from behind us and picked up a pillowcase and a suitcase full of money, and we jumped in the back seat and Roger drove us out."

Craft asked whether, after they had left Fleming-Neon and were driving down the road, there was any discussion among themselves as to what had happened at the Acker house. Bartley said there was. They had gone over whether they were sure that the old man and the girl were dead:

"Roger told Benny that he knew the doctor was dead. He had looked at him himself. He said, well, I know the girl is dead because the knife went all the way through to the floor."

"Who made the statement about the doctor?" Craft asked.

"Roger."

"And who made the statement about the girl?"

"Benny."

After hearing Bartley describe these events again, Danny Webb was more than ever convinced that this was the more or less true version. Their haste in leaving was the key to Hodge's homicidal frenzy. Even if Bartley had ended up with blood on his shoe, as someone had alleged, it could have been the doctor's blood. Frank Fleming, however, held to his different view.

Bartley's testimony had been more precise as to Benny's involvement than was the statement Bartley had given previously to Mike Caudill: the reference to the reason Benny was sure the girl was dead was, among other less crucial elements, not in the statement Caudill had recorded. Thinking they might have found an opening, Lester and Mitchell now demanded to see the full text and notes of the original FBI interview with Bartley. If they could find further omissions and inconsistencies there, Bartley's credibility could be seriously shaken.

Rod Kincaid, who was in the courtroom and prepared for this turn of events, quickly produced all materials relating to Bartley's original confession. To their disappointment, Lester and Mitchell soon realized that virtually everything Bartley was now saying was contained in Kincaid's original notes and summary. Bartley's only point of vulnerability seemed to be that he could not remember whether Epperson had handed, tossed, or thrown the knife to Benny down the hallway. When he began cross-examining, Mitchell bore in on this and on the curious suggestion that Benny, supposedly after first trying to kill the girl, had said, "She's not dead," after which Roger gave him the knife.

Mitchell failed to rattle Bartley, who insisted not only that he had not killed Tammy but that he had not had any idea of the savagery with which she had been stabbed until his attorney had shown him photographs of the body.

It remained for Lester to try to get to Bartley. Lester's technique was that of a fisherman. He had to bait the hook, let Bartley take it, let him run with it for awhile, play with him, then begin to reel him in. The bait consisted of a soft, inquisitive tone; the running and playing were a series of factual questions about which there could be little disagreement. Then came the reeling in and what Lester hoped would be the landing, the gutting, and the putting on ice. Lester began:

"When you got into the bedroom, Mr. Bartley," Lester said to him slowly, hovering over each word, "I want you to describe—in detail—what you did to that little girl, Tammy Acker."

Bartley supplied a minimal account of telling her to lie down and tying her up and removing her watch and bracelet. That was not good enough for Lester. He asked Bartley to reply precisely to a series of questions designed to place in the jurors' minds the image of a brutal, heartless little man who was himself the killer. To these questions, Bartley answered with two or three words each:

"You told her to lie down? ... And she obeyed your command? ... How was she lying? ... What was the condition of the room? ... Where did you ask that little girl to lie down in that room? ... Was she on her back or stomach or side? ... I'm to understand that you tied her hands? ... Like this? ... What did you tie her hands with? ... Did you put a gag in the little girl's mouth? ... And you tied that little girl's hair right up in that gag, didn't you? ... Did she cry or plead with you? ... Did she wrestle or fight or try to get away? ... She was just a peaceful, harmless, beautiful little girl, wasn't she? ... Was she a pretty girl? ... She was a beautiful girl, wasn't she? ... She didn't have those holes in her back, either, did she? ..."

Other than the initial introductions of the photographs of the body, this was the most emotional moment of the trial so far. Lester's questions were going to the black heart of the case. He stalked his prey, hobbling back and forth before the stand, then moving directly in front of him, blocking the jury's view:

"Why are you crying?" Lester asked him.

"I'm not crying," Donnie said.

"You're not crying?"

"No, I'm not."

"Well, you should be!"

Lester forced Bartley to look at the photographs: "Is that her? Is that her? Is that the kitchen that her lovely father, the old man, the fine gentleman and doctor—that she and he met you all in? Take a look at it! Is that the blood of her daddy on the kitchen floor? Did her back look like that? Is that what you gagged that beautiful young lady with? Didn't she tell you, don't bother my poor daddy, Mother just died?"

"She told me that on the way back to the bedroom."

"You say you've been worried and you can't sleep?"

"Yes."

"Haven't you been playing the guitar in your cell? Worried and can't sleep? You look like you've gained a lot of weight, to me. Didn't you tell me a few moments ago that I didn't see tears coming from your eyes?"

"I'm not crying, sir."

"You should be crying, shouldn't you, young man?"

When it was all over, Donald Bartley had not broken down, had not changed his story, and had left the defense lawyers with little to do in their closing statements but to attempt to ridicule the credibility of Lawrence Anthony Smith and of Bartley.

Realizing how little he had to go on in terms of exculpatory evidence, Lester tried to gain the jury's sympathy in any way he could. If they didn't care for his client, maybe they would vote for Lester Burns and against Donald Bartley. He began his oration by enacting a kind of evangelical healing service, as if he had been struck into wholeness by the light of truth. He threw away his crutches.

"If I may, I'm going to try to stand here without that crutch. I would like to thank each of you personally for Roger Epperson and his family and myself for the awesome burden that's been placed upon each of you by serving as a juror in this case. I would like further to thank the Commonwealth, the prosecutors—each of them—and the Court, the sheriff's office, the Kentucky State Police and every official in this courtroom and this county. I have never been treated more kindly or nicely," Lester said, and went on in praise of Dr. Acker. "That is one man before God Almighty in this County of Letcher who has nothing to tell but the truth! I submit to you before God Almighty as I stand here this morning that Dr. Roscoe J. Acker told you the truth!"

The specific truth to which Lester had referred was the one he had evoked during his brief cross-examination of the doctor, that nothing Dr. Acker had heard backed up Bartley's contention that a conversation had occurred in the kitchen in which Benny Hodge volunteered to kill the girl. Momentarily Lester broke out of his humble, thankful demeanor to scream at James Wiley Craft, "Shame on you, Mr. Commonwealth! You let the rat escape! Shame on you for not trying that skunk in this courtroom!"

Lester reminded the jury that there was "only one perfect man" in history and that even Lester Burns could make mistakes. He had mis-read Lawrence Anthony Smith's rap sheet because his eyes weren't very good. But he was glad he would not be making a more serious mistake. No one would be able to blame him for pulling the switch on the wrong man in the electric chair.

"Ladies and gentlemen," Lester concluded, "I would submit to you—and then I'll sit down—I'm not going to be able to find my seat—I just broke my glasses right in the trifocal—please find Roger Epperson not guilty of aiding and abetting in the murder of Tammy, Acker. Please find him not guilty of the attempted murder of Dr. Acker. On the other counts, do justice as you see fit. Regardless of what the verdict is, I'm your friend and I want to thank you for the job you've done."

In his final statement, James Wiley Craft reminded the jury that they were not trying Smith or Bartley. He emphasized that Tammy Acker's body was lying on a heap of clothes, arguing that this proved that she had been killed after Bartley had ransacked the room, while Bartley was in the kitchen choking the doctor. Craft cited Shake-speare's line about all the world's being a stage to portray the story of this case as a tragedy written, staged, costumed, and directed by the Straw Boss (Bartley had cited Sherry's epithet), Epperson. Benny Hodge, the strongman, had played the part of executioner. Now it was time for the jury to play their parts as the audience and to judge this play and show they understood its meaning. They should know that the tragic hero was Dr. Acker, who like King Lear had loved his daughters and had been made to suffer cruelly because of that love. In his final exhortation, Craft introduced another literary reference:

"I thought of a poem by Longfellow that I will quote to you. And I thought that if I could be permitted the insertion of just an extra phrase that it would be appropriate. And it is as follows: 'Wisely improve the Present,' for as I close, 'it is thine. Go forth to meet the shadowy Future, without Fear, and with a manly heart.' Justice must be done! The law must be enforced! Thank you."

28

A S IN MOST STATES, capital cases in Kentucky are tried in two phases, the first determining innocence or guilt, the second, if the jury reaches a guilty verdict, determining the penalty, which is set by the judge on the recommendation of the jury. At 11:30 A.M. on Friday, June 20, after receiving instructions from the judge, the jury retired to deliberate the outcome of the first phase, and Judge Hogg cleared the courtroom.

Down the hallway in the jail, Sherry took Ben Gish in to see Benny Hodge, who agreed to an interview because Sherry had told him that Gish was a good fellow and a sympathetic one. After taking a photograph of Sherry and Benny sitting together against a wall, arms and hands entwined, gazing into each other's eyes and managing to smile, Gish asked Benny how he felt at that moment, with his fate in the jury's hands. Was the death penalty on his mind?

"I think about it every day, twenty-four hours a day," Benny said. "When you wake up in the morning, you don't know if you're going to fall to the sane side or the insane side." He thought it was unfair that he had been pinpointed as the one who had done the stabbing. "The fact that I enjoy lifting weights doesn't make me guilty. I've never used my strength to hurt anybody."

He spoke about meeting Sherry when she was a prison guard and how she had changed his life. Things had been going fine until he had allowed himself to get involved in plans to commit the Acker robbery.

"I was minding my own business until someone came and gave me a sob story." If he had it to do all over again, he would never have come to Kentucky. "I'd have made Booger chain me to the bed so I couldn't've left that house."

He was anxious to tell what had really happened at the Acker house, but his attorney had advised him not to. All he could say was that Bartley was lying about the stabbing.

Ben Gish's impression, which he did not include as part of the story he wrote but confided to his parents and friends, was that Benny Hodge was not the brute he had been made out to be, and that he and Sherry genuinely cared for one another. It was difficult for Gish to reconcile the love he thought he saw between this pair with the image of someone who could murder a girl so viciously. As for Sherry, whatever she was, she was thoroughly, even obsessively devoted to this man, for whom she seemed willing to sacrifice her entire life.

Sherry did not tell Gish that she had already purchased two cyanide pills, which she was carrying concealed in her purse.

The jury, ten men and two women, deliberated for only an hour and forty minutes. At 1:30 P.M. Judge Hogg reconvened the court and read out the verdicts. The jury found Roger Epperson and Benny Hodge guilty of murder and guilty on each of the three other counts, to which they sentenced the defendants to the maximum of twenty years on each. It remained for them to retire again to decide whether aggravating circumstances merited that death be imposed as the penalty for the murder convictions.

The defense attorneys were permitted to make pleas to the jury to save Epperson's and Hodge's lives. Often during this procedure before sentencing in a capital case, witnesses testify to mitigating aspects of character and personal history that might sway the jury's sympathies. But Sherry had already taken the Fifth and could not be called; no other family or friends of Benny's were present. Carol had also taken the Fifth; she might not have made a persuasive character witness anyway. Epperson's family was in the courtroom, but none of them came forward. It remained for Judge Hogg to say that these men did have wives who loved them, and children, and that they had held jobs. Only Mitchell's and Lester's eloquence could now keep the defendants from execution.

Lester reminded the jury that many Biblical figures—Moses, King David, St. Paul—had done wicked things and had recovered to do great ones. Hadn't Moses been eighty years old when he received the Ten Commandments? Lester also provided a detailed account of the actual process of electrocution, with reference to wattage and the smell of burned human flesh.

Carried away perhaps by his own rhetoric, Lester at one point, in a hissed aside not caught by the court recorder but heard by the jury, accused James Wiley Craft of being willing to do anything to win this case because of his ambition to be elected state representative. As soon as Lester finished his speech and the jury retired once more to deliberate, Craft exploded at Lester, calling his remark "the cheapest shot I've ever endured in all my years as a lawyer." Lester, with reporters gathered round, apologized, saying Craft had presented his side brilliantly and calling him his friend.

It was nearly seven o'clock that Friday evening as the jury began their final, morbid task. They had the options of choosing any of four possible penalties: twenty or more years in prison, to add to the sixty already imposed; life in prison; life without possibility of parole for twenty-five years; or death. This time, they were gone for only forty minutes; it took nearly that long for the foreman to fill out the sentencing forms.

They chose death.

Judge Hogg read the verdict, polled the jurors individually, announced that defense counsel had waived any presentencing hearing, said that there was reason to believe that both defendants would kill again, and asked Epperson and Hodge with their attorneys to approach the bench. Neither defendant wished to make a statement. The judge pronounced the sentence of death.

"I believe we're finished," Judge Hogg said.

Frank Fleming had been standing directly behind the defense table. Now, as the convicted men were being handcuffed, Fleming walked up to Epperson and whispered into his ear:

"Roger, you still say Donnie stabbed Tammy?"

"Yeah," Epperson said. "Ask Benny. Benny, tell him who did it."

"Donnie did the stabbing," Benny said. No one but Fleming heard him.

Sherry, sitting in a back row and crying as she watched Benny being led away, did not rush up with the cyanide. In the hours between the verdict and the sentencing, she and Benny had scrapped their plan for suicide. There was the chance of a successful appeal, wasn't there? If that failed, they could kill themselves.

On condition of anonymity, jurors spoke to the press. There had been no disagreement among them about any significant aspect of the case. "We all felt that Hodge did the killing," one said. His strength had been the persuasive factor. They had believed Bartley as well as Lawrence Anthony Smith, because Smith had mentioned things he could only have learned from Hodge, the jury was convinced. "And according to the way they wrote our instructions up, Epperson is as guilty as Hodge."

Outside the courthouse, Lester spoke to Tawny and Dr. Acker. They agreed that this had been a sad business for everyone. Dr. Acker said that he had no hard feelings against Lester, who had only been doing his job.

Sherry, standing around outside with no one to talk to, then wandering back inside the courthouse, upstairs to the deserted courtroom, did not know what to do with herself. She approached the jailer, who told her that she could not see Benny now. Police were preparing to take the prisoners to the state penitentiary at Eddyville. They would be leaving in an hour or so, out the side exit. She might be able to see Benny then.

She wandered back toward the courtroom, past Judge Hogg's chambers, and found herself outside the Commonwealth Attorney's office. Through the glass in the door she could see a light. She stepped into the small, empty waiting room and sat down on a tattered couch. She began singing a song. It was Billy Joe Royal's "I'll Pin a Note on Your Pillow," about how a lover will let it be known that he is gone. She sang the first few lines and kept on mumbling and humming the rest. The door to the inner office opened and James Wiley Craft came out. His shirtsleeves were rolled up; he was holding some papers.

"Hello, Sherry," he said. "I know that song."

"Oh, yeah?" she said.

"It's about being lonely, isn't it?"

"I reckon."

He stood looking at her. He wondered if what he felt for her was wrong. He had seen her around the courthouse, always alone, so devoted to this man. There was something about her. She was that song. It seemed a waste. She was still humming.

"Sherry," Craft heard himself saying, "you ought to get on with your life." He cleared his throat. She looked up at him through her glasses. He had the impulse to say more, but did not.

She got up and left.

Outside again, around to the side of the courthouse, she sat down on the curb and smoked cigarettes as the darkness became complete. It was after ten by the time a Department of Corrections van pulled up.

Soon there he was, her man, handcuffed and shackled to Roger, being led down the steps toward the van. No one tried to stop her as she rushed up to him and threw her arms around his neck and covered his face with kisses and tears.

"Benny, I love you. Benny."

They loaded them into the van. It drove slowly off. Sherry balanced on the curb, waving.

Suddenly she remembered that her car was parked around the corner, and she ran. She jumped in, found her keys, and gunned it, tearing off in the direction she knew they were going. She caught up to the van at the intersection where Highway 15 goes toward Hazard.

They seemed to be the only ones on the road. Did they know she was following? She was crying so, the taillights ahead were a red blur. Benny was in that van. If this was the closest she could get to him, she would follow all the way. She would see him taken out and into the prison. It would make it better for him if she did that.

Half an hour passed on the good, two-lane road. Through part of Hazard, closed stores, a light or two in houses. She followed them down the on-ramp and onto the Daniel Boone Parkway heading west. It was so easy not to miss the turn when you were following someone. She checked her gas gauge: half-full. She would have to stop for gas somewhere, but so would they. Eddyville was way to the west, almost to Missouri. If she had to stop first, she could always catch up to them. Him. She kept on, beginning to sing, crying.

Somewhere before Manchester the van slowed and veered onto the shoulder and stopped. She pulled up twenty or thirty yards behind and switched off her lights. The driver stepped out. He flicked on a flashlight and shone it in her direction.

She remembered that she had left her clothes and her music tapes back at her motel. She gave up and turned around.

*   *   *

Back with her parents in Harriman, Sherry talked to Ben Gish over the telephone and told him that Benny and Roger had been "railroaded."

"I don't agree with anybody being killed, but at least let's try to be fair about it," Sherry said. "I hope that everybody that had a helping hand in taking these two men's lives has nightmares every night." She continued through tears: "Taking two more lives is not going to bring back the one that was took."

She thought that the jury's spending so little time deliberating meant that they had already made up their minds and had not listened to the evidence. The way things had turned out, she could only hope that Judge Hogg would sentence Donnie Bartley to die, too. "It would tickle me to death. If it's good enough for two, it's good enough for all three of them. Bartley put those two boys in the electric chair. He took Benny's life and Roger's. Every statement he made contradicted every other witness. If that ain't railroading, I don't know what is. He killed that girl and lied to save himself."

There were rumors, Gish told her, that Bartley had linked all three of them to other robberies and murders.

"Well, if that's true," Sherry said, "then why did this one bother him so bad if he wasn't the one who did it? I wonder if he can sleep good now, knowing he's killed two more people. If the other one bothered him so bad, then why in the hell didn't he give the doctor back his money? I'm dying, too. When you take someone away from the person they love, that is death. If I could take Benny's place in the chair, I'd do it. I love the man that much, and he loves me the same way. I won't quit fighting till I got no fight left."

She had no idea what had happened to all the missing money: "All I know is, I don't have it. And unlike Bartley, I don't lie. Even if I had it, that money's nothing compared to Benny's life. I'd give it to them in a New York minute. I don't have nothing against the doctor and that other daughter of his. If I was them, I'd probably have feelings, too."

Grateful for her candor—neither she nor Benny had spoken to any other reporter—Gish sent her a year's subscription to the *Mountain Eagle*. He wasn't sure quite why, maybe it was her steadfast devotion to Benny, maybe it was the way she stood alone, but he believed her. He hadn't found anyone else who did. Aside from the defense attorneys, everyone else who had been at the trial seemed certain that Benny Hodge was the killer.

Sherry began a weekly commute to Eddyville, a distance of nearly eight hundred miles round-trip. Saturday was visiting day; the Eddyville regulations for death row inmates were more lenient than most. As did Roger and Carol, Sherry and Benny met in a picnic area, closely watched, allowed one kiss. At the end of July, the wives rented apartments in the same building in Eddyville, figuring they would save motel money by doing so; Sherry paid her advance rent with four one-hundred-dollar bills. Carol, who wrecked two cars in two weeks, spent more time up there than Sherry did.

In Harriman, Sherry had to fend off questions from her parents.

"When are you going to give up on Benny?" E. L. asked her over dinner one night. "You're wasting your life. He'll never get out."

"I know he won't," Sherry said. "I love him. Do you dump someone you love just because he's in jail and is going to die? Would you run off from someone who's sick? What kind of a woman does that? Benny made some mistakes. I have, too."

"What if he got out? What if Benny escaped? Would you go with that Biggin?"

"Of course I would," Sherry said, knowing how much this pained E. L. "I'd follow Benny to the ends of the earth."

"Then you haven't learned nothing," E. L. sighed.

Sherry was sure that her days of being able to visit Benny every week were numbered. That was the reason, apart from devotion, that she went to see him as often as she could; and that was why she was spending more time with Renee than she had in more than a year. Unless Benny could escape and they could disappear together—it seemed impossible—she knew that it was only a matter of time before she was arrested.

She tried to prepare E. L. and Louise for this event; she could not bring herself to tell Renee. The day would come, she told her parents, when the Feds would take her away, she did not know for how long. "I've done some things," she said, "don't ask me no questions, and I'll have to pay for them." She wanted her parents to know that she did still understand the difference between right and wrong and that she was prepared to take responsibility for her actions. She hoped her parents could still love her. She was grateful that they had let her move back in with them. She was abiding by their condition, that she not bring any of her trashy friends around.

Meanwhile, waiting for the inevitable, she piled up the miles between Harriman and Eddyville, rushing back after seeing Benny to receive the collect call he always made to her on Sundays. He also managed to call during the week—Sherry's portion of the family phone bill for July was nearly five hundred dollars—but Sundays were special. She went to church with her mom and dad and, after the big Sunday dinner, waited for the phone to ring.

The phone calls and the visits—and the faint hope that Benny might escape—were all she felt she had to live for. Now that the reality of his sentence had sunk in, she could think of nothing else, and it seemed about to overwhelm her. She had no appetite. Every song, every place she drove around Harriman reminded her of him. She developed a monstrous headache that never seemed to go away; she went to bed with it and woke up in the middle of the night with her head pounding. It was then that the remorse got to her.

Everyone said that the cruelest thing you could do to your child was to kill yourself. She wondered. What kind of a mother was she? What chance did she have to redeem herself? Her going to prison would only make things worse for Renee, the biggest disgrace of all. Often Sherry got up in the silence of the early hours and stared at herself in the bathroom mirror and hated what she saw. She held a razor blade to her wrist on the scar Benny had made. Maybe Renee would be better off without her, but not Benny. Her love was all he had left. Better to wait until he was dead, then do it.

The headaches became unbearable; she went to the family doctor about them. When he asked her what she thought might be causing them, she told him about Benny and admitted that she was so depressed that she was thinking of killing herself. His response was swift. He told her that she had two choices: either to get psychiatric help immediately, or expect to deal with the police. It was his professional responsibility, the doctor said, to insist that any patient who was seriously considering suicide get help at once. He would give her twenty-four hours to seek counseling, or he would inform the police.

You bastard, Sherry thought. Now I can't even go to the doctor without having the cops on my ass. She considered the doctor a blackmailer. Reluctantly she made an appointment at the Ridgeview clinic once again.

She was more open in talking about Benny this time, but she said nothing about the stolen money or about facing prison herself. Follow-up sessions were advised, transactional analysis recommended, an emergency number provided, and she was given a prescription to relieve headache and muscle tension.

"35 year-old white female," the diagnostician, a woman in this instance, wrote on the profile sheet, "average intelligence—pleasant presentation—depressed, tearful over an identifiable stressor. Dealing with issues of loss of husband who is in prison and may be electrocuted—underlying anger at him. Some suicidal ideation but 'won't do it because of daughter & her sister.' Pessimistic outlook but beginning to make plans for the future—job hunting etc. Some guilt whenever she is enjoying herself and thinks of him in prison." The category on this visit was "Adjustment Reaction & depressed (*DSM* 309.00)."

When Sherry found out that the pills she had been prescribed were heavily laced with codeine, she threw them away. That is really sick, she thought, trying to turn me into an addict. I've come this far on my own; I better rely on myself. She did not return for further therapy.

For a year now, ever since Benny's Florida arrest, Sherry had been taping his calls. She kept the microcassettes in a box on a shelf with her dolls; each night she tried to coax herself into sleepiness by listening to one or another of their conversations. Assuming that the FBI had her line tapped wherever she was, she devised a code so that she could refer to certain matters without being detected. The code for money was anything to do with Renee's toys or clothes. When she saw Benny in person and they could speak without being overheard, she referred to "our" money. As if ownership had been transferred, the spoils were never the Acker money. They had earned it, hadn't they, at an expensive price?

She taped his calls so that she could hear his voice at any time she chose and feel closer to him and remember what it was like to make love with him. Whenever she managed to be alone talking to him on the phone, she said things to excite him, sometimes using words she avoided in regular conversation; he would talk about the things they had done together and wanted to do; she told him what she craved and how excited she was becoming hearing him, touching herself with only him on her mind.

Sherry believed that no two people in the world had ever been more open with one another about sex or had ever talked about it in such an uninhibited way. She knew from her first marriage and from girlfriends how different she and Benny were from other couples; she knew it from her days of cutting hair, when the women bitched constantly about their slam-bam-thank-you-ma'am husbands and boyfriends. She wished she and Benny could tell the world a thing or two; they might loosen folks up and bring happiness. Some might call it dirty; some might say some of the things they talked about were strange or weird or even perverse. They were puritans and hypocrites. You did what you had to do. Maybe the FBI were getting their rocks off listening. So what? Nobody understood.

How many people had done what she and Benny had together, tearing down a road after an armed robbery and making love in a jailhouse and being on the run and loving each other more the deeper in they got? She loved him now so completely, she wished she could chain herself to him with unbreakable chains so they would have to strap them into the chair together with her legs around him and the two of them screaming as some fool pulled the switch.

All she had to do was hear Benny's voice to get so worked up that she couldn't breathe. In her room, her parents asleep, she saw his face, his perfect body. She would reach over in the dark and pick out a tape at random and put on her earphones and start. It brought him to life. She'd have to force herself not to do anything but listen for a few tantalizing minutes, hearing his voice and her own teasing him, taunting him, with Benny becoming wilder and angrier, neither one of them holding back at all, until she couldn't take it any more, sweating in her bed full of him or almost. Exhausted at last, she'd cry herself to sleep with her face buried in Big Ben the pink buffalo.

29

ONCE THE CONVICTIONS CAME DOWN in the Acker trial, Rod Kincaid devoted all of his time to trailing that money. There was something mysterious about the Acker hoard, not merely that so much of it had vanished. Mike Caudill said that if anyone ever wrote a book about this case it should be called *Kentucky Moonstone;* he was referring to a novel written more than a hundred years ago by Wilkie Collins, *The Moonstone,* which was the name for a diamond that brought misfortune to everyone who came into possession of it. Maybe the Acker money was cursed.

According to Tawny Acker, everyone in her family had known that her father kept money in the house, a million or more, she had never been sure how much. Some of it was so old that it had dark marks on it from rubber bands; some was new. She, her father, and her late sister, Tawny said, had often touched it; their fingerprints should be on the bills and wrappers. Tawny did not say that her sister had died because of that money.

At least two of the men who had stolen it would now die young; the third would spend his life in prison. Rod Kincaid was confident that at least two of the three wives of these men would end up in jail, along with at least a couple of the lawyers. That made ten people whose lives had been ended or wrecked by that money; Kincaid was sure there would be more.

There already were, in a less drastic but still painful way. One day that summer, Danny Webb was talking to a Whitesburg neighbor of his, an elderly lady he had known all his life, who said to him, "Danny, ain't you going to get yourself one of them cars?" What cars? Webb asked. Why, the cars from the Acker case, the woman said. Hadn't he heard? All the police who had worked on the case were ending up with the automobiles that had been in evidence. She figured Danny would get the Corvette.

Had the lady finally gone around the bend? Webb told her about the recent negotiations that had finally returned some of Dr. Acker's property, including the cars, to him. It was one of many asinine quirks of the law that the cars and other items that had been in evidence could not automatically be turned over to the doctor after the trial. A separate, civil action was required to determine which of the seized property had been purchased with the money stolen from his house, which objects themselves had been taken from the house, and which had belonged to the defendants prior to and separate from the robbery. Had Epperson and Hodge simply agreed to give up claim to everything, this would have been a simple matter; but they had not. At a meeting between the parties, which had required transporting the prisoners from Eddyville to the Hazard KSP post, Epperson had, amazingly, insisted that the Corvette had been bought with money other than Dr. Acker's, and both convicted killers had quibbled about other items. Dr. Acker had no use for such things as a golden coke spoon, but he was not about to permit insult to be added to tragedy and stood his ground, backed up by James Wiley Craft, who was acting for him now as his personal attorney, not as Commonwealth's Attorney, as was permitted by Kentucky law and custom.

Many stolen items had vanished, among them Tammy's bracelet, black pearls, and Rolex—this last, according to what Bartley's mother had told police, tossed into a river. Dr. Acker was able to prove by serial numbers that some of the guns were his. The cars were the principal items of dispute. The argument grew rancorous. Craft shouted to Epperson that no jury in the world, if it came to that, would side with him; Frank Fleming lost his cool and called Roger and Benny sons of bitches. The meeting resolved nothing, but a week later, on the advice of their attorneys, Epperson and Hodge gave in.

So what was this about the *police* getting the cars? It didn't take Danny Webb long to find out that Dr. Acker, rather than selling them, had decided to do something nice for the policemen who had fought to get the cars back and had been so attentive and helpful in bringing his daughter's killers to justice. He had offered one to Frank Fleming and another to Lon Maggard at what the doctor considered wholesale but was far below their worth: Fleming took the 300 ZX for forty-seven hundred, Maggard the MR2 for forty-five hundred. Neither officer had even that much cash to his name, so they had agreed to pay Dr. Acker at the rate of a hundred a month, with no interest.

Danny Webb was incensed. Department regulations were specific: no officer was permitted to accept outside payment or gifts in connection with the performance of official duties. Fleming and Maggard were tooling around in these sports cars to the amusement and malicious gossip of everyone in Letcher County. Some zealous lawyer handling Epperson's and Hodge's appeals could jump on this as evidence of collusion between the police and the victim. Innocent as Dr. Acker's gesture was, a public defender could construe it as a payoff. As Webb knew all too well, and as Fleming and Maggard ought to have remembered, the Department of Public Advocacy was staffed by true believers, zealots so personally and ideologically opposed to the death penalty that they would go to extraordinary lengths to try to get a death sentence overturned. One of them was already after James Wiley Craft for representing Dr. Acker in the civil case.

Danny Webb could not remember a worse moment in his life as a policeman. He was these detectives' superior officer, responsible for everything that they did. His good name and the KSP's were on the line. He instituted proceedings to have Fleming and Maggard fired.

When the detectives learned that their heads were on the block, they immediately sold the cars, after having had them for only four days, and gave the cash received for them to Dr. Acker—a total of some twenty-three thousand dollars, as it turned out. When Fleming and Maggard found out that a KSP major had bought the '85 Corvette and was not selling it, they were resentful. Was there a different standard for higher-ups?

No, Danny Webb explained to them, the major had paid a price for the Corvette that was equal to its actual value, about nineteen thousand. Still exasperated, Webb relented. He had known Maggard and Fleming forever and had considered them friends. He decided to forgive them for being just country boys who had been carried away by all the wealth and automobiles involved in the trial and had suffered a lapse in judgment, though a costly one. They had been foolish, not corrupt, and both were remorseful. He withdrew his request to have them fired. But his relations with them were never again quite as they had been; both knew that their chances for promotion were at an end. Within a year Fleming and Maggard retired from the KSP—worn out, they said, by too many homicide investigations—and went to work as detectives for the CSX railroad. He was getting paid more, but Frank Fleming especially missed being a trooper; it had been everything he had ever wanted to be. He dropped by the Hazard post often and was glad when his new job sometimes let him work again with Danny Webb.

When Rod Kincaid heard about the incident, he filed it in his mind as further proof of the Acker money curse, not that he had much sympathy for the detectives; an FBI agent would have been fired on the spot. It was another instance of the difficulties he faced trying to cooperate with local officials, too few of whom were like Danny Webb. What was he to make, for instance, of the use Lester Burns had made of Pulaski County sheriff's deputies? Of the sheriff himself? There was nothing illegal about hiring off-duty policemen as guards. Why bribe them when all you had to do was hire them? The more Kincaid investigated Lester Burns, the more astounded he was by the network Lester had established over the years. He was everywhere! Everyone seemed to owe him favors of one kind or another. So many of these obligations stemmed from legitimate work Lester had done for people for free or from other favors Lester had bestowed, large and small. The numbers of people to whom he had given hams or farm machinery or what have you were countless. Lester was always picking up the check, sometimes for an entire restaurant. Lester Burns, Kincaid began saying, has corrupted half of Eastern Kentucky for the price of a steak dinner!

Lester's enormous material success made all the more mysterious why he had risked everything to accept what for him was peanuts in stolen money. He had been completely reckless, leaving footprints all over the place. Having learned from Sheriff Adams and others that Lester had made a big cash deposit immediately after returning from Florida last August, Kincaid had now obtained copies of deposit slips, currency serial numbers, and IRS cash transaction forms showing the amount as ninety-two thousand. It was obvious what he had been doing, trying to pretend he thought the money was legitimate. From Bartley, and from Donnie's mother and sister, Kincaid could assume that Lester's fee had been much larger than that. On the Comer–McNeal tapes, Lester himself bragged about four hundred thousand.

How much had gone to the other lawyers? Other than a cancelled cashier's check for five thousand, Bartley and his family had no proof of the two hundred thousand-plus they claimed had gone to O. Curtis Davis before he was fired. As for Dale Mitchell, a deputy had stated that Mitchell had been present when a car with a woman in it, undoubtedly Sherry Hodge, had arrived from Tennessee one night at Lester's farm. By the Bartleys' account, including that of the new Mrs. Bartley, Sherry was the banker. Physical evidence that she had controlled the money, however, consisted of only one item, the receipt from an express-delivery package Sherry had sent the Bartleys from Florida and that they claimed had contained several thousand in cash. There was also one small piece of evidence that she retained some cash: paperwork involving a two-thousand-dollar cashier's check that Sherry had tried to draw in favor of Dale Mitchell at an Oliver Springs, Tennessee, bank back in March. She had presented the teller with the cash and requested the check. Suspicious of the bills, which appeared uncirculated and possibly counterfeit, the teller had asked Sherry to wait, had informed a bank officer, and had stalled Sherry while security at the bank's Knoxville headquarters could be notified. Knoxville instructed the branch manager to refuse the money on the grounds that the customer did not have an account and to have someone take down the suspect's license tag number. The bank passed Sherry's tag number on to the FBI. Agents questioned Sherry at her parents' house a few days later. She explained that she had borrowed the money from a friend who was helping her pay Benny's lawyer.

By comparison, Lester Burns had made tracing a large part of his share of the money far easier, chiefly because he had already been under investigation. Initially through Dr. Billy Davis, who had decided to plead guilty in the Comer–McNeal–Burns insurance scam, Kincaid discovered the roles of Lillian Davis and Houston Griffin, who cooperated in interviews: they were not in jeopardy, since Lester had not told them that they were facilitating a crime. The boys at Max Flynn Motors, the folks at the 7 Gables Motel—Lester had managed to incriminate himself in numerous ways. And there was plenty of evidence against Carol Epperson. By August, Kincaid decided that it was time to ask a Lexington grand jury to act against Sherry, Carol, and Lester. Kincaid was betting that what was not already known about the whereabouts of the money would then come out. He remained pessimistic only about getting evidence against Pat Mason; so far, there was nothing on her. Was it possible that she had actually won her million-plus by chance? At this point he could not say yes, but legally there was not one reason to say no.

Lester had been expecting it. He had prepared his family. But when he actually read this latest indictment against him, he was mortified. On August 20, the grand jury proclaimed that Lester H. Burns, Jr., Carol Ann Epperson, and Sherry Loraine Hodge "knowingly did conspire together and with each other, and with Roger Dale Epperson, Benny Lee Hodge, Donald Terry Bartley, and with diverse other persons to the Grand Jury known and unknown, to commit offenses against the United States, that is, they did conspire to transport ... to receive, conceal, store, barter and dispose of stolen money.... It was a part of the conspiracy that Epperson, Hodge, and Bartley would and did commit an armed robbery/murder at the residence of one Dr. Roscoe Acker, Whitesburg, Kentucky, and did steal approximately $1.9 million from Dr. Roscoe Acker.... It was a further part of said conspiracy that Lester H. Burns, Jr., Carol Ann Epperson, and Sherry Loraine Hodge would and did agree to conceal, hide, wash, clean-up and launder said stolen money so that it would not be detected by law enforcement officials."

What horrified Lester was that, the way the indictment read, it not only implied but appeared to state that he had been in on the robbery and murder to begin with. He wondered how many people would read it that way; he vigorously protested, to no avail. In those dark moments, feeling as if the prison gates had already clanked shut behind him forever, his only solace was his family. To his deep gratitude, one of his sons-in-law accompanied him to Rod Kincaid's office in London, where he was photographed and fingerprinted. Watching Lester go through the demeaning routine, Kincaid took no pleasure in it.

Lester was already scheduled to go on trial in October on the various counts against him from Project Leviticus, to all of which he was pleading not guilty. That procedure would have to be postponed. On August 28, he appeared in U.S. District Court in Lexington for his arraignment. On the surface he had regained some of his bravado, although his demeanor before the magistrate was meek, and he kept repeating "thank you very kindly." Dressed in full Western regalia, he entered a plea of not guilty and posted a fifty-thousand-dollar bond.

Outside the courtroom Lester faced a squad of reporters shouting questions and shoving microphones at him. Swaggering a little, shoulders pulled back, cocking his head, every inch the cattle baron, he said that he had no doubts that he would be vindicated. To this day he did not know whether his fee had come from stolen money or not.

"You are asking the wrong person," Lester advised, referring to Sherry Hodge and Carol Epperson, both of whom were being held in the Fayette County Correction Center. Carol had been unable to make bond; Sherry had been denied bond, on evidence that she had the means to leave the country. Lester suggested that Carol, if she did not get out of detention within a few days, would probably make a statement. As for him, he was confident.

"Lester Burns," he declared, his voice rising, his hand sweeping the horizon, "will ride the ship of truth! The ship of justice will speed me to the shores of freedom!"

Carol, accompanied by her father, had surrendered to the FBI at the Clinton Police Department on the day the indictment was issued. That night Sherry learned that she, too, had been charged, when Dale Mitchell telephoned her to say that he would not be representing amyone in this matter, because of conflict of interest.

The next morning, Sherry was on the phone with Benny when Louise, who was alone in the house with her, said that three men dressed in suits were walking up to the front door.

"Let them in," Sherry said. "It's the Feds. I told you they'd be coming sooner or later." She asked Benny to hold on and peered out the window. It was Burl Cloninger, Scott Nowinski, and an agent she did not recognize. Cloninger she liked better than any other law officer she had ever met. He was straight but fair, had never lied to her, and, for an FBI guy, was almost kindly. Nowinski she despised. During a previous encounter with him, Nowinski, in front of Louise, had referred to Benny as a son of a bitch. Sherry had blown up, screaming, "He ain't done nothing to you, you dumb Polack! You don't call the man I love a son of a bitch to my face!"

Louise ran into the kitchen. Sherry opened the door.

"Sherry," Burl Cloninger said, "we've come to arrest you."

"You got a warrant?"

"No, but we can get one."

"Wait here a minute. I'm on the phone."

The agents stood in the doorway as Sherry, in the kitchen, picked up the receiver again. She told Benny what was up and asked him if she should cooperate.

"Get off the phone!" Cloninger called to her.

"I'll get off when I'm done talking!"

"Get off now!"

Benny advised her to do what the agents said. She said that she'd be in touch with him when she could.

Sherry told the agents to come in. Cloninger advised her that she was charged with conspiracy to transport money across state lines.

"What money?" Sherry said.

"Sherry, the best thing you can do is just come along and stop being a smart aleck."

"I ain't no smart aleck. I ain't got no money, I ain't had no money, and I ain't done nothing."

Cloninger read her her rights and asked her to sign an "Interrogation, Advice of Rights" form, but she refused, saying she would not be making any statements right then.

"Do you live in all this house?" Cloninger asked.

"How big do you think I am?"

"Which room do you sleep in?"

"My bedroom. What do you all think?"

"Well, where is your bedroom?"

"Yonder." She pointed upstairs. Cloninger asked if she would agree to sign a "Consent to Search" form for her bedroom and her car. She agreed, on condition that the agents disturb nothing else in the house. "It's bad enough, you all coming here like this upsetting my mom. You all ought to be ashamed of yourself."

Cloninger sat with her and Louise in the kitchen while the other agents searched her room and confiscated several items as evidence. These included letters from Benny; seven cashier's checks from five separate banks payable to Dale Mitchell, totaling thirty-five thousand dollars; pages of figures that looked like code; a gold pendant in the shape of a lion's head; and ninety-eight microcassette tapes.

Downstairs, Louise was crying.

"Don't worry, Mom," Sherry said. "I knew for a year this was going to happen. I told you I was going to jail."

"So you knew you were going to jail, did you?" Cloninger asked.

"I figured you all was going to come after me."

"Well, what have you done?"

"I ain't done nothing. I just knew how you people works."

After more than an hour, the agents came down and presented Sherry with an inventory of the items they were taking away. Sherry examined the list.

"Looks like you boys come up with a whole lot of nothing," she said. "How come you didn't take my dolls? Some might talk."

"Sherry," Cloninger said, rising to his feet, "we're going to have to take you in."

"You ain't taking me nowhere till I wash my hair and put on some clothes."

Cloninger smiled. He reached for her arm. She shrank back. They stood there staring at each other, hunter and hunted.

"No, Sherry," Cloninger said.

"You say no, I say yes. I do not wear shorts in public and I am not going out with dirty hair. Tell those boys of yourn to fetch me a pair of fresh jeans and a T-shirt. And tell them to turn their heads, or I'll undress in front of them. I ain't going to no jail in no shorts."

The anonymous agent, who looked like a rookie, brought her clothes, and he and Nowinski went to search her car. Cloninger sat down again and chatted with Louise as Sherry washed her hair in the kitchen sink and descended partway down the back steps for privacy to get dressed.

Louise was sitting with her head in her arms at the kitchen table. Sherry went to her, put hands on her shoulders, and kissed the top of her head.

"Aren't you ashamed of yourself?" Cloninger asked. "Look at what you've done to your mom and dad."

Sherry burst into tears, grabbing a dishcloth to cover her face. "Please leave my mom and dad out of this," she sobbed. "They ain't done nothing.... They ain't responsible for nothing I've done or been accused of doing ..."

"You should've thought of that," Cloninger said.

"You should've ought've learnt you some manners. Leave me alone. I got to go to the bathroom."

Cloninger asked Louise to go into the bathroom with her. He must think I'm going to kill myself, Sherry thought. I wouldn't give him the satisfaction.

When she came out, Cloninger produced handcuffs. Sherry begged him not to cuff her in front of her mom. He did not. She hugged Louise and asked her to call her brothers and not to tell E. L. while he was at work. Better to break the news to him that evening.

Cloninger ushered Sherry out the door and down the steps. "Don't put her in the back seat with that Polack," Louise called. "She'll beat on him."

The house sat on the side of a wooded hill overlooking the Clinch River, which meandered into a wide arc at that point on its way to meet the Tennessee. There was no bridge. A little ferryboat that crossed every twenty minutes to the opposite shore was the quickest way to the highway to Knoxville. Handcuffed now, Sherry waited in the car as the ferry, a chugging, rusty old thing that held only five cars, approached. She tried to make light again of the belongings seized from her bedroom and car and said she hoped she would get one item back. The lion's head had been a present for one of Benny's birthdays. She had spent seven hundred dollars for it and would hate to lose it.

"Nice day," the ferryman said as he collected the toll.

Theirs was the only car on the ferry's eastward crossing. Sherry sat in the back beside the rookie. Cloninger opened all the windows to let in a breeze. As the ferry gurgled slowly away, Nowinski turned around and looked down at Sherry's hands:

"You think you can swim with those cuffs on?"

"No," Sherry said. "I can't even swim with them off."

"Hey," Cloninger said, "I can't swim either."

Sherry stared out at the dark, swirling water, at the tangled bank ahead.

30

THE FBI LEFT HER AT THE KNOX COUNTY JAIL. At four that afternoon she was arraigned; the judge told her that he was refusing bail because she had access to over a million dollars and had rented a boat in Florida, something that was news to her, although she assumed Roger Epperson had done so a year ago. Asked whether she could prove indigence, Sherry took the Fifth to that, as to all questions. That night, still in Knoxville, she found herself in a cell opposite Carol's.

All of her animosities against Carol surfaced. She accused her of ratting on her, being an ingrate—hadn't she given Carol eight hundred dollars only the day before?—and a no-good snitch from day one who deserved to go to the chair just as much as Roger did. In the middle of that night Sherry awoke to find a matron fixing a deadbolt lock to the cell door. The inmate across the way, the matron said, was afraid Sherry would escape and kill her.

But when the state marshals came to get them at five the next morning, guards chained Sherry and Carol together for the ride up to a truckstop at Corbin. Truckers gawked and whistled as Kentucky marshals transferred them to another van and drove them to the detention center at Lexington. They were permitted to keep their own underwear; otherwise they wore issued blue jumpsuits and shower shoes. On the way to her cell, Sherry noticed a hand-lettered sign on the wall outside the Head Matron's office:

EPPERSON AND HODGE
NOT TO BE TOGETHER.

Immediately after Carol's arrest, Roger Epperson began telephoning the FBI, who accepted his collect calls, first to Cloninger, who referred him to Rod Kincaid. Carol would talk, Roger said, if only a call could be arranged between him and her. He too was willing to turn state's evidence and to become a prosecution witness in the Jackson County double homicide for which he, Benny Hodge, and Donnie Bartley had now been indicted. He told Kincaid that Lester Burns had received more than two hundred thousand of the stolen money and that he was firing Burns, who was in enough trouble himself. Kincaid advised him during this and several other calls over the next few days that the FBI was not in a position to help him, but Roger kept supplying information, and Kincaid listened. Benny Hodge had told him that Dale Mitchell had signed a receipt for money Sherry gave him and that Sherry still had possession of it. Roger telephoned Kincaid at least eleven times between August 25 and the end of September. He mentioned each time that he feared for Carol's safety because of retribution from Sherry, especially once she figured out that he and Carol were cooperating with the FBI. Sherry had the money to pay another inmate to kill Carol, Roger insisted.

In fact, as Sherry had suspected after the judge refused her bail, Carol had started cooperating with the FBI the moment she was arrested. By the time Burl Cloninger arrested Sherry, he had already interviewed Carol for more than two hours, during which Carol among many other assertions blamed Donnie Bartley for the Moon Mullins murder and said that she had been receiving regular payments of cash from Sherry ever since the Florida arrests. Subsequently Rod Kincaid conducted several lengthy interviews with her at the detention center in Lexington, where she lost no opportunity to suggest that Sherry controlled whatever was left of the money—an amount Kincaid, deducting all known and estimated expenditures, estimated must be somewhere between four and five hundred thousand dollars, maybe more. Since the amount originally stolen could never be determined for sure, what was left would always be guesswork; but it had to be plenty.

On September 19, Carol was moved from Lexington to the Laurel County jail, "for safekeeping," Big John Bowling said. The press reported that "another Lexington inmate" had been planning to kill her. Rod Kincaid continued to talk to her, extracting more and more information, especially about Lester Burns's fee. Finally, having agreed to testify against both Lester and Sherry at their trials, Carol changed her plea to guilty on the conspiracy charges, in return for which the original facilitation charge against her was dropped. She entered her plea on October 4 and in federal court told U.S. District Judge Eugene Siler that she had paid Lester Burns out of stolen money and that the attorney knew—was explicitly informed by Roger Epperson—that the money was stolen. It made all the papers.

Sentencing would come later for Carol. In the meanwhile, even though her court-appointed attorney was from Lexington, she asked to be permitted to stay on at the Laurel County jail, and the judge granted this request on the grounds of the prisoner's safety. It would be up to Big John Bowling to keep her apart from Donnie Bartley, who was still being held there, waiting to testify about the Gray Hawk murders.

At Lester's farm, a brilliant yellow sun beat down on all the colors of a Kentucky autumn. On a knoll above the farmhouse, under a huge old oak gaudy with saffron and crimson, Lester Burns stood on top of a picnic table delivering a harangue to Rod Kincaid, who looked up at him from a seat on one of the table's benches. This unlikely pair had come together to try to work something out. More specifically, Kincaid was there to persuade Lester that the legal situation for the Commonwealth's most famous attorney was hopeless. They had already been talking for three or four hours. At first, when Kincaid had arrived, impressed by the beauty and grandeur of the scene, the sprawling house of hand-chipped Tennessee redstone, the fat black cattle, the lake below, Lester had been surrounded by three pals of his wearing sidearms. Kincaid was not afraid of them, or of Lester, whom he knew was a showman, not a gangster. Soon Lester sent his goons—really just local boys, two farmers and a school superintendent whom Lester had rescued from one mess or another—away, saying that he needed to confer with "my friend from the FBI" alone. Alternately sitting and standing on the table top, while Kincaid, who spent half his life listening, kept to his inferior position on the bench, Lester seized the advantage in height and would not surrender it. But Kincaid had all the marbles.

Kincaid's difficulty was in getting a word in edgewise. He would bring up this or that piece of damning evidence—something from the one hundred and seven Comer–McNeal tapes, for instance—and Lester, after a disquisition on state and federal statutes relating to entrapment, would launch into some anecdote from his triumphant past. As the shadows lengthened and a chill wind began to blow in from the lake, Lester told Kincaid about a famous victory, the time he had defended a woman who had shot her husband to death.

"I thought she had a pretty good chance of getting off on self-defense," Lester said, lowering his voice to convey his personal disgust at the brutality of the husband. "He beat her black and blue. The trouble was, he was the second husband. She'd killed the first one, too. Knifed him to death. But I made sure when I made my closing argument that she brought her baby into court. At just the right moment, I snatched that infant from her arms and held it up in front of the jury. 'Take a good look at this child!' I was shouting, right into the baby's ear. 'If you send this woman to prison, you'll be condemning this baby to life without a mother!' I was hoping that baby would start bawling, but it didn't make a peep. I thought it was going to sleep. So I just slipped my hand under its diaper, like this, and gave it a pinch on its bottom. It let out a wail and a shriek like you never heard, and I shouted over it, 'Are you going to rip this child from its mama's arms?'

"I knew I'd won when the jury brought out their handkerchiefs. The woman walked, God bless her, and she hasn't killed another husband since!"

By twilight Kincaid had managed to convey to Lester most of what the government wanted him to know, offering no deals but implying without promising that, in return for an admission of some guilt, Lester might possibly avoid spending the rest of his life behind bars. Unstated was the assumption that he would be willing to testify against Dale Mitchell and Sherry Hodge. Kincaid declined Lester's invitation to dinner but agreed to meet him for breakfast at Jerry's Restaurant.

There were many meetings between the two. At one in Kincaid's London office, he was taking a phone call when he saw Lester's hand reach slowly toward a document that was lying on the desk. Kincaid grabbed it. Lester grinned as if to say, "I was just testing you." The man would not give up. He began telephoning Kincaid at home, even dropping by the agent's house—just to chat, he said, feeling lonely and, well, rather worried about his future. Kincaid enjoyed hearing Lester talk so much that he didn't really mind, but he had to cut him off at last. After all, this was the FBI, and Lester would have to make a decision, finally, on his own.

On November 10 Lester went before Judge Siler and entered guilty pleas on two of the nineteen counts against him. He admitted conspiring with Dr. Billy Davis to defraud two insurance companies by faking an automobile accident; and he pleaded guilty to knowingly receiving stolen money and transporting it to Kentucky. On the second count he asked that the record show that in no way was he pleading guilty to having known beforehand of the plans for the Acker murder and robbery. The judge accepted this, and agreed to the U.S. attorney's motion that all other charges against the defendant, including that he had conspired with a since-convicted judge to stage a car theft, be dropped. He was guilty of nothing other than what he had admitted, Lester said.

He described having taken too much whiskey and too many painkillers during the previous year, because of his hip, but denied that these had influenced his judgment. He had simply been an idiot. Had he been suffering from some mental problem?

"Your Honor, to be frank, I know where my life is. It's in your hands. Now, I believe I do have a mental problem—a total lack of sense. I'm disgusted with myself."

Lester's family and many of his friends were in the courtroom, along with Kincaid, James Wiley Craft, and Tawny Acker. Everyone found it a melancholy occasion. Danny Webb, reading about it in the papers and noting that for the first time anyone could remember, Lester refused to talk to the press, said it must have been more like a funeral than a conviction. It was hard to accept that Lester Burns was finished. It was like seeing a great tree fall.

Lester asked that his sentencing be postponed at least until April 15, so he could make arrangements for his mother and the rest of his family and make restitution to Dr. Acker. The judge agreed. Just before the New Year—in time to take the deduction on his 1986 taxes—Lester sent Dr. Acker a check for one hundred and seventy-five thousand dollars. James Wiley Craft, who was still Commonwealth's Attorney but continued acting as Dr. Acker's lawyer, received the check, deducted fifteen thousand for his fee in negotiating the settlement, and presented the balance to the doctor. BURNS RETURNS MONEY, said the *Mountain Eagle*.

Lester also made a separate deal with Craft, trading him the Rolls-Royce in exchange for Craft's Jaguar sedan plus twenty-five thousand dollars. "Glad to get that clunker off my hands," Lester said privately.

Four days before Lester entered his guilty pleas, concluding that she no longer had any choice, Sherry agreed to talk to Rod Kincaid. He interviewed her for nearly three hours at the Lexington detention center and was impressed by the precise detail of her accounts of everything that concerned the Acker case. She appeared to have every dollar received accounted for in her head, a veritable hillbilly Meyer Lansky. As for her attitude toward what had happened, Kincaid could not fathom it. She had isolated the murder of Tammy Acker as if it had been an unfortunate by-product of an otherwise straightforward robbery and only turned her head aside when Kincaid showed her photographs of Tammy's body, trying to test her for some reaction. She was insistent that Benny could not have done it.

Why had she allowed herself to be misled by Benny? Kincaid tried to probe her attachment and loyalty to this man.

"Ain't nobody misled me," she bridled. "People's always blaming everything on Benny. My folks does. They don't know me. Nobody knows me. I have always knowed what I was doing. Let me tell you something. I'm no Patty Puritan."

Kincaid could not get this last phrase out of his mind. It was, in all her bravado and self-knowledge and matter-of-fact criminality, her motto. It had its humorous connotations; it had the virtues of bluntness and honesty and self-irony; all the same, it was chilling.

It was because of her candor that Kincaid believed her when she said that only a few days after the Florida arrests, she had given more than half a million of the stolen money to a Detective Gene Foust of the Oak Ridge police force. She had flown back to Tennessee with the money in what she called her pilot's case, had distributed the Bartleys' share to them, and had put the remainder in a garbage bag and given that to her brother to store under his house. The sum was somewhat greater than her and Benny's share because, she admitted, she had "conned" some extra from Carol. After all, the banker deserved some sort of fee for her work, didn't she? She then contacted Gene Foust, who agreed to help her invest or launder the money. She met her brother at an abandoned airport, took the money to Foust at a Knoxville motel, and gave it to him. He planned to set up a phony company, Sherry claimed, called Triangle, with himself, her, and a friend of his as partners.

Subsequently, Sherry continued, Foust gave her back more than two hundred thousand of the money to pay Dale Mitchell and, along with the other Triangle partner, accompanied her to Lester Burns's farm to give Mitchell his fee. She had asked Foust and his friend to come along as protection because she did not trust Lester Burns or anyone else.

It was true that, incredible as it seemed, Mitchell had given her a receipt for the one hundred and fifty thousand. She had told him that she had torn it up, but if there was one thing she wasn't, it was stupid. She described the doll and indicated its location on the shelf of her bedroom. It had tickled her to death when the FBI had torn her room apart without thinking to check the dolls, although she doubted they would have found the receipt, the way it was hidden. It had been all she could do to keep from telling the agents how they had been fooled.

Since paying Mitchell, she had not been able to extract another dime from Foust, she said, and no longer trusted him. She believed that he had some of the money stashed in a safe under the carpet in his house. The safe was makeshift, dug into the foundation and covered with wire mesh and gravel. Foust kept the combination on the back of one of his credit cards. When the FBI got around to checking this out, they would know she was telling the truth about where the money went. How else would she know about the safe?

Sherry claimed to know nothing about the Gray Hawk killings. As far as she knew, the boys may have raided a poker game that night. Someone was trying to blame them for an unsolved crime if they were being blamed for that, too.

Kincaid recalled, without mentioning it, that Carol had accused Sherry of having been the one to urge that the boys leave no witnesses. To Gray Hawk? To Fleming-Neon? Or was Carol lying about that? What Sherry really had known and said was probably beyond knowing or proving in its totality.

She kept insisting that Donnie Bartley must have killed Tammy. He had come back to Florida with blood on his shoes. That could have been Dr. Acker's blood, Kincaid said, and Sherry scoffed.

Kincaid asked her to describe in detail the scene at the condo after the boys had returned. Were they all crazy? Had anyone indicated what had actually happened at the Acker house?

"I'll tell you how crazy," Sherry said. "I told Benny he should kill the rest of them."

"Roger and Donnie?"

"The women, too."

"Why did you suggest that?"

"So's me and Benny could run."

"Mass murder?"

"That kind of money can make you real strange," Sherry said. "I guess you wouldn't know about that."

In his car on the way home to Somerset, Kincaid tried to gain some perspective on what he had heard. This woman had been willingly involved with the lowest of the low. He had heard from colleagues in the Bureau and from others who had dealt with Sherry the opinion that she had actually been the brains behind the whole gang. Kincaid thought this only partially true. If she had been, they probably would not have been caught so quickly.

Her frankness was disarming. Her love for Benny Hodge was the most confounding thing about her. Women loving outlaws was a common enough theme, but this was something else besides, and somehow love did not seem the right word. Obsession? Compulsion? This was a woman with some grievance, some anger at something in her past that must have twisted or erased a part of her. But she was no ordinary psychopath. Her self-knowledge was too complete.

What he remembered from the tapes that had been confiscated from her bedroom told a lot about the kind of relationship she had with Benny. The tapes were so rank, so vile, that Kincaid had chosen not to listen to more than excerpts from them, leaving it to others to try to decipher anything incriminating that might be in them. Aside from their grossness, Kincaid interpreted them as examples of Sherry's and Benny's mania for mutual self-destruction and thought they sounded more like war than love. If love was life, this dark passion was death. "I'm no Patty Puritan"—she wasn't kidding. And she collected dolls!

Kincaid informed Burl Cloninger about the doll. It was exactly as Sherry had said, with the receipt tucked away and signed by Dale Mitchell. Cloninger then organized a raid on Gene Foust's house and found the safe. It had little in it other than some counterfeit watches and other costume jewelry. The agents did seize, however, twenty-four hundred in cash, a Bronco, a Cadillac Seville, a Corvette, and, later, a twenty-thousand-dollar motorboat at a Knoxville marina. Not bad for a detective. Foust was immediately suspended from the Oak Ridge force and, when he was indicted for receipt, concealment, and disposal of stolen money, he was terminated. For the time being he turned his attention to Rings And Things, a gift shop he and his wife opened.

On January 28, 1987, Sherry and Carol received nearly maximum prison terms. Facing a possible five years each, Carol got four, Sherry four and a half. It was the original crime itself, Sherry's lawyer, who had told her to expect the maximum, reasoned. Less than that meant that the judge had taken into account Sherry's cooperation with FBI investigators. But where the money had come from, that was what the judge must have been thinking—and about Tammy Acker.

During that week when Sherry and Carol were sentenced in Lexington, snow was falling up in the mountains, the first real blizzard of that winter. On Friday night, January 23, Dr. Acker, after another long day at his clinic, was asleep in his bedroom. About two A.M. he awoke suddenly to see a flashlight shining into his room from the hallway.

He grabbed the loaded pistol he now kept on his bedside table and shouted, "I've got a gun!"

"I've got a gun, too," a male voice replied from behind the light.

"Well, one of us is going to die, then," Dr. Acker said.

The intruder left. Dr. Acker called the sheriff, who found two sets of footprints in the snow. The men had smashed the glass on the patio door to get in. Frank Fleming, still with the KSP, told the *Eagle* that he was sure that the burglars were local people who had read or heard about the money Dr. Acker had received from Lester Burns. Everyone should know that Dr. Acker no longer kept money in the house. The money from Lester Burns was already in a trust fund.

Five months later Lester stood before Judge Siler for sentencing. Dr. Acker was not in court for the event, but a letter from him was read to the judge by an attorney (not James Wiley Craft) representing the doctor. Dated May 13, 1987, it urged leniency:

I, Roscoe J. Acker, M.D., through counsel have been informed that Lester H. Burns, Jr., has been very cooperative in attempting to recover property stolen from me. This cooperation has been in the form of [his] returning $175,000 paid to him as a fee by the defendant Roger Dale Epperson and making himself available to my attorneys in an effort to collect and recover the remaining sum stolen from me. In addition, Mr. Burns has agreed to continue his cooperation beyond his prior efforts and has stated that he will do everything possible to assist in the recovery of these additional sums. I believe Mr. Burns realizes he has done wrong, and it is my opinion that a man with many years of public service could perhaps serve society in a more meaningful manner through some form of public service work rather than detention in a federal correctional institution. It is my desire and wish that this statement be read into the record at the sentencing hearing ...

Dr. Acker's attorney added that, in his own opinion, Mr. Burns was extremely remorseful for his act: "I believe it's destroyed his life."

James Wiley Craft also spoke on Lester's behalf. He had known the defendant for many years, Craft said, believed him to have been a brilliant attorney, especially in the early years, but felt that recently his effectiveness had declined, possibly because of an alcohol problem. Mr. Burns had been in pain during the Acker trial, but had carried on at a very high level. Since then, he had helped recover stolen property and had assisted the U.S. government in identifying a police officer who had allegedly received stolen money.

Another attorney testified to Lester's abhorrence of drugs. The surgeon who operated on Lester's hip stated that the other hip was also in need of replacement. Lester's own attorneys, both of them women, spoke of how many people he had helped, of how impeccable his record had been until the lapses to which he had pleaded guilty, and of how he had already suffered humiliation and degradation. They argued for community service. And on his own behalf Lester, in a lengthy, somewhat rambling discourse, argued that he had been tricked by Comer and McNeal and even then, acceding to the insurance scheme out of compassion for Comer and believing in "that fine fellow" McNeal, he had refused their other enticements. He had been recorded by McNeal making many statements that were obviously nothing but empty, false boasts, and many exculpatory statements of his had either not been recorded or had been erased.

Judge Siler said that in many ways he thought Mr. Burns was a perfect candidate for community service, but deterrence had also to be considered. The maximum on the two charges was five years each. Lester would remain free so that he could testify in the upcoming Dale Mitchell trial. He would also have time to undergo a second hip operation before entering prison in August. "With a heavy heart," Judge Siler said, he was sentencing him to four years on each count, the terms to run consecutively.

Lester had not been optimistic; he had tangled with Eugene Siler years ago and had feared that ancient rancors might prove an influence. But *eight years?* He was stunned. He felt as if his entire life, all that he had achieved, had been wiped out—as if he had spent his days down a coal mine and had been condemned to die in one.

"They say the night comes before the dawn," was the best he could come up with for the reporters. "This must be night." He had already resigned his license to practice law; it no longer seemed practical, after receiving such a harsh sentence, to think about getting the license back someday. "I'll just have to pay my penalty. I'll make a good prisoner. I'll return to society and make a good citizen. Of course I'm disappointed, and my family is. But I'm a big old man."

31

T HERE WAS A LAST HURRAH FOR LESTER, although he called it "the worst day of my life." For an afternoon he turned the Dale Mitchell trial into his own farewell performance. The subject of his testimony was ostensibly Mitchell's guilt. But Lester's soliloquies—neither prosecution nor defense could stop the flow, and the judge did not try— were a tragicomic tour de force.

Irritating Mitchell's lawyer by repeatedly addressing him by his first name, an indecorous familiarity implying that they had all been cozy in conspiracy together, Lester exasperated him with relentless apologies—to the judge, the jury, his friends, the bar, his mother, and other members of his family dead and alive, to his Divine Maker—for his sins. "Are you through apologizing, Mr. Burns?" Mitchell's counsel finally broke in.

"No, Richard, I could never stop apologizing. I am ashamed."

To the simple question of whether he had asked to have the date on which he was to enter prison put off so he could testify against Mitchell, Lester responded:

"The reason I have not reported, Richard, is that I'm undergoing major surgery as soon as it can be set up in September. My total hip replacement was last March, and I'm having the same thing on the other hip in September. As soon as I recuperate I'm reporting—I have orders to report—to Eglin Federal Correctional Center at Eglin Air Force Base in Eglin, Florida. Richard, I've had back surgery. I've had hip—it's this right shoulder, grew back in low. I had a hip joint that's been replaced and one out and I had to testify and it's federal orders, if I'm in prison they have to put shackles on my ankles and legs and they have to handcuff me and bring me to court and I'm not physically able for it. And I'm not violent, never have been violent, and I have to sit in a little walled-off cold cell staring at the wall and it would be an inconvenience to my health. The government has not had to send me back here with armed marshals in an airplane and it's saved the government money and it's been a great personal relief to me to have the opportunity to have my surgery and not to go through any more. I've been going through a pretty rough time and still am, right now."

While he was not appearing voluntarily, Lester said, he was committed to telling the truth: "I have told many a tale, but never under oath." He knew that he had taken stolen money; he had warned Mitchell about it; he had bragged about it; he had acted out a plot gone haywire.

Sherry, in court wearing her usual pressed jeans and T-shirt, talked of how she had made Mitchell give her a receipt—which was then introduced into evidence—and had lied to him about tearing it up. She said she had warned him not to spend all the money in one place, because the serial numbers ran consecutively. There was no doubt in her mind that Mitchell knew where the money had come from; she had never pretended it was legitimate.

What impressed Rod Kincaid about both Lester's and Sherry's testimony was that, with all of Lester's dramatics and with all of the lying each had done, they were capable of telling the truth and did so, Kincaid believed, in convincing detail. He thought Sherry, who went straight to the facts and had complex figures down cold, was especially effective. She would have made a crackerjack agent.

In the end it was up to the jury to decide whether to believe the two convicted felons or Dale Mitchell, who was his own principal defense witness. Mitchell told the jury that he had jumped at the chance for his "dream," a big fee such as the ones Lester Burns always got. By asking for three hundred and fifty thousand, nearly as much as he then believed was the total stolen from Dr. Acker, he assured himself that his fee could not be part of the criminal proceeds. He denied that Lester had told him that the Acker take was over a million, as Lester had testified. On the contrary, Mitchell insisted, he was led to believe that Sherry and the others were fabulously wealthy people, with property all over Tennessee and Florida. When Sherry offered a Miami house as part of her payment to him, he took this as confirmation of her legitimate wealth.

Mitchell swore that he had not deposited any of his fee in a bank only to conceal that he was splitting it with Lester. Since he had signed a receipt for a hundred and fifty thousand, someone might have questioned why he was putting only half that amount in the bank. The fee-splitting arrangement would have come out, jeopardizing his old pal and benefactor.

He had asked Mrs. Hodge whether the money was stolen; there was "no problem" with it, Mitchell claimed she had said. As for accepting cashier's checks for the rest of his fee, he had done this on advice of counsel so as to show the source of the money, rather than taking more cash, which would have looked suspicious.

He had believed then that he was innocent, and he believed it now. Unlike Lester Burns, he had refused to plea bargain, because he was confident of his own blamelessness. Not only was it wrong to accept stolen money, it was against his "upbringing."

As far as Rod Kincaid knew, Mitchell had never been offered any plea bargain. What would Mitchell have had to offer in the way of information or testimony, now that everyone else except Gene Foust was either convicted or no longer under investigation? An investigation of the third lawyer, O. Curtis Davis, had gone nowhere: it was Davis's word against the Bartleys'. Two out of three was pretty good, Kincaid thought. Waiting for the verdict, he could not accept that the jury would swallow Mitchell's story. Yet you never knew.

The jury believed enough of it to acquit Dale Mitchell on each of the thirteen counts against him. "Reasonable doubt," the foreman called it.

Because he was officially innocent of having accepted stolen money, Mitchell was under no legal obligation to make restitution to Dr. Acker. Nor did he.

At the request of surviving members of the Morris family, who had attended the Acker trial and become close with the doctor and Tawny, James Wiley Craft agreed to prosecute Epperson and Hodge for the Gray Hawk murders. A second set of convictions would be a safeguard against the remote possibility that the Acker verdicts would be overturned on appeal. The compelling reason to prosecute, however, was to give the Morrises justice.

This would be the last of the crimes for which the gang would be tried: there was no sense in pursuing outstanding Georgia and Kentucky robbery charges; and as for the late Moon Mullins, his occupation suggested that he had already received the justice he deserved.

Other than that Donnie Bartley would act again as the key government witness, the Morris and Acker cases differed sharply from one another. In Gray Hawk no fingerprint had been found at the scene; neither had any stolen money, jewelry, or firearms been recovered; nor would Bartley be able to say that he had actually been inside the house as the crimes were taking place. Not even the murder weapon or weapons were in evidence. If Craft were to win the Gray Hawk case, he would have to do so relying entirely on circumstantial evidence.

As it turned out, there would also be a very different sort of man on the bench. Jackson County Circuit Court Judge Clay Bishop was eighty-four years old by the time the case went to trial in November 1987. One of Lester Burns's ubiquitous cousins, Judge Bishop was a sweet old fellow off the bench, but on it he was a terror, notorious for his intolerance toward defense attorneys. Becoming more irascible with each passing year, Judge Bishop continued to resist suggestions and demands for his retirement, which was overdue by at least a decade. His rulings, unlike Judge Hogg's, were frequently overturned and criticized by higher courts.

If the defense had requested it, Judge Bishop would likely have denied it, but this time James Wiley Craft agreed that a change of venue was advisable. A random telephone poll showed that virtually every citizen in Jackson County was already convinced of Epperson's and Hodge's guilt; most had avidly followed the Acker trial. As the county had only twelve thousand people living in it, an accurate sampling of opinion was not difficult to compile. In addition to the impossibility of finding an unbiased jury, the late Bessie Morris's brother was the County Sheriff, and one of her sons, Bobby, had become the circuit court clerk.

The trial was moved to London. Twice the size of Jackson in population, Laurel County was also more diversified socially and economically. It was contiguous with Jackson, however, and its newspapers and television stations had carried extensive coverage of the

Acker trial and had already reported that in the Morris trial, the prosecution would argue that the murders had been staged within the county, at Laurel River Lake. Judge Bishop would hear none of this, refusing to permit attorneys to question prospective jurors about the effect of pretrial publicity on their predisposition toward the defendants. As far as the judge was concerned, the trial had already been moved once; that should be enough for everyone, period.

The judge was intensely exasperated by Benny Hodge's attorney, Oleh Tustaniwsky of the state's Department of Public Advocacy, pronouncing or mispronouncing the lawyer's name as if it were some repulsive foreign food. The very sight of Tustaniwsky, a slight, bespectacled, scholarly fellow, seemed enough to turn the judge's jowls a deeper shade of red and send his gastric juices into revolt. He frequently admonished him with less than judicial restraint: "Mr. Tustenoughsky, why do you continuously want to do things you know are improper?" and "Don't get yourself in a mess and then expect the Court to pull you out. There are too many smart alecks, that's the trouble with this world," and "You'd better not get out of line again."

Pleased as he was to have a judge sympathetic to his side, James Wiley Craft was alarmed as much as he was amused by the judge's attacks on Tustaniwsky, who was an entirely competent advocate and was doing nothing to provoke them and whose principal offense seemed to be that his ancestors had clearly not ridden with Daniel Boone. And Craft was embarrassed when Judge Bishop, unable for once to make up his mind about how he should rule on a defense motion, turned to the prosecutor and asked, "What's *our* position on this?"

Only one defense move, or the lack of one, puzzled Craft. When at last it was time for both sides to use their preemptive challenges to dismiss jurors likely to be prejudiced, Tustaniwsky and his colleagues left a KSP trooper on the panel. Were they doing this in order to lay grounds for an appeal? To obviate that possibility, Craft would have used one of the prosecution's challenges to unseat the trooper, had they not already been exhausted. Craft could not recall ever having had a state policeman on a jury before.

The trial lasted only five days, it took that little time to present the relatively sparse evidence there was against Benny and Roger this time. Of the physical exhibits—bullets, pillows with bulletholes in them, various bloodstained household items including Mrs. Morris's

Bible with its four-leaf clovers—the most emotionally wrenching was the videotape taken by police of the murder scene. Even this, however, did not equal in power Jerry Morris's account of his discovery of his parents' bodies that morning after Father's Day in 1985. He broke down several times. The jurors kept their composure, but many spectators wept.

The other, most important witnesses included Bobby Morris, who testified that he had encountered Roger Epperson and Benny Hodge at a car auction near London about three weeks prior to the murders; a ranger from the Holly Bay campground who produced her logbook for that June showing that Carol Malone had registered there during the crucial period and had departed immediately after the killings; Harold Clontz, who had to be transported from prison to testify, who described sharing his moonshine with the defendants and admitted having loaned Roger a van on the evening of June 16; two young men who told of having nearly been hit by a similar van that had pulled out of the Morrises' driveway around eleven-thirty. And there was Donald Bartley's story of his role as lookout, of the disposal of the weapons and clothing, of Benny's admissions, and of the getaway to Florida.

Tustaniwsky and his colleagues made no attempt, as Lester Burns had, to break Bartley down, choosing instead to underline that, even if Bartley's account were true, he was less than an eyewitness, having heard the shots but not seen them. Much of the rest of his testimony was hearsay. Very little if any evidence corroborated Bartley's account, Tustaniwsky argued, and a defendant could not be convicted solely on the testimony of an accomplice.

Big John Bowling had his hands full that week, with both Epperson and Hodge back in the Laurel County jail. It was a likely time and place for them to try to escape, perhaps their last best chance, as the dozen or so troopers guarding them had been instructed. The prisoners had nothing to lose by trying. All of the grounds on which the appeal of the Acker verdicts and sentences had been based—judicial error and incompetency of counsel among them—had already been rejected by a higher court by the time the Morris trial commenced.

Big John's task was simplified, however, in that Donnie Bartley, whom the others would surely have tried to kill, was no longer resident at Bowling's jail. For safety's sake, Bartley was moved to a nearby halfway house. Big John had come to know Donnie and the other Bartleys well; they were almost family together by that time. While Donnie was still his guest, Big John had graciously let the inmate's parents manage the Old Mill motel and restaurant, which the jailer owned. Louise and Donald Bartley, Sr., remarried to one another, brought together by adversity or perhaps by something beyond common knowledge and understanding, seemed to be enjoying a degree of prosperity, on the evidence of automobiles registered to them and to Donnie's sister and observed parked at the Old Mill. These included an older Olds sedan leased from Avis, but also a 1986 Subaru GL sports car, a 1985 Cadillac Eldorado, and a classic 1957 Thunderbird, this last alone worth more than most new cars.

The Morris jurors chose the KSP trooper as their foreman. After hearing closing statements—the defense stressed the lack of physical evidence; Craft quoted Mark Twain's line that a human being's most precious possession was his or her last breath on earth—they retired to deliberate. They were gone about an hour before reporting that they had reached guilty verdicts on all counts, recommending twenty years each for robbery and burglary.

The emotions in that sweltering courtroom—the air conditioning had broken down, and it was unseasonably warm, eighty-four degrees inside; the jurors fanned themselves with their parking passes—were heightened by the presence of so many family members, relatives of victims and killers alike. Once so close, the Eppersons and Morrises now avoided each other except for an occasional bitter exchange. Troopers stood behind the defense table, in every corner, and at the doors. Outside, they were on guard with shotguns.

In contrast to the Acker trial, the defense chose this time to call witnesses during the penalty phase in an attempt to sway the jury against the death penalty. Benny Hodge's mother, identified as Eula Burkhart, was the first to take the stand to plead for mercy for her son. She described the hard life with Billy Joe Hodge, the beatings, the shooting of Benny's dog. She characterized Benny as a sweet boy who loved Christmas.

"Do you know why Benny would kill old people?" James Wiley Craft asked her. She denied his guilt. As did one of his sisters and his daughter by his first marriage, who called him a wonderful father, stressing the presents he gave and his cooking. Craft inquired of her what she had given him for Father's Day in 1985.

A preacher who had counseled him in jail stated that Benny had described how his stepfather had punished him by trying to force him to eat his own feces. It was the reverend's opinion that Benny still had hopes and dreams. A psychologist testified that Benny had told her that his present wife had taught him how to love. His sixth-grade teacher remembered him as a good boy who sometimes came to school with bruises on his face. Benny's second wife described how he had made a chocolate wedding cake with cherries on top for their nuptials at Brushy Mountain. Craft asked why, if she loved Benny so much, she had divorced him. Wasn't it true that he had run off with a prison guard?

All of Roger Epperson's immediate family members asked the jury to be merciful. Of them, his mother was the most emotional, his father the least. In her closing argument one of his lawyers described her client as a man with a drug problem and an alcoholic who was really "generous, considerate, a man who would put a Band-Aid on a bunny rabbit or try to save a bird who had flown in the window."

As the jury again retired, now to decide on life or death, James Wiley Craft wondered whether any of them could possibly be affected by the hearts and flowers they had just heard. After an hour, he began to worry. After two more hours, the trooper-foreman emerged to inform the judge that they had not been able to agree. It was past five-thirty. Perhaps if they had a quick meal it would put them into a mood for unity. The judge agreed.

Craft happened to glance through a window that looked into the corridor outside the jury room. Apparently taking a breath of air after their snack, the six men and six women were milling about the hall-way. The trooper was leaning down to talk earnestly to an older woman, one who Craft remembered had voiced misgivings about the death penalty during voir-dire examination, although she had said that she could imagine herself voting in favor of it. Unable to hear anything, Craft deduced that she was the lone holdout and that the trooper was trying to convince her to join the others arguing for death, the man of law reasoning against false sentiment. Letting him on the panel could prove to be a fatal defense mistake.

Just after six o'clock, the jury returned. They had chosen death for both defendants.

The Morris family cried from relief. Bobby Morris, responding to a reporter, said that his parents deserved no less than what the jury had decided. His heart went out, however, he added with tears streaming down his face, to the Epperson family.

James Wiley Craft studied the reactions of the jury. The trooper had his arm around the woman who Craft had guessed had been the holdout. She was crying, and the big man was trying to comfort her.

There were tears being shed over in the jailhouse, too. For humanitarian reasons, authorities at the federal prison in Lexington had permitted Sherry and Carol to be with their husbands on this day. Sherry was waiting in Big John Bowling's office as a pair of troopers led Benny in.

"What is it?" Sherry asked.

"Death, again," Benny said.

They embraced. Suddenly, as they were kissing, old Judge Bishop popped his head in.

"Say, Hodge," the judge said. "I forgot to tell you. Those twenty years you got on the robbery and burglary? They'll run consecutively."

Now that his purpose for the government had been fulfilled, it was time for Donnie Bartley to learn what punishment was to be his. Back in May of that year, he had stood before Judge Hogg and, on the advice of his attorney, refused to waive his right to a trial by jury. James Wiley Craft had asked for a sentence of two hundred years, abiding by his agreement not to seek the death penalty in return for Bartley's testimony. A jury would be bound by the limitations of Craft's request; a judge sitting alone would not, and would remain free to condemn Bartley to death.

But on December 15, immediately after a Letcher County jury was chosen, Bartley ignored his attorney and asked that Judge Hogg alone decide his fate. His reasoning was unclear. Judge Hogg asked him whether he understood that he could still be sentenced to death, despite any agreements that had been made.

"I never committed the murder," Bartley said in a near-whisper.

The judge continued to question him for some thirty minutes.

"I plead guilty," Bartley finally said, "but I didn't kill Tammy Acker. Benny Hodge committed the murder."

Judge Hogg announced that his own inclination was to give Bartley the death penalty, since he considered him equally as guilty as his cohorts, whether he had personally killed anybody or not. He had tried to kill Dr. Acker, as he himself had admitted. But an extraordinary thing had happened. Just that day, Dr. Acker and his surviving daughter had come to the judge's chambers and asked him to spare

Donald Bartley's life. Maybe their hearts were filled with mercy; more likely, they could not face the ordeal of another trial, in which Dr. Acker once again would have to relive that awful night. Only last month the doctor and Tawny had sat through most of the Morris trial, out of bonds of love and commiseration that had sprung up between them and the family of other victims of Bartley and his friends.

Bartley was a lucky man, Judge Hogg said. Out of respect for the Ackers, the judge sentenced him to life in prison without possibility of parole for twenty-five years.

Bartley did not feel lucky. He had been tricked, he maintained to anyone who would listen. He claimed to have understood that he would be eligible for parole after eight years. He began serving his long, possibly terminal stretch at the State Reformatory at La Grange—bitter, dreaming of revenge, considering himself one of life's victims. "I'd rather be homeless," he said, "sleeping under a bridge, than in this cell." He passed the time lifting weights and "making love to my guitar."

32

S HERRY SPENT THIRTY-SEVEN MONTHS and six days in prison, nearly all of that time at the Federal Correctional Institution in Lexington, before she was paroled. She was glad that she knew as much about prison life as she did, because her experience helped her to adjust. She dealt with the inevitable racial conflict during her first week in her own fashion. A large black woman challenged her to a fight. When the guards finally pulled them apart, Sherry's opponent was nearly unconscious and had lost some teeth. After that they became, if not friends, then peaceful toward one another.

Her experience also helped her to know how to control and conceal the marijuana and the green money she managed to acquire. She hid her currency by stuffing it into a full bottle of shampoo. She got into trouble only because during the first year and a half of her stay the Lexington prison was coeducational, with men and women on different floors and in different buildings but permitted to mingle with one another during meals and recreational activities. This experiment in prison reform proved as disastrous for the institution—the illegitimate birth rate soared—as it was for Sherry, who was disciplined for three charges relating to unauthorized contact with males. One involved kissing a guard; the other two had to do with prisoners and were of a more intimate nature.

"You all are crazy," she told the warden and her accusers. "You think I'm some kind of a Linda Lovelace?"

Her punishment was forty days in the hole, or solitary, without privileges.

Of privileges there were many available to those on good behavior. The prison had a movie theater, outdoor basketball and tennis courts, a running track, miniature golf, racquetball courts, a gymnasium, and roller skating on Tuesday and Friday nights. For the artistically and intellectually inclined there were classes in painting, leathercrafts, and ceramics; and there was a library. Sherry read the first book in her life, a romantic novel, while in prison; she also kept up with the outside world by reading the Roane County paper and the *Mountain Eagle*. On a typical day she arose at five, showered, and had breakfast at six-thirty. She worked in the physical therapy department of the prison hospital through the morning, lifted weights following a regimen Benny had devised for her, and, after lunch, returned to her cell to write him a letter every day. Sometimes she would send him a poem when she was feeling lonely:

> *What could be more beautiful*
> *Than watching Spring arrive*
> *And seeing all the world awake*
> *And Nature come alive?*

> *What could be more wonderful*
> *Than spending Easter Day*
> *With someone who will*
> *Not let the sunshine slip away?*

> *What could be more special*
> *Than to share all this with you—*
> *My Husband. My world. My dearest friend.*
> *My Joy my whole life through!*

It sounded like a greeting card, but she claimed it as her own.

After an early dinner, shared usually with two Mexicans with whom she had become friends, she reported for work at the prison's industrial plant. At first she stitched men's underwear; later she operated a press in a shop that printed court documents; eventually she became secretary to the supervisor of the entire industrial operation, earning a dollar twenty-five an hour. Twice she was named

"Employee of the Month" and received a fifty-dollar bonus. She was in bed by midnight.

For all this activity, however, Sherry was not among those who found life on the inside more appealing than the brutality of the street. She longed for the free world, marking each day served on a calendar, her earliest possible release date always in mind. Had Benny not also been confined, she might have tried to escape. Although not as often as to Benny, she wrote regularly to her parents, brothers, and daughter. All except Renee came to visit: Billy Pelfrey did not think that seeing her mother behind bars would be healthy for the girl.

Sherry's only excursion away from the prison was just before Christmas in 1987, when she was subpoenaed to testify at Donnie Bartley's sentencing hearing. She relished the chance for a day on the outside. She enjoyed seeing Ben Gish again and some of the others she had met around the courthouse.

It was dark by the time the prison van made it back to Lexington. She dreaded returning behind the walls and, having amused them for hours with her stories and repartee, prevailed on the marshals to drive around the city so she could see the Christmas lights. They stopped to buy her a cheeseburger and fries and, joking with her that this was her chance to run, let her off by herself at the front gate. She walked in alone, unhandcuffed and unshackled.

"I been out on a date," she said as she signed in.

During that day down in Whitesburg, Judy Jones Lewis, a young reporter for the *Lexington Herald-Leader* who had heard about Sherry from Ben Gish and others, talked to her for a while at the jail and noticed how men were drawn to her. Policemen, lawyers, jail employees, they all stopped by to chat, looking for an excuse to be near her. Judy Lewis asked her about it.

"I always liked males more than females," Sherry said. "Women are treacherous. I've always had a way of getting over with men—you know, being cutesy and flirty."

Judy Lewis wrote in her notebook: "Sherry folds her legs under her, like an Indian princess holding court, and men filter in and out of the room. They awkwardly find a seat in one of the vinyl chairs in the jailer's office and listen to her story." She was so fascinated by Sherry that she asked her if she would be willing to give her a full interview sometime. Sherry said, why not?

The story covered the top half of the front page of the *Herald-Leader* on a Sunday in January 1988, with a color photo of a smiling

Sherry and the headline LOVE, GREED AND EXCITEMENT LED SHERRY HODGE ASTRAY. It continued over an entire second page, with such tantalizing subheads as "A Robber's Wife" and "Marrying on the Phone." "There are three people I would die for," Sherry was quoted as saying. "My daughter, my dad and my husband. My dad told me, 'When you meet the man you love, do everything in the world for him, and he'll return it.'"

Sherry had opened up to Judy Lewis with startling frankness, mixing thrills with proclamations of undying love and hints of, if not quite remorse, at least regret: "You don't really gain anything from crime. Everything you make you have to spend to keep yourself out of trouble. I did it for a quick dollar, Benny's love and the excitement. If it came to the point of execution and they said, 'Sherry, if you'll take his place, we'll let him be a free man,' I would do it."

Benny's lawyers were horrified. Sherry's descriptions of the joyful life of armed robbery could be highly damaging to his chances for appeal and retrials. Benny did not care much for the story either when Sherry sent it to him. He was incensed by the paragraph depicting her as an Indian princess with men at her feet.

Sherry was released on parole on September 27, 1989, resentful that she had spent nearly a year longer than Carol in the pokey. One of the conditions was that she find a job within ten days. She went first to Roane Hosiery, not happy at the prospect of returning to crotch-slitting but willing to take anything. When she told the plant manager where she had been, however, he refused to hire her.

She tried an employment bureau, which sent her to Rockwood Sportswear, a factory located in an old hangar of the abandoned airport. The company manufactured leather jackets and coats, high-quality goods mostly for export to Europe. There the manager, an expansive New Yorker whose family owned the business and had opened the Tennessee plant because of low wages and tax breaks in the state, told her in his heavy Hungarian accent that he did not give a damn that she had been in prison and wanted to hear nothing about what had put her there. His business was garments, not moral judgments. The Christmas rush was on; he needed somebody who could operate a big sewing machine. Everybody deserved a second chance in life; he had had one or two of them himself. She could start work immediately at six seventy-five an hour.

The factory employed as many as sixty and as few as five workers, depending on demand. Nearly all of them were women. The huge workroom was well lit, clean, and air-conditioned, divided into rows of different sorts of machines that brought the outerwear, as it was called, from the stage of tanned hides to finished garments ready for shipping.

Sherry never missed a day's work and quickly learned to perform every task in the plant with greater speed and efficiency than anyone else. There was a high rate of absenteeism: workers were always calling in sick or simply not showing up, wandering off to other jobs or welfare. Sherry was assigned different tasks from day to day, which helped counteract the boredom, the lack of a getaway car. When orders slackened seasonally, the manager always kept Sherry on. "If I had five Sherrys," he liked to shout, shaking his fist at the incompetence of most employees, "I could fire these other slobs! This woman has *standards!*" Her refusal to join the union did not displease him, either. "A union is for sheep," she said. "I've always got on better with management. What can a union do for me except steal my pay and bring me down to everybody else's level?"

She was living with E. L. and Louise again. Renee came to stay on weekends. And Sherry accepted Benny's phone call every Sunday.

She still proclaimed her love, still felt it, but she began to waver now and then. Whenever she hinted to him that maybe she should think about getting on with her life, however, Benny would grow angry and threaten her. She was afraid of him. All he would have to do was tell some prisoner who was getting out that she was sitting on a pile of money, and she'd end up being found in some alley. She also feared many of the drug dealers whom they had ripped off together, now that Benny was not around to protect her. She steered clear of Lake City and other danger spots. But it was Benny who frightened her more, either by hinting that he would put a contract out on her if she abandoned him or by saying that if she did, he'd kill himself. When she drove up to see him on the Fourth of July and other holidays, memories came back and the fear went away and she loved him all over again.

To others, she was quick to defend him. In church one Sunday the minister, the same one who had performed the telephonic nuptials, was preaching about sin and punishment when he made the remark that everyone on death row deserved to be there. After the service Sherry went to him and gave him hell. How dare he say such a thing, knowing that the man she loved was only a few steps from the chair. The minister explained that what he had meant was that we are all sinners, not just those on death row, and that we all deserve eternal damnation and would suffer it, except for God's grace and the sacrifice of Jesus Christ. Sherry was mollified, and she prayed hard that night for her own salvation.

But at last, one day early in 1991, she went to a lawyer in Kingston, the same one who had handled her divorce from Mr. Wong, and asked him to help her file for divorce from Benny. Her understanding was that because of Benny's situation in another state, the action could be completed without his knowing. She began calling herself Sherry Sheets again, except when she signed in at the Eddyville prison gate.

When, agreeing that Judge Clay Bishop had made reversible errors, notably in refusing to permit adequate questioning of potential jurors, the Kentucky Attorney General ordered that the Morris case had to be retried, Benny was hopeful. Sherry knew that this was foolish, that he would be convicted and sentenced to death again, if he weren't executed first. All of his state appeals in the Acker case were exhausted, and only the federal courts stood between him and death. No one had been executed in Kentucky for more than thirty years, but times had changed, people were ready to pull that switch again. Benny was probably thinking that at a new trial, he could escape. Sherry now wondered whether she would want to run off with him. On most days, she thought not. She was becoming more determined to stay straight, free, and alive. The strain of being illegal was too great.

In July 1991, she had to testify at the trial of Gene Foust and his wife, which had been delayed until then while the FBI and the IRS continued to investigate the couple's finances. Foust's former police chief testified that he had begun to suspect that Foust was dipping into department funds in the fall of 1985, when the detective had begun acquiring expensive cars and clothing. Burl Cloninger, since retired from the Bureau, stated that he had been after Foust even before Sherry had named the policeman as the person to whom she had entrusted over half a million dollars. Foust, Cloninger said, appeared to be living above the level of his pay and, as the head of several narcotics-sting operations, had access to cash.

In her testimony, Sherry was more startling than ever. She

claimed that Foust had used the Acker money to finance a second unsuccessful campaign for sheriff. She also stated that Foust had promised to bring Benny down to Anderson County on a writ and to help him escape. And while freely admitting to a life of crime, she described how she had urged Benny to kill their four accomplices.

Other than Foust's cars and boat, which he swore had been purchased from savings, the government had not been able to discover anything the cash might have been used for and had located none of the missing money itself. Because of this failure, and because Foust's principal accuser was a woman of dubious repute, the case against the Fousts was weak. After fifteen hours of deliberation, the jury acquitted them on all counts. One juror spoke of Sherry as "less than savory."

The whereabouts of some money remained a mystery. Among those close to the case, opinions about where it had gone were not unanimous, but almost no one believed that Sherry still had access to any cash. If she did, she was doing a conscientious job of pretending otherwise, living with her folks, driving a seven-year-old car, and sitting all day at her machine in the factory. Like Rod Kincaid, most agents believed that Sherry had told the truth.

One day that summer a woman who was doing research for a book on the Acker case came to visit Sherry at Rockwood Sportswear, curious to observe at work this enigma who, only a few years before, had been on the run with satchels full of money. The woman had already listened to Sherry through several evenings, had taken her to dinner and heard her size up everybody else in the crowded restaurant—occupations, incomes, estimated worth of watches and jewelry, which ones were running around on their spouses. Sherry took delight in enumerating examples of human folly in that room. The researcher also pored over Sherry's family photo albums with her and watched her weep when talking about her parents, her daughter, and, even still, Benny Hodge—but there had been no tears for Tammy Acker or Ed and Bessie Morris.

Originally she had been afraid to meet her. Wasn't Sherry, after all, or hadn't she been, what people used to call a gun moll? The sessions with her told a lot and resolved nothing. A psychiatrist would label her this or that; someone else would spot in her an example of working-class resentment; another kind of anger would identify her as a feminist victim; some preacher would call her forward to proclaim sin. Sympathetic one minute, scary the next, the word for her might be prismatic. She spoke of Jesus Christ and the fear of hell. What sort of God did she believe in? As in some medieval grotesque in which a demon and an angel entwine where the tail snakes under a wing, she was something mysterious all right.

Was she in the end only a fool? Was she misguided, or a criminal mastermind after all? It was difficult to say. Was Lady Macbeth misunderstood? Experts disagree. She may have been a goddess or a fiend.

The woman found Sherry that morning dressed in jeans and a Mickey Mouse T-shirt, sewing the seam on a suede jacket. The stranger snapped a photograph and, saying good-bye, without thinking bent down to take Sherry's hand, grasped it, and talked of children, at last finding herself saying that she wished Sherry well. She hoped that Sherry would stay out of trouble. Maybe with her brains and hard work, she could make something of herself. Forty wasn't that old these days.

"Don't forget," Sherry said above the noise, those eyes clear and unblinking behind her glasses, "I'm only a hillbilly."

33

THE GRASS WAS KNEE-HIGH; soon it would be time to start bringing in the hay. Lester sat in the driver's seat of the big yellow bulldozer and thought how fresh everything looked, his hills and fields, the lake twinkling below, the high clouds and sky—it was as if he were seeing them all for the first time, as in a sense he was. It was May of 1991 and he had only been home from prison since just before Christmas. Everywhere the ground was smiling at him with wildflowers, except when the farmhouse came into view. He hated looking at it. He no longer even cared for the color of the stone walls he had laid himself years ago. He switched on the engine of the dozer and took aim.

Lester may have felt like a goner when he had heard his sentence pronounced four years ago to the day, but accepting defeat had never been a part of his nature. By the time he entered that prison at Eglin, on the Gulf Coast between Pensacola and Panama City, he was ready to start fighting again. Eglin had amenities and rooms instead of cells, and there was only a white line at the perimeter in place of a guarded wall. But he thought the line was worse, because you could see the world beyond, tempting and taunting. Often he stood with toes on the chalk, gazing out. He immediately got himself appointed law librarian and, when not helping other inmates with their writs and petitions, started preparing his own attempt to have his sentence reduced. This required a great deal of research as well as correspondence with friends up in Kentucky, whom he dispatched to dig up long-buried documents, some of which he knew certain people did not wish to see exhumed.

After several months, Lester petitioned the U.S. District Court in London, arguing that Judge Eugene Siler was prejudiced against him. The gist of the argument was that back in 1969, when he was a county attorney and Lester was defending a woman charged with murdering her husband, Eugene Siler had been part of a conspiracy to rig the jury selection process, resulting in the conviction of the defendant, whose farm was thereby inherited by one of Siler's relatives. To prove the conspiracy, Lester had obtained affidavits from the court clerk and her assistant, who swore that the clerk had pulled jurors' names from an envelope hidden in the selection box, rather than drawing names at random. The judge on this case, later appointed to the Kentucky Supreme Court, had been so enraged by Lester's accusations that he had convened a "court of inquiry," to which Eugene Siler had issued subpoenas. A state bar association investigation, however, had cleared Lester and concluded that jury fixing had taken place, although nothing was ever done about it. Wounds from this battle, Lester claimed, still festered and had affected Judge Siler's sentencing of him.

Lester's petition, because it involved such shocking accusations against a sitting federal judge and a past Supreme Court justice, and because it was filed by Lester Burns, made him front-page news again in Kentucky. Judge Siler recused himself from ruling on the matter but mocked the accusations, saying that he could scarcely remember the old case, doubted that he had issued subpoenas for the "court of inquiry," and had not even known that the woman inheriting the defendant's farm was a Siler. The federal judge who did rule on the petition dismissed it, accusing Lester of "dredging up" a lot of dubious old material and pointing out that he had already received very fair treatment, since he had been permitted to plea bargain and would otherwise have faced a far longer stretch in prison.

Resentful and discouraged, Lester was yet not entirely displeased. He was in the news again, which meant that he was still an actual person and not just a numbered item of federal property; and, he believed, he had caused Judge Siler some discomfort. If the action had failed, for a few months it had given Lester hope.

He did the rest of his time as a model prisoner, receiving the highest marks for his library work, attending church services each Sunday, and spending many hours discussing issues of crime, guilt, and punishment with the prison chaplain, who he thought was the only man in the place concerned about what would happen to inmates when they got out. As the jailhouse lawyer he won reductions in terms for other prisoners, including a Mississippi judge who invited him to come fishing some day. He took some mischievous glee in forcing the government to send him W-2 forms for his ninety-cents-an-hour wages as the antibureaucratic gadfly. He counted each day until the next visit from Asonia; he saved and often reread cards and letters from well-wishers and kept track of the several so-called friends who abandoned him, including a minister who explained that visiting Lester Burns in prison might be misunderstood by the congregation. When Dr. Acker sent sympathetic cards, Lester replied at length.

He spent his last month before parole at the federal prison in Lexington, the most unpleasant phase of his incarceration, locked up in the state he loved and had dominated. On the bus that took him there along with other manacled felons, the driver recognized and greeted him—"Hey, Lester! Come on up here and ride shotgun!"—a kindness that buoyed and humbled him.

Then the homecoming. Would they be glad to see him, or would having him around now be only an embarrassment? When he saw that his daughter who lived in New Orleans was there to greet him with her husband and his other daughter and son-in-law and the grandchildren and neighbors waving and shouting, he had to hide his face in Asonia's shoulder. A new Ford Explorer wrapped in yellow ribbons stood in the driveway. She had picked it out herself, Asonia said, but the car was to him from all of them, to let him know how they felt.

When spring came Lester's friends threw a big party for him out at the farm. It seemed as if half the people in the county showed up. A Greek neighbor butchered a lamb and they roasted it with a little porker on a spit outside, and there were banjos and fiddles and guitars. It had been no fun at all with Lester away, everybody said, and he proposed a toast:

"To justice! I believe in justice! I have fought for justice all my life! And I have received justice! I have had so much justice, *it's giving me diarrhea!*"

It was on that night that Lester decided that the farmhouse had to go. He could not bear to be inside it, there were so many ghosts, voices from the past, not least of all his own. And he wanted to have the pleasure of knocking it down himself. He had built it, he would wreck it, and he would build a new one in its place.

Pals of his standing nearby that afternoon when he sat on the bulldozer warned him not to hit the house straight on or too fast; he could ruin the blade and knock himself for a loop. But Lester was not in a cautious mood. He backed off farther, revved that engine, threw her into gear, and headed for the corner like one of Patton's tanks. He smashed into the stone at an angle and took a good chunk out, sending chips flying and cracks spreading in every direction. He let out a whoop and reversed to make another run.

A year later, the new house—of brick, two stories, higher up for a better view of the lake—was ready. He called it "Asonia's Monster." She had designed it and ordered every fixture and persuaded him that they should sell their other place and move to the farm full-time. He knew how right she was.

Not being able to practice law frustrated Lester, along with having to report to a parole officer; but he kept as busy as ever farming, developing a shopping center, attending land auctions and buying up property around his old law office, tinkering with a Chevy Eagle coupe that was nearly as old as himself and had a wooden trunk strapped to its rear that he joked would be perfect for holding cash. He planned to apply someday for the return of his attorney's license, for symbolic reasons, even if he never used it. "I hate criminals," he said. "God, how I hate them. But it's nice to think you're good for something. Just making money is a useless kind of life, although it beats not making it."

At the party to celebrate the new house, somebody noticed an old violin case with Lester's name pasted on it in silver block letters, lying in a corner.

"An old man gave that fiddle to me," Lester said. He opened the case and began the story.

SOURCES AND ACKNOWLEDGMENTS

F. Chris Cawood, an attorney practicing in Kingston, Tennessee, who acted for Sherry Sheets in two of her divorces, began gathering material for a book about her and the Acker crimes several years ago. I am grateful to him that when he decided not to write the book himself, he turned over his materials to me and continued to help with the research through the completion of my manuscript. His initial interviews with Sherry were invaluable and formed a basis for my subsequent talks with her. Mr. Cawood also was my guide on my first trip through Eastern Kentucky and East Tennessee, and my wife and I wish to thank him and his wife, Sara, for their hospitality.

Most of the research for *A Dark and Bloody Ground,* notably the extensive interviews and exploring of the territory, was carried out jointly by my wife, Suzanne O'Brien, and myself. We alternated asking questions and taking notes, comparing impressions and conclusions afterwards. She organized itineraries, made follow-up contacts, and was the first reader. Her contributions have affected every aspect of this work.

Sherry Sheets talked to me and eventually to Suzanne through many evenings. In explaining why and how she could be so open and detailed about personal and criminal matters, Sherry said that she wished to have her story known so that her daughter and other young women would not be tempted into her mistakes. I have tried to convey the spirit as well as the facts of her part of the story.

Lester Burns contributed to this book simply by existing, but he also gave freely of his time, supplied important documents, and was an inexhaustible source of Kentucky lore and of the history of his fascinating life. I also thank Asonia Burns for permitting me to stay in her home and for enduring my phone calls. Coming to understand her devotion to her family was most important to me.

I must thank Donald Terry Bartley for talking to me at the State reformatory at La Grange and on the telephone; thanks also to Jim Irwin of the Kentucky Department of Corrections for arranging this contact. On the advice of their attorneys, Roger Dale Epperson and Benny Lee Hodge refused my requests for interviews.

While I attempted to interview surviving members of the Acker family, Dr. Roscoe J. Acker and his daughter preferred not to relive their tragedy once again, it being already well documented in court transcripts, police records, and the press. Some months after the trial, Tawny Acker married KSP Trooper Tim Hogg, who works out of the Hazard post and is a cousin of Judge Byrd Hogg's. My impressions of the late Tammy Acker are derived from various sources, all of whom asked not to be identified. I wish to thank Mr. Jonathan Taylor of Harvard University for helping me obtain information and documentation relative to Dr. Acker's background.

Special Agent Wilburn R. Kincaid of the FBI was the person who suggested that I ought to meet Lester Burns, because of my interest in local color and idiom as well as for the sake of the story itself. For that alone I am indebted to him, but Mr. Kincaid also enlightened me about the FBI's role and provided me with his own analysis of everything relating to ACKMUR. Through him I was also able to interview Florida agents William Fluherty III and Charles Boling. I also wish to thank Belinda Maples of the Bureau's Washington, D.C., headquarters, who cleared my FBI contacts and was helpful in leading me to other sources. I must add that the Bureau's personnel as a whole were extremely courteous and helpful, doing everything within legal and practical limits to help me.

Lieutenant Danny Webb of the Kentucky State Police was most generous with his time and insights. Although Kentucky's "open records" law makes all case documents, including police reports, available to the public, actually obtaining these without help would have been another matter; nor would I have known what to look for had Lieutenant Webb not guided me. Bits and pieces of his knowledge and opinions are scattered throughout the last third of the book. At the present writing, the lieutenant continues to hold a pair of my reading glasses in custody, but I am sure they are safe at the Hazard post.

Detective Frank Fleming, formerly of the KSP, was very helpful and candid about a case that proved emotional and difficult for him; he is the obvious source of material that could only have come from him and that, until now, was known only to him and a handful of others. He and his wife also let me borrow their file of press clippings on the Acker and Morris cases, without my even asking.

When Alice Cornett, an editor, reporter, and biographer from London, Kentucky, learned that I was researching this book, she took the trouble to write me in care of my publisher, offering to turn over to me all of her files on the Acker and Morris cases, both of which she covered as a reporter and photographer. I must say that I remain at a loss to explain this generosity, so uncharacteristic of writers, which turned out to be of invaluable help. I was also able to benefit from talking to her in person and on the phone. She had at one time thought about writing about this case herself, but turned instead to completing a biography of the novelist James Jones, a much anticipated work.

Equally generous were Tom and Pat Gish, owners and publishers of the *Whitesburg Mountain Eagle,* and their son Ben Gish, who gave me copies of the relevant editions of their remarkable newspaper and permission to use photographs, and offered insights based on intimate knowledge and love of their native grounds. Close friends of the late Harry M. Caudill, the Gishes lead the campaign to build a library in his name, which will add to Whitesburg's distinction as the cultural center of Appalachia.

In Whitesburg I also must thank Judge F. Byrd Hogg, Commonwealth's Attorney James Wiley Craft, and Assistant Commonwealth's Attorney Mike Caudill. Mr. Caudill and his wife were the first people my wife and I interviewed there and helped us make other contacts; Judge Hogg responded in person and through correspondence; Mr. Craft granted us an interview and was invariably responsive to follow-up inquiries.

In Kentucky others who were helpful included the Hon. Elizabeth Meyerscough, Assistant Attorney General, of Frankfort; Gary E. Johnson, Assistant Public Advocate; Judy Jones, formerly with the *Lexington Herald-Leader,* who recommended background reading; and John and Donna Ward of Lexington, who helped in a most timely and crucial way.

I also wish to express gratitude to Jack C. Oxley of Tulsa, Oklahoma, who first introduced my wife and me to Kentucky many years ago and who provided transportation and hospitality for us throughout our research, solving logistical and other problems with his usual kindness and grace.

In Tennessee I wish to thank Gil Monroe, Warden of Brushy Mountain State Prison; Catherine Still and Eldridge Douglas, both formerly of the Anderson County Sheriff's Department; and several residents of Roane and Anderson counties who asked not to be identified.

I wish to thank the following people for specific help: Robert W. Davis, chairman, F & M Bank of Tulsa, for information on federal banking regulations; Charles B. Clement for guidance on Southern legal and business practice; Gailard Sartain and Brent T. Beesley for contributions involving local speech patterns and idioms; Guy Logsdon and John Wooley for help with folk and country music; Gary DeNeal for historical background; Blanche Hausam for information on techniques of Southern cooking; O. B. Hausam for answering important questions about early techniques of building-foundation construction; Gary Casey for Kentucky lore; Kevin Cavaness for facts about firearms; and Molly O'Brien for ideas on narrative structure.

I also wish to thank my colleagues in the English Department and the administration at the University of Tulsa for their continuing enthusiasm and support for my work.

The printed sources for this book include material from many big-city and small-town newspapers throughout Kentucky, Tennessee, Georgia, and Florida, the most important of which was the *Whitesburg Mountain Eagle.* These were obtained through personal files, various county libraries, the McFarlin Library of the University of Tulsa, and the libraries of the newspapers themselves, especially that of the *Louisville Courier-Journal.*

For historical background, I consulted numerous works: the literature of Kentucky and Tennessee is voluminous; writers have always found those states alluring. For me the two most helpful books have been Harry M. Caudill's *Night Comes to the Cumberlands* (New York, 1962) and David E. Whisnant's *All That Is Native & Fine* (Chapel Hill, 1983), subtitled "The Politics of Culture in an American Region."

Transcripts of the following trials and legal proceedings have been invaluable: *Commonwealth of Kentucky Versus Epperson and Hodge,* Letcher Circuit Court, 1986; *Commonwealth of Kentucky Versus Epperson and Hodge,* Laurel Circuit Court, 1987; *United States of America Versus Lester H. Burns, Jr.,* London, Kentucky, 1987; and *U.S. Versus Dale B. Mitchell,* Lexington, Kentucky, 1987. Other transcripts, depositions, appeals briefs, and various official documents examined are voluminous and seem too cumbersome to list here.

It remains for me to thank the two people who, after my wife, have been most important to the inception and completion of this book.

Robert Gottlieb, Senior Vice President, Member of the Board, and Head of the Literary Department at the William Morris Agency, has been my agent and friend for many years. He is a man of ideas who has made writing a far less lonely activity. It is a pleasure to express my continuing gratitude to him.

My editor, Susan Moldow, who is Vice President, Associate Publisher, and Editor-in-Chief at HarperCollins Publishers, expressed such faith in this project to begin with that writing it became a challenge to try to fulfill her expectations. If I have come close, it is largely owing to her support as well as to her suggestions for corrections and realignments and her insights into the characters and the culture portrayed. I feel fortunate to have found her.

D. O'B.
Tulsa, 1992